Touring
the Carolinas'
Civil War Sites

TO Tom -
Robin says this
will give you
some good reasons
to come up &
visit and a
chance to get
out of South
Florida.
Florida Native
Clint Johnson
12 - 18 - 96
God bless the
South & the USA

Touring
the Carolinas'
Civil War Sites

Clint Johnson

John F. Blair, Publisher
Winston-Salem, North Carolina

DESIGN BY DEBRA LONG HAMPTON
MAPS AND COMPOSITION BY LIZA LANGRALL
ALL PHOTOGRAPHS BY AUTHOR, UNLESS OTHERWISE NOTED

*The paper in this book meets the guidelines
for permanence and durability of the Committee
on Production Guidelines for Book Longevity
of the Council on Library Resources.*

Photographs on front cover, clockwise from top left—
Fort Sumter, Salisbury Confederate Statue,
5 East Battery in Charleston, Rose Greenhow's grave,
Bennett Place, Fort Fisher.

Library of Congress Cataloging-in-Publication Data
Johnson, Clint, 1953–
Touring the Carolinas' Civil War sites / by Clint Johnson.
            p.   cm.
ISBN 0-89587-146-7 (alk. paper)
1. United States—History—Civil War, 1861–1865—Battlefields—
Guidebooks. 2. North Carolina—History—Civil War, 1861–1865.
3. South Carolina—History—Civil War, 1861–1865. 4. Historic
sites—North Carolina—Guidebooks. 5. Historic sites—South
Carolina—Guidebooks. 6. North Carolina—Tours.
7. South Carolina—Tours. I. Title.
E641.J64 1996
973.7'09756—dc20   96-6236

*T*his book is dedicated to two bibliophiles:
my father, Clinton Johnson, Sr., a farmer
who relaxes by reading; and my
father-in-law, Marvin "Muggs" Gedemer,
who was a noted history traveler.

Table of Contents

Preface

All native Southerners run into them at some point, Northerners who ask the same question: "Why are you people still fighting the Civil War?"

My answer is always the same: "I'm not fighting the Civil War. I just remember it."

The Civil War, still called the War For Southern Independence by many people, was the defining moment in this nation's history. As author Shelby Foote has pointed out, the "United States" did not become a common term until after the war. The war created a coast-to-coast nation that would forever be united. Though we may not always understand each other, we are not fighting each other. There are very few nations on earth that can say that today. As Americans, we are all the better for it.

Southerners have also benefitted from the war. Yes, the Union Army did great damage to the South, sometimes simply for its own amusement. But, the war also forced the region to abolish slavery, to diversify its economy, to share its land resources, and to think of itself as a part of a whole rather than a nation unto itself. All in all, there are some good things that came with the invasion of the bluecoats.

Despite the destruction visited upon the South, it has been able to keep the best qualities—the qualities that molded the region. Southerners had to be clever and inventive to fight an overwhelming foe, and even when they were cold and hungry, they still lived with honor and grace. And the Southerners were fighters. Boy, were they fighters. In almost every battle they fought, including the battles on their own soil, the men of North and South Carolina were usually vastly outmanned and outgunned. They were rarely outsmarted. With a few exceptions, the officers from these two states were among the finest the South put on the field. That fighting spirit is still found today in the armed services, on sports fields, in the classroom, in the boardroom—everywhere that Carolinians, and all Southerners, gather.

This book looks at places where the men and women of the Carolinas and the rest of the South (and even a few from the North) displayed those kinds of qualities. These nineteen different tours visit all of the major Civil War sites in both North and South Carolina, and many of the minor or forgotten locations.

The tours are arranged chronologically by state when possible. For example, North Carolina's first tour starts on the Outer Banks, since the first battle in the state occured there. More obviously, South Carolina's first tour is in Charleston, where the war officially started when Confederates fired on Fort Sumter.

Each tour includes a map and photographs to give travelers some idea of what they can see along the route. There is also a bibliography for those who would like to read more about the Civil War in North and South Carolina. An appendix lists agencies that can supply more detailed maps and information.

Touring the Carolinas' Civil War Sites was compiled with the help of local historians, people who know best what can be seen in their communities. In selecting the tours, I started by reading comprehensive histories of the war in both states. I then sat down with a road map and a historical-marker guide to find the places mentioned. Then I contacted the chambers of commerce in towns that had a significant Civil War history and asked them to put me in touch with local Civil War historians. Every town has one, and their contributions were invaluable to finding hospitals, skirmish sites, earthworks, and houses. The professional historians at the states' national and state battlefields and historic houses also provided very helpful details. I even found two professional historians in Charleston and Wilmington who conduct Civil War tours.

Finding all of the dead generals buried in the Carolinas was more challenging, but if you can believe it, someone had already written a directory to the cemeteries containing the graves of all the Union and Confederate generals.

Some local historians will be disappointed that I did not make it to the Civil War sites in their communities. For that I apologize. The reasons for not including every possible site are varied: Those sites may not have fit into a tour route; I did not hear about them; including them would have lengthened an already long tour; or they may have been on inaccessible private property. There were literally hundreds of skirmishes fought in both states, and most of them are on private land that landowners are trying to keep from relic hunters.

All of the tour roads suggested in the book, with just two short exceptions, are paved so access to all of these sites is no problem. The major difficulty will be trying to see everything on the tours. Many, while listed as one tour, are best taken over two days.

The most trouble will be experienced by people trying to find graves in large cemeteries that have not named their crisscrossing roads. Most city cemeteries have maps that can be obtained during weekday office hours. If possible, get these maps before trying to follow my directions.

To my surprise, only a handful of generals' graves are on inaccessible private property. To my pleasure, many of them have very interesting tombstones, though their inscriptions often include some of the worst poetry I have ever read. Many tombstones, even those of famous men, are neglected and slowly eroding away. The inscriptions are often illegible. Some of the graves are very sad, such as the one of the general and his wife who were surrounded by the graves of their three infant children. One general seems to be buried by himself, without any family members. I wonder if it had anything to do with the fact that it was his regiment that accidentally shot Stonewall Jackson. While it may sound morbid to some, please do not neglect visiting the graves of these men (and three women). My favorite stop of all nineteen tours was the grave of Lieutenant General Richard Heron Anderson, an often overlooked general who commanded the division in which my Florida Confederate ancestor served before losing his arm at Fredericksburg.

Sadly, many Civil War sites have simply disappeared with time and progress. Older historians tell stories of how their fathers would visit the Charlotte home of Stonewall Jackson's widow. They would stare, awe-struck, at the general's saddle draped over the stair bannister. That house was torn down long ago and is now no more than what I call a "historic flat spot." This is literally true, as there is a marker laid flush in the concrete sidewalk marking the site of Mrs. Jackson's former home. Also gone in Charlotte are the houses where Jefferson Davis held cabinet meetings on his flight south; the relocated Naval shipyard, where munitions were manufactured; and the North Carolina Military Academy, from where North Carolina's first soldiers marched to the first major land battle in the war.

The threat of losing more Civil War sites is always real. Recently in Columbia, South Carolina, someone in power wanted to tear down an old building. There is nothing new about that. However, it happened to be the building where Confederate money was printed during the war, and where paroles were printed afterwards. Historians protested, and the site was saved from the wrecking ball. At least for now, the building still stands.

So visit these sites now, while you can. See these places that survive from the Civil War, and think about the men and women who lived, fought, and died here. It is because of their sacrifices that people of the United States can proudly call themselves Americans.

Acknowledgments

This book would not have been possible without the help of local historians. These are the people who study and preserve Civil War sites and who tell great ghost stories. Readers should thank them for keeping history alive. The following historians helped me research these tours. I particularly want to thank Jeff Stepp, colonel of the 26th North Carolina Regiment Civil War reenactment group, for his help in developing a list of sites that should be included, and my friends in the 26th for showing me the Civil War history in their communities.

NORTH CAROLINA:

Asheville—Jim Taylor (26th N.C. Regiment)
Boone and Linville—Lyle Bishop (26th N.C. Regiment) and Greg Mast (26th N.C. Regiment)
Averasboro—the Smith Family, owners of Lebanon (the hospital on the battlefield)
Bentonville—John B. Goode, site manager of the Bentonville Battlefield
Chocowinity—Bob Grimes

Elizabeth City and South Mills Battlefield—Raymond Sheely and William Forehand

Fayetteville—Les Monroe (26th N.C. Regiment)

Fort Branch near Hamilton—Henry Winslow, owner of Fort Branch

Goldsboro—Mary Grady and Emily Weil of the Wayne County Historical Society

Hertford—Ray Winslow

High Point and Jamestown—Billy Horne (26th N.C. Regiment)

Kinston and the CSS Neuse—Dan Blair and Eugene Brown

Lenoir—Skip Smith and Thomas Smith (26th N.C. Regiment)

Morganton—Randal Garrison (26th N.C. Regiment)

Morehead City and Beaufort—Jack Goodwin of the Carteret County Historical Museum

New Bern—John B. Greene III, curator of archaeology and historic structures for Tryon Palace

Plymouth—Harry Thompson, curator of the Port O' Plymouth Historical Museum

Raleigh—Brenda McKean (26th N.C. Regiment Soldiers Benevolent Society), Chet Whiting (26th N.C. Regiment)

Roanoke Island—Dick Armstrong (26th N.C. Regiment) and Hubie Blevin

Seven Springs—Carolyn Price

Siloam—Marion Venable of Surry County Community College

Tarboro—Monika Fleming

Washington—Fred Mallison

Waynesville—Jule Morrow (26th N.C. Regiment)

Wilmington—Chris Fonvielle, who conducts a Civil War tour of the city and its forts; Marcella K. Rippel of the Bellamy Mansion; Jane Patterson of the Wilmington Convention and Visitors Bureau; Jamie Credle of the Cape Fear Museum; Ted Lynch and Tom Prisk (26th N.C. Regiment)

Wise's Forks—Donnie Taylor (1st N.C. Battalion)

SOUTH CAROLINA:

Beaufort and the Sea Islands—Gene Norris; Wyatt Pringle; and Emory Campbell, the Penn Center Executive Director

Broxton Bridge—G.D. Varn, Jr.

Camden—Joseph Matheson, curator of the Camden Archives and Museum

Charleston—Jack Thomson, who conducts a dramatic two-hour "Civil War Walking Tour of Charleston"; Lynda Heffley of the City of Charleston; and Amy Blyth of the Charleston Convention and Visitors Bureau

Cheraw—Sarah Spruill of the Cheraw Visitors Bureau

Chester—Scott Coleman of the Chester County Historical Commission

Columbia—Ray Sigmon of the Historic Columbia Foundation; Jack Martin of the South Carolina Confederate Relic Room; and Roger Stroupe of the South Carolina State Historical Museum

Georgetown—Paige Sawyer

Parris Island—Steve Wise, curator of the United States Marine Corps Museum

Union—Dr. Alan Charles of the University of South Carolina at Union

Winnsboro—Tim Lord

Thanks to my professional photographer friend Lenny Cohen for taking my photo for the book's back cover.

I also need to thank Carolyn Sakowski, president of John F. Blair, Publisher, for taking on this book; Andrew Waters for editing it; Liza Langrall for drawing the maps from my pencil scrawls; and all of the staff at Blair for correcting my grammatical, spelling, and capitalization inconsistencies. Just when the writer thinks the manuscript is perfect, those darn typos and misplaced or missing commas leap onto the paper to mess it up. It takes a team of publishing professionals to find them all.

And, most importantly, thanks to my Wisconsin-born wife, Barbara, a rare Yankee in my family's 270-year Southern history. She has stood by me through thick and thin, visited Civil War battlefields (that really were just that—fields), walked through musty old museums, and been there when I needed her. I could not have received more from anyone.

Touring
the Carolinas'
Civil War Sites

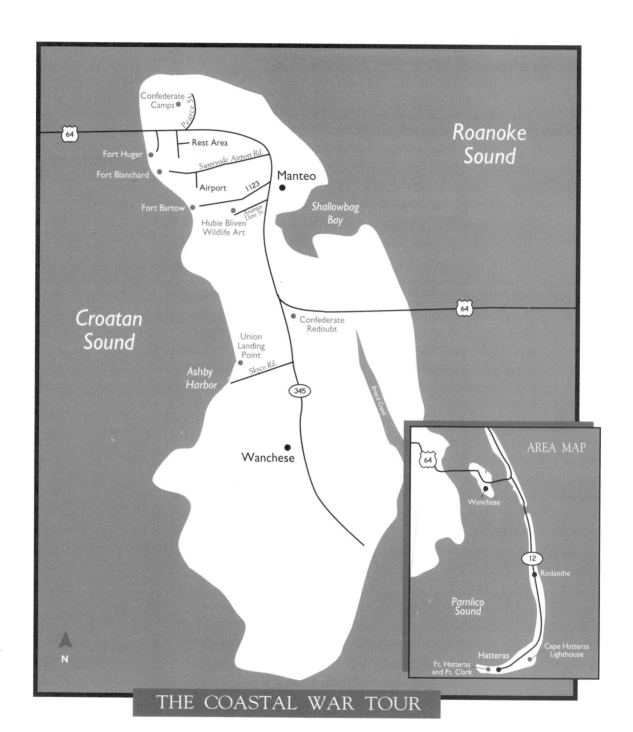

Confederate
Camps

Pearce St.

Rest Area

Fort Huger

Fort Blanchard

Sunnyside Airport Rd.

Airport

1123

Manteo

Fort Bartow

Ananias
Dare St.

Hubie Bliven
Wildlife Art

Shallowbag
Bay

Roanoke
Sound

64

Croatan
Sound

Confederate
Redoubt

Union
Landing
Point

Skyco Rd.

64

Ashby
Harbor

345

Broad Creek

Wanchese

AREA MAP

64

Wanchese

12

Rodanthe

Pamlico
Sound

Hatteras

Cape Hatteras
Lighthouse

Ft. Hatteras
and Ft. Clark

N

THE COASTAL WAR TOUR

The Coastal War Tour

This tour focuses on Roanoke Island, home to the present-day towns of Manteo and Wanchese, and includes a side trip to the Outer Banks. In February, 1862, the Union Army attacked Roanoke Island. A series of Confederate forts protected the island, but they proved no match for the overwhelming Union invasion. There is not a lot to see on Roanoke Island since the forts have washed away, but there is a preserved redoubt that was the scene of fierce fighting. The tour also includes a private relic collection open to the public, and the site where the Federal invasion landed. The side trip to the Outer Banks includes visits to Oregon Inlet, Hatteras Inlet, and the village of Rodanthe.

Total mileage: approximately 100 miles, counting the side trip to the Outer Banks. With beach traffic, this is an all day trip.

Though it was the tenth state to secede from the Union, North Carolina was the second state, after Virginia, invaded by the Union Army. The invasion occurred in August 1861 along the Outer Banks, the long string of low, sandy islands on North Carolina's coast.

The attack on the islands was a brilliant maneuver by an otherwise dim bulb, Union Major General Benjamin Butler. Butler, a politician with no formal military training, correctly recognized that by controlling the few inlet passages from North Carolina's sounds to the ocean, the Union could bottle up most of the state's long coastline. If it controlled the coastline, the Union could mount inland attacks when it wanted. Butler presented his plan to President Lincoln just after the Union defeat at First Manassas in July 1861. By August, the Union attack plan was put in motion.

When the war started, there were no forts on the Outer Banks. However, it quickly became clear the Confederacy needed to protect the three crucial inlets that allowed ships to pass through the Outer Banks. The three inlets were Oregon Inlet, Hatteras Inlet, and Ocracoke Island. Whichever side controlled these three locations controlled the potential invasion of mainland North Carolina from the sea.

The Confederates started using these inlets as bases for privateering. They acquired and armed small ships that could run out of the inlets, raid Union ships, then run back to safety behind the banks.

To protect this officially sanctioned pirate fleet, and to guard against Union attack, the Confederates started building forts on the Outer Banks. Fort Oregon was a small fort built on the south side of Oregon Inlet, near today's Herbert C. Bonner Bridge. Fort Morgan was built on Beacon Island in the Pamlico Sound, off Ocracoke Island. It mounted twelve guns, but was designed to handle fifty if the Confederacy ever got around to supplying them.

The more important forts were built near the town of Hatteras at the Hatteras Inlet. In 1861, Hatteras was a thriving port. It handled more shipping than Beaufort, North Carolina, and almost equaled Wilmington. Fort Hatteras was built of dirt, one-eighth of a mile from the inlet. Most of its twelve 32-pounders aimed into the Pamlico Sound.

Fort Clark was built east of Fort Hatteras, closer to the ocean. Most of its guns pointed out to sea. It mounted five 32-pounders, and two smaller guns. The placement of the guns at Fort Hatteras and Fort Clark created an overlapping field of fire across the sound that was supposed to keep Federal vessels from even thinking of attacking.

One did. On July 10, 1861, the USS *Harriet Lane*, fired three broadsides at the slave workers building at Fort Hatteras. This marked the first time the United States Navy had fired a shot in anger since the war began in April. The fire was also a harbinger of things to come. The first major land battle of the war, First Manassas, would come eleven days later.

Other than angering the workers, the shelling of Fort Hatteras by the *Harriet Lane* did little damage. The millions of mosquitos and sand gnats were more deadly. Some men were assigned to do nothing more than swat bugs.

Being new at war, Confederate authorities on the Outer Banks made a rather basic mistake. They allowed two captured sea captains to have run of both Fort Clark and Fort Hatteras. These two men carefully noted the forts' design, outdated cannons, low ammunition stores, damp black powder, and the demoralized condition of the few hundred troops assigned to the blazing hot post, miles away from the comforts of the mainland. When the two captains were freed in a prisoner exchange, they went right to the Federal fleet commander and told him the forts would be a pushover. On top of that, they told him they could help any Federal invasion ships run past the shoals around the islands.

On August 27, 1861, Confederate spies telegraphed authorities in North Carolina that Butler's force was heading south. The Union fleet consisted of warships mounting 149 guns and transports carrying nearly 1,000 infantry. Facing them were less than 600 Confederates, split between Fort Hatteras and Fort Clark.

When it became clear that the Federals' target was the Hatteras Inlet, the forts' commander sent word to the 250-man garrison at Portsmouth, North Carolina, an island south of Hatteras, to come up and help.

The Federal shelling of the forts went on for hours, then the first landing boats headed for shore. However, disaster struck as the soldiers tried to land. The surf suddenly began to churn and several landing craft were dashed on the beach. More than three hundred Federals landed safely, with no one drowning, but the rest of the troops pulled back rather than risk overturning in the heavy surf. As the drenched, hot soldiers gathered on the beach, lookouts on the gunboats spotted Confederate cavalry bearing down on the soldiers. A broadside was leveled at the charging horses, which turned out to be just that, horses with no riders. The "cavalry" turned out to be a herd of wild Hatteras horses running from the gunfire at Fort Clark. No one ever recorded casualty figures for the horses.

During the afternoon, the soldiers of Fort Clark fired all of their rounds and expended their powder. Without ammunition, they abandoned the fort. Under heavy Federal fire, they raced across the open dunes to Fort Hatteras.

Federal lookouts, seeing the running Confederates, thought that both Fort Clark and Fort Hatteras had been abandoned. The USS *Monticello* boldly entered the channel to take possession of Fort Hatteras. Her captain should have looked closer. The thrilled gunners of Fort Hatteras riddled the *Monticello* with artillery fire before she could put back to sea.

That night the stranded Federal soldiers spent the night in the abandoned Fort Clark, almost within hailing distance of the Confederates at Fort Hatteras. For reasons still unknown, the Confederates did not attack the thirsty, dispirited Union soldiers. It was a fatal mistake. Since Fort Hatteras's guns pointed toward the Pamlico Sound, they could not repel a Union attack from the ocean.

By morning, it was too late to do anything. The Federals started bombarding Fort Hatteras at first light. By 11:00 A.M., the Confederate commander surrendered.

The casualties in the two-day fight were light. No Federals were killed, and only one was seriously wounded. Seven Confederates were killed and about forty were wounded. More than six hundred Confederates surrendered, including the reinforcements from Portsmouth who arrived in the night and should have been used to recapture Fort Clark.

After the fall of the forts at Hatteras, the rest of the Confederate forces on the Outer Banks abandoned their posts. There were a few more minor actions, but for all effective purposes, the Outer Banks now belonged to the Union. General Butler's plan was a success. The Union forces now turned their attention towards Roanoke Island.

Roanoke Island is primarily known as the site of the "Lost Colony," the first English settlement in the New World, whose residents disappeared in 1587. In 1862, Roanoke Island could have been called just as easily the "Lost Confederate Opportunity." The island sat between Roanoke Sound on the east and Croatan Sound on the west. It was also directly in the path of the crucial Albemarle Sound to the north. If the Federals could capture Roanoke, they could use it and New Bern, to the south, as bases for attacks on crucial coastal locations. The strategic location of Roanoke made it an island that could not be bypassed; a fact obvious to the Federal high command in Washington, but ignored by their counterparts in Richmond.

However, North Carolina's military planners did recognize the strategic importance of Roanoke. For six months after the fall of the Outer Banks defensive forts in August 1861, they warned Confederate officials that Roanoke Island would be the Union's next target.

"Send us men, ammunition, cannons, and generals experienced in dealing with naval assaults!" was the essence of dozens of messages from North Carolina's governor and military leaders to the Confederate war-planners in Richmond. No one listened. The Carolinians could make no one in the Confederate bureaucracy understand that the capture of Roanoke Island would bring the entire upper North Carolina coast under Federal control. Dozens of rivers and sounds that might have been safe havens for blockade runners would be lost. If the island was lost, Union ships could bring in troops who could then make advances deep into the heart of the Confederacy.

Certainly, the Union leaders understood Roanoke Island's strategic importance to the entire war effort. Brigadier General Ambrose Burnside proposed that he lead the mission to capture the island. On January 7, 1862, General George McClellan ordered Burnside to capture Roanoke Island. McClellan's orders directed Burnside to follow the capture of Roanoke Island with attacks on New Bern and other strategic points in eastern North Carolina.

By late January 1862, Burnside was ready to personally lead the invasion of Roanoke Island. The Union fleet contained more than sixty-seven transports and warships carrying more than thirteen thousand troops, the largest amphibious force the world had ever seen to that point. Burnside chose the smallest ship, the USS *Picket*, as his flagship, on the theory his troops would be inspired if their commander was not afraid to brave the storm-tossed seas off the Outer Banks in a tiny ship. The inspiration worked. It took more than two weeks of riding heavy waves before the fleet could move into North Carolina's Pamlico Sound. Whenever the tiny *Pickett* moved past the much larger transports, the seasick soldiers saw their commander on the bridge wearing his trademark—a tall, round-crown, wide-brimmed hat. They would cheer him loud enough that he would wave or salute. Inspired by his courage, they would do anything for Burnside.

Finally, the storms subsided. By February 4, 1862, all of the Union ships were across the sand bars off Hatteras. There was no Confederate resistance since the forts at Hatteras had been captured in August 1861. The boats moved into the calmer, deeper water of the Pamlico Sound, and the Union Army readied itself for invasion.

The Confederate Army was not ready to receive them. Most of the forts on Roanoke Island were constructed at the northwest end, on the Croatan Sound–side of the island. No forts were constructed on the south end of the island, the logical direction of any Federal attack. Only one, 2-gun battery aimed into Roanoke Sound. The forts were placed on the northwest end so that guns could fire on the Federal ships as they made their way up the Pamlico Sound from the Hatteras Inlet. The reasons for this lapse in strategic planning are unclear. Historians speculate that the island's commander considered the south end of the island too marshy to build a fort. He built his forts on the higher ground at the north end, where the construction was easier. Those forts were not necessarily where any fighting would be, of course, but they were easier to build.

The northernmost fort on the island was Fort Huger. Three hundred yards south of that was Fort Blanchard. Fort Bartow was three hundred yards south of Fort Blanchard. These three sand forts had a total of twenty-five cannons. The unnamed, two-gun battery pointing into Roanoke Sound on the east side of the island was at Ballast Point, just below Shallowbag Bay.

Protecting the island's only north-to-south road was a redoubt (a small enclosed dirt fort) armed with three cannons. It was located in the center of the island, two miles southeast of the coastal forts. On either side of the redoubt were swamps that the Confederates hoped would protect their flanks.

Manning all of these fortifications were fourteen-hundred North Carolinians and Virginians, under the command of General Henry Wise. Wise was the former governor of Virginia who had executed John Brown after Brown's Harper's Ferry raid in 1859. Like many politically appointed generals, from both the North and the South, Wise was no match for a professional warrior like Burnside. On top of that, Wise was sick on the day the Federals landed. Overall Confederate command went to Colonel H.M. Shaw, a transplanted Yankee. A subordinate described Shaw as "not worth the powder and ball it would take to kill him." Needless to say, the average Confederate soldier on Roanoke Island did not draw inspiration from his commanders.

The only Confederate naval support came from seven, small wooden gunboats, derisively called the "mosquito fleet." Once their commander saw the nineteen large warships facing his little force, he wisely decided to stay out of their range and hide behind a line of sunken boats and driven pilings that was supposed to protect the north end of the Croatan Sound.

On Feb. 7, 1862, at 10:30 A.M., the guns of the Union fleet began pounding Fort Bartow. As the southernmost fort, Bartow was the only fort that could conceivably hit Federal transport ships as they unloaded troops at Ashby's Harbor, about three miles south. The other two forts were out of range, and they could not bring their guns to bear that far south.

Twice, the mosquito fleet ventured past the cover of their pilings into open water, before turning around and running. They were attempting to lure the Federal ships into range of Fort Huger and Fort Blanchard, as well as Fort Forrest, a small fort located on the mainland across from Fort Huger. However, the ploy didn't work.

As night fell, the Federal transport ships began landing their troops at Ashby's Harbor. Ashby's Harbor was selected as the landing point because of its shallow, sandy bottom and narrow beach. The selection was probably made by a runaway slave boy, Thomas Robinson. Robinson was in the advance wave of Burnside's attack, which guided the main force ashore. Robinson grew up on Roanoke Island and knew that points further south were without roads and too marshy for a landing.

The landings on Roanoke Island likely looked much like amphibious landings in today's army. A steamer headed toward the shoreline at full steam, towing surf boats behind it. As the steamer neared the shore, it veered off. The boats' lines were cast off, allowing the landing crafts' momentum to carry them to the beach.

Remarkably, at least two hundred Confederates, under the command of a timid colonel, watched the initial landing operation from the woods around Ashby's Harbor. The Confederates did not fire a shot. They quietly retired to the safety of the three-gun redoubt about a mile away, where they joined two hundred other Confederates to prepare for the attack they knew would come in the morning.

In less than thirty minutes, more than four thousand Federals and a six-gun artillery battery were ashore. By midnight, more than ten thousand Federal soldiers were around the woods at Ashby's Harbor, trying to keep warm on the damp, cold night.

When dawn broke, the Federals broke camp and started their cautious march north. Robinson, their guide, had probably warned them about the three-gun redoubt guarding the road less than a mile away.

The fight for the redoubt began at 8:00 A.M., with the three Confederate cannons firing down the center of the road. Confederate Colonel Shaw failed to reinforce the redoubt, even though the thousand Confederates manning the forts were useless now that the Federals had landed.

The first regiment to attack the Confederates was the 25th Massachusetts Regiment. In an effort to avoid the rifle and artillery fire coming down the road, members of the 25th would rise to fire then flatten themselves on the ground to load their muskets. The 23rd and the 27th Massachusetts Regiments plunged into the swamp to the right of the road in an attempt to move around the Confederates' left flank. The swamp did its job. The men could not reach dry land, and they found themselves wading in waist-deep water and thick briars.

More Federal regiments pushed into the thick woods on the Confederate right, and again the swamp enveloped them. One soldier, perhaps a veteran of the Seminole Indian Wars, proclaimed the swamp "worse than the Ever Glades of Florida, where we were half the time to our knees in mud and water."

Still, sheer numbers and time were working against the four hundred Confederates holding the redoubt. They could hear the Federals crashing through the woods and slowly surrounding them. As quietly as they could, the Confederates abandoned the redoubt and retreated.

At the moment the Confederates pulled out of their redoubt, an undeserved legend was born. The 9th New York Zouaves, under glory-seeking Colonel Rush C. Hawkins, charged the empty redoubt. They must have been a sight. While all of the other Federal regiments were in regulation uniforms—sky blue trousers and dark blue sack coats topped by dark blue billed caps—the 9th New York Zouaves were dressed in dark blue pantaloons and dark blue short jackets with bright red piping. Instead of caps, they wore red fezzes with long, red tassels.

For the rest of the war, Hawkins proudly claimed that his charge drove the Confederates out of the redoubt. Not so. Not only did the Confederates abandon the redoubt, but other Union regiments were probably already there as well. A member of the 21st Massachusetts claimed his regiment was already in the redoubt when "the 9th New York came running up the narrow corduroy road and with a great shout of 'Zou, Zou,' swarmed into the battery for all the world as if they were capturing it."

The retreating Confederates ran up the road toward their camps on the north end of the island. Couriers informed the three forts and the Ballast Point battery that the Federals were now in their rear. Since the forts' cannons pointed toward the sounds, they could not defend against a ground attack. The numbers were overwhelmingly against the fourteen hundred Confederates, especially without artillery, and they realized further resistance was useless.

The Battle of Roanoke Island was over without Fort Huger, Fort Blanchard, or the Ballast Point battery firing a shot. Confederates reported 23 killed, 58 wounded, 62 missing, and 2,200 captured, including some 800 reinforcements from Nags Head, who landed just in time to be captured. One of those killed was General Wise's son. Only a few members of the mosquito fleet were wounded. Federal ground losses were put at 37 killed, 214 wounded, and 13 missing. Several Federal sailors were killed and wounded, meaning the defenders at Fort Bartow had at least drawn some blood from the Federal fleet.

The Federals were unimpressed with the appearance of the captured Confederates. A member of the 25th Massachusetts wrote: "The prisoners are a motley looking set, all clothed (I can hardly say uniformed) in a dirty looking homespun gray cloth. I should think every man's suit was cut from a design of his own. Their head covering was in unison with the rest of their rig, from stovepipe hats to coonskin caps; with everything for blankets, from old bed quilts, cotton bagging, strips of carpet to buffalo robes."

The fall of Roanoke Island sent shock waves through the Confederacy. One very perceptive lady diarist wrote that the island fell because of "mismanagement that looks like treachery." The Confederate Congress in Richmond did what politicians always do—they established a committee to try to figure out why Roanoke Island fell so easily. These were, of course, the same bureaucrats who ignored North Carolina's constant pleas for men and arms before the battle.

The Roanoke Island Tour starts on the three-mile-long U.S. 64/U.S. 264 bridge heading from the mainland to Roanoke Island. While crossing from the mainland, look to the right, or south, and imagine what sixty-seven Federal war ships must have looked like to the Confederate defenders huddled in their sand forts. The water's surface would have

Fort Blanchard, looking south to where the Federal fleet would have been

been obscured by the hulls of ships. The sky would have been dark with coal smoke.

As you near the shore of Roanoke Island, look at the land to the immediate right of the bridge. The shoreline, and the trees growing on it, should look unnaturally tall. This raised land is the last remnant of Fort Huger. Immediately after crossing the bridge, make a hard right and turn into the small parking lot beside the bridge. Historic markers in the lot describe Fort Huger and Fort Blanchard.

Walk along the beach for about fifty yards, then walk inland. The slope will noticeably rise, and you may find survey stakes buried in the ground marking the rear wall of Fort Huger. Fort Huger was the only true enclosed fort built by the Confederates on Roanoke Island. The front part of the fort washed into Croatan Sound long ago. In the water in front of the site of Fort Huger are the remains of wooden pilings. These pilings may have been part of the fort.

Fort Blanchard was three hundred yards south of Huger. A walk in that direction does not yield any evidence of the fort. It, too, has washed away. Still, the walk south gives a good perspective on what Confederate troops must have seen on the day of the attack.

Return to your car and continue south on U.S. 64. Drive 0.1 mile and take the next right into a rest area. The rest area has a detailed map marker showing the locations of all the forts, accompanied by a concise description of the battle.

After reading the map marker, drive 0.3 mile south on U.S. 64 and take the next left onto Pearce Street. Drive into a housing development called Heritage Woods. The Confederate camps were located throughout these woods. It was in this area that Federals, seeking a commanding officer to officially surrender the island a few hours after the land battle, found Colonel Shaw sitting in front of a fire calmly smoking his pipe. The Confederates built their camps in this area because it was the highest point on the then-swamp-covered island. The National Park Service has bought the woods on either side of Pearce Street in front of Heritage Woods.

After driving through the housing development, return to U.S. 64 and turn left, or east. Drive 1.2 miles and turn right onto Airport Road. This road ends at the Dare County Airport. Park and walk toward a white picket fence that is located near the runway in the middle of the area where the airplanes are tied down. Inside the picket fence is likely the only Confederate soldier buried in the middle of an active airport. The soldier was Thomas Fitzpatrick of the Burke County Guards, 3rd Georgia Volunteers, who died on October 19, 1861. He was thirty-nine years old and probably died of disease. Local historians do not know the location of the graves of the Confederate dead. Federal graves were probably moved to New Bern after that town was captured in March 1862.

Get back on Airport Road and return to U.S. 64. Turn right, or east, again onto U.S. 64. Drive 1.8 miles and turn right, or southwest, onto Burnside Road, or S.R 1123. Burnside Road is located next to the Dare County Library. Within 0.2 mile, the road will fork. Take the hard-right fork to stay on Burnside Road. Drive past Payne Road on the right, 0.8 mile after turning onto Burnside Road.

The land past this point on Burnside Road was heavily shelled by Federal gunboats firing on Fort Bartow. Relic hunters continue to find both shell fragments and, occasionally, unexploded shells in the woods. Before new construction starts on this part of the island, relic hunters track down the owners of the land and ask permission to search their lots with metal detectors. Civil War relic hunters, and anyone else for that matter, must be very careful when they find artillery shells. Fused artillery shells from the Civil War can be as deadly today as the day they were manufactured. Careless relic hunters have learned that lesson the hard way. Some have been killed when they drilled the fuses from old shells.

After crossing a small creek on Burnside Drive, turn right, or southwest, onto Bartow Drive. This turn is about 1.4 miles since leaving U.S. 64. This area, now covered by a housing development, was the site of Fort Bartow, the only fort to fire on the Federals. The Confederate gunners at Fort Bartow actually did pretty well. They hit three Federal ships, killed six Federal sailors, and wounded seventeen.

Retrace the route to U.S. 64 and turn right. Drive 0.1 mile to Anamas Dare Street and turn right, or west, at the Manteo Baptist Church. Drive 0.2 mile on Ananias Dare Street to Hubie Bliven Wildlife Art on the right. A sign is in the front of the house. In back of the house is a separate building where Blevin sells his paintings and maintains a public display of

Civil War artifacts from the battle. Bliven's collection contains musketballs, cannonballs, rusty muskets, buttons, and a sword he found under the water in Croatan Sound.

From Ananias Dare Street, drive 1.8 miles on U.S. 64 to the intersection with N.C. 345, located just before the U.S. 64/U.S. 264 bridge to the Outer Banks. Turn right, or southwest, onto N.C. 345 and pull over immediately into the dirt parking lot. Park the car and cross the road to read the map marker inside the white picket fence.

This is the site of the three-gun Confederate redoubt, where the heaviest fighting took place during the battle. Face southwest behind the remaining portions of the redoubt to see the Confederates' perspective on the attack by the Massachusetts, Connecticut, and New Jersey soldiers. The map marker provides good detail on the movements of the soldiers.

Three Confederate cannons faced down the road, which is generally in the same place today as it was during the battle. The trees along the road today would have been cut down to provide a clear field of fire, and to

Confederate redoubt at N.C. 345

Federal hospital at Ashby's Harbor

form the core of the dirt redoubt. Explosive shells were fired when the Federals first came into sight. As the Federals drew closer, the Confederates switched to firing canister, essentially a can full of round balls that was like firing a giant shotgun.

The swamps that were on either side of the redoubt seem to have dried, but the woods are still thick, making it easy to see how the Confederates thought they were well protected.

After reading the map marker, continue southwest on N.C. 345. After driving 0.8 mile, turn right, or west, onto Skyco Road, or S.R. 1134, and continue until the road ends at Croatan Sound. This is Ashby's Harbor, the landing point of the Federal forces. The remodeled, two-story house on the left, just before reaching the sound, was there during the war. It was used as a Federal hospital once fighting erupted at the redoubt. On the night of the landing, the woods surrounding the harbor were filled with

Federal soldiers huddling to stay warm and trying to start fires fueled by fence rails.

At this point, Roanoke Island seems to make a slight indentation inward, a natural shield that helped protect the troops from Fort Bartow's shelling. According to reports, the landing went so flawlessly that most of the soldiers waded in water barely over their ankles to reach the beach.

Retrace your route to U.S. 64. This concludes The Coastal War Tour.

From here, you can continue on to the Outer Banks. Due to the constant shifting of the elements on the Outer Banks, almost none of the original Civil War sites still exist. The ocean has long since reclaimed the Confederate forts on the Outer Banks, but that is no reason why history travelers cannot go and see where the forts would have been. Their capture, as well as the capture of the forts on Hilton Head Island in November 1861, were the first major Union victories during the war. The capture of these forts proved to skeptical Union leaders that the Federal blockade could work if key Southern defenses were rendered useless.

The loss of the forts at Hatteras was a disaster for the South. Confederate authorities in Richmond bemoaned the loss, and wondered publicly why the soldiers didn't fight better. State authorities in Raleigh wondered privately why Richmond had ignored its requests for decent gun powder. North Carolina officials had constantly warned Richmond that the gunpowder at the forts was old and damp, and the state's pleas for better powder were well documented. However, Richmond had refused to divert anything away from the armies in Virginia.

After the forts at Hatteras fell, the little forts at Ocracoke and Oregon Inlets were abandoned without firing a shot. This was a source of further embarrassment for North Carolina's leaders. The abandonment of these forts made it even easier for Federal forces to attack Roanoke Island, since they did not have to worry about attacks on their ocean supply line in the area.

Union Admiral David Porter, writing after the war about the battle for the forts at Hatteras, said, "This was our first naval victory, indeed our first victory of any kind, and should not be forgotten. The Union cause was then in a depressed condition, owing to the reverses it had experienced. The moral effect of this affair was very great."

Historical speculation about the battle has always centered on what would have happened if the Confederates had retaken Fort Clark and kept captured Federals inside. Would the Federal Navy have shelled the fort, knowing they would be killing their own men? If the Navy had retired, the Union would have suffered its second straight defeat, and its first naval loss. The North might have thought long and hard about sending another invasion force after such dismal results.

The only other real action seen on Hatteras Island came on October 5, 1861, near the present-day village of Rodanthe. In the Civil War the town was called Chicamacomico.

After Fort Hatteras and Fort Clark were taken, General Butler put Colonel Rush Hawkins of the 9th New York Zouaves Regiment in command of Hatteras Island. Hawkins, afraid that Confederate forces would try to sneak onto the island and attack him at the forts, ordered the six hundred men of the 20th Indiana Regiment to occupy Chicamacomico.

On October 1, 1861, the USS *Fanny* set out from the forts at Hatteras Inlet with supplies for the Federals at Chicamacomico. Along the way, it was captured by several small Confederate ships. When the Confederates learned about the isolated Hoosiers at Chicamacomico, they sailed to Roanoke Island and loaded up every available man. On October 5, six Confederate steamers appeared on the sound off the Federals' Chicamacomico camp. When the Federal colonel saw the ships, he ordered a general retreat back to the safety of the town of Hatteras. This retreat is remembered in Civil War history as the Chicamacomico Races.

The Federal retreat soon turned into a headlong flight. Chasing the 20th Indiana were members of the 3rd Georgia Volunteers, who were wearing Union overcoats captured from the *Fanny*. From a distance, it must have looked like Federal soldiers running in dark blue sack coats were being chased by Federal soldiers in light blue overcoats.

To make the scene even more bizarre, the Confederate ships were racing the Federals as well. The Confederate ships were trying to get ahead of the 20th Indiana and land troops to cut off the Federal retreat. For some reason, the Confederate troops never landed, and the Federals made it to the Cape Hatteras Lighthouse around midnight. They ran almost eighteen hours and covered almost twenty miles.

The Confederates, concerned that the Federals were now entrenched at the lighthouse, made camp south of the village of Kinnakeet and prepared to return to Chicamacomico the next morning. During the chase, they killed eight Federals and captured forty others. When the Confederates broke camp in the morning, they saw the 9th New York Zouaves rushing toward them. The races were on again in the opposite direction, with the Confederates the ones chased this time. A Federal gunboat also chased the Confederates and shelled them as they ran. The Confederates made the twenty-mile-run back to Chicamacomico with only a few light casualties and returned to Roanoke Island.

The Chicamacomico Races proved nothing, except that running in sand for twenty miles while wearing wool uniforms sure makes a man hot and thirsty.

The last Outer Banks island to see any Civil War activity was Portsmouth Island. At the beginning of the war, there was a small Confederate garrison there. The garrison was sent to reinforce the Confederates at Hatteras and was captured during the battle there. When the Federals invaded the island, they were surprised to find a fat lady stuck in her front door. When the woman heard the Yankees were coming, she was so terrified she rushed through the front door, forgetting that the back door was the only door large enough to accommodate her.

Today Portsmouth is a preserved, though abandoned, town, administered by the National Park Service. All of the buildings there are post Civil War. It is reachable only by ferry from Ocracoke.

To start the Outer Banks tour, leave Roanoke Island by heading east over the U.S. 64/U.S. 264 bridge. Drive approximately 3 miles to the intersection with N.C. 12, the main road on the Outer Banks. Turn south. Drive 9.5 miles to reach Oregon Inlet. After driving over the 3.5-mile-long Herbert C. Bonner Bridge, pull into the parking lot on the left side of the road. Somewhere in this vicinity was Fort Oregon.

Continue south on N.C. 12. About 14 miles from the bridge is the village of Rodanthe. During the war, this was Chicamacomico. The races took place along the Pamlico Sound beach, through the town of Kinnakeet, to a point near the Cape Hatteras Lighthouse. Drive about 21 miles south of Rodanthe to the Cape Hatteras Lighthouse. The museum at the lighthouse has an exhibit on the Civil War on the Outer Banks.

After visiting the lighthouse museum, continue south on N.C. 12 to the Hatteras-to-Ocracoke Ferry. A historic marker at the ferry station describes how the forts were 2 miles southwest of that point. Both forts, made out of sand and grass, have long since disappeared into the ocean. All of their guns were captured by the Federals.

Take the ferry. After docking, drive the 12 miles on N.C. 12 to the next ferry stop, which goes to Cedar Island. This ferry will pass by Portsmouth Island, which was occupied by both Confederate and Union soldiers.

This concludes the sidetrip to the Outer Banks.

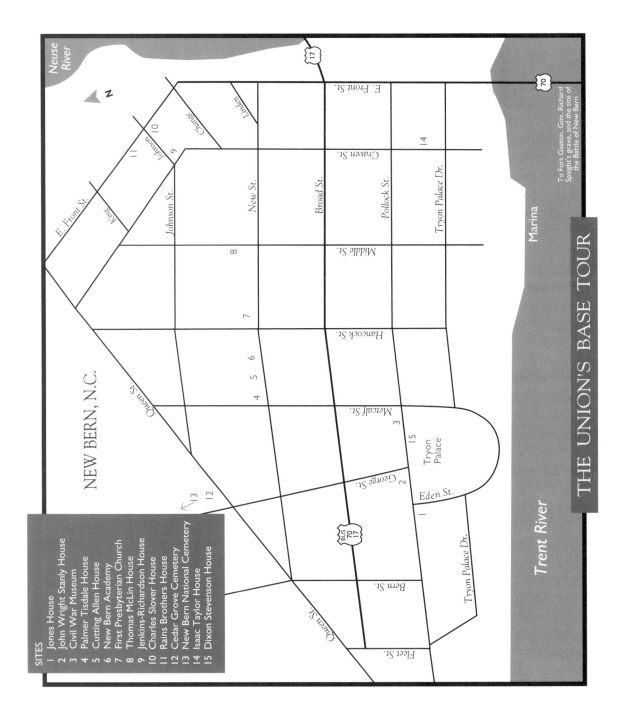

NEW BERN, N.C.

SITES
1 Jones House
2 John Wright Stanly House
3 Civil War Museum
4 Palmer Tisdale House
5 Cutting Allen House
6 New Bern Academy
7 First Presbyterian Church
8 Thomas McLin House
9 Jenkins-Richardson House
10 Charles Slover House
11 Rains Brothers House
12 Cedar Grove Cemetery
13 New Bern National Cemetery
14 Isaac Taylor House
15 Dixon Stevenson House

Neuse River

Trent River

Marina

To Fort Gaston, Gov. Richard Spaight's grave, and the site of the Battle of New Bern

THE UNION'S BASE TOUR

The Union's Base Tour

This tour covers New Bern and the forts and battlefields outside the city. Most of the city's houses were occupied by Federal troops throughout the war. That kept the houses from being burned and lost to history. The tour includes the house where a wily Confederate female spy was imprisoned, the birthplace of a Gettysburg hero, the home of a friendly soldier ghost, and the setting of a Mark Twain story. The tour also includes a preserved Confederate earth fort and the few remains from the Battle of New Bern.

Total mileage: approximately 23 miles. Plan for at least a day in New Bern.

After his easy capture of Roanoke Island on February 8, 1862, Union Major General Ambrose Burnside was on a roll. He immediately made plans to capture New Berne (the present-day spelling is New Bern), the old colonial capital of North Carolina and an important port city located at the confluence of the Trent and Neuse Rivers. It would be the Union's first attack on the North Carolina mainland.

Facing Burnside, a professional soldier in command of a eleven-thousand-man army that had just taken Roanoke Island by force, was Confederate General Lawrence O'Bryan Branch and four thousand untried troops. Branch, a Princeton-educated lawyer, was a former United States congressman who used his political clout to secure a field command. He did not have a single day of military training.

When he took command at New Bern in November 1861, Branch inherited Fort Thompson, a thirteen-gun dirt fort on the Neuse River six miles south of New Bern. A line of breastworks extended out from the fort. There were also six smaller dirt forts around the city, all designed to defend against a river attack. Not a single fort was designed to defend against land approaches, a planning mistake that one Confederate wrote was "the greatest failure of all. They (the forts) are a disgrace to any engineer."

Branch did the best he could in the limited amount of time he knew he had. He placed advertisements in area newspapers asking plantation owners to send him slaves to help build up the fortifications. One slave was sent in response. He asked Raleigh and Richmond for reinforcements, but as other Confederate commanders before and after Branch would learn, none came.

On March 11, 1862, it was too late to dig or reinforce. Burnside's fleet pulled into the mouth of the Neuse River at Slocum's Creek, about twelve miles south of the city. The location was a good six miles south of Fort Thompson, and many miles away from the guns of the other forts that were supposed to protect the town.

Burnside's troops landed unopposed the next day, using the same amphibious techniques they had perfected at Roanoke Island. Steamers towed landing boats close to land before veering off and casting the boats free. The landing boats' momentum carried them to shore. The landing went off without a hitch, and without any Confederate resistance.

As the soldiers marched north, they were surprised to pass over a line of abandoned Confederate trenches. What the Federals would have liked to have known was that Branch didn't defend the line because he didn't have enough men.

That night, the Federals camped in the pouring rain. A popular parody of the time may have been written that night: "Now I lay me down to sleep in mud that's fathoms deep; If I'm not here when you awake, Just hunt me up with an oyster rake."

Waiting for the rain-soaked Federals, in trenches running across the road to Morehead City, were the North Carolina regiments. Twelve cannons were on the Confederate line, an advantage since the Federals had not yet landed their artillery.

For some reason, Branch put his least experienced troops in the center of the line, next to an old brick kiln that had been built along the railroad line running between New Bern and Morehead City. Those troops were a local militia unit that had been formed only two weeks earlier, when it became obvious that Burnside was coming. They had no uniforms, and more importantly, they had not been issued military arms. They carried only shotguns and hunting rifles brought from home. Placing such troops at the center of the line, which was already broken by the kiln and the railroad tracks, was a mistake a professional military man probably would not have made.

On the morning of March 14, 1862, Burnside divided his force into three columns in preparation for the attack. The first column, commanded by Brigadier General John Foster, rushed the Confederate positions before the second Federal column could even get into position. That might not have been the most prudent thing to do. The land-facing guns of Fort Thompson cut Foster's men down. More Federals were killed by "friendly fire" from the Union gunboats in the Neuse River. The naval commander later explained that he did not mind killing Union soldiers if the effect was to demoralize the Confederate defenders. Union Navy commanders were not always popular figures among Union Army soldiers.

The second column, commanded by Union Brigadier General Jesse Reno, had better luck. Spotting the gap in the lines at the railroad, Reno personally led the 21st Massachusetts Regiment in a direct attack on the militia. In response, the local militia ran as hard as they could to the rear, exposing the flank of the 35th North Carolina Regiment. When the members of the 35th saw the advancing Federals, they broke as well and took off after the militia.

The 33rd North Carolina Regiment, which had been in reserve, rushed into the gap. They, along with the 26th North Carolina Regiment on the other side of the railroad, poured fire into the Massachusetts troops, successfully sealing the break in the Confederate line. The 21st Massachusetts, now caught behind Confederate lines, had to shoot its way out.

When he made his way to safety, the commander of the 21st Massachusetts reported to his commander that the Confederate center was weak. The Federals called up their reserve third column and rushed them toward the brick kiln. Again, the center of the Confederate line crumbled. Noticing that the Confederate center was collapsing, Foster ordered a bayonet charge that captured the breastworks in front of his column.

With his left flank and center disintegrating, Branch quickly issued orders for the whole Confederate line to retreat. The orders never made it to the 26th and the 33rd North Carolina Regiments, who were still fighting Reno's Federals on the far right of the Confederate line. Those two Confederate regiments were left behind on the battlefield while their buddies were hightailing it back to New Bern.

The abandoned 33rd North Carolina and the 26th North Carolina cut west into the swamps. When the regiments reached Brice's Creek, Colonel Zeb Vance of the 26th plunged into the water astride his horse to demonstrate how safe the crossing was. Vance was unhorsed and sank like a brick. The future governor was saved from drowning only after several men dove in after him.

A Black body servant scouting the bank found an old boat docked on the creek and reported it to the officers. Only eighteen soldiers at a time were able to cross the creek in the boat. Lieutenant Colonel Henry Burgwyn, Jr., of the 26th and a lieutenant kept the crossing orderly by making everyone march under their crossed swords into the boat. These two officers were the last to cross the creek.

General Branch and the main group of the retreating Confederates made their way back to New Bern by way of the bridge over the Trent River. The bridge had already been rigged for burning, and as the last man crossed, the match was set. Branch, apparently thinking that he would not be able to hold New Bern, had already made plans to set up shop in Kinston, about forty miles east. Some of the retreating Confederates did not stop running until they had made it to the last train at the depot.

The next day, Federal ships docked at New Bern's town wharf. The only person to meet them was an elderly slave, who greeted them warmly with the news that all of the Confederate soldiers had fled.

For the rest of the war, New Bern was occupied by Federal troops, an unhappy occurrence for the secessionists who had homes in the town, but a great thing for today's history traveler. The Federals obviously intended to stay for the duration of the war. Instead of burning houses and stores, as the Union Army frequently did when it captured Confederate towns, the Federals posted guards so that nothing would be destroyed. These houses and buildings are preserved today due to the Federals' good care.

Another happy occurrence for the history traveler is that almost as soon as the Federals moved in, photographers followed. Many, if not most, of the houses in New Bern were photographed during the war, both for historical records and as souvenirs that soldiers could purchase to send home to their family. Many of the surviving photographs show soldiers hanging out windows and off the balconies of local homes. Some officers are shown posing with their wives, who came down to live with the officers in the very comfortable homes graciously evacuated by New Bern's citizens.

Federal-occupied New Bern came under Confederate attack twice during the war. The first time came on March 13, 1863, when Confederate Major General D.H. Hill launched a three-pronged attack against the city. Hill ordered Brigadier General Junius Daniel to attack from the east and Brigadier General B.H. Robertson to attack from the south. At the same time, Brigadier General James Johnston Pettigrew was supposed to capture Fort Anderson, a dirt fort on the east bank of the Neuse River opposite New Bern. Daniel pushed the Federals back, but Robertson's attack failed to do much of anything.

On the other side of the Neuse River, Pettigrew fired a few rounds into Fort Anderson, then asked for the fort's surrender. The Federal commander asked Pettigrew for time to study the idea. While they were "thinking about it," the Federals were telegraphing Federal gunboats. By the time Pettigrew figured out that he had been tricked, the gunboats were there to stop the attack. All of the Confederates were forced to pull back, and an embarrassed Hill turned his attention to besieging the town of Washington, North Carolina, forty miles to the north.

Things were quiet for another nine months until January 1864, when Robert E. Lee heard a rumor that the Federals had stockpiled huge amounts of supplies in the city. Lee detached thirteen thousand men from his Army of Northern Virginia to capture the supplies.

Unfortunately, but not unexpectedly, Richmond's Virginia-centric view of the abilities of Confederate generals doomed the mission from the start. Instead of giving command of the expedition to Brigadier General Robert F. Hoke of North Carolina as Lee had suggested, the Confederate War Department insisted the responsibility go to Major General George Pickett of Virginia.

Pickett, who barely finished last of fifty-nine members in his 1846 West Point class, was never accused of being a military genius. Thus, when Hoke reluctantly offered his own plan to take the city by a coordinated attack from three directions, Pickett endorsed the plan as his own idea.

On February 1, 1864, Hoke's division of North Carolinians attacked and captured the fortifications around Batchelder Creek west of the city. They moved to within a mile of New Bern, where they paused and waited for the sound of firing from the Virginians in the east and south. The Tar Heels could have waited forever. Both of the other commanders chickened out when they saw the fortifications they were supposed to attack, even though they had the element of surprise. When those two commands failed to attack, all the Confederate forces pulled back.

The only real Confederate victory of this expedition was the capture of a Union gunboat, the USS *Underwriter*. The *Underwriter* was taken in a daring raid by Confederates in small boats. The ship was burned when the Confederates discovered it did not have enough steam to allow them to quickly slip by the Federals in New Bern.

In the attack on New Bern, Federal losses were put at about a hundred killed and wounded, while the Confederates suffered about forty-five casualties. The operation, which was launched to capture supplies for Lee's army, came away with fewer than 250 small arms and, according to Pickett's official report, "a quantity of clothing." Pickett made all kinds of excuses about his failure, including claims that the plan relied on too many "contingencies." Hoke wondered what would have happened if he had been in command of his own plan.

Start The Union's Base Tour by parking in the Tryon Palace parking lot, just off the intersection of Eden and Pollock Streets in New Bern. Walk to the Tryon Museum Gift Shop, also known as the Jones House, at 231 Eden Street on the corner of Pollock and Eden Streets. The gift shop is located just outside the Palace grounds. Built in 1809, this two-story, wooden house was used as a jail for Emeline Pigott, a suspected Confederate spy (See The Fall of Fort Macon Tour for details on the career of Emeline Pigott). Emeline was imprisoned in the Jones House for only a short time. She threatened several "pro-Union" men in New Bern that she would expose them as Confederate sympathizers unless they used their influence to free her. She was apparently not a woman to trifle with because the men soon persuaded the Federals to let her go.

The Jones House where Emeline Pigott was imprisoned

Walk east on Pollock Street. The Dixon Stevenson House, less than a block away on the southeast corner of George and Pollock Streets, was used as a hospital by the 9th Vermont Regiment.

Continue walking east on Pollock Street for one block to the corner of Metcalf and Pollock Streets. The New Bern Civil War Museum is at this intersection. The museum has a very good collection of Civil War muskets, carbines, pistols, and other artifacts. Included in the collection is a medical kit belonging to the surgeon of the 54th Massachusetts, the famed Black regiment raised in Boston in 1863. Other artifacts include a Confederate Bowie knife with "Yankee Slayer" carved into the handle, a sniper's rifle with shaded cross hairs at the muzzle, and a rare double-hammered, single-barrel Lindsey musket. Only one thousand of these muskets were manufactured. The rifle had two separate chambers, in theory, at least, giving the soldier twice the firepower of a man with a traditional single-shot musket. The better designs of the multi-shot Spencer carbines and Henry rifles no doubt limited the market for this unusual looking weapon.

The only artifact at the museum that does not really fit may be one that movie buffs will most want to see. The museum has the officer's uniform that actor Leslie Howard wore when he played Ashley Wilkes in *Gone With The Wind*.

Return to the Tryon Palace parking lot and pick up your car. Turn right onto Pollock Street heading back towards the museum. At the museum, turn north onto Metcalf Street. Continue two blocks, crossing over Business U.S. 70/Business U.S. 17, and turn right, or east, onto New Street. Park along New Street. On the northeast corner of New and Metcalf Streets, at 520 New Street, is the Palmer-Tisdale House.

The Palmer-Tisdale House was built in 1769, and was the war-time residence of Edward Stanly. In 1862, President Lincoln appointed Stanly, a former North Carolina congressman, to the post of "military governor" of North Carolina. Lincoln believed North Carolina could be brought back into the Union once its people saw how easily the eastern part of the state was taken by Union forces. He hoped Stanly's appointment would start a Unionist movement throughout the rest of the state. If nothing else, Stanly would be a good example of how the Federal goverment was trying to restore some order.

The New Bern Academy

Stanly was a native of New Bern who had moved to San Francisco to practice law in 1853. He was a strong proponent of the Union, but Lincoln's advisors neglected to check his attitude toward slavery. Stanly was all for it. After Lincoln issued the Emancipation Proclamation on January 1, 1863, Stanly resigned. He had served less than nine months. Lincoln concluded that appointing a sham governor while the real governor was still in office was a dumb idea. He did not try to find a successor.

Beside the Palmer-Tisdale House is the Cutting-Allen House at 518 New Street. Built in 1793, this house was moved from another site. It is one of the many houses captured in war-time photographs literally covered with frolicking Federals poking out from every possible place.

Beside the Cutting-Allen House is the New Bern Academy, a history museum operated by Tryon Palace. The building was used as a hospital by Federal forces. The museum houses a fine collection of artifacts tracing the history of New Bern and its architecture. One of the artifacts is a backpack used by a Federal soldier, Martin Payne. The backpack was discovered stuffed in a wall at a nearby house.

The Cutting-Allen House

Return to your car and continue east on New Street. Stop at the First Presbyterian Church at 418 New Street. The church, built from 1819–1822, was designed by a local architect to match similar churches in New England. During the war, Union forces used the church as a hospital. The Federals laid planks across the tops of the pews to create double-deck bed space and operating tables.

First Presbyterian Church

Continue east on New Street for one block and turn left, or north, onto Middle Street. At 507 Middle Street is the Thomas McLin House, built in 1810–1815 and moved to its present location in 1894. Local experts say the house is unique in local architecture due to its symmetry and small scale. This is the house where Martin Payne left his backpack to be discovered by future generations.

Continue to the next block and turn right onto Johnson Street. Follow Johnson Street to the intersection with Craven Street. On the southeast corner of this intersection, at 520 Craven Street, is the Jenkins-Richardson house, built in 1848. This attractive house is the setting for a touching story about a benign ghost who liked chatting with children.

Several years ago, a couple with a preschool-age boy lived in the house. One day, the child started talking about his new friend who came to visit him at night. The bemused parents assumed the child was going through his "invisible friend" stage. As the days passed, the child continued to tell stories about how his new buddy kept him company until he drifted off to sleep. The parents, perhaps a little concerned that someone might be sneaking into the house, asked more questions. The child referred to his friend as "the soldier man." The parents asked for more details, and soon elicited a description of a Union soldier. In one version of the story, the soldier told the child his name. Supposedly, a check of regimental records found the same name among New Jersey soldiers who had used the house as a hospital in 1863. Either the child had learned how to use the library's microfilm machine to check regimental rosters, or the dead Union soldier really did visit the house.

Continue in the same direction on Johnson Street to the southeast corner of Johnson and East Front Streets. The large, brick, Greek Revival house on this corner, at 201 Johnson Street, is the Charles Slover House, built in 1848. Although the official New Bern historic-homes-and-sites

The Slover House

map says this house was General Burnside's headquarters, Civil War historians more often refer to it as Union General John G. Foster's headquarters. Foster was in command of Union forces in North Carolina for more than a year while Burnside returned to service in Virginia after capturing New Bern.

Another interesting owner of the Slover House was C.D. Bradham, who bought it in 1908. Bradham invented "Brad's Drink," which became a little more popular when it was renamed Pepsi Cola.

Park along Johnson Street and walk north on the west side of East Front Street two houses up to 605 East Front Street. This is the childhood home of Brigadier General Gabriel James Rains and his brother, Colonel George Washington Rains. A historic marker is in front of the relocated house. If any two men could be considered critical to the Confederate war effort, they were the Rains brothers.

The Rains brothers, although rather lackluster commanders of men, were geniuses with gunpowder. Gabriel, an 1827 West Point graduate, invented "torpedoes," called "mines" in today's military. The first use of torpedoes came in 1862 during the Peninsula Campaign. Several unsuspecting Union soldiers marching towards Richmond stepped on the buried artillery shells, blowing them, and everyone around them, to smithereens.

Officers on both sides, who had no qualms about blasting men using cannon shells fired above the ground, found shells buried six inches below the ground unethical. However, desperation eventually forced the Confederacy to accept Gabriel Rains's lethal invention. He then adapted the land torpedo to water. By 1863, Confederate torpedoes were protecting ocean and river approaches all over the South. Union Admiral David Farragut's famous quote, "Damn the torpedoes! Full speed ahead!" was shouted in Mobile Bay, Alabama, just a few minutes after Federal sailors watched the ironclad USS *Tecumseh* strike a mine, roll over, and sink with her entire hundred-man crew.

Hundreds more Union sailors would die and dozens of Federal ships would sink during the war thanks to the high quality of Rains's torpedoes. Oddly, the United States government did not have hard feelings toward him after the war. From 1877 to 1880, he served as a clerk in the United States Quartermaster Department in Charleston.

While Gabriel was making the torpedoes, George was making the powder to go in them. An 1842 graduate of West Point, George was running an iron works in Newburgh, New York, when the war started. He gave up his business and returned to the South, where he was wisely assigned command of the Confederate Ordnance Bureau. Using his chemical background, George spent the war manufacturing gunpowder at Augusta, Georgia, not far from where nuclear bombs are made today. By the end of the war, he was credited with overseeing the production of nearly three million pounds of black powder.

George's most ingenious invention was a special explosive that could be molded into what looked like a lump of coal. A bomb of that type was successfully delivered by spies to the Federal ammunition dump in City Point, Virginia. On August 9, 1864, the bomb went off and a portion of the dump exploded. More than forty Federals were killed in the explosion. One man who was almost killed was Union General Ulysses S. Grant.

After the war, George taught chemistry in a medical school in Atlanta. He eventually returned to Newburgh, New York, and died there in 1898. One wonders how his New York neighbors treated the man who made enough gunpowder to keep the war going for four years, killing more than 350,000 Northerners.

After viewing the Rains brothers' home, walk back southeast on East Front Street, crossing Johnston Street, to see the low, long building behind the Slover House. Today, this building is a private home. During the Civil War, it was a kitchen and servants' quarters for the Slover House. It was also the setting for a Mark Twain short story titled, appropriately enough, "A True Story."

According to Twain, his postwar housekeeper, Aunt Rachel, was once a Virginia-born slave whose family was broken up and sold at auction. The last time Rachel saw her youngest child Henry, he swore he would run away and find her again to buy her freedom. They were separated when he was sold away to one plantation, and she was sold to another family who took her to New Bern, where she became a cook at the Slover House. When the Federals occupied the town, she continued to cook for them.

In time, the "big officer" living in the Slover House asked her if she had any family. She told him it had been thirteen years since she had seen

Henry, but she still remembered every detail of his face, down to the scar on his forehead. The sympathetic general told her that maybe Henry's dream of freedom had come true and that he was living in the North. The thought came as a shock to Rachel. She still thought of Henry as a little boy, not a fully grown man.

One night, the general had a big party for his officers, and a Black regiment was assigned to guard the house. The kitchen was filled with so many soldiers that Rachel finally yelled "Get along with you—rubbish!" One soldier stopped dead in his tracks and stared at her. She ignored him and threw all the men out of her kitchen.

The next morning, Rachel was bending down to look into the stove. The soldier who had been staring at her the night before approached her from behind on his hands and knees, the height of a small child, and shoved his face into her line of sight. It was then she saw the scar on the soldier's forehead. The soldier had recognized his mother by her angry use of the word "rubbish." Henry had found Rachel after thirteen years. Twain swore it was a true story.

Opposite this house, on the northeast corner of Johnson and East Front Streets at 529 East Front Street, is the Jones-Jarvis House, built in 1810. During the war, the Federals built a walkway between the house's two chimneys as a flag-signaling station to ships in the harbor.

Walk one block southeast on East Front Street, then turn right, or southwest, onto Change Street. The house at 209 Change Street is the Smallwood-Howard House, built in 1815 and moved to its present location in 1904. The house was photographed during the war with Federal officers and their wives.

Continue walking up Change Street one block to the intersection with Craven Street. Some locals have made up their own versions of historic house signs. One house in this neighborhood has a sign reading, "This house occupied by a Yankee, but he is a nice guy anyway." Another house sign reads, "On this spot in 1790, absolutely nothing happened."

On the northwest corner of Craven and Change Streets, at 501 and 505 Craven Street, is the house and office of Dr. Edward E. Smallwood, built in 1841. During the war, this was the headquarters for Foster General Hospital, a Union hospital named after General Foster. This hospital once

Dr. Edward Smallwood's office

covered the whole block bordered by Craven, Broad, Middle and New Streets. Today, the only other remaining evidence of the hospital is the Coor-Gaston House, a huge house on the southwest corner of the same intersection, at 421 Craven Street.

Return to your car. Drive northwest on East Front Street until it makes a hard left and becomes Queen Street heading southwest. Drive four blocks, then park along Queen Street near the arched entrance to Cedar Grove Cemetery on the right. Walk into the cemetery.

If it has been raining, be careful as you walk under the Weeping Arch of Cedar Grove. The coquina arch absorbs water, and legend says that anyone struck by drops falling from the arch will be the next person interred in the cemetery.

After entering the cemetery, turn right, or east, at the first dirt cross street, next to a light pole about 40 yards in from the entrance. Walk to a lane next to two large obelisks, one with a cross on top of it, and turn left, or north. Walk about 50 yards on this lane. Major General Robert

Major General Robert Ransom's grave

Ransom, Jr., is buried on this lane, just past one of the small, red-brick "holding" tombs. When facing Ransom's grave, the Confederate monument is a about 25 yards to the west.

Ransom, an 1850 West Point graduate, is often called "the other Ransom" in deference to his more capable older brother, Matt. Robert served credibly, if unspectacularly, during the early part of the war. He commanded the cavalry on Jubal Early's raid on Washington, and was likely one of the few Confederates who could say he saw the new United States Capitol, then under construction, during a battle. However, within viewing distance was as close as Early's raid got. Ransom spent much of 1864 back in North Carolina due to illness. After the war, he was a civil engineer in New Bern until his death in 1892.

Walk west to examine the Confederate monument and what may be the only Confederate crypt in the Carolinas, perhaps the whole old Confederacy. The mound underneath the Confederate monument is actually a hollow tomb with an eight-foot-high ceiling. Laid out on the crypt's floor in neat rows are the skeletons of more than sixty Confederate soldiers. Most were killed during the Battle of New Bern, and some were postwar veterans who asked to be entombed with their comrades. The names of most of the entombed soldiers are listed on the monument. Soldiers from both Carolinas, Alabama, Florida, and Georgia rest inside. Several years ago, relic-hunting vandals broke into the crypt. They swept the bodies with metal detectors in search of buttons, scattering the rib cages of the Confederates. The graverobbers were not caught by the authorities. Perhaps the ghosts of the dead haunt the relic hunters' dreams.

The monument, erected in 1885 after the crypt was built in 1867, depicts a rather cool-looking soldier. He has long hair and a long handlebar mustache, and is leaning on his musket. For some reason, his canteen is not standard issue.

Return to your car and continue driving southwest on Queen Street to the intersection with George Street. Turn right at the traffic light onto George Street. In about 0.75 mile, George Street curves to the left, or west, and becomes National Avenue. Cross over North Street and look for the New Bern National Cemetery on the left side of National Avenue behind a wall. The cemetery is about 1.0 mile from Cedar Grove Cemetery.

There are more than two thousand Federal troops buried in the New Bern National Cemetery, including many who died in a yellow fever epidemic. New Bern was one of the first national cemeteries where Black soldiers were buried. The states of New Jersey, Massachusetts, and Connecticut have erected monuments to their dead soldiers on the cemetery grounds.

It is at places like New Bern's National Cemetery where visitors can pause to experience the sadness of war. That sadness is illustrated by the letters of Private Durand W. Snow of the 46th Massachusetts, who died in New Bern. Snow wrote to his parents on June 10, 1863: "I am in the hospital now with the diarrhea and a slight fever. I am gaining strength and shall come home with the regiment. Do not worry." On July 1, 1863, a friend wrote Snow's parents: "The day before he died he told me his God was with him and he was prepared to die and he expressed his most earnest wishes to meet all his friends in heaven." Another friend wrote to Snow's parents: "He passed away like the rose that blooms in the spring." Snow's complete diary, including his description of the fighting at Kinston and Goldsboro, is at the New Bern library. Snow was probably buried in the New Bern cemetery, but he was apparently moved back north after the war. His name does not appear on the list of Federal soldiers buried in the national cemetery.

Return to your car and retrace your route to George Street. After returning to George Street, drive 0.3 mile to the John Wright Stanly house near the corner of George and Pollock Streets. The house is located immediately behind the Tryon Palace Visitor's Center. This house is open for visitors and is operated by the Tryon Palace.

Because it was built in 1783 and owned by a prominent Revolutionary War patriot, the tour at the Stanly House focuses on the eighteenth century. However, the house does have Civil War significance. It was the birthplace of both Edward Stanly, the military governor appointed by President Lincoln, and his cousin, Confederate Brigadier General Lewis Armistead. Armistead is famous as the only Confederate general to make it over the wall during the Pettigrew-Pickett-Trimble Assault at Gettysburg, more popularly known as Pickett's Charge. He died of wounds inside Federal lines. As much as North Carolina would like to claim him, Armistead is a Tar

Heel by birth only. His mother moved back to Virginia within weeks of his birth, and the general always considered himself a Virginian.

Return to your car and turn left, or east, onto Pollock Street. Drive four blocks and turn right, or south, onto Craven Street. Drive to the middle of the block. The three-story, brick house on the left, at 228 Craven Street, is the Isaac Taylor House. It was built in 1792. According to local legend, Federal soldiers occupied the first two floors of the house when they captured the city, forcing Taylor's two elderly daughters to move to the third floor. The women refused to leave the third floor or have anything to do at all with the Yankees in their home. Food was sent up to them by means of an outside pulley. Waste products were sent down the same way.

A ghost story claims that Miss Fanny, one of the spinster sisters, can sometimes be seen sitting in the first-floor front window. Apparently, now that the Yankees have been gone for 130 years, she has found it more convenient to haunt the first floor of her house.

Continue driving south on Craven Street to Tryon Palace Drive and turn left, or east. Drive one block to Business U.S. 70 and turn right, or southeast. Drive over the drawbridge spanning the Trent River.

After crossing the river, turn right at the first traffic light onto Mattamore Road, or S.R. 1004. During the war, this area was one large Federal camp. A short distance away was James City, a settlement for freed slaves. Drive 1.2 miles on Mattamore Road and pull off the main road onto an unmarked dirt road. To the right of the dirt road there is an average, modern, brick ranch house built in the middle of an earthen Civil War fort. The otherwise perfectly preserved earthworks have flowers growing on them. This is Fort Gaston, the earth fort that protected the Trent River bridge leading to New Bern. This was the bridge Confederate Brigadier General Branch burned on his retreat from the Federal attack on the city.

Return to Mattamore Road and continue in the same direction. Drive 0.6 mile to a small driveway next to a historic marker. This is the gravesite of former North Carolina Governor Richard Dobbs Spraight, Jr., who was killed in a duel by Congressman John Stanly in 1802. Spraight was a signer of the Declaration of Independence and the first native-born Tar Heel governor, serving from 1792–1795. During the war, a drunk Union soldier dug up Spraight, dumped his remains on the ground, and stole his fancy metal coffin. The official Union account says the coffin was returned and the governor reburied. A local diarist wrote that never happened. She claimed the Yankees stuck Spraight's skull on a fence post, and the grave was left open.

Retrace your route to U.S. 70 and head east toward Morehead City. Drive 3.9 miles after getting on U.S. 70 to the Craven County Fairgrounds on the left. Carefully cross two lanes of oncoming traffic and pull into the fairgrounds.

The fairgrounds were built on the trench line running from Fort Thompson on the Neuse River north to the Trent River. This was the trench line the Confederates defended against the Union attack that captured the city. Fort Thompson is now on private land and is inaccessible. All traces of the trench line on the fairground property are gone. The brick kiln is at least 0.5 mile west of this spot. Other remnants of the battlefield are on private property in the thick woods across the highway.

This concludes The Union's Base Tour.

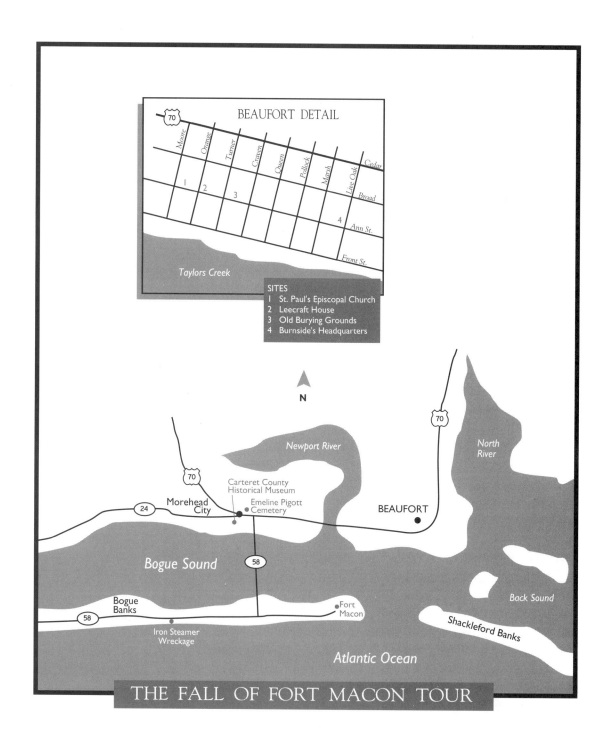

BEAUFORT DETAIL

70

Moore
Orange
Turner
Craven
Queen
Pollock
Marsh
Live Oak
Cedar
Broad
Ann St.
Front St.

1
2
3
4

Taylors Creek

SITES
1 St. Paul's Episcopal Church
2 Leecraft House
3 Old Burying Grounds
4 Burnside's Headquarters

N

Newport River

70

North River

58

24

Morehead City

Carteret County
Historical Museum

Emeline Pigott
Cemetery

BEAUFORT

Bogue Sound

58

Bogue Banks

Fort Macon

Back Sound

Shackleford Banks

58

Iron Steamer
Wreckage

Atlantic Ocean

THE FALL OF FORT MACON TOUR

The Fall of
Fort Macon Tour

This tour starts at the Carteret County Historical Museum in Morehead City, North Carolina, and continues to the grave of a Confederate female spy who is buried beside her unnamed lover. It then moves to the picturesque little town of Beaufort, North Carolina. Sites in Beaufort include a memorable Civil War monument, a church constructed by local shipbuilders that was used as a Federal hospital, and a cemetery with Confederate graves. From Beaufort, the tour moves to Fort Macon, an isolated fort that fell only after the brave Confederate defenders put up a spirited fight. Today, Fort Macon is North Carolina's best preserved brick fort from the Civil War.

Total mileage: approximately 29 miles. Leave plenty of time to explore Fort Macon and the town of Beaufort.

Morehead City and Beaufort are located on Bogue Sound, where the Newport River runs into the Atlantic Ocean. The war came early, but relatively gently, to these two towns. Nearby Fort Macon got a much ruder awakening.

With the fall of Roanoke Island on February 8, 1862, and the occupation of New Bern on March 14, it was only a matter of time before Union Major General Ambrose Burnside turned his attention further south. He quickly focused that attention on nearby Fort Macon, just thirty-three miles down the road. In fact, Burnside had been issued orders in January directing him "to reduce" Fort Macon in order to capture the Atlantic Ocean port at Morehead City.

Fort Macon, a brick fort on the tip of Bogue Banks across the sound from the town of Beaufort, was garrisoned by a 450-man force. The garrison's problem was obvious to both Confederate defenders and Union attackers—the fort's island location made any attack from the mainland a sure success. The garrison either would be starved out or blasted out.

Colonel Moses J. White, Fort Macon's commander, recognized his predicament, and he tried the same thing that commanders on the Outer

Banks, Roanoke Island, and New Bern had tried: he pleaded with Confederate government officials in Richmond for more men, weapons, and ammunition. And, like the others before him, he was turned down. Once again, Confederate war planners in Richmond failed to recognize the strategic importance of the North Carolina coast.

White knew he was being ignored, and he knew that his fort would be overwhelmed easily. However, he also knew one more thing. He would not give up without a fight—to do less would be dishonorable.

Burnside's Union forces reached the outskirts of Morehead City on March 21, 1862, and took the town without firing a shot. Beaufort also surrendered without a fight. One of the first things the Federals did after capturing the towns was to send an offer to accept the fort's surrender. White turned them down, and the siege of Fort Macon began.

Over the next several weeks, the Federals landed on Bogue Banks and steadily built a beachhead of supplies and men that moved closer and closer to the fort. The Confederates rationed their food, drilled every day, filled

Fort Macon

sandbags, and kept close watch over their enemy. By April 12, 1862, the Federals had placed siege mortars within thirteen hundred yards of the fort. On April 24, the Federals again asked for the fort's surrender. Again, White politely refused.

On the morning of April 25, 1862, the Federals started firing their mortars behind the protection of sand dunes. The gunners on the walls of Fort Macon could not even see their attackers, much less hit them with their cannons—guns that were designed to fire on ships in the harbor. Since Fort Macon lacked mortars to return fire on the land, its gunners concentrated on shooting at the Federal ships in the harbor. After some early hits and near-hits, the ships moved off.

That small measure of success could not sustain the fort. By the end of the day, White surrendered. He had known for a month that he would have to surrender, but he could not give up without a fight. Fort Macon, the last corner of Confederate resistance on the North Carolina coast, had fallen.

Mortar at Fort Macon

This tour starts in Morehead City at the Carteret County Historical Museum, located at 100 Wallace Street just off U.S. 70, or Arendell Street. The museum is on the south side of the road, just inside the city limits.

The first thing any visitor notices about the museum is the huge anchor in front. Found several years ago buried in ocean sand off Beaufort, the anchor once belonged to a blockading ship of the United States Navy. The identity of the ship has never been determined. That anchor may have, should have, caused a Union ship captain some grief, in the view of local historians who have theorized why a perfectly good anchor went to the bottom of the ocean.

At one point during the war, there was a rumor that the Confederate Navy was going to make a major attack on the Union blockaders. At the time, it was standard Navy procedure for a ship's captain to cut loose his anchor when under imminent attack. This saved the ship's crew from going through the time-consuming procedure of cranking the anchor to the surface and securing it onboard. Apparently, one fearful ship's captain cut loose his anchor and hightailed it to the open ocean.

The problem was that the attack never came. The fate of the Union Navy captain who intentionally dropped his only anchor to the bottom of the Atlantic Ocean without a Confederate ship in sight may never be known.

Behind the museum is a stout, wooden livestock fence estimated to be at least 165 years old. Built by slaves on a nearby plantation, the fence likely was used around a vegetable garden to keep out livestock. It is constructed without nails and is as solid today as the day it was put together. It is just one example found throughout the South of the construction skills of the slaves who worked on the antebellum farms and plantations.

Inside the museum are some photographs of a handsome woman named Emeline Pigott, a North Carolina spy who has never enjoyed the publicity bestowed on Virginia's famous women spies, Rose Greenhow and Belle Boyd. Only twenty-five-years old at the start of the war, Emeline lived on a farm just north of the small village of Morehead City. Early in the war, she became involved in helping nurse sick soldiers. She fell in love with one of her patients, a soldier who later died at Gettysburg. Upon hearing of his death, she dedicated her life to working for the Confederacy.

Emeline built up an extensive spy network that ran from Morehead City all the way to the nearest Confederate outpost at Kinston, more than seventy miles away. One of her most successful ploys was sending fishermen out to the blockading Federal fleet on the pretense of selling them fish. While one fisherman would haggle over price, the others would be chatting with the crew to learn the ship's tonnage, armament, cargo, and port of call. The fishermen would report back to Emeline, who carried the written descriptions to Kinston.

Emeline also organized her own mail service, keeping the residents of Federal-occupied Carteret County in touch with their Confederate relatives in the field. She would walk deep into the woods and leave letters and what medical supplies she could steal from the Yankees under a certain tree stump. Her contacts would come to the spot and exchange letters under the stump.

Eventually, Emeline's reputation reached the Union Army, and she was arrested in Beaufort. She refused to be searched by anyone but a white woman. While the chagrined officers went to find someone to conduct the search, Emeline ate the spy note she had concealed on her body and tore the mail she carried into little bits.

She was transferred to New Bern to await trial. While imprisoned in a New Bern house with her cousin, legend claims a vengeful Federal officer tried to kill them by releasing a large quantity of chloroform into the room. The two women broke open a window for fresh air and were not harmed.

Emeline escaped the gallows by threatening some influential men she knew in New Bern. She sent word to the men that she would expose them as Confederates rather than the pro-Union supporters they claimed to be. These men persuaded the Federals to release her without trial.

Federal ship anchor in front of the Carteret County Historical Museum

Emeline apparently stopped her spying, but not her nursing. She fell in love with another Confederate soldier, who died while in her care. Although she almost certainly knew his name, she had him buried in the family cemetery as an unknown soldier. Emeline, her heart broken by the death of her two loves, never married. She died in 1919, a true Confederate to the end. Even at the age of eighty-three, she was active in the local chapter of the United Daughters of the Confederacy.

Leave the museum and turn right, or southeast, onto U.S. 70. Within 0.2 mile is a historic marker describing Carolina City, a large Confederate Army training camp that was abandoned before the Federals captured it on March 21, 1862. At 0.4 mile from the museum, there is a large historic marker on the right side of the road that gives detailed information on the siege of Fort Macon. Pull into the nearby parking lot to read this helpful display. It describes how Morehead City was peacefully occupied on March 22, and Beaufort on March 26, 1862.

Continue east on U.S. 70 past Twelfth Street, the original town limits of Morehead City. At one time, the entire town was fenced to keep foraging livestock from roaming city streets.

At the intersection of Eighth Street and U.S. 70, on the one-way part of U.S. 70 heading west, is the Admiral's Quarters, an office building that local historians say may have been built as a hospital for Union troops. The fact that it was built from scratch indicates that the Federals had no intention of ever giving up the ocean port of Morehead City. Most Union hospitals were in houses and churches taken over for that purpose.

Turn around on U.S. 70 and head west back to Twentieth Street. At Twentieth Street, turn right, or north. Drive about 0.2 mile and take the first left onto Emeline Place. Take the next left onto Yaupon Drive. On the left side of Yaupon Drive is the Pigott family cemetery, located on land that was once part of their farm. The cemetery is padlocked, but Emeline's grave can be viewed from the road, as can the grave of the man the historic marker calls "the unknown boyfriend."

Follow Yaupon Drive around until it intersects with Emeline Place again. Retrace your route back to U.S. 70. Carefully cross the divided highway and turn left, or east, onto U.S. 70 towards Beaufort.

After crossing the bridge to Beaufort, take a right at the first light onto Turner Street. Signs will direct you to the historic downtown area. Within a block, you will pass the Carteret County Courthouse, which has a Confederate monument on its grounds. While many Confederate statues are inscribed with flowery language and, sometimes, bad poetry, this statue has a simple, memorable message: "Not even time can destroy heroism." The monument was erected in 1926, sixty-one years after the war.

Many of the local men the monument honors were fishermen. Surprisingly, the independent fishermen of Carteret County seemed to support the Confederacy, though very few owned any slaves. Most of the men in the nine villages east of Beaufort went into the Confederate Army, perhaps for no other reason than the fact they did not like the idea of the federal government telling North Carolina what to do. These men stayed at their posts to the very end. According to local historians, the last Confederate cannon shot at Appomattox on the day Robert E. Lee surrendered was fired by a five-man cannon crew from Carteret County. These feisty fishermen were loading a second round when a Confederate officer ran up to them waving his arms, telling them the war was over.

After leaving the courthouse on Turner Street, turn right, or west, onto Ann Street. Drive one block to the houses at 305 and 307 Ann Street on the right side of the street. These virtually identical houses were owned by the Leecraft brothers, who commanded an infantry unit called the Carteret Rifles during the war. Their father, a wealthy Beaufort merchant, lived next door to the houses he built for his sons.

Continue driving west on Ann Street. In the next block, at 209 Ann Street, is St. Paul's Episcopal Church, built in 1857 by local shipbuilders. Local historians say the church was used as a hospital by the Union Navy. The church was consecrated on May 21, 1861, just one day after North

Leecraft houses

Carolina seceded from the Union. Assisting in the ceremony was Reverend David D. Van Antwerp of New Bern and Reverend Alfred A. Watson of New Bern. Van Antwerp would become a Federal chaplain assigned to the captured Fort Macon. Watson would become a Confederate officer. After the war, Van Antwerp helped reestablish the church. A stained-glass window is dedicated to his memory.

The inside ceiling beams of St. Paul's look like an upturned boat, as might be expected of a church built by shipbuilders. Today, church members take great pride in how uncomfortable their pews are. Built by the same shipbuilders, the pew seats are way, *way*, too narrow for the buttocks of modern-day worshipers. Those pews, meant to be temporary until better seating could be purchased by the congregation, have been in the church for 139 years.

Turn around and head east on Ann Street to the Old Burying Ground, located on Ann Street between Turner and Craven Streets. Many Confederate soldiers are in the cemetery. Matthew Gooding, a successful blockade runner, is also buried there.

Continue on Ann Street to Live Oak Street and turn left. Drive to the corner of Live Oak Street and Brevard Street. The Reverend Ben Jones's house, located on this corner, was occupied by General Burnside while he was in Beaufort.

After viewing the Jones house, turn around on Live Oak Street and drive towards the water one block to Front Street. Turn right, or west, onto Front Street and drive three blocks to Queen Street. The Inlet Inn, at 601 Front Street on the corner of Queen and Front Streets, is on the site of the old Hammond Hotel. During the war, the hotel served as a hospital staffed by Roman Catholic nuns. The hotel was destroyed by a hurricane after the war.

Continue on Front Street to the North Carolina Maritime Museum, at 315 Front Street. The museum does not have any displays about the Civil War, but it offers good exhibits on boat building, and how and why people made their living on the ocean. It has a small library with a few Civil War books, including some that detail the size and armament of ships operating in the area at the time.

After leaving the museum, you may wish to enjoy the colonial-era homes and shops in Beaufort. When you finish visiting the shops, return to Morehead City on U.S. 70 West.

In Morehead City, continue west on U.S. 70 to Twenty-third Street. Turn left onto Twenty-third Street and drive over the bridge that connects Morehead City with Bogue Banks, following the signs for N.C. 58. About 0.5 mile from the bridge is the intersection with N.C 58. There is a traffic light at the intersection. Turn right, or west, onto N.C. 58. At 1.2 miles west of the traffic light is a historic marker showing the location of Hoophole Creek, where the Federal forces first landed to mount their siege against Fort Macon.

At 5.4 miles from the traffic light is the Iron Steamer Hotel and Fishing Pier. Just off the fishing pier, and sometimes visible at extremely low tide, is the wreck of the blockade runner *Pevensey*. The *Pevensey* was a five-hundred-ton, iron-hulled sidewheeler that ran aground to avoid capture in June 1864. Its cargo was not quite as dramatic as gunpowder, cannons, muskets, or gold. Instead, it was carrying twenty tons of bacon. When the *Pevensey* ran aground, the bacon was thrown overboard to keep it out of Yankee frying pans. There is a charge to park at the fishing pier, so stop at the hotel instead.

Turn around and head east on N.C. 58. Continue straight through the traffic light and follow the brown signs for Fort Macon. At 3 miles east of the traffic light there is a historic marker showing the location of the siege mortars Federals used to attack Fort Macon.

Drive 0.7 mile from the marker to the entrance of Fort Macon and park in the parking lot.

Fort Macon was built over four years, from 1824 to 1828. The construction of the fort used 1.3 million bricks. The design was typical for coastal fortifications of that time, but the fort was rendered instantly obsolete when ships obtained rifled cannons whose shells could bore holes through brick before exploding. Confederate forces seized the fort from its small United States Army garrison on April 14, 1861. However, Confederate leaders likely considered the fort doomed once they knew Union forces intended to attack coastal facilities.

The fort never got any respect from the Confederacy. Its commander, Colonel Moses J. White, never received any mortars to defend against ground forces, nor was his small garrison ever reinforced. In fact, his garrison was weakened when he was ordered to send some of his men to New Bern in a fruitless effort to defend that city against invasion.

White didn't even receive any fresh gun powder. He was forced to make do with the thirty thousand pounds of black powder that was already in the fort when it was captured by the Confederates. White calculated that, if attacked, he would have enough powder to fire his fifty-four cannons no more than three days. That was assuming, of course, that the powder would explode. It had been in the fort for years, and much of it was damp and old.

The story of Colonel White's career is a sad one. A native of Vicksburg, Mississippi, he graduated second in his class from West Point in 1858. He stayed in the United States Army until February 1861, when he resigned to follow his state. Photos of White show him to be thin and sickly. Records indicate that he suffered from epilepsy, a disease that must not have been diagnosed until after his graduation from West Point. He died on January 29, 1865, days before he was to take an overseas assignment in England. White had sought the assignment because he read that the world's foremost expert on epilepsy lived in London. The colonel never married, although there are stories that he loved a young woman in New Bern.

But even constant sickness did not diminish White's will to fight. Facing his 450 men in Fort Macon were more than 1,500 Union soldiers commanded by Union Brigadier General John G. Parke, a subordinate to the overall commander Burnside.

When Union forces first occupied Beaufort and Morehead City in March, Parke asked White to surrender. White politely refused. For the next month, Union forces moved closer and closer to the fort, finally setting up mortars that could drop 88-pound shells into the fort's interior.

When the Federal attack was imminent, General Burnside himself offered to let White surrender. Again, White politely refused. The attack was called for dawn on April 25, 1862.

The Union attack came from gunboats and mortar shells launched from behind the protection of the sand dunes. Against the land forces, White tried to compensate for his lack of mortars by dismounting six, old, thirty-two-pounder cannons from their carriages. He dug pits in the fort's parade ground and elevated the guns' muzzles as high as he could, attempting to make them act as mortars.

While there was little White could do against the land forces, he must have smiled when the four overconfident Federal ships pulled in close to the fort to start their shelling. He quickly let the boats have it with his cannons. His well-trained gunners hit two of the four ships within a few minutes. Within an hour, all four Federal ships had pulled out of range.

While he could beat the ships, White could not beat the Union mortars. A Federal officer watching the action at Beaufort helped Union artillerymen guide the mortars. After each shot was fired, the officer would signal by flags for the artillerymen to make corrections in their aim. Of the more than 1,150 rounds fired by the Federals, nearly half landed inside the fort. Within hours, nearly a quarter of the fort's guns had been dismounted, and the powder magazine was dangerously close to being exposed. Seven of White's men were dead and at least fifteen were wounded, while his gunners had managed to kill only one Federal soldier and wound three. White, realizing further resistance was futile, finally surrendered in the afternoon.

White, extremely emotional at the surrender, could not have done better than he did. A letter on display in the fort from a Union officer to his wife tells of practicing with the fort's guns using the old Confederate powder. The letter states the old shells burst almost as soon as they left the cannons' muzzles.

Fort Macon's courtyard features two Federal mortars of the type used to pound the fort into submission. The museum at the site features a good artillery shell display, other artifacts, and a slide show about the fort's construction and the battle. Colonel White's room has been recreated, as have the barracks of the average soldier from both the Civil War and World War II.

The fort was first opened as a state park in 1934, then reoccupied by United States Army coastal artillery units until after World War II. The World War II history of North Carolina's coast is represented by a large map display detailing the location of dozens of ships lost to German submarines.

Another interesting display is of letters written by soldiers stationed at the fort. One letter, written on June 7, 1861, reads: "There don't seem to be much chance of ever having a fight down here. We are well prepared for the enemy." The letter describes a typical day: Get up at 5:15 A.M. Drill in the morning and afternoon. Lights out by 10:00 P.M. On Sundays they would "have preaching, sometimes once, sometimes twice." Another Confederate letter, written on July 7, 1861, says, "I am very much dissatisfied, but I am into it now and no way to get out. I do not know when I can come home, but when I get clear of this war, I shall never engage in another." North Carolina had seceded less than two months earlier.

While it is open from 9:00 A.M. to 5 P.M. every day except Christmas, Fort Macon seems to be active all day and all night. For some reason, ghost stories about the place abound. Many are told by Civil War reenactors who occasionally spend the night on the fort's courtyard. These reenactors have seen mysterious soldiers walking picket duty along the fort's walls. When they rush to the top of the wall, the soldiers disappear. One night when there was a full moon, four reenactors who were chatting noticed that five shadows were being cast on the ground. Doors have been known to slowly swing shut, and lights that staffers know they turned off have been found burning.

There are even treasure stories associated with Fort Macon. According to one legend, a shifty Federal officer spent much of his military career collecting gold from different sources. For some reason, he melted his booty down into a cannonball and painted it black, apparently to disguise his wealth from his shipmates. During the heat of battle, someone grabbed the cannonball and fired it at Fort Macon. According to the legend, it was never recovered.

This concludes The Fall of Fort Macon Tour.

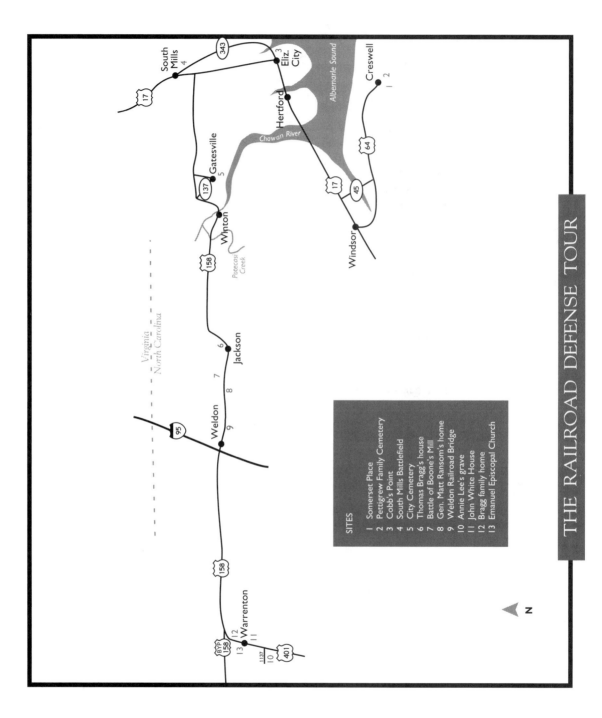

SITES

1 Somerset Place
2 Pettigrew Family Cemetery
3 Cobb's Point
4 South Mills Battlefield
5 City Cemetery
6 Thomas Bragg's house
7 Battle of Boone's Mill
8 Gen. Matt Ransom's home
9 Weldon Railroad Bridge
10 Annie Lee's grave
11 John White House
12 Bragg family home
13 Emanuel Episcopal Church

THE RAILROAD DEFENSE TOUR

N

The Railroad Defense Tour

For the Union forces in upper northeast North Carolina, much of the Civil War action can be reduced to a simple command: Destroy The Railroad. From 1862 until 1865, a major objective of the Federal forces operating in this part of the state was to burn the Wilmington & Weldon railroad bridge over the Roanoke River. The bridge was located at the small town of Weldon, more than 175 miles northwest of the Union base on Roanoke Island. If the bridge were destroyed, and the town held by Union forces, the supply of food, clothing, and ammunition flowing from North Carolina to Confederate forces in Virginia would be cut off. Without these supplies, Lee's Army of Northern Virginia would quickly fold.

Capturing the bridge at Weldon was the goal of Union General Burnside after winning the Battle of Roanoke Island on February 8, 1862. However, before he could take the bridge, he had to make sure the Union Navy controlled all of the rivers and sounds in the region. A look at a map showed him that the Pasquotank, Chowan, and Roanoke Rivers cut deep into the state. If he could use those rivers to transport troops on gunboats, he would save days of marching, lessening the natural dangers of being on enemy soil.

This tour starts in the remote northeast portion of North Carolina, at the Pettigrew State Park near Creswell. Pettigrew State Park includes the grave of General J.J. Pettigrew and Somerset Place, a plantation that remains as a testament to the slaves who built it. From there, the tour moves to Elizabeth City and the site of the Battle of South Mills. In the battle, a handful of Confederates defeated three thousand Federals. It then travels through the small towns of Gatesville, Winton, and Jackson. Sites in Jackson include the Boone's Mill battlefield, where naked Confederates fought back advancing Federals. From there, the tour travels through Weldon to Warrenton, where the home of Braxton Bragg and the former grave of Annie Lee, General Robert E. Lee's daughter, can be seen.

Total mileage: approximately 200 miles. Most stops will be short, although a visit at Somerset Place and Pettigrew's grave can take up most of a morning.

The first task would be to swat the pesky little "mosquito fleet" that had harassed his gunboats at Roanoke Island. (See The Coastal War Tour for details on the mosquito fleet.) Burnside knew the Confederate ships had run up the Pasquotank River to Elizabeth City. He sent several warships in pursuit.

The Confederate commander of the little band of boats—most armed only with one or two mismatched cannons—was Commodore William F. Lynch, a Virginian who had resigned his captain's commission in the United States Navy. While rearming his boats at Elizabeth City, Lynch put ashore at a dirt fort on Cobb's Point, south of the town. He intended to rouse the fort's troops for the coming fight.

Lynch found the four old cannons at Cobb's Point were manned only by eight inexperienced militiamen. A full complement would have been at least twenty men, just to man the cannons. While Lynch was ashore trying to figure out what to do, the Federal fleet appeared, coming full speed ahead up the river. As soon as they saw the Federal ships, the militiamen turned and ran.

Lynch frantically signalled to his ships for men to crew the guns. The volunteers made it to shore in just enough time to get off two cannon rounds at the speeding Federals, who swept by them in pursuit of Lynch's six ships.

The tiny Confederate boats were no match for the Union ships. The CSS *Black Warrior* was set on fire by her own crew in a cove directly across from Cobb's Point. The CSS *Seabird* was rammed and sunk by a Federal ship. The crew of the CSS *Ellis* fought hand-to-hand with the crew of the USS *Ceres*. The CSS *Fanny* was run aground, and the crew headed for the swamp. The CSS *Beaufort* turned tail and ran up the Dismal Swamp Canal, hoping to make it all the way to Confederate-held Norfolk. The *Beaufort* was followed, for a while anyway, by the CSS *Appomattox*. Her captain discovered too late that his boat was just a bit too wide for the canal. The *Appomattox* would not fit, so the captain burned the boat as her crew ran into the woods.

The naval battle for Elizabeth City was over in minutes. Only two Federals were killed. Four Confederates were killed, several were wounded, and thirty-four were captured, not to mention the loss of the last Confederate boats in coastal northeast North Carolina. The "battle" was another Confederate disaster.

The Federals took Elizabeth City and nearby Edenton without any civilian resistance. Scouts were sent to look at two other immediate objectives: the locks of the Dismal Swamp Canal, located at the small hamlet of South Mills, about 12 miles north of Elizabeth City; and the little Chowan River town of Winton.

Burnside recognized the Dismal Swamp Canal could be a valuable path leading to and from Virginia. He thought it could be used to transport Federal troops by boat into Virginia.

Winton was an important river town. Burnside saw that Winton could be used as a base for an attack on the important railroad bridge at Weldon, as well as for other operations.

On February 18, 1862, just ten days after the fall of Roanoke, Federal forces began their attack on Winton. A thousand Federal soldiers, made up of Colonel Rush Hawkins's 9th New York Zouaves and the 24th Rhode Island chugged up the Chowan on eight gunboats. The four hundred Confederates in Winton decided the only way they could win against those odds was to lull the Federals into a false sense of security, then surprise them.

Winton was built on a high bluff overlooking the Chowan River. The bluff was so high that the town could not be seen from the wharf below. The Confederates wanted the Federals to dock at the wharf so their boats' cannons could not be elevated high enough to fire on the bluff. Once the Federals had tied up their ships, the Confederates would spring from their high ground and shoot down on the Federals like fish in a barrel. The plan was to get a local woman to wave the boats ashore.

As the gunboats neared Winton, Federal soldiers could see the woman waving a white cloth at them, motioning them ashore. The gunboats headed her way. The boats were almost ready to dock when the lookout high in the mast of the leading vessel, Colonel Hawkins himself, spotted sunlight glinting off muskets behind some trees in town. He then spotted two cannons.

Shouting for the vessels to move away from the dock, Hawkins swung down from the high mast so fast that some Confederates later wrote he was shot down. The Federals veered into the river and shelled the bluff, driving the Confederates off.

The next morning, a decidedly peeved Hawkins returned to Winton. He almost hanged the woman but believed her story that she was forced into the deception.

The town was sacked and burned, the first instance during the war when Federal soldiers destroyed private property and residences. The burning of Winton was not good public relations for the Federals in general, and Hawkins in particular. At the same time Hawkins was burning Winton, other Federals were passing out leaflets around eastern North Carolina telling residents that the Old Union was finally there to protect them. Once the residents heard about the burning of Winton, the propaganda campaign failed.

Hawkins was personally embarrassed by the burning. A fund-raising drive was underway in New York to create medals commemorating his Zouaves' charge at Roanoke. Once news spread about Winton, donations dried up.

However, the Winton burning did not mean Hawkins gave up his dreams of glory. Later in the year, Hawkins and his men, who had fought in all the early battles in North Carolina, were transferred to the Army of The Potomac. They achieved their long-sought-after glory at the Battle of Sharpsburg, also known as Antietam. A large monument was later erected to them there. Hawkins, the brash New York City lawyer/soldier, lived until 1920. He was always eccentric and did everything with a flourish, even dying that way. He was run over by a car.

The next action in upper northeast North Carolina came in April 1862. More than three thousand soldiers under the command of Union Brigadier General Jesse Reno set sail from New Bern to Elizabeth City. Their mission was to take care of Burnside's second goal, the capture or destruction of the locks at South Mills. (Though under Federal control, Elizabeth City never became a major base for the Federals. They feared Elizabeth City was too close to Confederates forces in southern Virginia. The Federals preferred to concentrate their forces in New Bern, where supplies could be easily brought in by ships.)

The Federals landed at a natural harbor near Elizabeth City called Chantilly, the same spot where the CSS *Black Warrior* had been scuttled back in February. The ever present 9th New York Regiment, Hawkins's Zouaves, were sent ahead of the main force. A local mulatto was recruited to guide Hawkins to South Mills. The mulatto, whether intentionally or by accident, took Hawkins on a longer road that took the regiment right to a Confederate picket line. Hawkins had the man shot for his supposed deception. Hawkins finally found the right road to South Mills, but now the Confederates were warned.

Protecting the locks were three little cannons and four hundred members of the 3rd Georgia Regiment, the same intrepid landlubbers who had crewed the mosquito fleet. Their colonel positioned his men behind a long, wide ditch that he filled with fence rails. When he knew the Federals were close, he lit what would become known as "the roasted ditch." He kept the bonfire burning as he and his gallant four hundred waited for the three thousand Federals.

The Federals tried flanking the Confederates but were beaten back twice. Against orders, Hawkins tried a frontal assault, the same tactic he had used at Roanoke Island in attacking a Confederate earthworks. Hawkins's Zouaves lowered their bayonets and charged through the blazing ditch.

Unlike the Zouaves' charge at Roanoke Island, the Confederates at South Mills were entrenched in their earthworks and were waiting for the blue-and-red-clad Zouaves. The Georgians killed nine New Yorkers and wounded fifty-eight, including Hawkins. Some of the wounded caught fire when they fell in the roasted ditch.

Reno had enough. He retreated and marched back to his ships, inexplicably leaving his thirteen dead and hundred wounded on the battlefield. The tiny band of Confederates held out for more than five hours against a force eight times its size. The Confederates suffered only six killed and twenty wounded. Their success gave credence to the oft-repeated Southern claim that any Southerner—under certain circumstances—could lick a dozen Yankees.

It would be more than a year before large organized Federal forces would push their way into the interior of northeast North Carolina again, but that did not mean the area was safe for the Confederacy. The land between the Chowan and the Pasquotank Rivers, from Elizabeth City to west of Winton, came under the control of irregular Confederate deserters,

Unionist sympathizers, and bushwhackers. These irregulars collectively came to be called "buffaloes." The origin of the term is murky, but it may refer to the way the irregulars operated more like a free-roving herd than a military unit.

The buffaloes rarely engaged regular Confederate troops, preferring to raid secessionist farms and plantations to keep themselves supplied with food and ammunition. They killed an uncounted number of farmers who opposed them. Although a Confederate attack on a buffalo base on the Chowan River above Winton slowed the problem, it did not end it. The buffaloes remained a thorn in the side of the Confederacy for the rest of the war. Friction over their actions still exists today. Confederate descendants in northeast North Carolina say they still distrust buffalo descendants.

In July 1863, the Federals launched a series of raids in northeast North Carolina, burning bridges and stores in Warsaw, Greenville, Tarboro, and Rocky Mount. On July 26, 1863, two Federal regiments disembarked at Winton and marched for the bridge over Potecasi Creek several miles away. They were opposed for a short time by militiamen from Murfreesboro, but the fighting was short.

This Federal movement toward the Weldon railroad bridge attracted the attention of Confederate leaders in Virginia. They sent Major General Matt Ransom to deal with the attackers. Ransom was from the area, and the Federals were advancing in the direction of his own plantation. When Ransom arrived in North Carolina, he found only about two hundred militiamen and two cannons ready to oppose two battle-experienced Union regiments. Ransom ordered his men to dig in behind the pond at Boone's Mill, west of the little town of Jackson, North Carolina. Meanwhile, Ransom rode forward to see if there was anything else he could do to protect his exposed position.

Ransom was returning to his men when he heard "a great shout" behind him. It was Federal cavalry. Ransom spurred his horse toward the mill, ordering his men to pull up the bridge after him. The few who were clothed did. The rest of the naked crew were still swimming around the mill pond. Ransom ordered them to strap on their cartridge belts and start shooting. The only battle in North Carolina fought by nudists was underway.

Ransom resorted to some trickery to fool the Federals. As he leaped off his horse, he started shouting orders for specific regiments to move to different points on the battlefield. The Federals heard the orders and hesitated. What they did not know was that those Confederate regiments only existed in Ransom's imagination. The fighting went on for a few hours, until the Federals, perhaps demoralized at how well outnumbered naked men could fight, retired. They never dislodged Ransom's little force, even though the Federals had nine cannons to the Confederates' two little guns. Since the Confederate position was protected by swamps on either side, the Federals could only attack straight down the road. The concentrated fire of two hundred muskets on that narrow causeway kept the Federals from their objective. They withdrew to the cheers and jeers of the Confederates.

The Battle of Boone's Mill was small by Civil War standards of men engaged, but huge in its outcome. If Ransom's men retreated or had been overrun, the way to Weldon would have been completely open. The Federals would have burned or captured the bridge over the Roanoke Rapids. Lee's supply line, now needed even more since he was retreating from Gettysburg, would have been cut. Conceivably, if captured, the Weldon railroad bridge could have been used to send Union soldiers from New Bern deep into Virginia within a matter of days.

In December 1863, Union Brigadier General Edward Wild—a one-armed, Harvard-educated, former doctor—led "Wild's African Brigade" on a two-week-long raid through Camden, Currituck, and Pasquotank Counties. The two thousand Black soldiers of Wild's brigade freed more than twenty-five hundred slaves, and burned dozens of private homes. Even Wild's supporters considered his brigade's actions excessive. Most inexcusable was the way he held captive the families of men he suspected of being Confederates.

Wild's raid was the last major action by Federal troops in the far northern reaches of northeast North Carolina. As the war progressed, this land was spared, while attention shifted to places a bit more south like Plymouth and Washington.

This tour of upper northeast North Carolina starts in one of the state's most remote state parks, Pettigrew State Park in Tyrrell County.

To reach Pettigrew State Park from U.S. 64 in the small town of Creswell, turn south onto Sixth Street from U.S. 64. Turn left, or southeast, onto Main Street. Follow this road for about 2 miles, until reaching Thirtyfoot Canal Road. Turn right, or southwest, and follow Thirtyfoot Canal Road for about 6 miles all the way to Somerset Place. Somerset Place is a restored antebellum rice, corn, and wheat plantation that is in Pettigrew State Park.

First laid out in 1785, Somerset Place covered more than ten thousand acres and required the labor of more than three hundred slaves. Many slaves who already knew how to grow rice were brought directly from Africa to the plantation. The plantation thrived for the first fifty years of its existence under the ownership of the Collins family, merchants and entrepreneurs from Edenton. In 1835, Josiah Collins III, the grandson of the original owner of Somerset, built Somerset Place—the large, fourteen-room mansion that is now the centerpiece of the state park. Like his father and grandfather, Josiah was very successful in draining and cultivating the swamps on the plantation.

The Civil War doomed the plantation. By 1862, Federal soldiers had visited the plantation and taken all of the horses. Josiah Collins III died, leaving his inexperienced wife to run the huge property. Many slaves stayed on the property after they were freed, and she tried sharecropping with them. When that failed, she was forced to sell the property to a son-in-law, who also had little luck with the property.

The decline of Somerset Place can be taken as an example of how much the Southern economy was dependent on slave labor. Once the plantation lost its free workers, Somerset could not be supported. The state bought the property in 1939, restored it, and made it into a state park. The plantation house is open, as are many of the outbuildings. The state eventually plans to rebuild the slave cabins that once existed on the plantation.

Every two years, Somerset Place is the site for a unique family reunion. The descendants of Somerset's slaves, and the descendants of the plantation's slave owners, come from all over the country to celebrate their common heritage.

The furnishings at Somerset Place illustrate how wealthy the family was, but it is a second-floor portrait of a female Collins that many visitors find most interesting. Most portraits and photographs of women of the era depict them as rather plain-featured. This picture of Sally Jones Collins is fetching. The portrait captures her beauty, grace, and maybe even her sensuality.

Find the path to the Pettigrew family cemetery in front of the house. This may be the time to separate the true Civil War historians from the tag-alongs. It is a brisk twenty-minute walk through the woods to the grave of Confederate Brigadier General James Johnston Pettigrew. A round trip, with time to ponder the general's place in North Carolina history, can easily take forty-five minutes.

Pettigrew may be the most remarkable man North Carolina ever produced. Born on July 4, 1825, on Bonvara, the plantation bordering Somerset, Pettigrew entered the University of North Carolina at age fourteen and quickly distinguished himself as a mathematical genius. At age eighteen, he was awarded a professorship at the United States Naval Observatory (the present-day residence of the United States Vice President), where he cataloged the location of more than a hundred thousand stars. He then studied law and traveled all over Europe, learning to speak German, Italian, French, and Spanish, and to read Hebrew and Arabic. Somewhere he found time to learn how to play the piano.

In 1852, Pettigrew moved to Charleston, South Carolina, to practice law with his first cousin, James Louis Petigru (who insisted on using the old Scottish spelling). Petigru was South Carolina's leading lawyer. He was also a staunch, though slave-holding, Unionist, who preached throughout the war that secession would be the downfall of the South. There must have been some interesting conversations around the law office, since Petigru, the Unionist, owned slaves, and Pettigrew, the secessionist, did not.

On December 27, 1860, Pettigrew, a lieutenant in the local Charleston militia unit, led his men in what could be considered the first, if bloodless, act of the Civil War. Pettigrew and his men rowed to Castle Pinckney, a tiny fort in Charleston's harbor. There, they demanded and received the surrender of the fort from its six-man garrison.

When the war started, Pettigrew returned to North Carolina, where he was elected colonel of the 22nd North Carolina Regiment. He was wounded in the Peninsula campaign, captured, and exchanged within a few months. He returned to combat in North Carolina and participated in a failed attack on New Bern in April 1863. On June 1, 1863, Pettigrew's brigade

General James J. Pettigrew's grave

was transferred to the Army of Northern Virginia. On July 1, the first day at Gettysburg, his men drove the Federals out of McPherson's woods.

On July 3, Pettigrew was given temporary assignment to command Major General Henry Heth's division, as Heth had been wounded on the first day at Gettysburg. Pettigrew's five thousand men made up the left flank of what has always been known in North Carolina as the Pettigrew-Pickett-Trimble Assault. (Pickett's Charge is a name created by Virginia historians. Pickett was not in direct command of the men in Pettigrew's or Trimble's divisions.)

While Pickett sought safety behind some nearby barns, supposedly to "coordinate" the assault, Pettigrew personally led his men across the open fields to the stone wall on Cemetery Ridge. He took several rounds of grape shot through his hand. Pettigrew's men actually went further than Pickett's. Today, there is a spot marked on the battlefield with a monument to the 26th North Carolina Regiment. Unsupported and overwhelmed, all of the Confederates fell back.

On July 14, 1863, Pettigrew was part of the rear guard protecting Lee's recrossing of the Potomac into Maryland, when a force of Federal cavalry burst into their camp. A Federal corporal shot Pettigrew in the stomach. Enraged Confederates pulled the cavalryman from his horse and crushed his chest with a boulder.

Pettigrew was moved to a farmhouse. On July 16, 1863, an Episcopal priest offered to give him communion. The general refused saying, "It is not from a want of faith or a want of disposition, but from a feeling of unworthiness. I fear to incur the guilt of presumption." The next morning he whispered, "It is time to be going." He was thirty-five years old.

Follow the flat trail southwest through the woods, watching for the one turn to the north. The Pettigrew family cemetery is in a field on the edge of the woods. The general is buried under a simple Christian cross.

Return to Somerset. If you did not take water with you, refresh yourself.

Retrace the route to Creswell and drive west on U.S. 64 through Roper. Continue to the intersection with N.C. 45, about 5 miles past Roper. Turn right, or north, onto N.C. 45. (Plymouth, just three miles away from this intersection, is covered in another tour.)

Drive about 14 miles on N.C. 45 to the intersection with U.S. 17. Turn right, or northeast, onto U.S. 17. Just before crossing over the long, narrow bridge over the Chowan River, there will be a historic marker on the right describing the Battle of Batchelor's Bay on May 5, 1864. The battle occured 7 miles south of the bridge. In the battle, the ironclad CSS *Albemarle* fought seven Union ships, defeating them all. (See The River Cities Tour for more details on the *Albermarle*.)

Edenton, a picturesque little town, is on the north side of the Chowan River. The town has an expansive colonial history but virtually sat out the Civil War. It surrendered to the Federals two days after Elizabeth City, without firing a shot in its defense. Hertford, 12 miles north on U.S. 17, was once visited by Black troops. They burned the floating bridge over the Perquimans River, roughed up the local Episcopal priest, and fired a few shells into the town as they departed on their gunboats.

Continue on U.S. 17 to Elizabeth City, 13 miles northeast of Hertford on the Pasquotank River. Elizabeth City has several Civil War sites, including the Museum of The Albemarle, located at 1116 South U.S. 17, just south of downtown on the left side of U.S. 17. A Civil War display describes all of the actions that took place in northeastern North Carolina, including Hatteras Island, Roanoke Island, Elizabeth City, Edenton, Winton, and South Mills.

Continue north on Business U.S. 17, which becomes Ehringhaus Street. When Business U.S. 17 turns north, continue on Ehringhaus Street until it runs into Water Street. Turn left on Water Street. Beside the wastewater treatment plant pump station will be a monument to Pastor Forbes, who donned his clerical robes, just in case, to surrender the town to Federal forces. About 1.75 miles downriver and southeast of the waterfront is Cobb's Point. This was the site of the four-gun battery protecting the town that was abandoned when the militiamen saw the approaching Federal fleet. The site of the fort is now a private home. No evidence of the fort remains.

Elizabeth City has a number of fine antebellum homes, but since the town was not used as a base by either side, they do not have a great deal of Civil War significance. The Chamber of Commerce has a map showing the oldest homes in town.

If not visiting any of the antebellum homes, take Water Street along the waterfront until it intersects with Elizabeth Street, or U.S. 158/N.C. 34.

Turn right or north and cross over the Pasquotank River. It is 2.7 miles to Country Club Road, or S.R. 1139. Turn right and drive 0.7 mile and turn right onto Chantilly Road, S.R. 1138. After another 0.7 mile, the road dead-ends into Chantilly Bay, where the Federal troops landed on their way to South Mills. The wreck of the CSS *Black Warrior*, a mosquito-fleet boat, lies hidden beneath the water just offshore. Cobb's Point, the location of the Confederate fort that was supposed to protect Elizabeth City, is directly 1.0 mile across the river.

Return on Chantilly Road for 1.6 miles, passing over Country Club Road, until Chantilly Road intersects with N.C. 343. Turn left, or northwest, onto N.C. 343.

About 10 miles northwest on N.C. 343, after passing a small road labeled Sawyers Lane, is the battlefield of South Mills. A slight depression, running from right to left, in the fields across the highway may be the remains of the "roasted ditch." Nothing is at the site to identify it as the battlefield. The historic marker for the battle is in South Mills.

While the Federals officially reported they lost 13 men, legend says local farmers used more than an acre to bury the Federal dead. The three thousand Federals fled in the middle of the night after their defeat, frightened that the four hundred Confederates would attack them. The Federals even left their wounded on the field out of fear that the Confederates would hear their groans if they were being carried on a retreat.

Continue 3 miles on N.C. 343 into South Mills to view the Dismal Swamp Canal locks that both the Federals and the Confederates considered so important. The locks are visible when N.C. 343 passes over a rather unimpressive canal in South Mills. Ironically, the locks were actually too narrow and shallow to accommodate most of the ships that could help either side. Originally, Burnside attempted to capture the locks because he received a spy report claiming the Confederates were preparing to send ironclads down the canal to attack Federal forces. No ironclad would have made it, as the canal was only forty-feet wide and five-feet deep, far too narrow and shallow to allow the passage of an ironclad.

In South Mills, N.C. 343 will cross Business U.S. 17. Turn south on Business U.S. 17 and follow it to U.S. 17 South. Stay on U.S. 17 South for about 3 miles until it intersects with U.S. 158. Turn right, or west, onto U.S. 158 and follow this road for about 20 miles through the Great Dismal Swamp until reaching Business U.S. 158 to Gatesville. Follow Business U.S. 158 into Gatesville to the intersection with N.C. 37. Turn left, or south, onto N.C. 37 and follow it to the intersection with N.C. 137. Turn right, or west, onto N.C. 137. Drive about 0.4 mile. A small city cemetery is on the right. Confederate Brigadier General William Paul Roberts is buried in the northwest corner under a large obelisk.

Roberts, credited with being the youngest brigadier general in the Confederate Army, was only eighteen when the war started. He enlisted in the 19th North Carolina Volunteers. He was a colonel by age twenty-two and a general at twenty-three. General Lee is supposed to have presented his own gauntlets to Roberts in recognition of the young general's maturity and leadership. Before he died in 1910, he was one of the last living Confederate generals.

Leaving Roberts's grave, drive west on N.C. 137 for 7.8 miles, to the intersection with U.S. 158/U.S. 13. Turn left, or southeast, onto U.S. 158, and cross over the Chowan River. After crossing the river, turn left onto Mulberry Street. Mulberry Street leads to Main Street in Winton. Turn left onto Main Street. Drive to the end of Main Street to see the bluffs that unsuccessfully shielded the Confederates from Union ships on the Chowan River. A historic marker is in front of the courthouse on the bluffs.

Retrace the route back to U.S. 158. Turn west on U.S. 158 by driving straight across the highway. (Don't take the wrong road, U.S. 158 makes a confusing right turn at Winton then heads directly west.)

Continue on U.S. 158 to Potecasi Creek, 4.6 miles from the point where U.S. 13 splits off from U.S. 158. This was the site of a small skirmish between the Murfreesboro Home Guard and Federal forces on July 26, 1863. The Murfreesboro Home Guard stood their ground, however briefly, against a far superior and better trained Union force determined to capture the Weldon railroad bridge. The Federal forces captured the bridge and waited a day for their cavalry to catch up. They spent their time freeing the slaves on the surrounding plantations. The cavalry's delayed arrival allowed the Confederate forces extra time to set up a defense at Boone's Mill to the west. A historic marker at Potecasi Creek claims breastworks are in the area, but heavy woods may have taken them over by now.

Continue on U.S. 158 to the small town of Jackson, 32 miles west of Winton. In downtown Jackson, U.S. 158 becomes Jefferson Street, or Business U.S. 158. In the 200 block of Jefferson Street is a historic marker for Thomas Bragg's home. Turn right just past the sign onto Atherton Street. Drive one block. Turn right onto Calhoun Street. On the left, just after turning, is a unrestored, white, two-story house that is the home of Thomas Bragg. Thomas Bragg was a two-term governor of North Carolina and attorney general of the Confederacy for four months. He was the brother of General Braxton Bragg.

During his term from 1854–1858, Thomas Bragg was a good governor. He expanded the railroads and the roads in the state. However, he was a pessimistic Confederate attorney general, matching his brother's pessimism as a field general. As early as March 1862, Bragg was expressing public and private doubts about the survival of the Confederacy.

Drive one block on Calhoun Street and turn to the right to return to Jefferson Street. Continue in the same direction on Jefferson Street (Jefferson Street becomes U.S. 158 after leaving Jackson) for 1.5 miles to a historic marker for the home of Colonel Henry Burgwyn, Jr., the "boy colonel" of the 26th North Carolina Regiment. The marker states the home once stood 4 miles south of the marker. Burgwyn is probably North Carolina's most famous regimental colonel. He was wealthy, northern educated, and spoiled. This, and the fact he was a strict disciplinarian, caused his men not to like him at first. However, at the Battle of New Bern in March 1862, he was the last man to leave the battlefield, escaping only after he made sure all of his soldiers were across a swollen creek. His men began to think his discipline would help them on the battlefield.

On the first day of Gettysburg, July 1, 1863, Burgwyn was killed while trying to keep the regiment's battle flag from falling on the ground. He was twenty-one years old. Burgwyn was one of fourteen color bearers to be struck down in that one fight with the 24th Michigan regiment.

He was buried on the battlefield in a gun case, but his body was later transferred to Raleigh's Oakwood Cemetery, where it now rests under the tallest obelisk in the Confederate section.

Continue west on U.S. 158 for approximately 0.5 mile after leaving Burgwyn's marker to a historic marker for the Battle of Boone's Mill. This is where General Matt Ransom's buck naked brigade of Confederates defeated a much larger, fully clothed force of Federals on July 27, 1863. These were the same Federals who had just defeated the Murfreesboro Home Guard at Potecasi Creek. All traces of the mill are gone, but the mill pond where the Confederates were swimming is still there. A historic marker says trenches are there, but thick woods hide them from view.

For years after the Battle of Boone's Mill, Ransom would return to the site to visit a large tree where he had been standing when a cannon ball hit it. Had the tree not been there, Ransom would have lost his head. He put a fence around the tree and made sure it was watered and fertilized for the rest of his life. Ransom called the tree "a true friend."

Matt Ransom's plantation is just 2.5 miles west of Boone's Mill on U.S. 158. The plantation house can be seen about eight hundred yards south of the historic marker in an open field. Ransom is buried on the property, which is private.

Matt Whitaker Ransom was a lawyer and served as state attorney general and in the general assembly before the war. His brother, Robert, was also a Confederate general, and at one time, Matt reported to Robert. Matt Ransom was wounded twice at Malvern Hill, but returned in time to fight at Sharpsburg. He then served some time in North Carolina, but was eventually transferred back to Virginia in time to suffer in the trenches at Petersburg. He was wounded a third time at Drewry's Bluff, south of Richmond. He surrendered with Lee at Appomattox.

Ransom reentered politics in 1870. He spent twenty-three years serving as North Carolina's United States senator. For a short time, he was minister to Mexico. He died in 1904, at age seventy-eight.

Drive 3.2 miles from Matt Ransom's historic marker to where U.S. 158 joins with U.S. 301. Continue west on U.S. 158/U.S. 301 for 2 miles to the bridge over the Roanoke Rapids. This is the site of the crucial Wilmington & Weldon Railroad bridge. While the current bridge is modern, of course, it is near the same location as the Civil War–era bridge. Had this bridge fallen to the Federals, it is entirely possible that Lee might have given up. He needed the supplies that were coming from Wilmington and passing over this bridge.

After crossing the bridge, U.S. 158 splits off from U.S. 301. Follow

U.S. 158 west through Weldon, under I-95, and through Roanoke Rapids. Continue on U.S. 158 towards Warrenton. About 25 miles after passing under I-95, follow Business U.S. 158 into the city of Warrenton.

In Warrenton, turn left, or south, onto U.S. 401. Drive 5.3 miles from the intersection to a marker for Bridal Creek, the birthplace of the Ransom brothers. The house no longer stands. It is 9.7 miles from the intersection of Business U.S. 158 and U.S. 401 in Warrenton to the intersection with Annie Lee Road, or S.R. 1137. Turn right, or west, and drive 0.2 mile. Pull into the little parking lot. A few yards away is a small family cemetery featuring an obelisk over the former grave of Annie Lee, the daughter of General Robert E. Lee.

Annie, the shyest and frailest of the Lee daughters, died of a fever in White Sulphur Springs in Warren County on October 20, 1862. She was so shy that no photo exists of her. Some sources indicate she had a marred face that she did not want photographed. White Sulphur Springs was a Civil War–era "health spa," where Annie had been sent to try to cure her lifelong sickliness. General Lee, consumed with fighting the war, was devastated at her death, but he could not take the time to attend her funeral.

After the War was over, Lee accepted a position as the president of Washington College in Lexington. When it became obvious to the trustees that Lee was in failing health, they suggested he take a leave of absence to recover his strength. He readily agreed and made visiting Annie's grave his major goal. He knew it would be the only time he would visit her grave. "If I am to accomplish it (the visit), I must do it soon," he wrote to his son.

Annie Lee's former grave

On March 29, 1870, Lee and another daughter, Agnes, visited the little family cemetery where Annie was buried. Lee remarked that he was happy the spot where Annie was buried was so beautiful. It was the only time he would visit her grave. Lee died October 12, 1870.

In 1994, there was a controversy about Annie Lee's grave. Repeated vandalism at the cemetery caused some Lee-family members to request that her remains be exhumed and sent to Lexington, Virginia, where Lee, his wife, and most of the family rests. Reluctantly, the state agreed, but both sides of the controversy really won. All that was recovered from Annie's grave were the metal handles of her casket. Her body had long ago been

John White House, where General Lee slept the night before visiting his daughter's grave

absorbed into Warren County's soil. As Lee himself wished, Annie stayed in North Carolina.

Return on U.S. 401 north to Warrenton. At 9.9 miles after leaving Annie's grave, turn right or east onto Marshall Street. A historic marker for the house of John White, a Confederate commissioner who bought blockade runners in England, is at this intersection. Drive one block on Marshall Street to Eaton Street. The side of White's house is now visible directly ahead. The house faces Halifax Street, one short block to the left. Robert E. Lee and Agnes Lee spent one night in the house before making their visit to Annie's grave.

Turn left from Marshall Street onto Eaton Street, which runs beside the White house, and drive the short block to Halifax Street. Turn left onto Halifax. Within one block, the street makes a sharp turn to the right, or north, and becomes Bragg Street. The boyhood home of Thomas and Braxton Bragg is 0.6 mile away, at the intersection of Academy Place and Bragg Street.

Perhaps the dilapidated condition of Braxton Bragg's house is indicative of how North Carolinians feel about the highest-ranking Civil War general from the state. There are no Confederate generals as unpopular as this 1837 graduate of West Point. He was considered dour, humorless, vengeful, militarily unimaginative—and those were his good qualities.

Bragg started the war in command of Pensacola, Florida. He later served as a corps commander, and he was given command of the Army of Tennessee in 1862. He spent the next year-and-a-half depleting his army with defeats at Perryville and Stone's River. At Chickamauga, in September 1863, Bragg actually won a battle. However, he was so unaccustomed to victory that he failed to chase the Federals all the way back to Chattanooga. That was a fatal mistake. The Union army was able to regroup and grow stronger as it waited for relief from General Sherman's army. To be fair, some historians say Bragg's army was too badly damaged to drive the Federals farther back.

Bragg's old friend, President Jefferson Davis, brought him to Richmond as a military advisor. Bragg served in that role until Davis sent him to Wilmington to help hold that city against Federal attack. Within a month after Bragg's arrival, his mishandling of troop placement sealed the fate of Fort Fisher, the fort protecting Wilmington. The fort was lost to the invading Federals. Bragg finished the war fighting at Wise's Forks and Bentonville. He died in Galveston, Texas, in 1876 and was buried in Mobile, Alabama.

Turn left, or west, onto Academy Place, and drive one block to South Main Street. Turn left again onto South Main Street. Drive two blocks to Emanuel Episcopal Church at 229 North Main Street. On July 5, 1836, a young newspaperman named Horace Greeley married Mary Youngs Cheney in the church.

At the time Greeley was nothing special. In 1841, however, he founded the *New York Tribune*. By the time the Civil War started, the *Tribune* was the nation's largest and most influential newspaper. At first, Greeley supported the North's war effort, demanding that the abolition of slavery be made the central goal. By 1864, the seemingly endless slaughter on the battlefields made him rethink his position. When the war was over, Greeley put up bail for Jefferson Davis, an act that brought him many enemies in the North. Greeley ran for president in 1872, just the public forum his

Emanuel Episcopal Church

enemies wanted. They ran him and his ideas into the ground. He lost and died within a month of the election at age sixty-one.

This concludes The Railroad Defense Tour. To reach the beginning of the next tour, retrace your route to Weldon where U.S. 158 intersects with U.S. 301. Turn south on U.S. 301 and drive to Halifax.

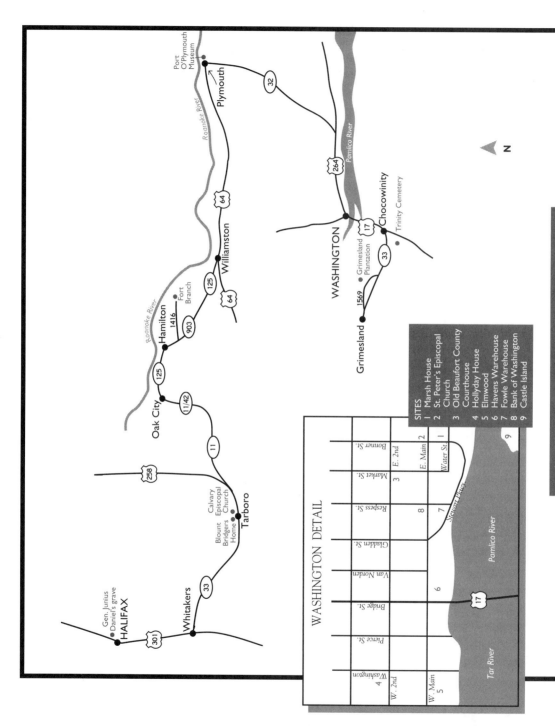

THE RIVER CITIES TOUR

N

Port O'Plymouth Museum
Plymouth
32
Roanoke River
Pamlico River
64
Williamston
125
64
Fort Branch
1416
Hamilton
903
125
Oak City
11/42
11
258
Calvary Episcopal Church
Blount Bridgers Home
Tarboro
Whitakers
33
301
Gen. Junius Daniel's grave
HALIFAX

264
WASHINGTON
17
Chocowinity
Trinity Cemetery
Grimesland Plantation
33
1569
Grimesland

WASHINGTON DETAIL

SITES
1 Marsh House
2 St. Peter's Episcopal Church
3 Old Beaufort County Courthouse
4 Hollyday House
5 Elmwood
6 Havens Warehouse
7 Fowle Warehouse
8 Bank of Washington
9 Castle Island

Bonner St.
E. 2nd
E. Main   2
Water St.   1
Market St.   3
Respess St.   8
7
Stewart Pkwy.
Gladden St.
Van Norden
6
Bridge St.
17
Pierce St.
Washington
W. 2nd   4
W. Main   5
Pamlico River
Tar River
9

The River Cities Tour

This tour starts in Halifax, North Carolina, at the grave of a Confederate general, and continues to Tarboro and another Confederate general's grave. It then travels to Fort Branch, outside Hamilton. Fort Branch is an excellently preserved earth fort that played a major role in protecting Robert E. Lee's supply line for more than three years. From there, the tour moves to Plymouth, a town captured by Federals then recaptured by the Confederates in a brilliant operation that combined army and navy forces. The tour then moves to Washington, a town captured, and later burned, by Federals. The tour ends in the community of Chocowinity, at the monument of an assassinated Confederate general.

Total mileage: approximately 205 miles. This tour may be better taken in two days, with extra time in Plymouth and Washington. Fort Branch is only open on the weekends and is a must-see to understand the war in northeast North Carolina.

As mentioned in The Railroad Defense Tour, the Federal goal in northeast North Carolina was to gain control of the rivers and sounds, then use them to push inland and destroy the state's interior railroads. It was not a complicated strategy, or a difficult one. The Confederates were slow to recognize the strategic importance of northeastern North Carolina. As a result, the Federals were able to capture Hatteras Island, Roanoke Island, New Bern, Fort Macon, and Elizabeth City with very few losses. The towns of Washington, located at the confluence of the Tar and Pamlico Rivers, and Plymouth, on the Roanoke River, fell with no Confederate resistance at all. Washington was surrendered without a shot on March 21, 1862. Union troops arrived in Plymouth on May 17, 1862. The residents of both towns claimed to have strong Union sympathies, so the occupying Federal soldiers put away their matches—for the time being.

While the towns themselves were secure for the Union, the countryside surrounding the towns was not. During the war, dozens of skirmishes were fought in the counties surrounding Washington, Plymouth, and New Bern. Sometimes the fighting was only sniping between pickets. Sometimes regiments faced off. Some of the engagements were large, such as the fighting at Tranter's Creek, about twelve miles northwest of Washington. The battle occurred on June 5, 1862, when the 24th Massachusetts squared off against the 45th North Carolina. Sizeable numbers did not necessarily mean long fighting. When the commander of the 45th was killed early in the battle, the Confederates immediately retreated.

Sometimes the battles had unusual twists. On July 9, 1862, the Confederate cavalry ambushed the Union navy. On that day, three wooden Union gunboats cruised up the Roanoke River to Rainbow Bend, two miles southeast of Hamilton. Suddenly, the Federals were showered with lead, mostly fired from the pistols of a forty-two-man Confederate cavalry unit concealed on the bank. Two Union sailors were killed and nine more wounded before the boats could turn around and scamper down the river.

Most of the action in the area occurred at, or near, the two largest ports in the area, Washington and Plymouth.

While the town of Washington gave itself up peacefully to Union forces in March 1862, the rest of its Civil War history was anything but placid. On September 6, 1862, a small force of Confederates charged into Washington from the west under cover of predawn darkness and fog. Fighting was street-to-street, one of the few times this occurred during the war. A Federal gunboat, the USS *Picket*, started shelling the Confederates, but it suddenly exploded, killing all but one of her twenty-one crewmen. Within a few hours, Federal reinforcements arrived on the scene, and the Confederates were forced to retire. Losses were heavy on both sides. Twenty-seven Federals were killed and fifty-eight were wounded. The Confederates lost at least that many.

On April 1, 1863, just two weeks after attacking New Bern, Confederate Major General D.H. Hill lay siege to Washington. Hill hoped to force the surrender of the twelve hundred Federals there, or at least to keep the Federal forces in town while his men foraged for supplies. One Union relief force came up the Pamlico River from New Bern in an attempt to relieve the city. However, the Federals saw a new Confederate fort on the river and turned around. Another Federal relief force marched up from New Bern. However, they met an entrenched Confederate force at Blount's Creek, several miles south of Washington across the Pamlico River, and were unable to advance to Washington.

Union Brigadier General John Foster, overall commander of all Union forces in North Carolina, was visiting Washington when the siege began and found himself trapped in the city. His attitude must have been, "If you want something done right, do it yourself." On April 16, 1862, he boarded the USS *Escort*, determined to run past the guns of the Confederate fort southeast of the city and get help. Just to be sure the boat's pilot did not intentionally run the boat aground, Foster stood in the wheelhouse with a pistol to the pilot's head. The *Escort* was hit dozens of times, but it passed the fort. The pilot, who had been loyal after all, was severely wounded. His dying words to Foster were that he promised to get the *Escort* down the river, and he did his job. Foster wrote that he broke down in tears when the man died.

Foster's breakout, and the knowledge that more Union troops would soon be on the way, broke Hill's will to fight. He said his men's lives were not worth Washington, and he pulled them all back.

After Hill's siege, Washington stayed relatively quiet until April 27, 1864. On that day, the Union forces in the city learned that Confederate Brigadier General Robert Hoke captured Plymouth less than a week earlier. For the next three days, the formerly benign, kind Federal forces ransacked Washington, then set fire to it. Not even that was enough. As Washington went up in flames, the retreating Federal gunboats shelled it for good measure.

Union Brigadier General Innis N. Palmer, commanding the district, was appalled at the conduct of his men. He wrote: "(Troops within his command) have been guilty of an outrage against humanity, which brings the blush of shame to the cheek of every true man and soldier. The town was fired, thus wantonly rendering houseless and homeless hundreds of poor women and children. All this was done by men in the military service of the United States."

Like Washington, the people of Plymouth hoped their pro-Union attitudes would be enough to keep war away. They were wrong.

After Confederate Major General Pickett failed to take New Bern in early February 1864, Brigadier General Robert Hoke was placed in command of the remaining Confederate forces in northeast North Carolina. (See The New Bern Tour for details on Pickett's failed attempt to capture

New Bern.) Hoke immediately made plans to capture Plymouth. On the surface, it would not be an easy task. The town had 2,800 Federal troops entrenched in a series of strong dirt forts. Protecting the forts' rear were four capable Union gunboats.

What Hoke did have was access to an ironclad, the CSS *Albemarle*, which was nearing completion on the Roanoke River at a place called Edwards Ferry.

The *Albemarle* was the brainchild of nineteen-year-old Gilbert Elliott of Elizabeth City. Despite his age, Gilbert was mature enough to capture the attention and imagination of Confederate authorities. He must have been brilliant. When Elliott needed to speed up the process of boring holes through iron plating, he invented the twist drill, cutting the time needed to drill a hole from twenty minutes to four minutes.

Hoke visited Edwards Ferry and persuaded the building crew to finish construction of the 152-foot-long *Albemarle* in time for his attack on Plymouth.

To keep their appointment with destiny, the *Albemarle*'s crew cast off from Edwards Ferry on April 17, 1864, and started down the river—backwards. The river was twisty and narrow near Edwards Ferry, and Captain James W. Cooke hoped it would be easier to steer if he could drag his bow anchor chains to slow his progress. As Cooke tried to steer, crewmen swarmed on deck, bolting the two inches of armor into place over four inches of pine planking. Twice, the ironclad was forced to pull over for repairs to its rudder. Along the way, the crew was drilled in the operation of the ship's two, 6.4-inch Brooke rifled cannons, the finest cannons the Confederacy could manufacture.

Somewhere below the Roanoke River–town of Williamston, it occurred to Captain Cooke that he had no idea what he was supposed to do when he reached Plymouth. General Hoke had not given any orders, or even suggestions.

About three miles above Plymouth, Cooke stopped the ship, unsure if the obstructions the Federals sank in the river would allow the ship to pass. Gilbert Elliot himself rowed to the obstructions and discovered that heavy spring rains put them more than ten feet below the surface. The *Albemarle*'s eight-foot draft would easily clear them. It was time to fight.

At 2:30 A.M. on April 19, 1864, the *Albemarle* barreled out of the darkness toward Plymouth past Fort Gray, a federal fort designed to protect the town from a river assault. The USS *Southfield* and USS *Miami*, chained together in an attempt to snare the Confederate ironclad between them, lay dead ahead. Cooke saw the trap, and he swung his ship to one side of the river. He then turned and came at the *Southfield* from the side at full speed. His armored prow sank deep into the *Southfield*'s wooden side, and she instantly went to the bottom.

On board the USS *Miami*, Commander Charles W. Flusser, a man who had served admirably in North Carolina up to this point, did perhaps the dumbest thing anyone ever did during the entire war. Before his men could stop him, he personally fired one of the *Miami*'s cannons at the *Albermarle* at point-blank range. The shell bounced off the *Albemarle* and landed at Flusser's feet. It had been charged with a ten-second fuse. Flusser likely stared at the hissing shell a few seconds, the cannon's lanyard in his hand, before he was shredded by exploding iron.

The USS *Miami* retreated south down the river, and the *Albemarle* pounded the Federal forts in Plymouth from the rear, a direction of attack the forts' builders never anticipated. In the morning, Hoke starting hitting the Federals with well-placed artillery rounds of his own.

The Federal commander at Plymouth, Union Brigadier General Henry Walton Wessells, surrendered on April 20, 1864. When the fifty-five-year-old Wessells met Hoke, he said, "General, this is the saddest day of my life." The twenty-seven-year-old Hoke replied, "General this is the proudest day of mine."

The goods taken from the Federals at Plymouth were tremendous. The Confederates captured twenty-five hundred Federal prisoners, twenty-eight cannons, five hundred horses, five thousand stands of muskets, seven hundred barrels of flour, and other stores. Hoke was rewarded with a promotion to major general, one of the youngest men to hold that rank.

On May 5, 1864, the *Albemarle* sailed from its new base at Plymouth to attack the Union fleet at the mouth of the Roanoke River. During the battle, the largest Federal ship, the USS *Sassacus*, was virtually destroyed when it tried to ram the *Albermarle*. The *Albemarle* was knocked off keel in the collision and was in danger of sinking, until it pivoted one of its guns toward the Federal ship and literally shot the enemy vessel free. The

Albemarle then pounded the other six Union ships, before returning to Plymouth for repairs. The engagement became known as the Battle of Batchelor's Bay.

The mighty Confederate ironclad finally met its match at Plymouth. The defeat did not come from a Federal Monitor-style ironclad, but from a wooden launch manned by a handful of sailors and a determined daredevil Naval lieutenant named William Cushing. On October 27, 1864, Cushing and his men brazenly chugged up the Roanoke River past the Confederate pickets. Their boat hit a floating log barrier at full speed and shot over it. Within seconds, Cushing lowered a boom mounted on the bow of the boat. Suspended from the boom was a torpedo, a waterproofed keg of black powder. Cushing ran the keg under the keel of the *Albemarle* and set it off.

The explosion tore the *Albemarle* apart. According to the *Albermarle*'s engineer, the hole in the ship's bow was "big enough to drive a wagon through." She sank slowly to the river bottom.

Cushing escaped and lived to lead other daring, unusual raids, gaining the admiration of both Federals and Confederates. Even the commander of the *Albemarle* admitted that "a more gallant thing was not done during the war." Cushing died in an insane asylum in 1874, perhaps broken in spirit because a country at peace no longer needed his daring escapades.

The history of the *Albemarle* was not quite over, but its real end seems sadder than being the only Confederate ironclad sunk by Federal forces. After the war, the Federals raised her and plugged the hole in her hull. In 1867, she was cut up and sold for scrap. Her Brooke guns now rest in front of NATO headquarters in Norfolk, Virginia. For years, irritated North Carolina historians have been trying to get the cannons back from foreign Virginia soil.

Plymouth would remain in Confederate hands only until October 31, 1864, when the Federals retook the town.

Hoke's attack and capture of Plymouth remains controversial. For the past 130 years, historians have debated whether Hoke's men executed Black Federal soldiers captured at Plymouth. The original charge was made by a Federal sergeant in July 1864. The men of the 101st and 103rd Pennsylvania, two white regiments captured along with the Black soldiers, said it never happened. Reports from Black soldiers who were there said it did.

The truth will likely never be known, but this is what may have happened: Hoke sent his men to scour the swamps across the Roanoke River for straggling Union soldiers. Many of the Black Federal soldiers at Plymouth were escaped slaves from Bertie County, who had joined the 2nd North Carolina Volunteers, a Union unit. After the battle, they would have tried to swim the river to get back to their homes. Confederates may have found Federals, including Black soldiers, in the swamps, and shot them for vengeance. There are reports that citizens heard occasional gunshots across the river in the days following the battle.

This tour starts in the historic colonial town of Halifax, about 7 miles south of Weldon. Start at the Historic Halifax Visitor's Center on Business U.S. 301, or St. David Street. The visitor's center has nothing on the Civil War, but it does have a great slide show explaining life in colonial North Carolina.

Leave the visitor's center on Business 301 South and head toward downtown. In one block, turn left, or northeast, onto King Street. The grave of Confederate Brigadier General Junius Daniel, surrounded by an iron fence, can be seen from the street, about a block down on the right. There is room to pull over or park on an intersecting street, a half-block further down.

An 1851 West Point graduate, Daniel was the son of a wealthy plantation owner. In 1861, he was elected colonel of the 14th North Carolina Regiment. He served in the Seven Days battles before being transferred to North Carolina, where he took part in the defense of Kinston in December 1862. He was transferred back to Virginia in May 1863. His brigade of three North Carolina regiments had the highest percentage of casualties of any brigade at Gettysburg. Daniel was fatally wounded while leading a counterattack from the Mule Shoe during the Battle of the Wilderness. He died May 13, 1864.

Turn around on King Street and head south through the business district. King Street becomes Business U.S. 301 heading south at the intersection with St. David Street. Business U.S. 301 intersects U.S. 301 within a few blocks. Turn left, or south, onto U.S. 301.

Turn left, or east, onto N.C. 33 in the town of Whitakers, 18.3 miles after leaving Daniel's grave. Please note: The North Carolina Department of Transportation has renumbered this road. Older maps will show it to be N.C. 44. It is now N.C. 33.

Drive about 38 miles on N.C. 33 to the outskirts of Tarboro. Stay on N.C. 33 into downtown Tarboro, where the road becomes St. Andrews Street. Turn right onto Walnut Street at the Hardee's and drive one block to Main Street. Turn left onto Main Street, or Business U.S. 64. Drive three blocks on Main Street to Phillips Street. Turn left onto Phillips Street and drive to the Blount-Bridgers House in the middle of the block.

This house museum was owned by Captain John Bridgers, the commander of the Edgecombe Guard. This was also the company of Private Henry Wyatt. In June 1861, at Big Bethel, Virginia, Wyatt became the first Confederate soldier killed in battle. Wyatt was buried in Richmond's Hollywood Cemetery as the South's first war hero. Inside the house is Bridgers's field desk and a large map of the battle of Big Bethel.

Return to the intersection with Main Street and turn left. Drive five blocks to the town square, between Park and Wilson Streets. The park contains a monument to Wyatt. Drive another two blocks on Main Street to St. James Street. Turn left onto St. James and drive three blocks to Calvary Church, at the intersection of St. James and St. David Streets. It is rumored that extra wood from the construction of the ironclad CSS *Albemarle* was used to build the altar inside the church.

In the right rear of the church's cemetery, at the foot of a large cedar tree is a cryptlike, concrete gravestone surrounded by cannon balls. It is the grave of Confederate Major General Dorsey S. Pender. His monument reads "Patriot by nature. Soldier by training. Christian by faith."

When the war broke out, Pender was a twenty-seven-year-old graduate of West Point. He had spent his early career fighting Indians in New Mexico. He joined the Confederate Army and soon got command of first the 13th North Carolina regiment. He then commanded the 6th North Carolina, a unit that would win fame as "The Bloody Sixth." He was promoted to general and given command of a brigade of North Carolinians. Although apparently popular with his men, he also had the reputation of being a strict disciplinarian. After Chancellorsville, he was appointed to major general and given a division command at the age of 29. At the time, he was the youngest Confederate major general. (Hoke later took that title.)

On the second day at Gettysburg, July 2, 1863, Pender was wounded in the thigh. Having been wounded three previous times with little ill effect, he slapped on a bandage and continued fighting. On July 18, infection prompted the removal of the leg, but it was already too late. Pender died the same day.

Lee saw something in Pender that he admired. After Pender's death, Lee often commented that certain reversals during different battles might not have happened if Pender was alive. West (closer to the church) and north (closer to the cemetery's outside wall) of Pender's grave is the grave of North Carolina Governor Henry T. Clark. In 1861, Clark was speaker of the North Carolina senate. When Governor John W. Ellis died in office in June 1861, barely a month after North Carolina seceded, Clark was appointed to fill out his term.

Clark is credited with helping North Carolina gear up for the war effort by establishing training camps and procuring arms, but he also took unwarranted blame for the Federal attacks on coastal North Carolina. He chose not to run in 1862. Zebulon Vance won the election that year. Clark returned to Tarboro and died there in 1874. Local historians say when the Federals raided Tarboro, Clark ran to the river and helped put out the fires.

Leaving the cemetery, turn around on St. James Street and turn right at the next block onto St. Patrick Street. The house at 407 St. Patrick Street, in the middle of the block, is Governor Clark's wartime home. It was built by his father in 1830. It is a private house.

Retrace the route back to St. James and turn right to reach Main Street. Turn left onto South Main Street and proceed over the downtown Tar River Bridge. This is the general area where Federal cavalry pushed into town on July 20, 1863. They destroyed a half-completed ironclad (The CSS *Tarboro*, a copy of the CSS *Albermarle*), two steamboats, a hundred bales of cotton, and considerable stores. The Federals did take time out to eat lunch at the local hotel, located at the corner of St. James and Main Streets. It is doubtful that they paid for lunch, or left a tip.

That afternoon, the Federals burned the bridge over the Tar River and started back for New Bern. It had been a successful raid.

As you cross the Tar River on Main Street, or Business U.S. 64, you will enter the town of Princeville. This town was formed by freed slaves, and has been historically black since 1865. It was incorporated as Princeville in 1885. Turn left onto U.S. 258 from Main Street.

After 0.2 mile on U.S. 258, turn right, or northeast, onto N.C. 111. (Older maps may show this road as N.C. 44.) About 10 miles after getting on N.C. 111, it will make a sharp turn to the left while N.C. 142 continues straight. (Yes, between renumbering and odd turns, the roads in this region are confusing.) Continue on N.C. 111 and follow it towards Oak City.

Outside of Oak City, N.C. 111 intersects with N.C. 11/N.C. 42. At this intersection, turn left, or north, on N.C. 11/N.C. 42 and drive a short distance. At the traffic light with a Texaco station on the corner, turn right, or southeast, onto N.C. 125 towards Hamilton. Drive 5.8 miles to Hamilton. In Hamilton, turn right, or south, onto N.C. 903.

If you care to make a brief side trip from Oak City, continue north on N.C. 11/N.C. 42 for about 4 miles until it intersects with N.C. 903. Turn north on N.C. 903. Drive approximately 18 miles to Scotland Neck. Turn right, or north, onto U.S. 258 in Scotland Neck and drive approximately 5 miles to the point where U.S. 258 crosses the Roanoke River. The location of Edwards Ferry is indicated by a historic marker just before crossing the river. This is the area of the shipyard where the CSS *Albermarle* was built. Retrace the route back down N.C. 903 all the way to Hamilton, about 25 miles.

Drive south through Hamilton on N.C. 903. Turn left, or east, onto Fort Branch Road, or S.R. 1416, 2.8 miles outside of Hamilton. Drive 2 miles to Fort Branch. Please note: A visit to Fort Branch should be taken only during Saturday and Sunday afternoons, as these are the only hours the fort is open. It is a privately owned state historic site, not a state-owned park.

The fort is roughly a squashed-star shape with its major gun emplacements facing down the Roanoke River. It was built in October 1862 and located at Rainbow Bend, the same high bluff where the Confederate cavalry attacked three Union gunboats earlier in 1862. The fort is near some earthworks constructed in February 1862, under the direction of Captain Richard Meade. Meade resigned his United States Army commission after being bombarded inside Fort Sumter by the secessionists in April 1861. He was the only Federal officer at Fort Sumter to join the Confederates after the bombardment.

The earthworks Meade constructed at Rainbow Bend in February 1862 were too small to be considered good protection against Union forces, so the Confederacy promised area residents they would build a larger, more effective fort. Confederate authorities realized that they had to have a good fort on the Roanoke River to protect the Wilmington & Weldon Railroad bridge about sixty miles upriver. Construction started on what would become Fort Branch (named after General Lawrence Branch who was killed at Sharpsburg) in late October 1862.

On the very day that construction was supposed to begin, a raid by Union forces took Rainbow Bend. However, the Federals abandoned the area, and by November 1862, construction started on the fort again. It was finished by February 1863.

The armament ordered for the fort included a rifled thirty-two-pounder, and three, smoothbore twenty-four-pounders. One day, a smoothbore thirty-two-pounder from Charleston showed up unannounced and unordered. The person who delivered the cannon agreed to leave it at the fort if the Confederate commander would "assume the responsibility."

The cannon was apparently treated like Civil War unclaimed freight. Fort Branch's garrison had it, so they thought they should be allowed to keep it. In Charleston, General P.G.T. Beauregard discovered he was missing a 32-pounder and demanded it back. The smoothbore, an obsolete cannon on its best day, was shuttled back down to South Carolina.

When Plymouth fell to the Confederates, the immediate importance of Fort Branch was diminished, but when the town was retaken by Federals in October 1864, the fort again became crucial. On December 9, 1864, fifteen hundred Federals left Plymouth to attack Fort Branch. The Federals quietly marched past Fort Branch during the night, thinking the garrison was asleep. In reality, no one was home. Almost the entire garrison was in Virginia chasing Federals. The fifteen hundred Federals marched on towards Confederates stationed at Butler's Bridge. One of the units facing them at Butler's Bridge was 70th North Carolina, a regiment of teenaged Junior Reserves.

A Confederate officer met the Federals in the dark and mistook them for an expected reinforcement from the Weldon Junior Reserves. Using that information, the Federals advanced on a Confederate camp, asking the pickets not to fire since they were Junior Reserves who did not know the passwords. That must have sounded interesting since the captain trying to affect a North Carolina accent was from New Jersey.

The Confederates were driven from their entrenchments around Butler's Bridge, and the Federals turned back to Fort Branch. By that time, at least seventy Confederates were defending the fort. These Confederates fired several musket volleys, and the Federals, low on ammunition, retreated.

Union gunboats, which were supposed to support the attack, never made it to the fort. In Jamesville, a little river town between Williamston and Plymouth, a Union gunboat and tug struck torpedoes and sank side by side. When the rest of the Union gunboats finally got past Williamston, they ran into more Confederate opposition. Afraid of torpedoes and tired of the constant sniping, the Navy pulled back. They are lucky they did. All of Fort Branch's guns were presighted at a bend in the river. The instant a Federal gunboat came into sight, it would have been in range. Fort Branch's rifled cannon would have been deadly against any wooden gunboat that tried to attack.

That battle marked the end of Fort Branch's military career, but the strong dirt fort on the bluffs of Rainbow Bend continued to frighten the Federals until the end of the war. It had done its job. In April 1865, the commander of the fort pushed all his guns over the bluff and into the Roanoke River. The troops dispersed. The war was over.

Reconstructed winter quarters at Fort Branch outside Hamilton

For a hundred years, Fort Branch was simply "the old fort," the playground of small boys. Trees and shrubs covered it; historians forgot about it. (It is not even mentioned in *The Civil War in North Carolina* by John Barrett, the "bible" of the war in North Carolina, published in 1962).

Then in the 1970s, some scuba-diving Civil War researchers from Alabama read Confederate records that described how the guns were dumped over the side of the cliff. The Alabamians came, dove, and discovered the guns were right where they had been since the war ended. They were in the process of recovering the cannons and taking them home when local Tar Heels discovered what was happening. A court order and a sheriff's deputy or two stopped them immediately, and another court order eventually awarded the guns to the fort.

The seven cannons on display at Fort Branch today were part of its original armament. This is one of the few places in the country where the guns originally assigned to a Civil War battlefield or fort are the same ones that can be viewed by visitors today. By comparison, only one cannon at Gettysburg, out of the hundreds on display, is known to be the same gun that was there during the battle. The rest simply came out of government inventory and were placed there as park displays.

Visitors to Fort Branch can see the cannons inside the visitor's center, as well as news clippings about the guns' recovery and other artifacts recovered from the site. The fort itself is open for a self-guided tour. A volunteer is building a fiberglass model of the 32-pounder. It will be mounted in its original gun emplacement on the bluff. Visitors will then be able to sight down the barrel to the bend in the river and see how dangerous Fort Branch would have been to any adventurous Federal gunboats. A Civil War reenactment is held at the fort every November, with the proceeds going to the preservation of the fort.

After visiting the fort, return down Fort Branch Road to N.C. 125. Turn left, or east, onto N.C. 125 to head to Williamston, 11.4 miles away. Follow N.C. 125 south through town to U.S. 64. Turn left, or east, onto U.S. 64 and drive to Plymouth, approximately 20 miles away.

In Plymouth, turn left, or north, from U.S. 64 onto Washington Street and head toward downtown. Drive 0.3 mile to a historic marker identifying the area as the location for "earthworks" that formed the main Union defense of the city. This is the location of the south side of Fort Williams, behind which the Federals huddled during the dual cannonade of Hoke and the CSS *Albemarle*.

Continue driving down Washington Street to the intersection with Third Street. On this intersection, at 302 Washington Street, is the Windley-Ausbon House, one of only four surviving houses in Plymouth built before the Civil War. Its Third Street side is pockmarked with dozens of bullet holes fired by Federal soldiers at a Confederate sniper who had commandeered the second-floor window during the aborted 1862 Confederate raid on the town.

The Windley-Ausbon House, pockmarked with bullet holes

Follow Washington Street to Water Street. Turn right, or east, and drive to the end of Water Street to find the Port O' Plymouth Roanoke River Museum in the old train depot. Before entering the museum, look to the east about 0.5 mile. Somewhere underneath the river is what is left of the USS *Southfield*, rammed to the bottom by the CSS *Albemarle* on April 19, 1864. Then look to the west. In the water, close to where Washington Street intersected with Water Street, was where Cushing sank the mighty *Albemarle*. Further up the river, where the paper mill is now, was the site of Fort Gray, the Federal fort that fruitlessly fired at the Albemarle as she passed down the river. Crewmen inside the *Albemarle* described the effect of the fort's fire on the ironclad as "no more than pebbles thrown against an empty barrel."

The Port O'Plymouth Roanoke River Museum is primarily devoted to the Civil War. Beside the expected exhibits of shot, shells, and photos of the *Albemarle*, are rare items like hand grenades, reported to have been used during the 1864 battle. The museum has one of the most complete Civil War belt-buckle and button collections in the country, including a rare CSN (Confederate States Navy) button. Most states had their own button and buckle designs. These artifacts are used by relic hunters and historians to determine which units were in particular areas of battlefields.

The museum is trying to draw more attention to the history of the 380 Black Union soldiers from Bertie County, located across the river. Historians say that four escaped slaves from Bertie County were with the 54th Massachusetts regiment when it made its famous attack on Battery Wagner outside Charleston in 1863. Other escaped slaves followed to serve in the Union Army.

The top of a powder keg with "USS *Miami*" stamped on the top reminds visitors of Flusser's impetuous pulling of the lanyard that brought a cannon shell bouncing at his feet. Displays of musket balls, period maps, and photos of soldiers who served in the city complete the display. Taken down for now are photographs made during the filming of a made-for-TV movie produced in the late 1950s that told the story of Cushing's daring attack on the *Albemarle*. A full-scale model of Cushing's ram was built for the movie, and shooting was done on location in Plymouth, with George

Peppard playing Cushing. For some reason, the show never aired, and CBS archivists claim they cannot find a copy of it.

Retrace your route to Washington Street, which becomes N.C. 32. Drive south on N.C. 32 to Washington, a distance of approximately 38 miles. Approximately 5 miles east of Washington, N.C. 32 intersects with U.S. 264. Turn right, or west, onto U.S. 264 toward Washington.

Follow U.S. 264 until it intersects with U.S. 17, or Bridge Street. Turn left, or south, onto U.S. 17 and follow it to the last traffic light before crossing the river. Turn left at the light onto Main Street. Drive two blocks and turn right onto Stewart Parkway, which runs along the Pamlico River.

Drive east on Stewart Parkway. Continue to the end of Stewart Parkway as it curves left to the intersection of Water and Bonner Streets. At this intersection, look for 210 Water Street, the Marsh House. Built in 1795, the Marsh House was used as quarters for Federal troops during the War. A cannonball that crashed completely through the Marsh House in 1864 is displayed in the second story of the house. The Myers House, next door, also housed Federal troops. Locals say the cannonball in the Myers House was added as a conversation piece and is not a real war relic.

Castle Island, the wooded island in the Pamlico River opposite the Marsh House, once had a four-gun Federal artillery battery. One Federal report said a cannon round fired from Castle Island brought down a Confederate officer perched in a treetop on the opposite bank of the river. The report says, "While he was indulging his curiosity, down he came, spyglass and all."

From this point, Fort Hill was about six miles downriver on the opposite bank. Fort Hill was the fort the Confederates built during their siege of Washington to keep Union ships from reaching the town. It was this fort that Union General Foster passed on the USS *Escort*.

Drive north on Bonner Street one block to the corner of Bonner and East Main Streets. The original St. Peters Episcopal Church stood on this corner, until it was burned by the Federals in 1864. According to townspeople, the church bell started tolling its own death knell during the fire, apparently due to the heat waves rising from the fire below. The present building dates to 1867.

Continue north on Bonner Street one more block to East Second Street. Turn left, or west, and drive one block. At the corner of Market Street

Beaufort County Courthouse

and East Second Street is the old Beaufort County Courthouse, now the county library. When the town was captured, the Federals ordered all of the townspeople to the courthouse to watch as the American flag was raised over the courthouse. The Federal commander warned of dire consequences if anyone insulted the flag in any way. An illustration of the moment ran in *Harper's Illustrated Weekly*, the nation's leading news magazine.

While the Federal commander would not allow any insults to the flag, he did not extend that same courtesy to the townspeople. A committee of women approached him to complain that they were the object of obscene comments from his men. He did nothing to punish his soldiers. He did order that no Southern songs could be sung in local taverns.

Continue west on Second Street. At the northwest corner of Second Street and U.S. 17, or Bridge Street, was a small Federal gun emplacement. It was from here that the Confederates made off with four brass cannons during their daring early morning raid in 1862. Drive another two blocks to 706 West Second Street to see the Hollyday House. This house was used as a hospital by Union forces.

Continue on Second Street until it dead-ends into Hackney Street. In this area was a large Federal wooden blockhouse that was part of the city's outer defenses. Turn left on Hackney Street, drive one block, then turn left again onto West Main Street and head back toward the center of town. At 731 West Main Street is Elmwood, a large, impressive home that was featured as one of the South's most distinguished homes in an 1857 *Harper's Illustrated Weekly* article. That did not keep it from being used as a hospital during the war.

Drive one more block on Main Street to Pierce Street. South of this point, under the Tar River (the river changes names from Tar to Pamlico at the U.S. 17 bridge) is the location of the USS *Picket*, the boat that exploded during the Confederates' raid in 1862. As noted earlier, the boat's magazine likely was reached by a stray spark fired from one of the Federals' own cannons, rather than from any action by the Confederates.

Continue on West Main, crossing over U.S. 17 to the Havens House on the next block at 404 West Main Street. The Havens House was owned by the same family that ran the brick Havens Warehouse across the street on the wharf. The Federals tried to set fire to the Havens Warehouse, but its sturdy brick construction survived. Turn right from Main Street onto Stewart Parkway again. Drive one block to Respess Street. At 112 Respess, on this intersection, is the Fowle Warehouse. The Fowle warehouse also survived the war, but it was saved only because Mr. Fowle and his daughters were able to muster a bucket brigade leading from the nearby river after the Federals set the warehouse on fire. The Federals had prepared for the fire by chopping up all of the fire hoses in the town and smashing the pumps.

Fowle's daughter, Martha, writing to a cousin, said, "The iron shutters were soon red from the heat of the fire. I distinctly remember that the trees on Main Street were on fire as we passed them."

Park the car along Stewart Parkway near the Fowle Warehouse and walk north on Respess Street to Main Street. (Parking can be at a premium on Main Street.)

Just north of the Fowle warehouse, at 216 West Main Street, is the Bank of Washington, now a gift shop on the northwest corner of Main and Respess. Built of block, and with a brick-lined roof, the 1864 fire skirted around the building. Virtually everything east of this point was turned to ashes in the fire. All of the churches in town were burned, as were more than half of the residences. Townspeople remembered watching one woman leave her house, then pause on her front steps as if she were deciding if she had time to retrieve something from inside. She ignored shouted warnings and turned back into the house. The firestorm arrived, and she never came out.

Walk back to the car. Drive down Stewart Parkway once more to Bonner Street. Turn left onto Bonner Street, drive two blocks to East Second Street, and turn left again. Drive one block to Market Street and turn right, heading north, away from the river.

Drive north on Market Street to get an idea of where the Federals and Confederates faced each other when Confederate Major General D.H. Hill besieged Washington in April 1863. He later wrote that his attempt to retake Washington was not worth the lives of his men.

Continue on Market Street to the intersection with Ninth Street. This intersection marks the outer ring of Federal earthworks during the 1863 siege. A slight raised area can still be seen at the southwest corner of Ninth and Market Streets. Drive on to the intersection of Market and Fifteenth

Bank of Washington

Street. On the right is a cemetery. The Confederates set up cannons on the hill where a Confederate monument is now. The Confederate dead from the siege now rest under that statue.

From the cemetery, turn around and drive back down Market Street to East Second Street. Turn right onto East Second Street and drive five blocks to Bridge Street, or U.S. 17. Turn left, or south, onto U.S. 17 and cross the bridge over the Tar/Pamlico Rivers to leave Washington.

At 3 miles after crossing the bridge, turn right, or west, onto N.C. 33 in the community of Chocowinity. Drive 1.1 miles from this intersection and look for the unmarked Trinity Cemetery on the left. In the back of the cemetery is a very impressive monument obelisk to Confederate Major General Bryan Grimes, who ordered the last Confederate assault on Federal troops at Appomattox on the morning that Robert E. Lee surrendered. It is this attack that is commemorated in the last part of North Carolina's war motto: "First At Bethel, Farthest to the Front at Gettysburg and Chickamauga, Last at Appomattox." The monument to Grimes lists the twenty-eight battles in which he participated.

Grimes was a wealthy, thirty-two-year-old planter and member of the state secession convention when he started his Confederate service as major of the 4th North Carolina Regiment. He was a fearless leader and plunged right into every battle with his men. When Lee wanted to see if he could still break out of Appomattox, Grimes stepped forward to try the assault. It could not be done. Lee surrendered.

Grimes was the last major general to be appointed by Lee, receiving his commission less than two months before the surrender. If Grimes had a fault, it was that he was not exactly magnanimous toward Yankees, before, during, or after the War. He described Federal prisoners as "the lowest scum of the Yankee population."

That unbending attitude caught up with Grimes on the night of August 14, 1880, when he was shot by an assassin. Grimes's killer was hired by some people who Grimes was trying to expel from Beaufort County. A twelve-year-old boy who was riding with Grimes in the carriage drove the dying general back to his nearby plantation home, Grimesland.

Grimes was buried in a family cemetery, with the intention he would be transferred to Trinity Cemetery. The transfer was never made, but Grimes is honored with the elaborate marker in the cemetery. On one side it reads: "Soldier sleep—Thy warfare is over." Another side reads: "Fearless, faithful, tender and true. An honest man, a brave soldier, a generous friend, a patriotic citizen, the hero of 100 battles." Another side reads: "His life was gentle and the elements so mixed in him that nature might stand up and say to all the world that this was a man." A cannon back-to-back with a plow is carved on the front of the monument. The word "assassinated" is in heavy type.

Leave the cemetery and continue west on N.C. 33. At 1.7 miles after leaving the cemetery is the crossing over Bear Creek where Grimes was shot. Drive 0.6 mile past Bear Creek to where Grimes Farm Road, or S.R. 1569, forks to the right. Veer right onto Grimes Farm road and drive towards Grimesland, Grimes's plantation. Grimesland is 4 miles from Trinity Cemetery, or 1.3 miles from the fork from N.C. 33.

Grimesland is a large plantation house a couple of hundred yards off the road to the right. Neither the house nor the family cemetery is open to the public. Descendants say Grimes's actual grave marker is very simple compared to the detailed obelisk in Trinity Cemetery.

Grimes's death was avenged. The assassin was dumb enough to return to the area in 1888, get drunk, and brag about his deed. Legend says the assassin's body was found hanging from a bridge with a sign reading "Justice At Last" hanging on his chest. The bridge was a toll bridge once owned by Grimes. One of the men who hired the assassin was found dead in South Carolina. The other was never heard from again.

Return to U.S. 17. From here visitors can return to Washington or head south to New Bern. This concludes The River Cities Tour.

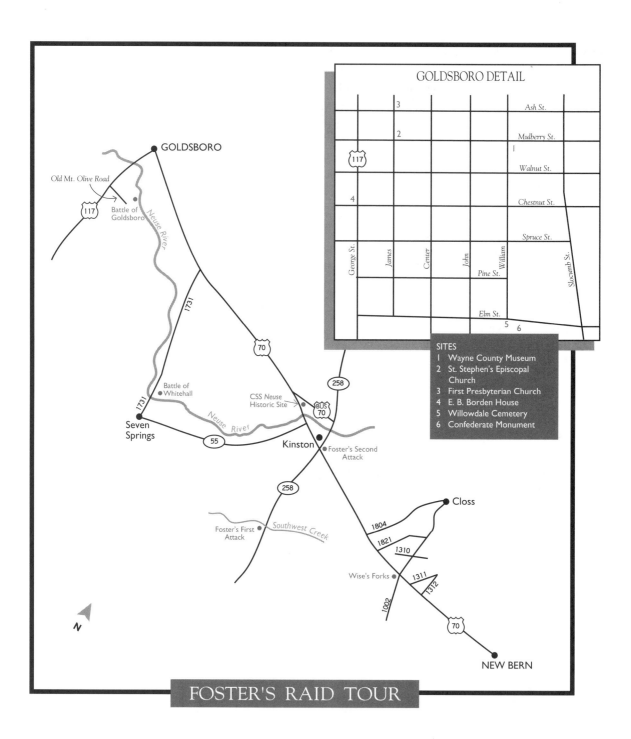

GOLDSBORO DETAIL

Ash St.

Mulberry St.

117

Walnut St.

4

Chestnut St.

Spruce St.

George St.

James

Center

John

Pine St.

William

Slocumb St.

Elm St.

5 6

SITES
1 Wayne County Museum
2 St. Stephen's Episcopal
  Church
3 First Presbyterian Church
4 E. B. Borden House
5 Willowdale Cemetery
6 Confederate Monument

GOLDSBORO

Old Mt. Olive Road

117

Battle of
Goldsboro

Neuse River

1731

70

258

Battle of
Whitehall

CSS Neuse
Historic Site

BUS
70

1731

Neuse River

Seven
Springs

55

Kinston

Foster's Second
Attack

258

Foster's First
Attack

Southwest Creek

Closs

1804

1821

1310

Wise's Forks

1311

1002

1312

70

N

NEW BERN

FOSTER'S RAID TOUR

Foster's Raid Tour

This tour begins outside of New Bern, then moves to the outskirts of Kinston and the site of the Battle of Wise's Forks, the second largest land battle in North Carolina. It continues into Kinston and the sites of the two bridges where Union General Foster tried to attack the town. In Kinston, the tour also stops at the CSS *Neuse*, a Confederate ironclad. From Kinston, the tour moves to the town of Seven Springs, where the Battle of Whitehall was fought and where the CSS *Neuse* was built. It then travels to Goldsboro, the site of the Battle of Goldsboro in 1862. Goldsboro is also the final resting place of more than eight hundred Confederates, the largest mass burial in North Carolina.

Total mileage: approximately 100 miles.

In December of 1862, Union Brigadier General John G. Foster, commanding the District of North Carolina from his headquarters in New Bern, was getting a little bored—there had been no military action in his area for several months. Washington, North Carolina, was captured without firing a shot in March 1862. Plymouth was occupied in May, also without firing a shot. Foster had sent out several small raids since then, but nothing truly big had been staged by the Union forces for some time.

Then Foster received a message from his old commander, Major General Ambrose Burnside. Burnside, now in command of the Army of the Potomac, was ready to attack Robert E. Lee's forces at Fredericksburg. He needed Foster to stage a coordinated attack in North Carolina to draw off any Confederate reinforcements.

Foster was happy to oblige. For some time, his eyes had been on an important railroad bridge over the Neuse River in Goldsboro. He had also heard that the Confederates were building an ironclad on the Neuse below Goldsboro, near the village of Whitehall. That was disturbing news. An ironclad could wreck the Federal fleet based at New Bern.

On a cold December 11, 1862, Foster set out from New Bern at the head

Neuse River Bridge at Seven Springs

of a formidable column of ten thousand infantry, more than six hundred cavalry, and forty pieces of artillery. The only forces facing him would be Confederate regiments scattered throughout the area, totaling only a little more than two thousand men. Most of the state's troops had been transferred to Virginia to reinforce Lee.

Two days of hard marching brought the Federals to Kinston, a small town on the Neuse River. The Confederates used Kinston as a staging area for patrols in the region. Foster had to attack Kinston in order to keep the Confederates stationed there from harassing him on the way to Goldsboro. There was also an important bridge over the Neuse River in Kinston. In the first engagement of the raid, the Confederates were easily flanked in a brief skirmish on Southwest Creek several miles southwest of Kinston. On December 14, the Federals turned east toward town and the bridge over the Neuse River.

The Confederates, under Brigadier General Nathan G. Evans, were well positioned behind earthworks, with their flanks protected by swamps. Evans, nicknamed "Shanks" because of his slim legs, had a good reputation coming onto the Kinston battlefield. At First Manassas in 1861, he detected the Federal flanking movement and held off the Federal forces until reinforcements could arrive, thereby saving the whole Confederate army. At Kinston, Evans fought well at first, hitting the Federals' much larger force very hard. Confused Union gunners dropped artillery rounds into their own ranks as they searched for the Confederate positions.

Then the Confederate left flank was turned, and it started a retreat across the Neuse River bridge toward town. For some reason, Evans's orders to retreat never reached the Confederate center and right flanks. It almost seems Evans forgot about these flanks because he started shelling their positions once his left flank regiments began crossing the bridge. Evans's "forgetfulness" might have been caused by heavy drinking. The bridge was set on fire before all of the Confederates were across, but the Federals still managed to capture it before it was destroyed. The Confederates retreated to the north side of town, leaving it to the Federals to ransack. More than four hundred Confederate prisoners and eleven pieces of Confederate artillery were taken during the battle.

Evans did not have time to ponder his poor performance. He started marching his men toward Goldsboro, hoping that a small force he placed at Whitehall could slow the Federals for a few hours.

Learning that Burnside's men had been cut down on the slopes of Marye's Heights in Fredericksburg, Virginia, Foster pushed on for Goldsboro. He was determined to get a solid victory for the North. His next objective was the hamlet of Whitehall (known today as Seven Springs), a small port town on the south banks of the Neuse River, about eighteen marching miles northwest of Kinston. Intelligence sources told him an ironclad, the CSS *Neuse*, was under construction there.

The overwhelmed Confederate force at Whitehall skirmished with the Federals through the town before retreating to the north bank of the Neuse. The Federals set up ten cannons on a high bluff overlooking the town and the riverbank, where the *Neuse* was still under construction. Ordinarily, such a position would have been enough to insure victory. In reality, yielding the high ground to the Federals was the best thing to happen to the Confederates. The officer in charge of the Federal artillery was the remarkably incompetent Colonel James Hewett Ledlie. Ledlie was a politically well-connected civil engineer who had raised his own regiment, the 3rd New York Artillery. He had no military training and knew nothing about artillery. That did not stop his friends in the War Department from regularly promoting him through the ranks until he was in charge of all the artillery on Foster's expedition. Ledlie short fused many of the rounds the Federals fired at the Confederates, meaning that the shells were bursting over his own men much of the time. Many, if not most, of the casualties Foster's men suffered at Whitehall came from "friendly fire."

The colonel of the 9th New Jersey, writing about Ledlie and Colonel Rush Hawkins of the 9th New York Zouaves Regiment, said, "If Colonel Ledlie or Colonel Hawkins perform anything credible before this war lasts, the good citizens of New York state will have reason to be thankful."

Despite the Federal mishaps, one Union soldier performed a very brave act during the battle. Private Butler of the 3rd New York Cavalry jumped into the river carrying a piece of the burning bridge to set fire to the ironclad. The Confederates saw Butler before he could reach the boat and opened fire. Miraculously, Butler was able to swim back without injury. A Federal writing about the courageous soldier said Butler was praised on the spot by his major "while in a situation not observable in civilized, unwarlike society." In other words, Private Butler was standing in front of his major naked as a jaybird.

The ironclad was shelled but not severely damaged. The Federals started heading northwest for their final objective, the important railroad bridge over the Neuse at Goldsboro.

While it would be nice to think that Ledlie was court-martialed for killing his own men, such was not the case. He was later promoted to brigadier general. In battle after battle, Ledlie proved to be a drunken coward, yet he was handed more and more responsibility.

Ledlie's most famous bender came at The Battle of the Crater in Petersburg, Virginia, in 1864. Ledlie's division was picked to spearhead the thrust into the enemy lines after tons of gunpowder had exploded in a mine shaft dug under the Confederates. While his men were being slaughtered in the crater, Ledlie was knocking back rum shooters in a bomb shelter behind his lines. Even that episode brought him only a mild rebuke. Ledlie did not leave the Union Army until January 1865.

Along the way to Goldsboro, a cavalry detachment was sent to the town of Mount Olive. The town had not even heard about the Union raid on Whitehall, just fifteen miles away. When the Federals took the train depot in Mount Olive, the ticket agent was still selling tickets.

By the time the Federals reached the Goldsboro bridge, the Confederates, including many of the same soldiers who had fought at Kinston, were ready for them. The Confederates had stripped the underbrush from the side of the river where the Federals would advance, leaving no cover for the Union troops. The Confederates also had something that was vaguely described by soldiers at the scene as a "Merrimac car," or a "Monitor car"— an armored railroad car that shelled the advancing Federals. This may have been the first recorded military use of a tank. Unfortunately, nothing more about the construction of this tank and what happened to it has found its way into the history books.

After several hours of trying to cross or burn the railroad bridge, the Federals abruptly left the battlefield. They appeared to be heading back for New Bern. A group of impetuous South Carolinians, thinking they could turn the Federals' orderly retreat into a rout, charged across the railroad bridge in hot pursuit. Too hot, it turns out. The Federal cannons, which had not moved out, cut the South Carolinians down with double loads of canister. Canister is an artillery shell that looks like a tin can full of small round shot. Firing a round of canister turns a cannon into a giant shotgun and is deadly against men charging into it.

One Federal wrote, "The enemy was allowed to get rather close to the battery. The rebels made this bayonet charge with great dash and courage, but not withstanding, they were repulsed with great loss of life and with an amusing and astonishing precipitancy."

The Confederates still had a few tricks up their sleeves. On the march away from Goldsboro, the Federals had to cross a dry mill stream near the Neuse River. The Confederates had closed the mill-stream gate several hours earlier, allowing millions of gallons of water to back up into a pond. The Confederates waited until a number of Federals were walking across the mill stream bed before opening the gate "allowing the water to rush down with astonishing impetuosity." Several Federal soldiers drowned.

The Battle of Goldsboro was a Federal defeat, but Foster never admitted it as one. Even so, the Federal soldiers knew they had been in a hard fight. A Federal chaplain, hoping to get some praise for God out of the men, asked one of the retreating soldiers if he had been supported by "divine inspiration" during the battle. The weary soldier, in no mood to praise a deity for his survival, replied, "No. We were supported by the 9th New Jersey."

Years after the battle, an old Union soldier visited Goldsboro. He asked an old Confederate to take him to the battle site. As they walked the battleground together, the Confederate's curiosity got the most of him. He asked the Federal why Foster had left the battlefield so abruptly when it appeared he was on the brink of taking the railroad bridge and the town.

"We were entirely out of ammunition. We did not have a round to the man and all of us expected capture. If twenty-five hundred Confederates had been thrown ahead of us at Kinston, they could have captured the whole fifteen thousand," the Federal replied. The official Union reports present it a little differently, but it is apparently true that Foster's men were low on ammunition by the time they returned to New Bern.

The ravages of war returned to Kinston in March 1865. The war was winding down. Lee was trapped at Petersburg. Wilmington had fallen. Sherman was about to enter the state from South Carolina. The Union was ready for the last big push.

Sherman sent orders to Union Major General John M. Schofield at Wilmington to gather supplies that would be transferred to Sherman's army near Goldsboro sometime in the coming month. In order to get the supplies safely to Goldsboro, Schofield had to secure the route from the Confederate forces stationed near Kinston. Schofield ordered Major General Jacob Cox to advance on Kinston with thirteen thousand troops.

Facing Cox, in trenches dug along Southwest Creek about five miles east of Kinston, was what remained of the evacuated Wilmington garrison. These forces were under the immediate command of Confederate Major General Robert F. Hoke and the overall command of General Braxton Bragg. Coming up in support were more Confederates under the command of Major General D. H. Hill. Hill was a bitter enemy of Bragg and had virtually refused to fight under him in Tennessee. In Hill's command were the North Carolina Junior Reserves, called "the seed corn of the Confederacy." These were barely trained boys, some as young as sixteen. All the Confederate forces in the area numbered less than ten thousand.

Action started on March 7, 1865, with Federal artillery probing Confederate defenses. In the early morning of March 8, Hoke and Hill moved their forces out of their entrenchments and attacked on both flanks. The tactic so surprised the Federals that one Massachusetts regiment ran and the 15th Connecticut, a unit of a thousand men, was captured outright. It was the last mass capture of Federals during the War. The only sore spot for the Confederates was that the boys of the Junior Reserves had been too frightened to be effective.

Although they still outnumbered the Confederates, the surprised remaining Federals dug their own trenches and stayed in them until reinforcements could come up.

In the early hours of March 10, 1865, Hoke tried a mirror image of the tactic that Stonewall Jackson had found successful at Chancellorsville. Hoke swung around the Federals' left flank and attacked them in their trenches, sending some running to the woods. Unfortunately for Hoke, not enough Federals ran. Soon, Hoke pulled his weakened force back. Hill, who had taken one line of trenches on the Federals' right flank during the action, also retreated. Bragg pulled his entire command back across the Neuse.

Confederate trench line at Goldsboro

This three-day battle goes by numerous names—Second Battle of Kinston, Battle of Southwest Creek—but it is most often called the Battle of Wise's Forks, named after a nearby crossroads. Judged by the total number of troops engaged over the three days, it was the second largest land battle in North Carolina.

From Kinston, the regiments under Bragg, Hoke, and Hill marched to the last and largest battle fought in North Carolina, Bentonville, which was to come just nine days later. (See The Bentonville Battle Tour for full details on the Battle of Bentonville.)

Start The Foster's Raid Tour in New Bern driving west on U.S. 70.

About 30 miles after leaving New Bern on U.S. 70, the Dover Road (S.R. 1005) exit will be on the right. Dover Road was one of the roads used by the Federals during their several advances on Kinston. Just north of here is Gum Swamp, the scene of several skirmishes, usually won by Federals patrolling out of New Bern. After passing the Dover Road exit while heading west on U.S. 70 toward Kinston, look for a small white house on the left. The house marks the approximate beginning of the Wise's Forks battlefield area.

About 1.4 miles after passing the Dover Road exit, U.S. 70 makes a slight curve to the left while Sky Road, or S.R. 1312, intersects it from the right. Turn right onto Sky Road. Cross the railroad track and turn left onto S.R. 1311, a gravel road. This is the same country road that one wing of the Federal forces marched down as they cautiously advanced toward Southwest Creek in March 1865. Off the road is an abandoned cemetery rumored to have unmarked Federal graves of soldiers killed by Confederate snipers.

About 1.0 mile later, the gravel road returns to U.S. 70. Turn right, or west, and travel 1.0 mile to Wise's Crossroads, where Wise's Fork Road intersects U.S. 70. A Texaco station is on the southeast corner. Turn right or north onto Wise's Fork Road, or S.R. 1002. Drive for about a mile and turn right, or east, at the stop sign onto S.R. 1310. The Federals camped throughout this area on the night of March 7, 1865, in preparation for doing battle the next day. Remnants of their trenches may be seen along S.R. 1310. Turn around and return to Wise's Fork Road. Turn right and head north until Wise's Fork Road dead-ends at a church and the intersection with Neuse Road, or S.R. 1804. This is the region where D.H. Hill moved in anticipation that Hoke's flanking maneuver would send all of the Federals towards Hill's troops on March 10, 1865. Turn left or west onto Neuse Road. Southwest Creek crosses under the road at this point. The main Confederate defensive line ran along the creek.

Neuse Road intersects with U.S. 70. Turn left, or east, onto U.S. 70, remembering this is a divided, four-lane highway. Within a hundred yards after turning is a two-story white house on the left that served as a hospital during the action in 1865. Cross over Southwest Creek again and take the next left, or north, turn onto British Road, or S.R. 1821. A large map marker on the northeast side of the intersection describes the Battle of Wise's Forks. Pull into the parking lot to read it. This is the area where Hoke rolled up the Federal flank on March 10, 1865. For more than a century after the battle, farmers plowing the fields beside British Road would hear the constant clatter of musket balls ringing off their equipment. Today, the area is residential.

Turn right at the British Road intersection with Wise's Forks Road. Drive back toward U.S. 70 and cross over it, remaining on Wise's Fork Road. This southwest side of U.S. 70 is still part of the area where Hoke attacked the Union flank. In the distance to the west is a white house that was used as a hospital during the battle. Rumor says that blood stains soaked the walls and floors and that Federal regiments wrote their names on the walls.

Return to U.S. 70 and turn left, or west, heading toward Kinston. Lenoir Community College will be on the left as you approach town. This area was a Federal staging ground for the December 1862 attack on the Neuse River bridge leading to Kinston. Across from the community college, on the north side of U.S. 70, is a Holiday Inn. Pull into the hotel parking lot, drive to the west side, and park. Walk just north of the Holiday Inn to the Business U.S.70/Business U.S. 258 bridge leading into downtown Kinston. Look over the bridge's east side, then walk to the east, along the river's edge. In the water under the bridge are the remnants of wooden pilings, indicating the current bridge is on the same site as the 1862 bridge. About fifty yards downstream from the bridge is a line of wooden pilings and rock obstructions stretching across the river. Local historians say these obstructions are part of the Confederates' defenses to keep the Federals from traveling up the river by gunboat.

The Federals actually fought the first skirmish with Confederates in the December 1862 raid at another bridge over Southwest Creek on December 13. There is nothing left of the original bridge, but to see the modern-day version, drive right or west out of the Holiday Inn parking lot and get immediately into the left turning lane for U.S. 258 South. On U.S. 258, drive 4.7 miles from the intersection with U.S. 70 and pull over at the bridge. There is no historical marker here, but Federal and Confederate trenches lie hidden behind fenced woods. Foster's men easily flanked the Confederates by wading the creek. The Confederates retreated to Kinston to join the defenses there, and the Federals followed to attack the Neuse River bridge near the Holiday Inn.

Turn around and head north on U.S. 258 to Bypass U.S. 70/Bypass U.S. 258. Turn left or west onto Bypass U.S. 70. Drive 2.5 miles to the intersection with Business U.S. 70 and turn right or northeast, toward Kinston. The CSS *Neuse* State Historic Site is 0.3 mile from the intersection on the right. The ribbed wooden hull of the ironclad rests in back of a small museum dedicated to artifacts from the *Neuse* and ironclad warfare in general. A helpful display compares the designs of Confederate ironclads with Union Monitor-style ironclads. There is also a mockup of how the *Neuse's* wooden planking would have been topped with railroad iron.

The *Neuse* was designed to do one thing: cruise down the Neuse River to Beaufort and smash the Federal wooden ships holding the port city. The ironclad was designed by the same nineteen-year-old mechanical wizard who built the successful Confederate ironclad CSS *Albemarle*, which operated on the Roanoke River. (See The River Cities Tour for more details on the very successful career of the CSS *Albemarle*).

The *Neuse* was 158 feet long and 34 feet wide, virtually a twin of the *Albemarle*. Both vessels drew 12 feet of water. This draft was no problem on the Roanoke River, but caused problems on the shallow Neuse. Compared to the Confederacy's first ironclad, the CSS *Virginia*, the *Albemarle* and the *Neuse* were small—158 feet long compared to the *Virginia's* 270 feet. The *Virginia* also drew 22 feet of water, much too deep to operate in most rivers or around ports.

The *Neuse*'s armor started with two base layers of yellow-pine lumber. According to the ship's design, two layers of 2-inch thick railroad iron was supposed to be bolted at a sloping angle on top of the lumber. The sloping iron would cause Federal shells to glance off the boat. The armament consisted of two, 6.4-inch Brooke rifled cannons, the best the Confederacy could manufacture at the Tredegar iron works in Richmond. The shells they fired weighed 66 pounds. The plans called for the Brooke cannons to be mounted back-to-back on semicircular iron bands, so each gun could be swiveled to fire from one of five gunports. There would be one gunport facing directly forward, one facing aft, and two facing at angles forward and aft. The crew numbered eighty-five, including cooks.

The *Neuse* was damaged in December 1862 by Foster's raid but construction continued for eighteen months afterwards. Construction was hampered by a lack of skilled labor and by the slowness of the Wilmington naval commander in sending the railroad iron that had been ordered for armor. The commander, William Lynch, did not believe in ironclads, so he was not moved to help prove that wooden ships were obsolete. This was the same man who had unsuccessfully commanded the tiny Confederate fleet of lightly armed wooden ships called the "mosquito fleet" at Roanoke Island in February 1862. He lost his whole force in a very quick naval battle at Elizabeth City just two days later, a distinction that hardly made him an expert on naval warfare. (See Coastal War Tour and The Railroad Defense Tour for more information on the "mosquito fleet.")

While the CSS *Albemarle* enjoyed a successful career smashing Union ships, the CSS *Neuse* never really got a chance to prove itself. She lay in Kinston almost a year waiting to be outfitted with armor and machinery. The only time she was really underway was April 1864, when she was supposed to attack the Union fleet at New Bern. There was one small problem. The river was too low to float much further than downtown Kinston. The ship ran aground on a sandbar and was stranded there for more than a month. It was the Civil War equivalent of building a sailboat in the basement before discovering the door was too narrow to get it out. The only shots the ship fired were at advancing Federals during the Battle of Wise's Forks.

The Confederates intentionally burned and sank the *Neuse* just a mile downriver from where she rests today under a protective shelter in the state historic site. The Federals never bothered to raise her, although they did recover her guns. In time, her engines and armor plating were stripped off and sold by local scavengers. The engines were being used in a local sawmill in 1870. In 1961, the state undertook an effort to raise the ship. The effort took more than two years, with the river periodically flooding and hampering the salvage.

The *Neuse* historic site is one of only three places in the country where visitors can see a Civil War ironclad. The USS *Cairo*, restored so that visitors can actually board her, is in Vicksburg, Mississippi. The wooden hull of the CSS *Jackson* is on display in Columbus, Georgia.

The *Neuse* had the capability to destroy the Federal wooden ships at Beaufort, and Confederate officials knew it. While Richmond-based officials rarely supported the transfer of troops from Virginia to North Carolina, they readily approved all plans to build the *Neuse*. That included complicated logistics such as ordering railroad iron from Atlanta and the Brooke cannons from Richmond, then sending these supplies to a tiny river village in North Carolina. Alas, even the men at the top could not deal with the lower-level bureaucrats who seem to control every war. Much of the holdup in the construction of the *Neuse* was caused by bickering and infighting among these lower officials.

The *Neuse* also played a role, although a slight one, in what some postwar Northern generals called a war crime.

Twenty former Confederates were captured in Federal uniform during the Confederate attack on New Bern on February 1, 1864. All of the deserters were former members of the 66th North Carolina Regiment, a unit raised in eastern North Carolina. Many of the men were recognized by neighbors who had remained loyal to the Confederacy. The men were tried without counsel and hanged in a field near Kinston's courthouse using hawser rope cut from the *Neuse*. (References record only that the field could be seen from the courthouse.)

A Congressional investigation after the war tried to have Confederate Major General George Pickett, the commanding officer who captured the deserters, brought up on war crimes for the soldiers' execution. However, Ulysses S. Grant personally dropped the charges, claiming that desertion to the enemy was a universal offense punishable by death in any army. Grant's critics grumbled that he let Pickett off the hook because they were very good friends. During the war, Grant sent Pickett congratulations and a gift when he heard that Pickett's wife had given birth.

After leaving the CSS *Neuse* State Historic Site, retrace your route on Business U.S. 70. Turn left, or east, on Bypass U.S. 70. After 1.1 miles, turn right, or west, onto N.C. 11/N.C. 55. After 3.2 miles, follow the N.C. 55 fork to the right. The town of Seven Springs (known as Whitehall during the Civil War) is about 12 miles west.

After entering the town limits of Seven Springs on N.C. 55, slow down and look for Church Hill Street to the left. It will be less than 0.5 mile after crossing the intersection with Drummersville Road. Turn left and drive up Church Hill Street to the front of the First Methodist Church. Park near the steps leading down from the bluff.

This is the high ground where the Federals placed their cannons during the 1862 raid. It was from this point that the incompetent Colonel James Ledlie attempted to fire on the CSS *Neuse* and Confederate soldiers in the woods 0.2 mile to the north on the opposite side of the river. This is great ground for cannon; higher than the target ground and wide enough to place several batteries wheel to wheel. It is hard to believe that Ledlie could screw up the barrage, but he did, dropping as many shells on his own troops as he did the Confederates. Still, enough shells hit the Confederate side that people into the 1920's wondered why the tops of the trees on the north side of the Neuse River were missing.

Leave the church, drive back down Church Hill Street and turn left onto N.C. 55. Take the immediate right onto Piney Grove Road. A fire station will be on the northwest corner. Drive north, noting the historic marker about the 1862 battle on the right side of the street.

Drive down to the Neuse River. This is the same area where the naked Private Butler tried to set fire to the *Neuse* in December 1862. Just before crossing the river, pull into the parking lot of Seven Springs Library on the right. A granite monument in front of the library commemorates the battle. Walk to the river and notice how the trees along the north bank all seem to be the same height, perhaps indicating that the trees there 134 years ago were all cut down at the same time to build the *Neuse*. Confederates writing about the battle said they were saved by hiding behind all the cut logs along the river.

Get back into the car and cross over the river on Piney Grove Road, heading north. Follow Piney Grove Road for 9.3 miles, to where it intersects with U.S. 70. Turn left, or west, onto U.S. 70. After 5.4 miles, bear left onto East Ash Street, or Business U.S. 70, which will lead to downtown Goldsboro.

After traveling 2.6 miles from the U.S. 70 intersection, turn left, or south, from East Ash Street onto North Claiborne Street. A small office building for Parker Advertising will be on the right side of East Ash Street at this intersection. Drive one block on North Claiborne Street. At the corner of Mulberry and North Claiborne Streets, in front of a house on the northwest corner, are preserved Confederate earthworks. A sign in the house's yard reads that the earthworks were constructed in 1862. These earthworks once stretched more than four miles. Continue south on North Claiborne Street one more block to Walnut Street. Turn right, or west. Drive 1.8 miles to the corner of Walnut and William Streets, the beginning of the Goldsboro historic district.

Turn right, or north, onto William Street. Drive one block to the Wayne County Museum at the corner of Mulberry and William Streets. A room opening in 1996 will be dedicated to the Civil War.

Turn left, or west, onto Mulberry and drive three blocks to the corner of Mulberry and James Streets. St. Stephens Episcopal Church, on the corner at 200 North James Street, was built in 1857. Turn right, or north, onto James Street. In one block, at the corner of Ash and James Streets, is the old First Presbyterian Church, built in 1856.

Turn left onto Ash for a block, then left onto George Street, or Business U.S. 117.

At 111 South George Street is the site of a house that belonged to Mrs. E.B. Borden. The Borden house is now gone and another house is on the property. In March 1865, when Mrs. Borden heard the Yankees were coming, she buried the family money in the back just a few days before Union Major General John Schofield appropriated her house. When Mrs. Borden looked into her backyard after the Federals moved into the house, she saw soldiers had pitched a tent directly over her money.

Over time, Mrs. Borden befriended the general, making sure he had every comfort he needed. Within a few days, she swallowed hard and told Schofield where her money was buried. The general walked out into the yard and had her dig up her savings. He then told all of the soldiers they would have to answer to him if he heard they were bothering her.

Drive three blocks south on George Street and turn right, or west, onto Elm Street. Follow Elm until it intersects with Bypass U.S. 117/U.S. 13. Turn left, or south. South of Goldsboro, Bypass U.S. 117 becomes U.S. 117. About 3 miles south of downtown is a bridge over the Neuse River. Take the first left after crossing the bridge at a traffic light for Old Mount Olive Road. A Hardee's restaurant is on the northeast corner.

The land from the rear of Hardee's to the river, and from U.S. 117 to the east, is the 1862 battlefield. No historic marker is on the site. Continue 0.4 mile on Old Mount Olive Road and cross the railroad tracks. Watching and listening for trains, slow down and look to the left, or north, toward the river. About 0.75 mile away is the modern railroad bridge that is likely on or near the spot where the vital railroad bridge existed in 1862. This is the area where the Confederate "Merrimac car" shelled the Federals.

It is also the area where the Federals killed scores of brave, if foolhardy, South Carolinians who charged straight into Union cannons loaded with double loads of canister.

After the battle in 1862, the Federals returned to New Bern with very little harassment from the exhausted Confederates. One hundred Federals were killed and nearly 500 were wounded over the two-week, 200-mile raid. More than 70 Confederates were killed, 270 were wounded, and nearly 500 were taken prisoner. The majority of Confederate prisoners were taken at Kinston when General Evans left them on the wrong side of the river.

There is no public access to the Battle of Goldsboro site at present, although the county now owns the land. Local historians hope the property will become a historic park. Other than the commercialization along U.S. 117, this is a pristine battlefield. Return to U.S. 117 and turn north, recrossing the Neuse River. Veer right, or north, onto Business U.S. 117, 2.2 miles after leaving Old Mount Olive Road. After 1.4 miles on Business U.S. 117, turn right, or east, onto Elm Street. An Exxon Station is on the corner. Drive three blocks on Elm Street to Willowdale Cemetery on the right. On entering the cemetery, bear left, then right, on the first road to get back to the old section. A large mound guarded by a Confederate statue contains the bodies of more than eight hundred Confederates, the largest mass burial of soldiers in the state. The monument's inscription reads, "On fame's eternal camping ground, their silent tents are spread. In glory guards the solemn round, the bivouac of the dead." In appreciation for the contributions of Northerners, another side is inscribed, "A generous foe contributed to the erection of this memorial." Most of the dead at this cemetery are from the Battle of Bentonville and from the burial grounds of North Carolina hospitals. The monument was erected in 1883 by the Ladies Monument Society. The trees flanking the monument look old enough to have been planted when the monument was first dedicated.

A few yards south of the Confederate monument is the grave of Confederate Brigadier General William Gaston Lewis, a former teacher and surveyor who worked on the vital Wilmington & Weldon Railroad for three years. Lewis's only military training came as a teenager in military school in Raleigh. He fought at Big Bethel, the first battle of the war, New Bern, Gettysburg, Plymouth, the Shenandoah Valley campaign, and Petersburg,

Mass grave of 800 Confederates at Willowdale Cemetery

and just about every major action of the Army of Northern Virginia. Most of his regimental service was with the 33rd and later the 43rd North Carolina regiments. In May 1864, he was promoted to brigadier general, serving under Major General Stephen D. Ramseur. Lewis was wounded and captured just two days before Lee's surrender at Appomattox. He served as state civil engineer after the war and died in 1901 at the age of 66.

In March 1865, Goldsboro was peacefully occupied by more than a hundred thousand Federal soldiers, as both Sherman's men and the Union soldiers from New Bern converged here. They were not exactly GQ magazine models. One of these soldiers wrote in his diary: "Probably one man in a dozen had a full suit of clothes. Many were bareheaded or had a handkerchief tied around their heads. Some had hats so holey that their hair was sticking out. Generally both legs on the trousers were nearly off to the knees."

After a review of his troops, Sherman turned to General Schofield (whose command had not participated in Sherman's March) and said, "They don't march very well, but they will fight."

Return to the front of the cemetery. William Street begins across from the entrance. Drive north on William Street six blocks to Ash Street. A right turn leads to U.S. 70.

This concludes the Foster's Raid Tour.

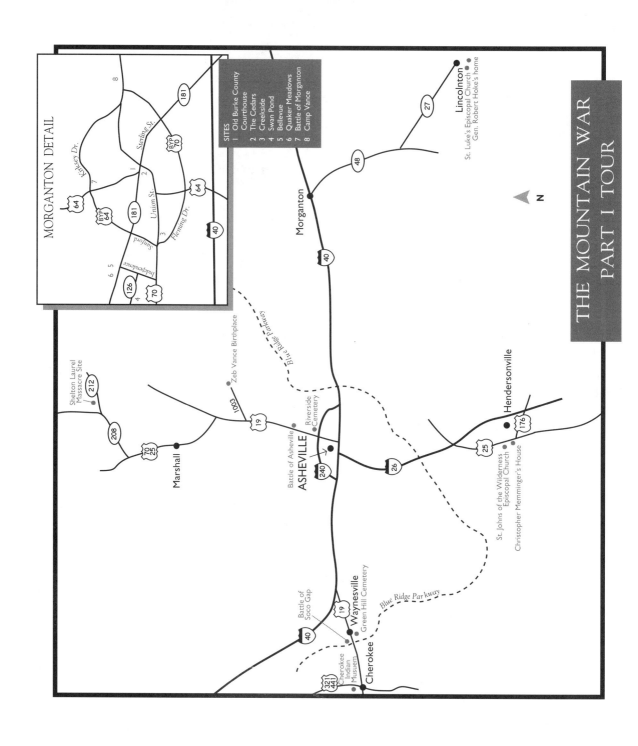

THE MOUNTAIN WAR
PART I TOUR

N

MORGANTON DETAIL

SITES
1   Old Burke County
    Courthouse
2   The Cedars
3   Creekside
4   Swan Pond
5   Bellevue
6   Quaker Meadows
7   Battle of Morganton
8   Camp Vance

Lincolnton
St. Luke's Episcopal Church
Gen. Robert Hoke's home

Morganton

Marshall

Shelton Laurel
Massacre Site

Zeb Vance Birthplace

Blue Ridge Parkway

Riverside
Cemetery

Battle of Asheville

ASHEVILLE

Hendersonville

St. Johns of the Wilderness
Episcopal Church

Christopher Memminger's House

Battle of Soco Gap

Waynesville
Green Hill Cemetery

Blue Ridge Parkway

Cherokee
Indian
Museum

Cherokee

The Mountain War
Part I Tour

This tour starts in Cherokee, North Carolina, where a unit that included Cherokee Indians fought the Federals. From there, it moves to Waynesville. A side trip travels to Flat Rock, near Hendersonville, where the Confederate treasurer maintained a home that was later bought by poet Carl Sandburg. From there, the tour moves to Asheville and includes the site of the Battle of Asheville. The tour continues to the birthplace of Zeb Vance, North Carolina's war-time governor. It then travels through Marshall to the site of the Shelton Laurel Massacre, where local Union supporters were murdered by Con-federate troops. It ends in Morganton, where Stoneman's raiders brushed aside the home guard defending the city.

Total mileage: approximately 310 miles, counting the side trip. It is best to take the tour in two days. Asheville may deserve a longer look and is a good halfway point.

While North Carolina ranked seventh among the Confederacy for the number of slaves within its borders, very few of them were in the mountains. There were some slaves scattered throughout the western part of the state, but many areas there were almost all white. The reason for the lack of slaves in the western part of the state was simple. There was nothing for them to do. The mountains were too steep, and the soil too poor to plant cotton. Rice, the other slave-labor-intensive crop, needed vast expanses of flat marsh, something most mountaineers had never seen in their lives.

When wealthy politicians started complaining that the election of Lincoln would lead to the emancipation of their slaves, the mountaineers shrugged. That would not make a single change in their lives. When the politicians said that tariffs kept European goods high in cost, they shrugged again. Store-bought goods, no matter where they were made, were always expensive in the mountains because transportation costs to bring them up the hills were high. These high costs were why mountain people had always been self-sufficient, making what they needed and doing without other luxuries.

And, despite the fact that one of their own, Zebulon Vance from

Buncombe County, built a national reputation as a politician, mountaineers were never too fond of any government. They did not care if government men came from Raleigh or Washington, D.C. They did not like them.

When the war came, the reaction among the people of western North Carolina was split along three lines. Some mountaineers immediately joined Confederate regiments. Others did nothing, believing the conflict was a "rich man's war and a poor man's fight." Some expressed pro-Union sentiments, and some of these Union supporters headed into East Tennessee once it was under Union control to join Federal units. Joining a Federal unit became known as "going over the mountain," a term that was the subject and lyric of many traditional folk songs.

After the Confederates started drafting men against their will, the negative reaction to the war escalated among the people of the mountains. Farmers who had ignored the call for volunteers now hid when the sheriff came around with the conscription agents. Confederate supporters started feuding with their pro-Union neighbors. Bushwhackers, both Union and Confederate, took to the hills, preying on isolated farm houses and nocturnal travelers. Citizens who thought war was something fought on distant battlefields learned it could be practiced right in their own communities when their houses and barns were robbed, their crops burned, and their livestock stolen.

While the mountain region saw its share of violence, there were no large-scale battles fought in the area. For one thing, no armies could pass through the mountains over the narrow, twisting, poorly maintained roads. Second, there was little of strategic value to be captured. There were no railroads, no river ports, no vast supplies of stores.

The battles that were fought in the mountains did not follow a time line, as the coastal battles did, and they were mostly small affairs between dozens, scores, and on rare occasion, a few hundred men per side. Raids conducted by either side were small affairs, designed to let the other side know the war was still raging in other places. The largest operation during the whole war occurred near the end. That was the month-long raid of Union Major General George Stoneman. From March to April of 1865, Stoneman and his eighteen hundred cavalrymen rode throughout the Blue

Ridge–mountain range. When he was opposed, it was rarely by more than a few hundred Confederate militiamen.

But the scale of military operations had nothing to do with the bitterness that could be generated by both sides. One action, brashly and horribly undertaken by two Confederate colonels in the winter of 1863, has left many mountaineers of North Carolina angry and suspicious of outsiders for the past 135 years.

Madison County, the county northwest of Asheville, is isolated from the rest of the state by a mountain range running north to south. This isolation led residents of Madison County to think of themselves more as Tennesseeans than as Tar Heels. The natural lay of the land and the French Broad River pointed towards Greeneville, Tennessee. To even get to the county seat in Marshall, North Carolina, meant climbing up and over a mountain. If North Carolina wanted to secede, that had little to do with the citizens who lived in the mountain hollows north and west of Marshall.

While this indifference may have been the attitude of many of Madison County's citizens, the state refused to absolve the region of its responsibility to raise troops. The 64th North Carolina Regiment was created and manned with volunteers and, later, conscripts from the region. Some of the regiment's members, particularly the wealthy officers who tended to look down on their hardscrabble soldiers, did not think kindly of their neighbors hiding out in the nearby hollows. The regiment was led by Colonel Lawrence M. Allen and Lieutenant Colonel James A. Keith. Allen and Keith were wealthy townies who had houses in Marshall rather than cabins hacked out of hillsides like most of their soldiers.

Salt was a valuable, life-sustaining commodity in the mountains. Without it, game shot during the fall could not be preserved for the long winters. With supplies running low throughout the South, what little salt reached the mountains through official government channels was supposed to be reserved for Confederate families. Union sympathizers could find their own supply; the Confederates did not care.

In January 1863, a small band of men, supposedly from pro-Union farms in Shelton Laurel, an isolated region of Madison County which ran along a tiny creek, raided Marshall to steal a supply of salt. While there, they broke into the home of Colonel Allen and roughed up his wife and

Skirmish site near Shelton Laurel

children. Two of the children were sick with fever, and some of the bolder, more spiteful raiders took the blankets from their beds.

When word of the raid reached Allen, who was on duty with the 64th North Carolina, guarding a larger supply of salt in Bristol, Tennessee, he asked his commander, Confederate Brigadier General Henry Heth, for permission to lead a raid into Shelton Laurel. Allen vowed to clean out this band of Unionists once and for all. Heth, a Virginian and close personal friend of Robert E. Lee, agreed. Although he later denied it, some witnesses believed Heth also gave an extra set of instructions to Allen and Keith—take no prisoners.

Heth was no stranger to disavowing his own actions. At Gettysburg, General Robert E. Lee himself commanded Heth to refrain from fighting until all of the Confederate Army was ready. Heth ignored the order, and his division started the battle several hours too soon. Had Heth followed orders, Lee might have swept the inferior Federal opposition aside, taken the high ground, and history may have seen a different winner at Gettysburg. Heth always denied that the defeat at Gettysburg was his fault.

Allen entered the valley of Shelton Laurel from the southwest with part of the 64th North Carolina. Keith entered the valley from the northeast with the rest of the regiment. Their approach was trumpeted by mountaineers blowing horns as signals. Unionist snipers fired down on the Confederates from hidden mountain perches. The snowy, frozen ground gave the soldiers frostbite. Finally, near the farm of a man named Bill Shelton, the two units came together. A short battle ensued, with several mountaineers being killed. Then the 64th made camp. That night, Allen rode back to Marshall, just in time to hold his dying daughter in his arms. His son had died one day earlier. Allen knew, just knew, that the salt raiders from Shelton Laurel had as much to do with the deaths of his children as the scarlet fever.

What happened next is hard to determine. Some reports say that a few Unionists were captured during the battle. Other stories say the 64th went house-to-house in the valley looking for men. The women in the houses may have been tortured to reveal the hiding spots of their kinfolk. In the end, fifteen men, one as young as thirteen, were taken prisoner. Their families were told the men would be marched to Knoxville, where they would stand trial for the crime of stealing the salt. Two prisoners escaped, leaving thirteen to walk to Knoxville the next day.

The men and boys did not walk more than a couple of miles. Without warning, but not without some obvious planning, the column, led at the time by Keith, halted. The thirteen prisoners were forced to their knees and shot dead. The spot, apparently chosen by Keith and Allen for this precise purpose, was a natural amphitheater. There must have been scores of Unionists watching the murders from the hills around the little killing field. Keith and Allen wanted to make sure these witnesses understood what happened to Unionists who defied them.

The Confederates buried the bodies in a very shallow grave. The next day, an elderly lady, a member of Bill Shelton's family, came to the site with a broken coal shovel and one helper. Together, the two removed the bodies and reburied them on a little ridge on her farm.

Governor Vance did his best to pursue Allen and Keith for war crimes, but both men escaped retribution for their actions. Both of them had the good sense to leave North Carolina and move to Arkansas, where they died old men.

However, not every member of the 64th North Carolina escaped payback. One of the two Unionists who had escaped capture recognized one of the 64th's members as a neighbor. The next day, he watched the shootings from a mountainside. The Unionist bided his time, and after the war, he killed his Confederate neighbor.

Perhaps the most interesting military force to come from the mountains of North Carolina was Thomas's Confederate Legion, sometimes erroneously called the 69th North Carolina Regiment. While most Confederate soldiers carried common names like Johnson, Smith, and Jones, some members of Thomas's Legion had names like Astoogatogeh, Ahmacatogeh, Cah hah, Cahtoquaskee, and Chunollegah. Thomas's Legion was made up of Cherokee Indians and white mountaineers. At different times, more than a thousand men served in the Legion.

William H. Thomas was a white man who served twenty-two years in the general assembly and in North Carolina's secession convention. He had lived among the Cherokees since his youth and was widely known as a proponent for the rights of the Cherokees in western North Carolina.

During the war, the Legion served in eastern Tennessee and as far north as the Shenandoah Valley. However, most of its service came as a home guard unit in western North Carolina, where it fought several skirmishes with Federal raiders.

Once, fifteen Cherokee soldiers were captured and taken to Knoxville, where they were told they could return without harm if they would bring in the scalps of Thomas and his officers. The Cherokees agreed, returned to camp, told the story around the campfire, and laughed at the Federals.

The oddest battle fought by the Legion occurred after General Lee had surrendered. The odd part was that both sides knew the war was over. On May 6, 1865, the Legion ran into a small Federal force west of Waynesville, North Carolina. The Legion fought the Federals, killing one Union soldier and driving them into town. These may have been the last shots fired in North Carolina during the war.

That night, the Legion surrounded the town. Cherokee soldiers built fires on the hillsides and filled the night with war whoops and drumming, making the Federals very nervous. The Confederates continued to play mind games with the Federals the next day. That morning, Thomas and Confederate Brigadier General James G. Martin, the commander of all the remaining Confederate forces in the mountains, entered Waynesville under a flag of truce. With them were twenty of Thomas's largest Cherokees, stripped to the waist with faces painted for war.

Thomas and Martin had Waynesville surrounded, but in light of the fact the Confederacy's two major armies had already surrendered, they agreed to give up to the Federals. Thomas's surrender created the unusual circumstance of a victorious force surrendering to a beaten one.

Thomas, a white man who had the greatest love and respect for his Cherokee friends, never recovered from the stresses of war. After the war, he lost his money and his mind. In 1893, he died in a mental institution at the age of eighty-eight.

General Martin, called "Old One Wing" since losing an arm during the Mexican War, must have savored that one last "victory." He had spent the early part of the war organizing North Carolina regiments. He itched to get into the field during most of the war, but his organizational skills kept landing him desk jobs. When he was given field command, he always did well. His health failed him, however, and at the end of the war, he was shuttled to the mountains to try to hold together scattered commands like Thomas's Legion.

Thomas's Cherokees, fierce fighters and expert trackers, put their leadership skills to work after the war. Several of the regiment's members eventually became chiefs of the tribe. Legion members proudly noted that, while their white officers formally surrendered to the Federals, many of the Cherokees simply left Waynesville without giving up their weapons. These Cherokees never actually gave up their war against the Union.

The best-known military action in the North Carolina mountains—Stoneman's Raid—also occurred at the end of the war. The raid had little military significance, but it did cover a great deal of ground and inflict a lot of damage. Like the old "Washington slept here" stories, Stoneman himself seems to have been in every hamlet and burned every barn on every ridge between Asheville and Salisbury.

Union Major General George Stoneman, an 1842 graduate of West Point, likely could have slipped into history unnoticed, or worse, a military joke, if it wasn't for his raid through western North Carolina in March and April of 1865. Stoneman first came to history's attention in April 1863, when General Joseph Hooker, commander of the Army of the Potomac, sent him on a raid to cut off Robert E. Lee's retreat from Chancellorsville. Stoneman tore up railroad tracks and bridges, and generally wreaked havoc behind Confederate lines while he waited for Hooker to send Lee his way. Unfortunately, Lee did not retreat. He attacked Hooker, sending the Union army reeling back toward Washington. Stoneman was left waiting in the woods.

Hooker, always looking for a scapegoat for his failures, picked on Stoneman. Stoneman was sent west to fight with General William T. Sherman. Serving under Sherman, Stoneman got permission to try to raid Andersonville prison in Georgia. Unable to cross one river, he tried taking Macon. Unable to do that, he tried retreating. However, he was trapped by superior Confederate forces; and Stoneman and five hundred of his men were forced to surrender on July 31, 1864.

Exchanged in October and desperate to restore his hurting image, Stoneman led a raid on the salt works at Wytheville, Virginia, in December 1864. He was finally successful, destroying millions of dollars of property including railroad stock, salt mines, and lead mines.

The success of this raid restored the Union Army's confidence in Stoneman's abilities. In March 1865, Sherman and Ulysses S. Grant agreed that the best way to cripple the spirit of the South was to send a mounted raid through North Carolina and Virginia. The object would not be to seek out battles, but to destroy material. Stoneman was ordered to enter North Carolina and to burn every factory he found. He was to let the Southern people in the mountains and piedmont know that resistance in their part of the state was futile, no matter what was happening with the Confederate armies.

On March 23, 1865, nine regiments totaling eighteen hundred riders, left East Tennessee bound for western North Carolina. In his saddlebags, each rider carried four extra horseshoes and five day's rations. Stoneman was in overall command of the expedition, with second-in-command falling to Union Brigadier General Alvan Gillem, a Tennessee native.

Stoneman's raiders moved fast, too fast for meager Confederate forces to mount any opposition. In his official report, Stoneman wrote that his forces swept past Banner Elk and into Boone, "capturing the place, killing nine, capturing 62 home guards and 40 horses." If postwar stories from area residents are to be believed, some of those killed by Stoneman were shot down in cold blood. One Boone resident who resisted was a fifteen-year-old boy. The boy killed two Federal soldiers in the fighting before escaping into the woods.

At Boone, Stoneman split his command into two columns on March 26. Stoneman himself went east with one column toward Wilkesboro, while Gillem's column cut south through Blowing Rock. Gillem's column burned some factory buildings at Patterson, in Happy Valley near Lenoir, then cut back east in order to link up with Stoneman at Wilkesboro.

After splitting up on March 26, Stoneman's column made one vast loop from Boone. He, or portions of his command, went all the way to Salem, Virginia, before swinging back down into North Carolina to raid Winston and Salem, Greensboro, Jamestown, Salisbury, Statesville, Lincolnton, Lenoir, and Morganton.

Following the exact route of Stoneman's Raid is virtually impossible because the brigades frequently split into regiments, then into companies, then into even smaller units when necessary. The Federals raided so many small hamlets and individual farms that a detailed account of exactly where all of Stoneman's troops went is impossible to report.

Stoneman's men were not the only Federal forces operating in western North Carolina in March and April of 1865. On April 6, 1865, the city of Asheville got its first taste of war. An eleven-hundred-man Federal force, operating independent of Stoneman, marched on Asheville from East Tennessee. The Federals, led by Colonel Isaac Kirby, passed through Warm Springs (now Hot Springs), North Carolina, on April 4 and continued toward Asheville, ignoring rumors of a large rebel force waiting for them there. As they approached Asheville on the Buncombe Turnpike, they were met by a home-guard unit waiting on either side of the road. The Confederates fired on Kirby's force and drove him back. Casualty details are sketchy, but they were light on both sides. Kirby thought better of a long fight. He soon pulled out and returned to East Tennessee. This engagement became known as the Battle of Asheville. The people of Asheville were relieved that their town had been saved, at least for the time being.

The people of Lenoir were relieved as well when Stoneman's men swept past them and east toward Wilkesboro at the end of March. Later, they heard that Stoneman was heading into the piedmont. However, the city's reprieve was short lived. On April 15, 1865, the Federals returned to Lenoir. With the Federal cavalrymen were hundreds of prisoners, most of them guards from the Salisbury prison. The prisoners, some as old as sixty, had not been allowed to eat for several days, so the townspeople of Lenoir tried to sneak them food.

At this point in the raid, Stoneman again split his command. He led his column on a return march to Tennessee, taking his prisoners with him. He left Gillem in charge of the remaining brigade.

Gillem turned his attention to Morganton, the seat of Burke County. There, he was opposed by eighty members of the Confederate home guard. The home guard held the high ground on top of a bluff west of Morganton. They also had the advantage of knowing where the fords across the Catawba River were located. The Federals brashly tried to cross the first ford they found, and left a number of bodies in the river as a price for their overconfidence. The home guard, though gallant in their defense, proved rather quickly that they were not the best soldiers. After firing their little howitzer a couple of times, the gun was dislodged—either by Union artillery or because the Confederates forgot to chock the wheels. Local historians say the cannon rolled all the way down the bluff. When that happened, the home guard ran away, and the Federals marched into Morganton. Union soldiers burned all the records at the courthouse and apparently plundered, but did not burn, private houses in the town.

From Morganton, Gillem's men turned toward Marion where they ransacked some houses. The Federals then moved toward Asheville; but on April 19, General James Martin moved his Confederate forces out of that city down the Swannanoa Gap to thwart them. Though there was some skirmishing, the Federals steered clear of the gap and Martin's men.

Part of Gillem's force then moved towards Rutherfordton and on to Hendersonville. Along the way, they passed through Hickory Nut Gorge and were awed by what is now called Chimney Rock and the Hickory Nut Falls. When they neared Hendersonville, the Federals heard about four cannons the Confederates were trying to save by taking them back to Asheville. The Federals caught up with the cannon crews and their infantry escort about twelve miles from Hendersonville. The guns were captured before the Confederates could put up much resistance.

Gillem's command included some Tennesseans who were not well-liked, even by their comrades. A Federal officer, commenting on the Tennesseans after Gillem's command passed through Rutherfordton, wrote: "They stole everything they could carry off, put pistols to the heads of the citizens, persuaded them to give up their pocketbooks, and even took the rings from ladies' fingers. The sympathy we used to feel for the loyal Tennesseans is being rapidly transferred to the enemy."

By April 22, 1865, word had reached Confederate General James Martin in Asheville that General Johnston had surrendered his army near Durham Station. Martin met Gillem near Hendersonville and agreed to allow the Federals to pass through Asheville unmolested on their way back to Greeneville, Tennessee. Although older by eleven years, Martin apparently knew Gillem from prewar army service in the West. Reports say the two men greeted each other as great friends, expressing regrets for the war that was finally over.

Then on April 26, 1865, the day after friendly Confederates had issued rations to hungry Federals under a flag of truce, the Union forces got word that Sherman's surrender terms with Johnston had been rejected by the United States government. Gillem was ordered to continue fighting, and Asheville was captured without a shot by Gillem's men. One of Gillem's brigade commanders, Colonel William Palmer, sent Martin a letter of apology, saying it was shameful that the United States government had not given Confederates warning that the town was to be captured.

Union soldiers, sensing that the war was ending, went on a plundering spree in Asheville. Several Federal soldiers rode their horses through the glass doors of a family home, beat the elderly judge who challenged them, and then fired a shot at the man, just missing his head. Another group captured a little girl's Shetland pony, then shot it dead when they knew she was watching.

Gillem's troops then received orders to rush to South Carolina and attempt to cut off the escape of Confederate President Jefferson Davis. Gillem's departure from Asheville marked the end of Stoneman's Raid. It cost North Carolina millions of dollars in destroyed property, but very few deaths. One thing it did accomplish was to fix forever Stoneman's image in the Union Army. He rode his popularity to the governorship of California from 1883 to 1887.

This tour starts at the Museum of the Cherokee Indian in Cherokee, North Carolina. The museum is located on U.S. 441 about 0.6 mile north from the intersection with U.S. 19 in downtown Cherokee.

The Museum of the Cherokee Indian has an extensive display on the history of the Cherokees, including portraits of past leaders of the tribe. Several of the chiefs were members of Thomas's Legion. Only one display case is devoted to the Legion. The case has a portrait of Thomas as well as a large photograph of his Legion at a Confederate veterans' reunion. In the picture taken at the reunion, some of the men are holding their battle flag. The same flag is on display.

Leaving Cherokee, head north on U.S. 19. This climbing, twisting road will pass under the Blue Ridge Parkway about 12.7 miles from Cherokee.

The intersection of U.S. 19 and the Blue Ridge Parkway is at Soco Gap.

This intersection was the site of a small skirmish involving Thomas's Legion and a group of pro-Union soldiers. The intersection is just north of the site of the Battle of Soco Creek, a small engagement where a company of Thomas's Legion ambushed Union Colonel George Kirk and his band of six hundred men on February 3, 1863.

Kirk was probably the most feared and disliked man in the Confederate mountains. A twenty-six-year-old native of Tennessee, he organized his own force of Unionists from East Tennessee and western North Carolina. He seemed to raid the mountains when he pleased, one time traveling as far east as Morganton. There, he captured a whole Confederate training camp without firing a shot. He was a horse thief, a bushwhacker, a raider, and maybe even a murderer. He was also a thorn in the side of Confederates.

The members of Thomas's Legion caught Kirk at the Battle of Soco Creek, but he escaped to fight another day. The Cherokees fought hard and gave ground grudgingly at Soco Gap because it was sacred to them—the great Indian organizer, Tecumseh, held a meeting of the different tribes at Soco Gap in 1812. Also near the gap was Quallatown, a Cherokee town where Thomas had his first job as a store clerk.

Continue on U.S. 19 to the outskirts of Waynesville. At 23.5 miles after leaving the Museum of the Cherokee Indian, turn right, or southeast, from U.S. 19 onto Business U.S. 276 toward downtown Waynesville. Drive 2.7 miles, then turn right, or southwest, from Business U.S. 276 onto Main Street, or Business U.S. 23. Drive 0.7 mile to Green Hill Cemetery. Colonel William Holland Thomas's grave is on the hill on the north end of the cemetery under a large, traditional, double headstone with a large brass plaque on the back. A white statue of a woman is nearby.

The plaque details virtually all of Thomas's life, including the fact that his father fought in the American Revolution at the Battle of Kings Mountain, that he was a cousin of President Zachary Taylor, and that his mother was a grand niece of Lord Baltimore, the founder of Maryland. Thomas is given credit for being a great friend to the Cherokee, spending some thirty years trying to help them acquire homes and land. He is also credited for his efforts to build roads and railroads in western North Carolina.

Retrace your route to Business U.S. 276. At the intersection of U.S. 276 and U.S. 19/U.S. 23/U.S. 74, turn right and head north on this combined highway. Drive 3.3 miles to the intersection with I-40 and turn onto I-40 East.

If you care to make a side trip to Hendersonville, follow I-40 East to the intersection with I-26 outside of Asheville. This will be 19 miles after getting on I-40 near Waynesville. Drive south on I-26 to Exit 22, the exit for Highland Lake Road, which is also U.S. 176. After 2.4 miles on Highland Lake Road, turn left, or south, onto U.S. 25. Drive 0.2 mile to St. Johns of the Wilderness Episcopal Church, pull into the parking lot, and walk to the cemetery.

The grave of Christopher G. Memminger, a treasurer of the Confederacy, is among the third set of graves up the steps from the parking lot. The grave is surrounded by a wrought-iron fence. Orphaned at age three, Memminger was raised by a man who would later become South Carolina's governor. Helped by his connections and his own hard work, Memminger was a wealthy lawyer by the start of the war. He helped draft the Confederate Constitution and, to his surprise, was named the Confederacy's treasurer.

His appointment also surprised many leading South Carolinians, most of whom had never heard of him. Some historians believe Memminger's appointment was a clumsy mistake that Jefferson Davis was too embarrassed to correct. Memminger served three years as treasurer, doing his best to create an entirely new monetary system based on little more than promises that the Confederacy would pay its bills. He resigned in 1864. After the war, he became known as the father of public education in Charleston, and he remained a champion of educating both whites and Blacks until his death in 1888.

Near Memminger's grave is the grave of Charles de Choiseul, a lieutenant colonel in the 7th Louisiana Infantry, a unit that served in the Army of Northern Virginia. Like many regiments from that state, the 7th Louisiana Infantry had an international flavor. Only half of the regiment's members were born in the United States.

De Choiseul once briefly commanded a gang of rowdies called Wheat's Louisiana Tigers, a regiment of Zouaves who wore pantaloons resembling black-and-white pillow ticking. It was while serving as the colonel of this unit that de Choiseul showed how difficult—or easy—it could be to command men.

Wheat's Tigers (named after their maverick, soldier-of-fortune commander Colonel Roberdeau Wheat) had the reputation of being some of the most uncontrollable soldiers in the Army of Northern Virginia. Many of them were thieves and ruffians who joined the army just to kill someone. One day, de Choiseul confronted a pair of Tigers who were walking out of camp without a pass. They ignored his orders to halt, so he knocked one of them to the ground. Other Tigers started to pull the colonel from his horse, so de Choiseul calmly pulled out his pistol and shot the nearest soldier in the face, blowing out all of the man's teeth.

"That quelled the riot," de Choiseul wrote in his diary. He also noted that the other Tigers left him alone from that point forward. The colonel was later killed at the Battle of Cross Keys, Virginia, presumably by Federal soldiers and not by grudge-holding Tigers. The Tigers became so unruly that their regiment was disbanded and its men scattered among other Louisiana units.

Leave the church cemetery and continue driving south on N.C. 25 for 0.4 mile to the intersection with Little River Road. Turn right, and then take a left into the parking lot for Connemara.

Christopher Memminger built this house as a summer home in 1838. In 1945, the house was bought by Carl Sandburg as a place to write his songs and poems. Sandburg's other Civil War connection was his four-volume history of Abraham Lincoln, which won the Pulitzer Prize in 1940.

Return to U.S. 25 and continue south for 0.5 mile to the Woodfield Inn. The inn was built in 1855 as a stop on the local stagecoach line. In February 1865, soldiers from the 64th North Carolina, the same regiment responsible for the Shelton Laurel Massacre two years earlier, were assigned to guard duty here. When Gillem's Federals rode through the area, the Confederates supposedly hid in a secret room. The old hotel is open today as a Civil War–era bed and breakfast.

Retrace your route to I-26. Get on I-26 North and drive towards Asheville. After passing over I-40, I-26 turns into I-240 East.

Take I-240 East into Asheville and take Exit 4C to Montford Avenue. Turn left, or north, onto Montford Avenue. At the first traffic light, take a

left onto West Chestnut Street. At the first stop sign, turn right onto Pearson Street. Take the next left onto Birch Street, the main entrance into Riverside Cemetery. Follow the main entrance to the office. A map detailing famous graves can be obtained during office hours Monday through Friday.

Civil War Governor Zebulon Vance and his brother, Confederate Brigadier General Robert Vance, are buried within about fifty yards of the cemetery office. Make a S-turn on the main road after leaving the office. A small metal sign will point the way to the Vance brothers' graves.

Zeb Vance, a famous and beloved colonel, governor, and United States senator, is buried under a simple family stone, with absolutely no mention of his background and service to the state. His wife, Adalie, for whom the blockade runner *Ad-vance* was named, lies beside him. Brother Robert lies in front of Zeb, under a military-issue stone.

Zeb, a native of Reems Creek just north of Asheville, started his political career at age twenty-two, when he won election for solicitor. It helped that the turnout for the election was small, and all his relatives voted for him. By age twenty-four, he was serving in the general assembly. By twenty-eight, he was a United States congressman. He was a Unionist at heart, and he believed his Northern friends when they told him Lincoln would withdraw the troops from Fort Sumter to avoid a confrontation. When that did not happen, and Lincoln ordered North Carolina to supply men to invade the seceding states, Vance wrote that he had raised his hand to the north in friendship. When it fell by his side, he continued, it fell at the side of a secessionist.

Vance raised his own unit, the Rough and Ready Guards, but he was soon appointed colonel of the 26th North Carolina. He fought in some early battles, including a valiant but losing effort at New Bern. His military career almost came to an abrupt end during the retreat from New Bern when he and his horse plunged into a creek to show his men it could be forded. Some of them had to dive in and pull him up from the bottom. He later led his regiment during the Seven Days battles around Richmond.

Vance was actually in the field when he was elected governor in August 1862. His whole campaign was masterminded by a Raleigh newspaper editor, who emphasized that Vance was too busy fighting the Federals to come back to the state to campaign.

Throughout the war, Vance told North Carolinians that his job as governor was to "fight with the Yankees and fuss with the Confederacy." That he did.

He constantly bombarded Richmond with letters and telegrams complaining about the way North Carolina soldiers and officers were being used. Despite his disgust with the ruinous attitudes of Richmond's politicians, he stayed loyal to the Confederacy. However, he stayed more loyal to his state. At the end of the war, North Carolina's warehouses were filled with uniforms that Vance would release only to North Carolina troops. Captured after the war, he spent nearly two months in prison in Washington before he was released.

After the war, Vance spent fifteen years in the United States Senate. Once, in response to a Rhode Island senator's derogatory comment about North Carolina, Vance rose and announced that he could easily urinate (Vance actually used a more familiar term) across Rhode Island, and that he would not mind demonstrating. Such quick action to defend North

Carolina made him one of the state's most beloved politicians. He died in 1894.

Zeb's older brother Robert was always in his brother's shadow. Robert was elected colonel of the 29th North Carolina early in the war. He was cited for coolness under fire at Murfreesboro, Tennessee, in 1863 and promoted to general in March 1863. In January 1864, he was captured while on a raid in East Tennessee, and he was not exchanged until March 14, 1865. Robert later served in the state legislature and was a United States congressman while his brother was a United States senator. Robert died in 1899.

Leave the Vance brothers' graves and walk back to the cemetery office. Facing away from the office, look for three obelisks about 50 yards away. Confederate Brigadier General Thomas L. Clingman, for whom Clingmans Dome in the Great Smoky Mountains National Park is named, lies under the furthest monument.

A career politician, Clingman served in the state house and the United States Congress before his appointment and, later, election to the United States Senate. Upon his resignation from the senate in 1861, Clingman was appointed a colonel of the 25th North Carolina Regiment. He spent most of the war on duty in the state until 1864, when he was ordered to duty around Richmond and Petersburg. There, he was wounded and unable to return to command. After the war, Clingman became interested in establishing the heights of the peaks of the Blue Ridge Mountains. Clingmans Dome was named for him because of his interest in the altitude of the mountains, not for his military service.

Return to your vehicle and drive along the main road of the cemetery, past the sign to Zeb Vance's grave. The road will curve around to the left. Confederate Brigadier General James G. Martin is almost directly behind Vance, near the intersection of the main road and a minor road to the right. Martin's tombstone is on the left side of the road.

Martin was probably the only Confederate general in either of the Carolinas who started the war less than whole. An 1840 West Point graduate, he lost his right arm in the Mexican War at the battle of Churubusco. That did not put him out of the United States Army. He resigned after a twenty-one-year career to join his home state as adjutant general. Credited by historians as the training and supply genius who prepared North Carolina for war, Martin quickly acquired the nickname, "Old One Wing," which he apparently did not mind.

Once the state's military machine was working, the old fighter requested and received a field command. Martin was never given major commands, but he was cited several times for gallantry. At Petersburg, his men once carried him around on their shoulders in an impromptu parade for his bravery. He ended the war in command of the Confederate forces in the mountains of western North Carolina. Martin's was the last command surrendered in the state in May 1865. He died in 1878.

Leave Martin's grave and continue on the main cemetery road to exit Riverside Cemetery. Retrace your route back to I-240. Get on I-240 West and follow the signs to U.S. 19/U.S. 70/U.S. 25 heading north. These highways intersect with I-240 just west of the Montford Road exit. Head north on U.S. 19 for about 1.5 miles. Take the next exit, Exit 4A, for Broadway Street, or N.C. 251. At the bottom of the ramp, turn right, back toward town. This is the Old Buncombe Turnpike and the site of the Battle of Asheville. In the battle, Union Colonel Isaac Kirby's eleven hundred Federals were turned back by a home guard force of three hundred. Where U.S. 19 and N.C. 251 intersect is about where the battle began.

Notice how the road is sunken, with hills on both sides. Federal soldiers must have noticed the same thing on the road in April 1865 when they experienced cannon fire from their right and rifle fire from their left. It did not take Kirby long to understand that he was the head fish in the barrel. He retired after several hours. Colonel Kirby had to do a lot of explaining about why his trained Federals could not overwhelm a ragtag home guard unit of Confederate shopkeepers. Asheville was saved for another few days.

Turn left off Old Buncombe Turnpike, or Broadway Street, at the first light. This will be just 0.2 mile since exiting U.S. 19. Then take an immediate left into the parking lot for the University of North Carolina at Asheville Botanical Gardens. From the parking lot, find a nature trail that leads behind the gardens and along a small stream. On a hill, below a dormitory for the school, are the unmarked remnants of the earthworks Confederates used to fire on Kirby's Federals. A mulch path leads through and near the earthworks, which were so eroded in 1995 that they were virtually unrecognizable. Still, it is easy to see how even a home guard commander could figure out the advantage of digging in on this hillside. Cannons were placed on the hill on the opposite side of the turnpike, behind what is now a hospital parking lot.

Walk back to your car and retrace your route to U.S. 19 North. Drive north on U.S. 19 about 2.5 miles to the Stock Road exit and turn right. Follow this access road to Business U.S. 19. Turn north on Business U.S. 19 and drive 0.8 mile, then turn right, or northeast, onto Reem's Creek Road, or S.R. 1003. Drive 5.2 miles on Reem's Creek Road to the Vance Birthplace State Historic Site.

The log cabins at the historic site are the actual buildings where Zebulon Vance spent his youth. The museum details important events in Zeb Vance's life and career, including the time he won his first political office by a vote of eleven to eight. The eleven were relatives, or friends who owed favors to relatives.

In Vance's first campaign for the state legislature, his opponent declared that a boy of twenty-four did not know enough to serve the people. Vance apologized for being so young and said he would have cheerfully been born at an earlier date, but his parents gave him no choice in the matter. He promised to do better next time. Such wit got him elected to every office he ever tried to achieve. A slide show details his entire career. Artifacts and excerpts from his speeches adorn the walls. The pistol he carried while with the 26th North Carolina Regiment is among the relics on display.

The next stops will be at sites associated with the Shelton Laurel Massacre. It requires a commitment of at least two hours, as the road is twisting and average speeds are slow.

Retrace your route to U.S. 19. Continue driving north on U.S. 19 until reaching the intersection for U.S. 70 West/U.S. 25 North. Turn northwest onto U.S. 70 West/U.S. 25 North. Drive about 8 miles, then turn onto Business U.S. 70/Business U.S. 25 heading into downtown Marshall. In Marshall, Business U.S. 70/Business U.S. 25 turns into Main Street. (If you need gasoline, get it in Marshall. There are no gas stations on the twisting road to Shelton Laurel.)

The simple frame house of Colonel Lawrence Allen, the commanding officer of the 64th North Carolina Regiment, and the man who ordered the Shelton Laurel Massacre, is next to the First Baptist Church on Main Street. It was this house that the salt raiders invaded in January 1863, frightening Allen's children and stealing their bed clothes.

Follow Main Street, or Business U.S. 70/Business U.S. 25, west through town until the road intersects with U.S. 70/U.S. 25. Turn left, or northwest, onto U.S. 70/U.S 25. About 12 miles after leaving Marshall, U.S. 70/U.S. 25 turns to the left. Do not turn. Stay on N.C. 208, which merges with the main highway at this point. Follow twisting N.C. 208 north for another 2 miles until it intersects with N.C. 212, approximately 14 miles outside of Marshall. At this intersection is a historic marker describing the Shelton Laurel massacre.

Turn right, or northeast, onto N.C. 212 and drive 6.8 miles. At this point, in an open field on the left where Hickey's Fork (creek) runs into the Shelton Laurel (creek), is where Colonel Allen, Lieutenant Colonel Keith, and the men of the 64th North Carolina Regiment carried out the Shelton Laurel Massacre.

The battlefield where local Unionists tried to make a stand against Allen's men the day before the massacre is 2 miles further up N.C. 212 on the right. The graves of the massacre victims are near the battlefield in a cemetery on private property.

As you retrace your route back down N.C. 212, notice how the road follows the flow of the creek and how the mountain range naturally points to East Tennessee, rather than towards Marshall and the rest of North Carolina. The war was brought to the people of this region, they did not seek it.

Retrace your route through Marshall and back to U.S. 19. Drive south on U.S. 19 towards Asheville, then follow the signs to I-240 and to I-40 East. Follow I-40 East for about 50 miles to Exit 105, the exit to N.C. 18. Drive north on N.C. 18 towards downtown Morganton.

Follow N.C. 18 to the intersection with Business U.S. 64/N.C. 181/U.S. 70. This intersection forms the town square in Morganton. The Old Burke County Courthouse Museum is located on the town square.

Stoneman's men burned the county's records from the courthouse, but did not burn the building itself. The building has a Confederate monu-

Burke County Monument and Old Courthouse Museum

TOURING THE CAROLINAS' CIVIL WAR SITES

ment on the grounds listing all of the county's Civil War soldiers, and a small museum is located inside.

Circle the old courthouse and start heading west away from the square on Union Street, or Business U.S. 64. Just one block away, across from the Belk's Department Store, is the Cedars, an old house at the corner of Union and King Streets. The house was built in 1855 by William MacRae. MacRae later served as a lieutenant colonel with the 6th North Carolina in the Army of Northern Virginia. This regiment earned the nickname "The Bloody Sixth."

Continue west on Union Street. At 1.7 miles from the town square, across the street from a Chevrolet dealership, is Creekside, a house built in 1837 by Colonel T. G. Walton of the Burke County Home Guard. Walton defended Morganton at least twice during the war, once from Colonel George Kirk's raiders and once from Stoneman's men. This house demonstrates how compact towns were in the 1860s. When it was built, it was a countryside plantation home.

Follow Union Street to the intersection with Sanford Drive, or Bypass U.S. 64, and turn right, or north. At the next light, turn left, or west, onto North N.C. 181. Drive 0.6 mile and turn left, or southwest, onto Independence Boulevard, or N.C. 126.

After 0.5 mile, N.C. 126 will fork to the right away from Independence Boulevard. Follow N.C. 126 for 2.4 miles, through land that is still used to farm the same crops it produced during the Civil War. Turn left onto Swan Pond Drive, which turns into a gravel road. Bear left until the road ends at Swan Pond. Swan Pond is located on the Avery family plantation. A historic marker at the pond notes a visit to the plantation by French botanist André Michaux in 1794. Though the gravel road is public, the plantation is private property. Please stay in the car.

During the war, the Averys lost three sons. One son, I.E., fell on the second day at Gettysburg. Before dying, he had just enough time to pen his father a bloodstained note that read: "I died with my face toward the enemy." The note was carried back to North Carolina and handed to his father. At one time, 122 slaves worked the crops around this 2,500 acre plantation, one of the largest in western North Carolina. No cotton and little tobacco were grown here.

Quaker Meadows

Retrace your route back to N.C. 181 and turn left, or west. Drive just 0.2 mile, then turn right, or north, onto Bost Road. Drive 1.8 miles on Bost Road. To the right of the road, under some large trees, is Bellevue, an 1823 plantation that once had fifty-five slaves. The plantation house is now owned by a corporation and is on private property.

Retrace your route back to N.C. 181 and turn right, or west. Drive 0.2 mile to the next light and turn right onto Maryes' Church Road. On the left, after driving 0.2 mile, is Quaker Meadows, one of the oldest properties in Burke County. The Overmountain Men once camped on the property on their way to the Battle of Kings Mountain during the American Revolution. The house dates back to 1812 and was owned by J.C.S. McDowell, a Confederate officer who was killed at Fredericksburg. It is being restored by a historic foundation and will one day be open as a museum.

Retrace your route to N.C. 181 and turn left, heading into Morganton. Turn left onto Kirksey Drive, formerly Sanford Drive, or Bypass U.S. 64. Drive through the intersection with U.S. 64. After passing this intersection, drive about 0.2 mile on Kirksey Drive to the end of a metal guardrail on the right. Pull over onto the shoulder of the road. This is the site of the Battle of Morganton, where the Burke County home guard tried to stop the advancement of Stoneman's raiders on April 16, 1865. The home guard was on a high bluff looking toward the Catawba River. The river is to the left of the road, hidden by trees.

The Confederates could see every move the Federals made, making it possible to shoot right down their enemies' throats—at least until their cannon rolled down the hill. Reports state that eight Federals were killed and twenty-five wounded as they tried to cross the river. They quickly fell back and looked for another crossing. They found it at Fleming's Ford, about a half mile beyond this point. Once the Confederates realized the Federals were flanking them, they scattered and the battle was over.

Continue on Kirksey Drive for about 5 miles until it intersects with U.S. 70. Turn left, or east, onto U.S. 70. Within 2 miles, watch for a road on the left called Sequoia Circle. The road is located across from a church with a historical marker for Camp Vance in front of it. The housing development on Sequoia Circle is built on what used to be Camp Vance, a training camp for Confederate draftees. It was raided in June 1864 by the Unionist troops of Colonel George Kirk. Somewhere near here, in a spot still unknown to local historians, was a train depot where Kirk destroyed a locomotive, three cars, and several buildings. He was talked out of burning the nearby hospital.

Kirk captured Camp Vance without firing a shot. He walked into the camp under a flag of truce and convinced the Confederates to surrender. What he said to the 123 conscripts and the camp's commanding officer that convinced them to give up without firing a shot has been lost to history. Kirk marched back to Tennessee with his prisoners. The Burke County Home Guard tried to rescue the prisoners, but were defeated by Kirk's men at the Battle of Winding Stairs, about twenty-five miles west of Camp Vance.

Retrace your route on U.S. 70 back to Kirksey Drive, and follow it back to the intersection with U.S. 64.

This concludes the Mountain War Part I Tour. The Mountain War

Part II Tour will start in the Caldwell County town of Lenoir, approximately 13 miles away.

If you care to end the tour with a side trip, turn left, or east, onto U.S. 64. This becomes Business U.S. 64/Business U.S. 70. At the intersection with N.C. 18, turn right, or southeast. Follow N.C. 18 about 21 miles to the intersection with N.C. 27. Turn left, or east, onto N.C. 27 and drive about 15 miles until it becomes West Main Street in Lincolnton.

Like so many towns in western North Carolina, Lincolnton was visited by Stoneman's Raiders. One of the raiders was shot and killed as he rode into what the Federals believed was going to be a quiet town.

General Robert F. Hoke's home

Follow Main Street through the downtown area to the Lincoln County Cultural Center, at 408 East Main Street, on the corner of East Main and Cedar Streets, four blocks east of the courthouse. The cultural center has a display on the history of the five Confederate generals who were born in the county. They were: brothers John and William Forney, Robert D. Johnston, Stephen D. Ramseur, and Robert F. Hoke. (See The Surrender Tour for a biography of Robert Hoke. See The Piedmont Invasion Tour for a biography of Stephen Ramseur.) The Forneys and Johnston moved to Alabama and are not buried in North Carolina, so their histories will not be addressed on this tour.

After seeing the modest displays here, travel north, on Cedar Street, which runs beside the cultural center. Drive to the intersection with Pine Street to see the grave of Confederate Major General Stephen Dodson Ramseur at St. Luke's Episcopal Church. Ramseur rests under a large white obelisk next to Cedar Street. His wife and daughter are beside him. This is the second monument to Ramseur at the cemetery. The first, identical to the second, was destroyed by a tree that was knocked over by Hurricane Hugo in 1989. The monument lists twelve battles that Ramseur participated in, including his last at Cedar Creek, Virginia, on October 19, 1864.

General Stephen Dodson Ramseur's grave

Turn left, or west, onto Pine Street and drive past the church cemetery to Aspen Street. Turn right, drive one block, and turn right again onto Chestnut Street. The house at 119 Chestnut Street used to belong to General Robert F. Hoke. Hoke is buried in Raleigh. Retrace the route back to Aspen Street, which leads to the courthouse square.

At the courthouse square, find N.C. 150/N.C. 27 and head east. About

2 miles after leaving Lincolnton, N.C. 27 will fork to the southeast. Follow N.C. 27 and drive about 6 miles to the Mt. Vernon Baptist Church in the little community of Iron Station.

In the cemetery of the church is the grave of Adam Miller Moore. Moore represents a growing minority in Confederate history, a documented Black Confederate.

Born a slave, Moore was the friend of his white owner, Adam Miller Roberts. During the war, Roberts took Moore along with him as a body servant. Though it was against the law, Roberts armed Moore with a pistol. Moore built breastworks and cared for horses. Once he stumbled into a Union patrol, but did not take the opportunity to run away with them. Though his master was killed at Chancellorsville, there is some indication Moore stayed with the Confederate Army and surrendered at Appomattox nearly two years later.

When asked in 1938 why he had served without running away, Moore replied: "If the South won, my master promised freedom and if the North won, the Yankees promised Freedom." Moore died at the age of 108. (Rudolph Young, a Black historian from the region, has found at least six Black men from his county who served with the Confederacy. At least one was a free man who served for the entire war.)

This concludes the side trip to Lincolnton.

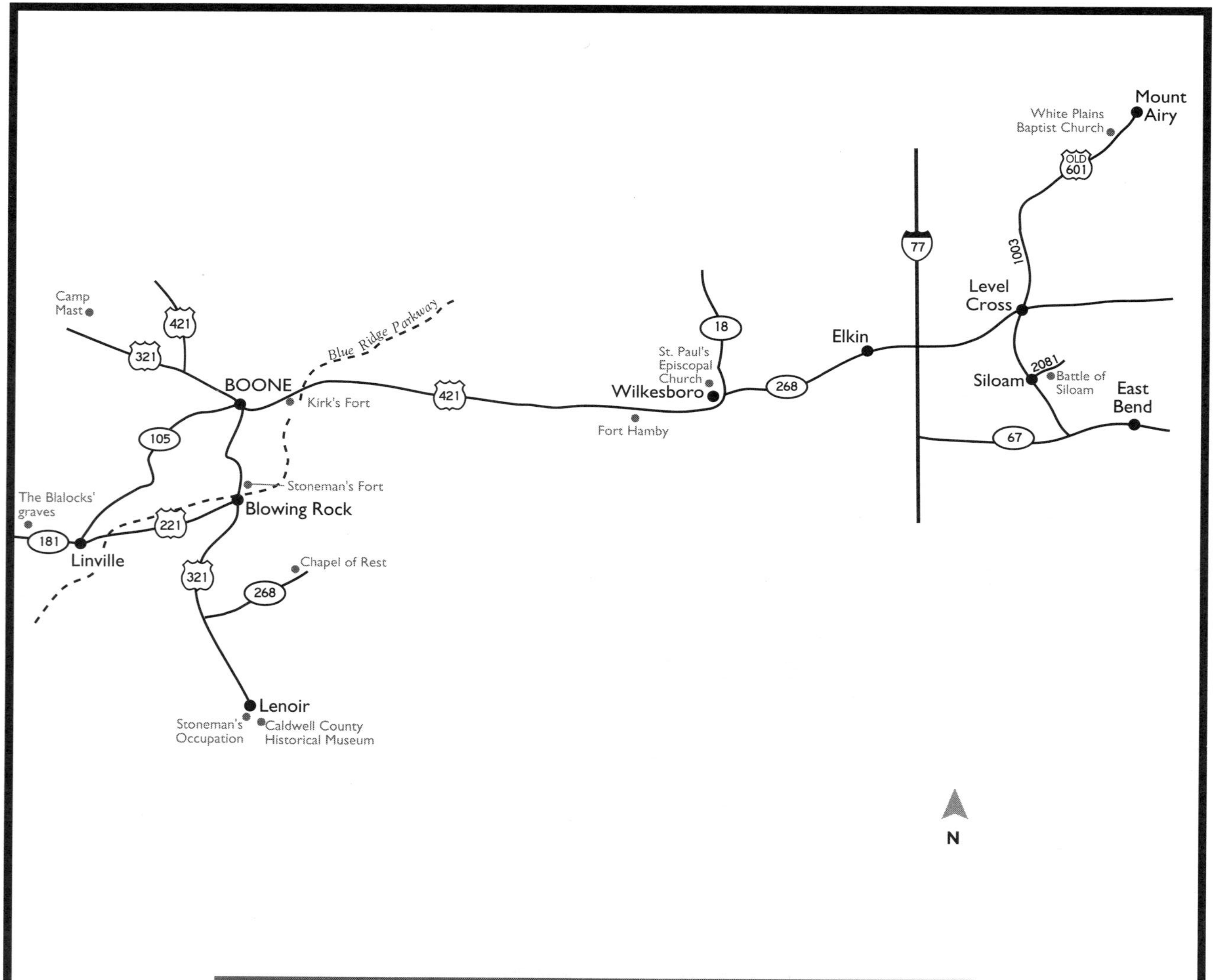

THE MOUNTAIN WAR PART II TOUR

N

Mount Airy

White Plains Baptist Church

OLD 601

1003

Level Cross

Siloam

Battle of Siloam

2081

East Bend

67

77

Elkin

268

18

St. Paul's Episcopal Church

Wilkesboro

Fort Hamby

421

Blue Ridge Parkway

Kirk's Fort

Stoneman's Fort

BOONE

Blowing Rock

Chapel of Rest

268

Lenoir

Caldwell County Historical Museum

321

Stoneman's Occupation

421

321

105

221

Camp Mast

The Blalocks' graves

181

Linville

The Mountain War Part II Tour

This tour starts in Lenoir, North Carolina, near the grave of an English-born general. It moves to Blowing Rock, then to Linville to the graves of North Carolina's Civil War version of Bonnie and Clyde. From there it travels to Boone, then to Wilkesboro and the grave of another general. It continues to Elkin and Mount Airy, where it visits the graves of two (almost one) of the most interesting slave owners in history. It ends in the community of Siloam, where two Confederates held off a whole company of Federal cavalrymen.

Total mileage: approximately 200 miles.

This tour picks up where the Mountain War Part I Tour ends, and continues to focus on Union Major General George Stoneman's raid through the western part of North Carolina. If taking this tour before taking the the Mountain War Part I Tour, read the historical overview of that tour to understand the war in the mountains and the purpose of Stoneman's Raid in April 1865.

From Morganton, take U.S. 64/N.C. 18 north about 11 miles to the intersection with Business N.C. 18 in downtown Lenoir, the seat of Caldwell County. Turn left onto Business N.C. 18 and follow it to the downtown square. Across the way is the Caldwell County Confederate monument, erected in 1910. The monument used to be in the center of the square, but numerous traffic accidents finally convinced government officials to move it to the corner where it now rests. Closer observation shows that the cannonball has been glued back together after its last collision.

Turn right onto West Main Street, or U.S. 321A. Go two blocks, then take a right onto College Street at the St. James Episcopal Church. In April 1865, this whole block was used by Stoneman's raiders to corral Confederate prisoners they had picked up in Salisbury. The prisoners, who were mostly old men and boys, had not eaten since leaving Salisbury. Though the Union soldiers tried to prevent it, the townspeople tossed food to the Confederates prisoners.

Across the street from the church on College Street is the Caldwell County Heritage Museum. To reach the museum, take the side road up the hill. The museum is housed in the last standing building of Davenport College, a girls school that Stoneman burned along with the Findley Academy boys school. The museum is open Monday, Wednesday, and Saturday. The museum is creating a Civil War room to house exhibits, including a display of all known photographs of Caldwell County soldiers. Both Stoneman and Gillem appropriated nearby houses for their headquarters while in town. Stoneman left from here to return to Tennessee with his prisoners. Local tradition says the prisoners were sent to Camp Chase, Ohio, but it seems unlikely that all of them went to Ohio since the war was virtually over.

From the museum, retrace the route to Business N.C. 18 and turn right. Drive two blocks to U.S. 321 and turn north.

About 5.5 miles north of Lenoir on U.S. 321 is a turnoff to the right, or east, labeled River Road. Follow River Road to where it intersects with

Caldwell County Heritage Museum

N.C. 268 and turn right. This is the beginning of Happy Valley. The Chapel of Rest church is on the left, or north, side of N.C. 268, 4.1 miles after turning off U.S. 321. Turn up the gravel road to the white wooden chapel. The chapel should be open for private prayer.

Behind the chapel is the grave of Confederate Brigadier General Collett Leventhorpe, the only foreign-born Civil War general buried in either of the Carolinas. A native of Falmouth, England, Leventhorpe was forty-five years old and already retired from ten years of service with the British Army when the war started. He was elected colonel of the 34th North Carolina, and by December 1861, he was leading a four-regiment brigade. His first real test of command came in December 1862, when he faced Union Brigadier General Foster during the Union's raid on Goldsboro.

In 1863, Leventhorpe was transferred to the Army of Northern Virginia. He was wounded on the first day of Gettysburg and later captured on the retreat south. He was released in April 1864, but his wound made his left arm useless. He spent the rest of the war protecting the Wilmington & Weldon Railroad with state troops. He died in 1889. His obelisk lies behind the church, shaded by a magnolia tree. The graveyard has several other Confederate officers, including a colonel of the 26th North Carolina.

Happy Valley was the location of the Patterson flour and corn mills burned by Stoneman. The Federals wanted to burn Fort Defiance, the nearby home of William Lenoir, a leader of the American Revolution. The home was saved from burning at the last moment when a Union officer, who was a Mason, noticed a Masonic symbol on Lenoir's tombstone in the family graveyard.

One of Stoneman's columns followed N.C. 268 east along the Yadkin River, all the way to Wilkesboro, to link up with the other column.

Retrace N.C. 268 back to the intersection with U.S. 321 and turn north toward Blowing Rock, about 12 miles away. A column of Stoneman's men, with their artillery, passed south through Blowing Rock on March 28, 1865. While there may have been a little sniping, there was no major action in the town.

Though he was not part of Stoneman's force, Union Colonel George Kirk built a fort in Blowing Rock to protect the mountain gap from a Confederate counterattack on Stoneman's Raid. Kirk's Unionist force of

Tennessee and North Carolina natives spent most of the war raiding the mountains and foothills of North Carolina. Much of the fort was constructed by pulling down the summer house of a man from Lenoir.

In downtown Blowing Rock, take the turnoff for Business U.S. 321. Follow Business U.S. 321 until it intersects with U.S. 221, just north of the business-district shops. Turn south onto U.S. 221 and follow it to the town of Linville. In Linville, U.S. 221 intersects with N.C. 181 and N.C. 105. From this intersection, follow N.C. 181 northwest for 1.6 miles. Slow down and look for a gravel road coming down from a hill on the right, or north, side of the road. There is a cemetery on top of the hill which is not visible from N.C. 181 as you head northwest. If you see a sign to the left pointing towards the community of Montezuma, you have gone too far. Turn around and drive back up N.C. 181, looking to the left. The cemetery should be visible from this side of the road.

Take the gravel road up to the top of the hill and stop about 20 yards after the entry road levels out on top of the hill. Get out of the car and walk directly into the cemetery. The graves of William McKeeson "Keith" Blalock and his "brother" Sam are on the eastern edge of the cemetery. Keith's bronze marker, flush with the ground, identifies him as a member of the 26th North Carolina Regiment, company F. This is a brazen statement considering he served no more than two months with the Confederacy. He was released after throwing himself into a patch of poison sumac. The resulting rash looked like a fever to the doctor, who released Blalock from service.

The same doctor also released Sam Blalock, who was described as a "good looking boy, aged 16, 130 pounds, 5'4", dark hair." Sam appeared to be normal. He picked up the soldiers' drill very well. The only thing Sam didn't do was go skinny-dipping in the river. He preferred watching the other boys swim.

The reason Sam did not go swimming, and the reason Sam got out of the Confederate Army with Keith, was that Sam's real name was Malinda, and "he" was really Keith's wife. There is no military marker for "Sam," but Malinda's normal stone marker is beside Keith's bronze military marker.

Malinda was twenty-two years old to Keith's twenty-four, when they both joined the Confederate Army. Historians believe Keith joined in order to get close enough to Union lines to defect. While drilling with his unit in Kinston, it occurred to him that he could die before that happened, so he faked his illness. Malinda apparently went everywhere Keith did. Only the man who recruited them knew the truth.

The story does not end with Keith and Malinda getting out of the Confederate Army. Malinda and Keith became the Bonnie and Clyde of the mountains. Besides acting as guides for Colonel George Kirk's band of Unionists, the Blalocks founded their own little band of bushwhackers. For some reason, they held a grudge against the recruiting officer who kept Malinda's secret. They raided his home twice, which was not a smart move for Keith. On the second raid, his eye was shot out.

The Blalocks continued raiding Confederate homes "under the Grandfather" (meaning near Grandfather Mountain) throughout the war. Malinda, who was always at Keith's side, was wounded at least once. The number of bushwhackings they participated in, either as instigators or victims, has never been determined, but both survived the war. In 1913, Keith died at age seventy-seven when he lost control of a handcar on a mountain railroad. Malinda had died twelve years earlier. A picture of Malinda holding a picture of herself in uniform is on display at the North Carolina Museum of History in Raleigh.

Retrace N.C. 181 back to Linville and turn left, or north, onto N.C. 105 heading towards Boone, about 19 miles away.

If you care to make a brief side trip, turn left, or north, onto U.S. 321 at the intersection of N.C. 105, U.S. 221, and U.S. 321. Stay on U.S. 321 after U.S. 421 splits off to the north and drive about 1.2 miles to the intersection with Old U.S. 421 in Sugar Grove. Turn right onto Old U.S. 421. On the right side of Old U.S. 421 in Sugar Grove is the approximate site of Camp Mast, a Confederate training camp established in 1863.

On February 5, 1865, about seventy Unionists captured Camp Mast by fire. Not by gunfire, but by fire. The Unionist commander built scores of campfires on the hills surrounding Camp Mast. When the sleepy Confederates rolled out of their tents in the predawn darkness, it looked like they were surrounded by the entire Union army. The Confederates surrendered without firing a shot. When daylight revealed they had been tricked by a handful of their neighbors, the Confederates seemed to go along with the joke. They were as happy to be free of military responsibilities to the Confederacy as they were to be prisoners of their neighbors.

Retrace your route back down U.S. 321 to the intersection with U.S. 421. Follow U.S. 421 south, through Boone heading east toward Wilkesboro.

If not going to Camp Mast, drive through the N.C. 105 intersection with U.S. 221 and U.S. 321. Follow N.C. 105 about 0.9 mile until it intersects with U.S. 421. Turn right, or south, onto U.S. 421 and drive toward Wilkesboro.

Continue on U.S. 421 to a historic marker in Deep Gap, 11.1 miles after leaving Boone, just before the overpass for the Blue Ridge Parkway and before starting down the mountain. Deep Gap was the location of another Union palisade. This one was also erected by Union Colonel George Kirk's band of Unionists. As noted earlier, Kirk and his men were not part of Stoneman's command, but they were used to hold mountain passes to protect Stoneman's route of retreat. Stoneman did not want to come back from his raid into North Carolina's piedmont and find the mountain passes in possession of Confederate home guards.

Many of Kirk's men were from North Carolina, so they naturally knew the country and the mountain gaps that needed to be protected. At least a hundred of Kirk's men held the Deep Gap fort for nearly two weeks before Stoneman's raiders returned. A tour through the thick woods beside the historic marker failed to turn up signs of the fort, but state archaeologists say it is there. In 1995, there was a controversy over whether to preserve what remained of the fort, or to allow the land to be used for the widening of U.S. 421.

Follow U.S. 421 down the mountain. About 15 miles from leaving the historic marker for Deep Gap fort, there will be brown state park signs for access to W. Kerr Scott Reservoir. At the sign, take a right from U.S. 421 onto Minton Road. The reservoir will be about 1.0 mile south. Somewhere on the western edge of this reservoir near where Lewis Fork Creek feeds into the Yadkin River, in a spot known to archaeologists, is the foundation for Fort Hamby.

Fort Hamby was not a real fort, but a two-story, log blockhouse that was the headquarters of a gang of bushwhackers led by a man named Wade.

Wade claimed to be a Federal soldier who had come through the area with Stoneman. Whoever he was, he and his buddies were dangerous men. They terrorized Wilkes and Caldwell Counties for weeks in the winter and spring of 1865. Mountain legends say they killed for sport and to practice their aim. One story claims the bushwhackers saw some children climbing a fence in the distance, so they used them for target practice and killed them.

Though the war was over in May 1865, the danger from Wade's gang was growing. Not a home in the area was safe from their invasion. A group of former Confederate soldiers sent word to the nearest occupying Federals that they would take care of the problem themselves. The former Confederates surrounded Fort Hamby and smoked the bushwhackers from their lair. Wade somehow escaped. The rest, at least twenty men, did not. The former Confederates saw no need to take these murderers to Federal authorities. They shot them on the spot. By the time a Federal cavalry company arrived, Fort Hamby and the bushwhackers were gone.

Return on Minton Road to U.S. 421 and turn right, or east. Continue east on U.S. 421 about another 5 miles. Take the exit to downtown Old Wilkesboro's Main Street, or N.C. 18. This is Wilkesboro, not North Wilkesboro. Do not make the mistake of turning onto Business U.S. 421, which leads to North Wilkesboro. Just before reaching the old courthouse on Main Street, or N.C. 18, in Wilkesboro, turn left, or north, onto Cherry Street. Follow Cherry Street one block to St. Paul's Episcopal Church. There, behind the church and surrounded by a wrought-iron fence, is the obelisk marking the grave of Confederate Brigadier General James B. Gordon, a distant cousin of the more famous Confederate Major General John B. Gordon of Georgia.

North Carolina's General Gordon enlisted as a private in 1861 and quickly rose through the ranks, becoming a general in 1863. A cavalryman with the 1st North Carolina Cavalry Regiment, Gordon won the praises of Wade Hampton and J.E.B. Stuart and earned a reputation for fighting alongside his men. The day after Stuart was killed at Yellow Tavern, Virginia, in May 1864, Gordon was wounded at Meadow Bridge, Virginia. He died May 18, 1864.

Retrace your route to Main Street, or N.C. 18. Look on the west side of the old courthouse for a one-story, brick building. This is the old Wilkes

General James Gordon's grave

County jail. Its most famous resident was one Tom Dula. That name may not be familiar, but the name Tom Dooley should be. "Hang Down Your Head, Tom Dooley" was a top-selling folk song in the early 1960s. Dula was a Confederate veteran who returned to the mountains after the war, only to lose his heart to Laura Foster. Dula learned Laura was carrying on with others in the neighborhood, so he "met her on the mountain and there he took her life." He tried to run but was caught before getting out of the state. ("If it hadn't been for Grayson, I'd be in Tennessee.") Grayson was a former Federal officer, now buried near Boone, who captured Dula and brought him back to trial. Former Governor Zeb Vance defended Dula in two trials, but the executioner eventually left Dula "hanging from a white oak tree."

Turn left onto Main Street, or N.C. 18. In front of the courthouse is a historic marker noting that Stoneman's raiders occupied the town on March 29, 1865. The Federal raiders, who split into two columns in Boone, reunited in Wilkesboro.

Follow N.C. 18/N.C. 268 north through an often illogical maze of streets in Wilkesboro and North Wilkesboro. Outside of North Wilkesboro, N.C. 268 finally turns to the right, or northeast. Turn onto N.C. 268 heading northeast. Drive about 19 miles to Elkin. Elkin was visited by Stoneman's raiders on April 1, 1865. Three mills in the town were put to work grinding meal for bread for the Union soldiers, and food found in a storehouse was quickly devoured. Stoneman himself went ahead to Jonesville on the other side of the Yadkin River.

The Confederates believed Stoneman would follow the Yadkin River from Elkin all the way to Salisbury, in an attempt to free the Federal prisoners there. The prison camp was about eighty miles away by following the river. Stoneman let the Confederates think that. By April 2, 1865, all of his columns were across the Yadkin River and on their way to raid southwest Virginia. Along the way, they surprised a Confederate supply-wagon train near Dobson and burned it. For years, the burned, iron wagon wheels were a local landmark in Surry County.

Continue east on N.C. 268 from Elkin for about 17.5 miles to the community of Level Cross. In Level Cross, turn left, or north, onto S.R. 1003. There is a church on the northwest corner and a little store on the southeast corner of this intersection. Drive 8.1 miles, then turn right, or northeast, onto Old U.S. 601. A gasoline station is on the right at this intersection. Continue in this direction for 0.7 mile to the White Plains Baptist Church.

In the church cemetery are the graves of two of the most interesting slave-holding secessionists in the South. Actually, they could be called two of the most interesting men in the entire world. They were Eng and Chang Bunker, twin brothers co-joined by a band of skin at the chest. The term "Siamese Twins" was coined for the Bunker brothers.

The Bunker brothers retired from their world exhibition travels years before the war, selecting Surry County, North Carolina, as their home after visiting it and nearby Wilkes County. The brothers had prospered since their retirement from the exhibition circuit, they were quite happy with their new lives.

The Bunkers, now forty-nine, had married sisters and become farmers with a knack for growing things, including children. They had two houses full of them. Every three days, the brothers would drive a buggy to the other's house. Chang made the rules in his house. Eng made the rules in his house.

The brothers became popular farming tutors to other growers in the region, and the locals quickly got over the Bunkers' unusual appearance. When the war started, the Bunkers owned more than seven hundred acres and thirty-three slaves (tax records were kept separately for the two). Each of the brothers had a son who joined the Confederate Army. Photographs show the boys' very distinct Thai heritage. Both boys survived the war, though one was slightly wounded and captured. He spent seven months in a prison camp in Ohio.

According to one local story, Eng was briefly "drafted" into Stoneman's raiders. Stoneman put the names of all local residents into his own draft lottery and drew Eng's name. Chang's name was not drawn. Once Stoneman realized who he was dealing with, he dropped the idea of taking one—or both—of the famous brothers.

The Bunker daughters proved themselves to be fighters like their brothers. When a Federal soldier grabbed at one of the Bunker girls while she was sitting on her front porch, he got a fist to the nose. From that point forward, none of the Bunkers were bothered by Union soldiers.

The war left the brothers in debt. The loans they had made to their neighbors were now worthless since the money was in Confederate dollars. The thirty-three slaves they had owned were now free. It was time to hit the exhibition halls again. By 1866, the brothers were touring. They died in 1874, at age sixty-three. Their graves are behind the White Plains Baptist Church, which they helped build.

Retrace your route on S.R. 1003, passing over N.C. 268. Drive 41.4 miles from the White Plains Baptist Church to the small community of Siloam. From S.R. 1003, turn left, or east, onto Hardy Road, or S.R. 2081, on the south side of the community. Drive 0.3 mile. Just across Hogan's Creek, on the right side of the road, there is a little white kitchen house that belonged to the Reeves family. This is the site of what could be called, in a stretch, "The Battle of Siloam."

At this site, in a house that no longer stands, two Confederate officers were recuperating from wounds when a group of Stoneman's raiders came calling. One Federal cavalryman demanded the surrender of the one Confederate he saw. His answer was a carbine ball through the chest. The two Confederate officers supposedly emptied a carbine, two double-barrel shotguns, and four revolvers at the Federals before running out the back door toward the nearby Yadkin River. The two Confederates made it to the river, where they lay on their backs among the reeds, submerged except for their nostrils.

A search by the Federals failed to find the two men. Accounts say that one Federal soldier was killed and two were severely wounded during the "battle." The soldier was supposedly buried on the site, but no trace has been found by modern researchers, who are trying to preserve the place where two Confederates held up an entire Federal cavalry column.

Retrace your route back to S.R. 1003 (also known from this point south as Smithtown Road). Turn left, or south, onto S.R. 1003. This road runs into N.C. 67 in 3.9 miles. Turn left, or east, onto N.C. 67 to reach Winston-Salem, 21 miles away.

This concludes the the Mountain War Part II Tour.

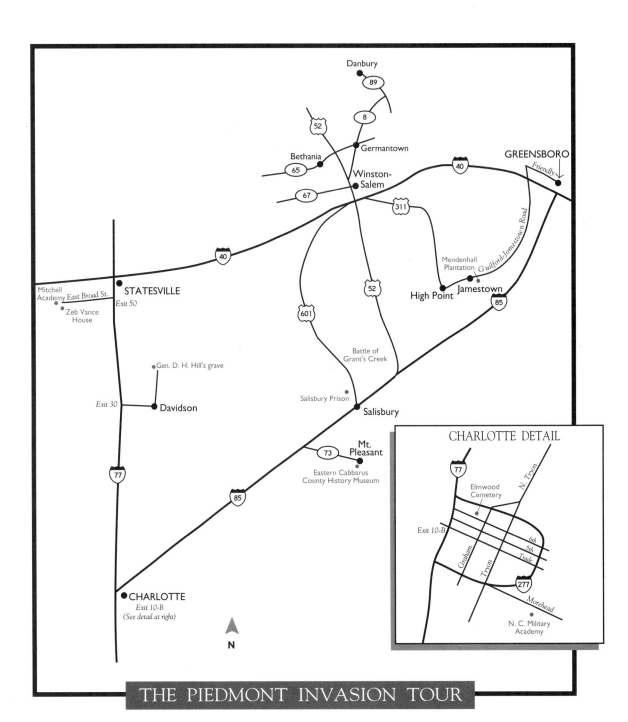

Danbury
89
52
8
Germantown
Bethania
65
Winston-Salem
67
311
40
GREENSBORO
Friendly
Mendenhall
Plantation
Guilford-Jamestown Road
40
High Point
Jamestown
52
85
STATESVILLE
Exit 50
Mitchell
Academy *East Broad St.*
Zeb Vance
House
601
Battle of
Grant's Creek
Gen. D. H. Hill's grave
Salisbury Prison
Salisbury
Exit 30
Davidson
77
73
Mt.
Pleasant
Eastern Cabbarus
County History Museum
85
CHARLOTTE
Exit 10-B
(See detail at right)
N

CHARLOTTE DETAIL

77
N. Tryon
Elmwood
Cemetery
Exit 10-B
6th
5th
Trade
Graham
Tryon
277
Morehead
N. C. Military
Academy

THE PIEDMONT INVASION TOUR

The Piedmont Invasion Tour

This is a lengthy, ambitious tour that starts in the remote town of Danbury, North Carolina, where Stoneman's raiders regrouped before invading the piedmont. The tour then travels to Germanton. A side trip visits the grave of a Black Confederate soldier in Pilot Mountain. The tour then proceeds through Bethania and into Winston-Salem. From there it moves to High Point, Jamestown, and Greensboro. From Greensboro, a lengthy side trip can be taken to Milton, North Carolina, to view the scenes of one of the Civil War's great romances. The tour then continues to Salisbury and the site of a Confederate prison camp. From Salisbury, the tour moves to Charlotte, Davidson, and finally ends in Statesville.

Total mileage: approximately 375 miles, including the side trips. This tour is best taken over at least two days.

After leaving Boone, North Carolina, Stoneman and his raiders targeted the lower towns of Virginia, which had seen little of the Civil War. North Carolinians breathed easier, thinking they had seen the last of the raiders. They were wrong. Stoneman's men swept back down into North Carolina after raiding the Virginia towns of Hillsville, Wytheville, Christiansburg, Lynchburg, and Martinsville. The raiders' objective in lower western Virginia had been to tear up the railroad. That accomplished, Stoneman set his sights on freeing the Federal prisoners in Salisbury, North Carolina. (See the Mountain War Part I Tour for an in-depth discussion of Stoneman's Raid.)

This tour starts at the old courthouse in Danbury, a small city in Stokes County less than 10 miles from the Virginia border and about 22 miles north of Winston-Salem. The courthouse is located downtown on N.C. 8/N.C. 89. If approaching Danbury from the south, the courthouse is on the right.

It was in Danbury, the county seat, that General George Stoneman regrouped his brigades after their raids through southwestern Virginia. Stoneman's men rode into Danbury around 4:00 P.M., April 9, 1865, not

Hotel occupied by Stoneman

Moratuck Furnace

knowing that General Lee had surrendered the Army of Northern Virginia earlier that day at Appomattox, not more than 150 miles away.

Stoneman and his officers spent that night at a two-story downtown hotel, still standing as a private residence just west of the courthouse. On the grounds of the old courthouse is a unique modern monument dedicated to the several companies of men who served in the Civil War from this area of Stokes County. It is unique because it lists the companies by their nicknames. When the companies marched off to war in 1862, they carried names like The Town Fork Invincibles, The Stokes Boys, The Danbury Blues, the Brown Mountain Boys, and the Mountain Boys.

Leaving the courthouse, drive 0.3 mile south along N.C. 8/N.C. 89. Turn left onto S.R. 1652, crossing over the Dan River Bridge. Make an immediate right into Moratuck Park, following a gravel road down to the river level. A softball field is on the right.

Ahead on the left, under the trees, is the Moratuck Iron Furnace, built in 1843. The massive rock structure, with its three fireplaces, processed iron ore for the Confederates throughout the war. Its outbuildings were burned by Stoneman's Union cavalrymen.

Return to N.C. 8/N.C. 89 and continue south for 3.2 miles to where N.C. 8 veers right, or south. Turn right onto N.C. 8. and follow it 13.2 miles to Germanton. At the intersection with N.C. 65, turn right, or west, and follow N.C. 65 through town.

Stoneman's raiders, who were followed by hordes of fleeing slaves, did not think much of this little town. One wrote that it was "without paint or whitewash and laziness was apparent all over it." Stoneman, fearing an upcoming fight with imagined Confederates, shed his command of the freed slaves. He sent them off down the road toward East Tennessee.

Just before leaving Germanton, N.C. 8 splits off to the left from N.C. 65. Stay on N.C. 65 to the right, or west. Follow N.C. 65 through the town of Rural Hall to the intersection with U.S. 52.

If you care to make a brief side trip to see the grave of a Black Confederate soldier, take U.S. 52 north from the intersection with N.C. 65. Drive about 18 miles to the Pilot Mountain exit, Exit 134, which leads to N.C. 268. Turn right or east onto N.C. 268. This road becomes Key Street. In downtown Pilot Mountain, turn right at the first light onto Main Street.

Drive two blocks, then turn left at the next light onto Depot Street. Three blocks from here, at the top of the hill, is Lovell's Chapel Methodist Church. The grave of William C. Revels, marked by a Confederate military tombstone, is in back of the church.

Scattered around North and South Carolina are the graves of Black Confederates, slaves and free Black men who went into the field with the Confederate Army. The slaves went mainly as body servants to their owners. Some would hold horses on the battlefield, retrieve water, cook in camp, or act as couriers. Many of the free Blacks acted as musicians. After the war, any Blacks who served regular duties in the army were eligible for, and received, Confederate pensions from the state. One such man was William C. Revels, a fifer in Company H of the 21st North Carolina. He was 23 years old when the war started. He apparently took part in all of the engagements of the 21st, which included most of the major battles with the Army of Northern Virginia. He died in 1915.

Retrace the route back to U.S. 52 and the intersection with N.C. 65 in Rural Hall. Exit and turn right, or west, onto N.C. 65 and continue to Bethania.

If not taking the side trip, continue west on N.C. 65 at the intersection of N.C. 65 and U.S. 52. Cross U.S. 52, ignoring the signs saying that N.C. 65 ends. Continue on this road until it intersects with Bethania-Tobaccoville Road. Turn left onto Bethania-Tobaccoville Road, the main street of the tree-shaded Moravian town of Bethania.

Stoneman's raiders rode through town in April 1865, but it was not the first time Bethania saw an invading army. The white house on the corner of the intersection of N.C. 65 and Bethania-Tobaccoville Road is traditionally called the Cornwallis House. The British Army marched through the town on its way to the Revolutionary War Battle of Guilford Courthouse, some 40 miles to the northeast. Legend says Cornwallis slept in this house.

Drive 0.1 mile to the Bethania Moravian Church on the left. Stoneman's raiders broke up church services here when they came through town. Turn left onto Grabbs Road, a small street beside the church. Drive all the way to the end of the street to God's Acre, the traditional name for a Moravian cemetery. This one dates back to 1760. As you face the cemetery, all the women are buried together on the left, and the men are buried on the right— a Moravian tradition. Three rows back and three tombstones over are two uncommon stones that stand upright. Moravian stones are usually flush with the earth and equal in size, according to their belief that death humbles all and makes rich and poor equal.

One of the upright stones is for J. Permania Schultz, a twenty-five-year-old member of the 21st North Carolina Regiment. He died in a Richmond, Virginia, hospital. The inscription reads: "Beneath this slab a soldier rests, who fought and fell among the brave. Let all who dared the foe to face, tred [sic] lightly round the hero's grave." The other upright stone is for Schultz's friend in the 21st, Augustus Conrad. It reads: "Here lies a mother's soldier boy, her darling son, her pride and joy."

Return to the intersection with Bethania-Tobaccoville Road and turn left. Drive 0.1 mile and make the next left onto Bethania Road. This is a blind corner with trees obstructing vision, so be careful of oncoming traffic. Drive 0.9 mile to Reynolda Road, or N.C. 67. Turn left onto Reynolda Road and head into the city of Winston-Salem. After 6.5 miles, Reynolda Road makes a s-turn to the left, changes its name to West End Boulevard for two blocks, turns back to the right, and then becomes Broad Street. (It sounds confusing, but stay on the main road and it will work out.) Continue on Broad Street, crossing over Business I-40. Turn left, or east, onto Academy Street, 7.8 miles from turning onto Reynolda. Follow Academy Street three blocks into Old Salem, a preserved Moravian town founded in the 1760s. The visitor's center is on the corner of Academy Street and Old Salem Road. Admission is required for some buildings.

The square at Academy and Main Streets, one block east of the visitor's center, was where several companies of the 21st North Carolina Regiment marched off to join the Army of Northern Virginia. The Old Salem Boys School (also called the Wachovia Museum) on the northeast corner contains a picture of the 26th North Carolina Regimental Band, reported to be one of Robert E. Lee's favorites. When they were not playing, they carried stretchers. All of the members of the band survived the war.

Across the square is Salem College, known during the war as Salem Academy. It is a school for girls operated by the Moravians. When Stoneman's raiders arrived in Salem, a girl leaned out of one of the second-story windows and gave a loud rebel yell. She was quickly pulled back inside. Her's was the only act of defiance in the city, and the Federal troops did not loot the town.

Visitors might like to take several hours visiting the colonial setting of Old Salem. When you are ready to continue the tour, drive north on Main Street for three blocks to Brookstown Avenue. At the intersection of Main Street and Brookstown Avenue will be a large metal coffeepot, a symbol of Moravian hospitality. A legend claims that one or two Confederate soldiers hid inside the coffeepot while Stoneman's men were in town. It would have been cramped.

Turn right from Main onto Cemetery Street, one block north of the coffeepot. The first cemetery encountered on the right will be God's Acre, Old Salem's Moravian cemetery. Like the markers in Bethania, the ones here are flat and identically sized. When Stoneman's raiders encountered this cemetery, they all dismounted, doffed their hats, and walked their horses along the narrow pathway. This unexpected show of respect must have made the nervous citizens of Salem feel a little bit better about their blue-clad visitors.

After passing God's Acre on Cemetery Street, take the first entrance into Salem Cemetery, which will have the traditional stand-up markers. Continue on the circular drive down the hill and stop at some steps on the left near a grave marker for the Loman family. Walk down the steps to the marker for Confederate Brigadier General William R. Boggs.

Boggs, an 1853 graduate of West Point, was from Georgia. He was at the Fort Sumter bombardment in April 1861, and the Fort Pickens, Florida, bombardment in November 1861. However, that was about the only combat he saw. He spent most of the war as chief of staff for General Edmund Kirby-Smith in the Trans-Mississippi Department. Kirby-Smith came to dislike Boggs, but Boggs seems to have performed a credible job. Boggs is another example of a general who looked good on paper but failed to perform in the field. He graduated fourth in his West Point class. In the same class were Union Major General Phil Sheridan, ranked at thirty-fourth, and Confederate Lieutenant General John Bell Hood, ranked at forty-fourth.

Leave Boggs's grave and walk back up the hill toward a plot surrounded by a wrought-iron fence. Inside is the grave of Major Henry Belo of the

Coffee pot rumored to be a Confederate hiding place

55th North Carolina Regiment. Normally, Belo would be just another officer, but he did something in May 1863 that makes him interesting.

In that month, the 55th was stationed around Suffolk, Virginia. One day a Federal raid on the Confederate lines captured some cannons. Two Alabama officers wrote official reports claiming that the 55th ran during the raid, allowing the Federals to take the guns.

Angered by the report, the colonel of the 55th and Major Belo challenged the two offending officers to duels. The Alabamians agreed and had the right to choose the weapons. The colonel's adversary chose double-barreled shotguns loaded with buckshot. Belo's adversary chose rifled muskets at 40 paces. Belo and his adversary went first. Belo's shot grazed the Alabamian's head, while Belo was missed entirely. According to dueling etiquette, a second round was in order. This time Belo missed, and the Alabamian sent a musket ball tearing through Belo's uniform just above the shoulder, but without injuring the major.

Before the other two officers could aim at each other with shotguns, cooler heads convinced the Alabamians to apologize for their "mistaken" report.

Leave Salem Cemetery and turn right, onto Cemetery Street. Follow Cemetery Street until it meets Salem Avenue. Turn right onto Salem Avenue. Drive 0.2 mile and turn east, or left, onto Stadium Drive. After passing under a railroad bridge, get on the entrance ramp for U.S. 52 South. After 2 miles, exit U.S. 52 onto I-40 East. After about 3 miles on I-40 East, exit onto U.S 311 South towards High Point.

At 12.6 miles after getting on U.S. 311, at the eighth traffic light, turn left, or northeast, onto Lexington Avenue. At 1.5 miles from this intersection is the High Point Museum. Since before the American Revolution, High Point and the surrounding towns were arms producers. During the Civil War, several arms factories operated nearby. Some examples of their muskets are on display at the museum. There is also a portrait of Laura Wesson, a young Virginia woman who died while nursing soldiers in High Point near the end of the war. She lies buried with her soldiers in a nearby cemetery.

Leaving the High Point Museum, turn left onto Lexington Avenue. Lexington Avenue becomes Greensboro Road.

If you care to make a brief side trip to see Laura Wesson's grave, turn right at the next traffic light onto Montlieu Street, 1.7 miles after leaving the museum. Drive 0.9 mile on Montlieu to reach Oakwood Cemetery on the left. Turn into the cemetery. Once inside the fence, take the first left turn, then the next right turn, and drive back to the old part of the cemetery. The twenty-year-old Wesson and the fifty Confederate soldiers with smallpox she nursed lie in the far southeast corner of the cemetery under a grove of pines.

Retrace the route back to the intersection of Montlieu Street and Greensboro Road. Turn right onto Greensboro Road and drive 1.8 miles to the Mendenhall Plantation on the right in Jamestown. Jamestown is an old Quaker village that was an active stop for runaway slaves on the Underground Railroad. The Mendenhall Plantation house was built in 1811. It was well known to Quakers and runaways as a place where slaves could always find refuge. Ironically, some historians believe Confederate Secretary of War John C. Breckinridge stayed in the house on the Confederate cabinet's flight south at the end of the war.

The exact history of the Underground Railway and the Quakers' important role in its operation will never be known. Historians guess that more than fifty thousand slaves were spirited out of the South over a period of thirty years. Many would have come through Guilford County, North Carolina, one of the centers of Quaker settlement in the South.

The prized possession of the Mendenhall Plantation is a false-bottom wagon, one of two known to exist in the country. At first glance, the wagon looks normal. A second look shows that the bed is more shallow than the sides of the wagon would indicate. Under the driver's seat is a pull-away board hiding a narrow chamber. As many as eight runaway slaves would hide in the chamber. Hay or heavy boxes were loaded onto the shallow bed, and young boys drove the wagon to Ohio or Indiana. This particular wagon operated out of Pleasant Garden, North Carolina, now part of Greensboro. The number of slaves the wagon liberated is unknown.

Turn right from Mendenhall Plantation and drive less than a mile to Ragsdale Drive. There is a Texaco Station on the corner. Turn right onto Ragsdale Drive. Less than 0.2 mile down this road is a bridge. Watch for traffic and slow to a crawl before crossing the bridge. Look to the left at an

Mill in Jamestown almost burned by Stoneman's raiders

old white mill, now on a private drive. In April 1865, Stoneman's raiders wanted to burn this mill but were talked out of it by the miller. He claimed all he was doing was grinding meal to feed women and children. Cross the bridge and turn around at the first opportunity. Return to Greensboro Road.

Turn right back onto Greensboro Road, or Main Street. Drive less than 0.5 mile to the next light and turn right onto Oakdale Road. About 0.75 of a mile down Oakdale Road to the right is Oakdale Mill Road. Drive to the end of Oakdale Mill Road to view the Oakdale Mill. In 1862 and 1863, this mill was converted into an arms factory that produced more than three thousand muskets. The factory is still in operation as a cotton mill, but it has been heavily modified through the years.

Retrace the route to the intersection with Greensboro Road. The old yellow house and antique store on the southwest corner of the intersection is the former Shubal Coffin house. During Jefferson Davis's flight south, he briefly stopped in the house. Confederate Secretary of the Treasury George Trenholm may have spent the night there.

Turn left, or west, on Greensboro Road. Turn right onto Penny Road, about 0.75 mile past Mendenhall Plantation. Drive north on Penny Road for about a mile until it passes over a finger of High Point City Lake. Turn around and slow down while passing back over the bridge. Traffic permitting, look to the southeast edge of the lake. About fifty yards away, at the water's edge, are the block foundation remains of another arms factory. This factory was attacked by Stoneman's raiders.

After viewing the foundation, return to the Greensboro Road and turn left, heading back towards the Mendenhall Plantation.

Continue on the Greensboro Road until reaching Guilford-Jamestown Road at an angle on the left. The Oakdale Road intersection is on the right. Turn left, or north, onto Guilford-Jamestown Road. Drive about 8 miles to the intersection with West Friendly Avenue in Greensboro. Guilford College occupies the northeast section of this intersection. During the war, this was New Garden Boarding School, a Quaker boarding school founded in 1835. No part of the original school survives. The school and the surrounding Quaker community of New Garden were probably the center of the Underground Railroad activity in North Carolina.

In 1789, the community of New Garden was the birthplace of Levi Coffin. Coffin was a devout Quaker who left North Carolina for Indiana in 1826. Though Coffin left New Garden, the community continued to play an important role in his life's work—running the Underground Railroad. Guilford College historians say the woods next to the school likely hid hundreds of runaway slaves. Hiding places in the woods included hollow logs and secret, lumber-reinforced pits covered by leaves.

The Quakers still tell legends about Levi Coffin and New Garden Boarding School, and how slaves escaped through Guilford County. Once, while he was still living in New Garden, Coffin met a man who had tracked his slave right to Coffin's door. Coffin spent the night plying the slave owner with liquor, while the slave ran to the next safe house. By the time the man sobered up, he had almost forgotten why he came to New Garden in the first place.

Another story revolves around Vina, a free Black woman who worked as a laundress for the school. When her husband died, she kept his manumission papers (official documents explaining that the bearer is a free Black man. The papers bore the description of the black person). For uncounted years, Vina would look over every male runaway slave who passed through New Garden. If he looked enough like her husband, she would lend him the manumission papers. The papers would be given to Levi Coffin in Freeport, Indiana, who sent them back to New Garden in one of the false-bottom wagons.

Helping one's fellow man leads to a long life. Coffin lived to be eighty-eight years old. He is buried in Indiana.

From the Guilford-Jamestown Road intersection, turn right, or east, onto Friendly Avenue and head toward downtown Greensboro. Friendly Avenue will intersect with Elm Street in about 6 miles, one block after crossing a major intersection with Greene Street. From Friendly, turn right, or south, onto Elm Street. Drive four blocks to the 500 block of South Elm Street. On this block, in a small open area to the left, will be three markers set in a small open area. Turn left onto Martin Luther King Street, park along this street, and walk to the open area to read the markers.

One marker describes the area as the place where Confederate President Jefferson Davis met with General Joseph Johnston to discuss surrender terms for Johnston's troops. Davis spent five days in Greensboro, starting on April 11, 1865. According to local legend, his train made its way over Reedy Creek north of town and to the safety of Greensboro not more than five minutes before a Federal cavalry column arrived to burn the bridge. The other markers list the battles in which the Confederate Army of Tennessee fought. One marker gives General Johnston's surrender address.

According to local historians, Johnston's army camped in a wide area around Greensboro, including ground now occupied by North Carolina A & T State University, a few blocks to the east. Johnston's headquarters was 1.5 miles west of this area, on what is now the campus of the University of North Carolina at Greensboro.

Johnston made his final address to his soldiers from the back porch of a house on Gorrell Street, not far from these markers. With tears streaming down his cheeks, he told them that "I shall always remember with pride the loyal support and general confidence you have given me. I now part with deep regret and bid you farewell with feelings of cordial friendship; and with earnest wishes that you may have hereafter all the prosperity and happiness to be found in the world."

More than thirty-nine thousand paroles were issued to the Confederate soldiers camped around Greensboro. This is an unusual number considering it is more than twice the number of troops Johnston had with him at the Battle of Bentonville in March. The paroles were issued over two days, May 1–2, 1865.

Perhaps the most unusual soldier in Greensboro during this time was really a sailor, Admiral Raphael Semmes. He was the former commander of the Confederate raider ship CSS *Alabama*. Semmes had been part of the James River Squadron in Richmond. Semmes and 250 sailors from the James River Squadron traveled to Greensboro after the fall of Richmond. Semmes, who had spent his entire career on the ocean, ended it as a dirt soldier in Guilford County guarding Reedy Ford on the north side of Greensboro. Semmes's pardon, issued in Greensboro, is made out to his name as both a rear admiral and a brigadier general in the Confederate Army. Semmes, always a precise man, wanted any Union officer who asked to know that he was pardoned both as a soldier and a sailor. He did not want to be considered a pirate for his service as a Confederate raider on the high seas.

Return to Elm Street and retrace your route, heading north towards downtown. At the 200 block of North Elm Street, turn right onto Summit Avenue. Directly ahead is the Greensboro Historical Museum. Park behind the museum. The museum is on the site of the First Presbyterian Church, which was used as a hospital for soldiers wounded at the Battle of Bentonville. The original building was removed in the 1920s, but the churchyard contains the graves of some Confederate soldiers.

The museum has a military hall on the second floor with displays from the Revolutionary War, War of 1812, Mexican War, Civil War, World War I, and World War II. The Civil War display focuses on the service of Company B of the 27th North Carolina, the "Guilford Grays." The members of Company B were recruited from the region. Out of the hundred or so men recruited, only twelve survived to surrender at Appomattox. An advertisement, or "broadside," offers a hundred-dollar bounty for men joining the Grays. Displays include the contents of a haversack, photographs of soldiers, several muskets manufactured in the area, and a rare LeMat (French) carbine, with a revolving cylinder for the rifle and a second barrel for a shotgun. A drum, apparently left by a drummer with the 114th New York, is also displayed.

One of the favorite artifacts of the museum staff is a Tarpley carbine, manufactured in Greensboro. The Tarpley was a breechloader that had two major flaws. It had no wooden understock to hold. After a few shots, the barrel became too hot to hold. Also, the poorly designed breech didn't allow gases to escape once the gun was fired. This created discomfort to the shooter and caused the breech to jam, due to the buildup of gun-powder residue. The flaws did not stop the manufacturer from printing an advertisement, also displayed, that called the weapon "one of the finest rifles on the market."

A whole display is devoted to Henry Clay Gorrell, a member of the Guilford Grays who was killed at Fair Oaks on June 14, 1862. A friend wrote and published the following tribute:

They laid him away on the cold, damp ground on the banks of a
    Southern stream.
Not so far from his own native land where the rays of a tropic sun gleam.

No coffin to enclose his mangled remains, no shroud save his uniform
  coat.
But his name is entwined with the laurels of fame and a memory's table
  'tis wrote.

From the Greensboro Museum, head west on Lindsey Street for three
blocks to Eugene Street. Turn north, or right, onto Eugene Street. Drive
four blocks, passing through the Battleground Avenue intersection. Turn
left, or west, onto Cleveland Street. Follow Cleveland into Green Hill
Cemetery.

The simple marker of General Alfred Scales is near the center of the
cemetery, in front of a large, tall, rough-hewn obelisk that has nothing to
do with him. Scales's grave is about fifty yards north of the Confederate
statue guarding the remains of three hundred unknown Confederates buried in the cemetery.

Scales was a prominent lawyer and state legislator before his election to
the United States House of Representatives in 1857. In 1861, he volunteered for the 13th North Carolina Regiment as a 34-year-old private. However, he was soon elected captain of the regiment. He served as a colonel
at Chancellorsville, where he was wounded, and was promoted to brigadier general soon afterwards. He was wounded again on the first day of
Gettysburg. He returned to service in 1864 and participated in the battles
for the Wilderness and the siege of Petersburg.

Scales's wounds never fully healed, and he left active service late in the
war. He returned to North Carolina and apparently was never formally
pardoned. In 1866, he was reelected to the state legislature. From 1875 to
1884, he again served in the United States House of Representatives. In
1884, he was elected governor of North Carolina for the first of two, two-
year terms. He died in 1892. His monument is small and unassuming for a
man who served in the legislature, the United States Congress, as a governor of the state, and as a general in the Confederate Army.

Leaving Green Hill, turn right, or south, onto Eugene Street. Drive seven
blocks to Washington Street. Turn right and go to 447 West Washington
to view Blandwood Mansion, the former home of North Carolina governor John M. Morehead. There are some indications that Morehead hosted

some parties for the Confederate cabinet in Blandwood while they were in town. Confederate secretaries of the treasury George Trenholm and Christopher Memminger stayed at Blandwood on their way south out of Richmond. This was also the last place General Johnston visited before leaving town after formally addressing his men for the last time. Mrs. Morehead wrote that the old general could not manage to say anything, and tears were streaming down his face. Over Johnston's shoulder, Mrs. Morehead saw the road filled with Confederate soldiers walking south towards their homes.

There is some question concerning whether President Davis stayed in local houses during his stay in Greensboro, or if he remained in his railroad car. Some historians say that the citizens of Greensboro did not welcome Davis out of fear that any house sheltering him would be burned by the Federals. Others say that Davis himself worried about the same thing, and that he stayed in his railroad car after turning down invitations to stay in local homes. There are reports that Davis at least visited some houses in the city, but there is no official recognition of any such residences.

At this point, you can take a side trip to view the site of one of the greatest romances of the Civil War. However, the trip is rather lengthy. If you care to make the trip, return to Eugene Street and follow it south to I-85. Get on I-85 North and follow it to Exit 127, the exit for U.S. 29 North. Drive 23 miles on U.S. 29 North to the intersection with U.S. 158 in Reidsville. Drive east on U.S. 158 for 21 miles to Yanceyville. In Yanceyville, turn left, or north, onto N.C. 62 and drive 12 miles to the tiny town of Milton on the North Carolina and Virginia border. At the intersection of N.C. 62 and N.C. 57, turn right, or south, onto N.C. 57 and drive 2 miles to Woodside Inn. The house was built in 1838 by Caleb Richmond, a native of Rhode Island who came to Caswell County in 1820 to grow tobacco.

It is doubtful that the Civil War produced a more romantic and tragic story than that of Confederate Major General Stephen Dodson Ramseur of Lincolnton and his cousin, Ellen Richmond of Milton. Ramseur, an 1860 graduate of West Point, started his career as a captain of artillery, but he was soon elected colonel of the 49th N.C. Regiment at the age of twenty-four. Wounded in the arm at Malvern Hill on July 1, 1862, he was sent to

Woodside Inn in Milton

his uncle's plantation at Milton to recover. It was at Woodside that he met his young cousin Ellen, or Nellie, as he called her. She called him Dod.

Love blossomed between the two as Ramseur regained his strength. After Ramseur was healed, the couple courted by letter for almost a year. On Christmas Day, 1862, Dod wrote: "You are the source of all my joys, how infinitely much I owe to you, how inexpressibly much I love you for all this new found happiness." After Gettysburg, he wrote: "The intensity of my love I felt more keenly in these times of danger." Finally, on October 23, 1863, they were married at Woodside.

Marriage did not make Ramseur any more careful. He was wounded a second time at Chancellorsville and a third time at Spotsylvania Courthouse. In the fall of 1864, he was promoted to major general the day after his twenty-seventh birthday. On October 16, 1864, while waiting for an upcoming battle near Cedar Creek, Virginia, Ramseur was handed a message that had been received from a signal station: "The crisis is over and all is well." Nellie had given birth to their first child. Ramseur broke down and cried at the news. He penned one more letter: "God bless my darling! May He soon reunite us in happiness and peace a joyful family." He then wrote a new will to include his child. He did not know if it was a boy or a girl.

On the morning of October 19, 1864, Ramseur pinned a yellow flower in his lapel in honor of his first child. As he formed his troops, he laughed and cried out to them to be prepared to push the Yankees. "Let's drive 'em for I must get a furlough to see my little wife and new baby!" he exclaimed.

Several hours later, during the Battle of Cedar Creek near Middletown, Virginia, Ramseur was mounting his third horse—after having two horses shot from under him. A bullet tore through both lungs, and he was soon captured by Federal troops. His captors took him to Belle Grove Plantation (today a house museum that preserves the room in which Ramseur was placed). He lingered for almost a day, constantly saying he wished to see his baby just once before he died. Several old West Point friends came to visit Ramseur before he died: Wesley Merritt, Henry duPont, and George Custer. All were Federal generals.

Finally, on October 20, 1864, twenty-seven-year-old Stephen Dodson Ramseur died, eight days short of his one-year wedding anniversary. For the next thirty-six years, until her death, Nellie wore black mourning clothes. Ramseur's daughter, Mary, died at age seventy-one. She never married. All three are buried side by side in Lincolnton, North Carolina.

Woodside was restored in 1985 and opened as a country inn and restaurant. The inn displays photos of Ramseur and his family.

Retrace your route to I-85 and turn south, driving back through Greensboro towards Salisbury, North Carolina.

If leaving from Blandwood Mansion, return to Eugene Street and follow it south to I-85. Take I-85 South for 51 miles to Salisbury. About 40 miles after leaving Greensboro, I-85 passes over the Yadkin River. Stoneman's raiders were beaten back here when they tried to burn a bridge located to the right of the interstate bridge.

From I-85, take Exit 76-B onto U.S. 52 North (Innes Street). Follow Innes Street into downtown Salisbury. Drive east on Innes Street for 1 mile then turn right, or northeast, onto Depot Street. Go two blocks to the Salisbury Visitor's Center, located in a restored train depot. At the visitor's center, pick up a free audio-tape tour of the Salisbury Prison (the tape must be returned).

From the visitor's center, drive up one block on East Liberty, then turn left onto North Main Street. Drive four blocks, then turn left onto East Bank Street. Crossing over the railroad tracks on East Bank Street puts the visitor inside the walls of what used to be Salisbury Prison.

At the beginning of the War, Salisbury's population of two thousand made it the largest town in western North Carolina. Early in the war, the Confederates bought a failed cotton factory, originally built in 1839. The Confederates intended to make the factory into a prison for no more than a thousand Federal soldiers. However, as the war progressed, the Federal government, aware that it had a greater supply of soldiers, stopped exchanging prisoners. By not returning Confederate prisoners, the Union hoped to further deplete the South's supply of men. As a result, prisoner populations soared. By August 1864, more than ten thousand Federals were crammed into the sixteen-acre Salisbury Prison. Men were dying at a rate of forty-five a day from diseases such as dysentery. The exact number of Federal soldiers who died at the Salisbury Prison will never be known, but the number is estimated to be in excess of five thousand. (A monument

Confederate monument in Salisbury on Innes Street

Josephus Hall House

mentioning ten thousand is considered by historians to be inaccurate.) By January 1865, most of the soldiers had been transferred away from the prison. Stoneman arrived in April expecting to set the prisoners free, but the majority were long gone. He burned all of the buildings, save one that now serves as a cemetery office.

Today, the site of the prison serves as a national cemetery. At the top of the hill, under a statue erected by the state of Maine, are the unmarked graves of the Union soldiers. During the week, the small office at the front of the cemetery is open with a display on the prison.

Retrace your route to the visitor's center to drop off the tour tape. Return to Innes Street from Depot Street and turn right, or west. Drive three blocks to the intersection of Innes and Church Streets. In the center of this intersection is one of the South's most beautiful Confederate monuments. The statue of a winged woman holding up a wounded Confederate soldier was erected in 1909. The widow of Stonewall Jackson came from her home in Charlotte to dedicate the monument.

Turn left, or south, onto Church Street and drive two blocks, then turn right onto West Bank Street. Drive one block and turn right onto South Jackson Street. On the corner of Bank and Jackson Streets, at 226 South Jackson Street, is the Josephus Hall House, built in 1820. Hall was the doctor for the Salisbury prison. The house is open for tours.

Drive two blocks on South Jackson Street to Innes Street. Turn left, or west, onto Innes Street, following the signs for U.S. 601 West. After 2.7 miles, U.S. 601 West will fork off to the right. Follow it past Catawba College. Just past the college on the right, and before reaching Grant's Creek, is a historic marker for a skirmish between Stoneman's raiders and a group of "galvanized" Irishmen fighting with the Salisbury Home Guard. The term *galvanized* means the Irishmen were Federal soldiers freed from Salisbury prison after they promised to join the Confederate army. When they heard that Stoneman was coming, the local Confederate home guard, with the Irishmen, threw up a defensive line on the Salisbury side of Grant's Creek.

It was not much of a fight. Almost as soon as Stoneman's men rode into view, the Irishmen started running. Not many shots were fired before the Federals swept past the home guard and entered the city.

What is more unusual is that another group of galvanized Irishmen guarding the Yadkin River railroad bridge on the north side of the city held firm. They put up a spirited fight when Stoneman's men tried to burn the bridge. The Federals tried to capture the bridge for more than five hours before finally withdrawing to Salisbury. They then headed back west toward the mountains. Had the Federals only waited a few days, they would have encountered President Davis passing over that same railroad bridge. Several weeks later, while almost back in Tennessee, Stoneman's raiders received orders to pursue Davis into Georgia.

Leaving Grant's Creek, retrace the route back on U.S. 601 East to Innes Street, then back to I-85. Get on I-85 South and head to Charlotte, approximately 35 miles away.

If you care to make a side trip, take Exit 55 off I-85 South onto N.C. 73 East. Follow N.C. 73 through the town of Concord to the town of Mt. Pleasant, approximately 12 miles from the interstate. In Mt. Pleasant, turn left onto Main Street. Drive one block to the Eastern Cabarrus County Historical Society Museum. The museum was once a Lutheran boys' school, built in 1852. During the War, North Carolina regiments used the building as a recruiting depot. Inside the museum is a Civil War room that includes pictures, uniforms, swords, and other weapons from the war. During the war, the Lutheran boys donated the carpets in their dormitory rooms to use as blankets in the field. The museum is open only on Mondays and the first and third Sundays of the month.

Retrace the route back to I-85 South and continue to Charlotte.

In Charlotte, get on I-77 South when it intersects with I-85 South. Drive three miles on I-77 South and take Exit 10B, the Trade Street exit. Head toward town. At the fourth light on Trade Street, turn left, or north, onto South Graham Street. This is the area where Mrs. Stonewall Jackson lived after the war.

Go two blocks, then turn left onto West Sixth Street, which is a one-way street heading back toward I-77. Pass under a railroad underpass, then turn right into Elmwood Cemetery, at 700 West Sixth Street. After entering the cemetery, take the left fork, then bear right around the Confederate cemetery. The Confederate cemetery contains the graves of more than a hundred Confederates who died in Charlotte hospitals during the war. The Barringer family plot is beside the road, just southeast of the Confederates.

Confederate Brigadier General Rufus Barringer was a well-respected lawyer and politician when the war started. He was a staunch Unionist before the War but joined the Confederate Army when North Carolina seceded. Elected a captain, he kept that rank for almost two years, though he fought well in all of the major battles. In June 1864, he was promoted to brigadier general and given command of four North Carolina cavalry regiments. His record of engagements lists three wounds and seventy-six different battles. He served in his last battle on April 3, 1865, when he was captured.

Barringer was in a tent awaiting transfer to prison when he heard a voice outside say, "Mr. President—Have you ever seen a live Confederate general in uniform? Here is one now." The tent flap opened, and Abraham Lincoln walked inside. Barringer and the President talked for a few minutes. It turned out that Lincoln had served in the United States Congress with Barringer's brother Moreau. That good fortune worked in Barringer's favor, as Lincoln wrote a note to Secretary of War Edward Stanton asking for fair treatment of Barringer.

Barringer was married to one of three Morrison girls. The other two sisters were married to Lieutenant General D.H. Hill and Lieutenant General Thomas "Stonewall" Jackson. Barringer returned to the practice of law after the war and became a Republican, which killed his political career. He died in 1895.

Buried close to Barringer is Brigadier General Thomas Drayton, the unfortunate commander of Hilton Head, South Carolina, in November 1861. Drayton was a 1828 graduate of West Point, the same class as his friend Jefferson Davis. After graduation, Drayton did not find much to do in the peace-time army. He resigned in 1836.

When Drayton was made a brigadier in the Confederate Army in 1861 and put in charge of Hilton Head, he had been out of active duty for nearly twenty-five years. Drayton never quite found a niche in the modern army. His headquarters was at his own plantation on Hilton Head, which he was forced to abandon when the Federals captured the island. Though he was in command of a brigade from time to time, he never won any praise from his superiors. After the war, he became an insurance agent. He died in 1891.

Leave Elmwood Cemetery and turn right onto Sixth Street. After a short distance, make an immediate left to head back toward the city on Fifth Street, a one-way street heading east. Turn right at the fourth light onto Tryon Street, the main street for Charlotte. When crossing over Trade Street on Tryon Street, look to the left. President Davis met with his cabinet at a house two blocks to the left on South Trade Street. The house was long ago knocked down. Beyond that one block was a factory where the Confederate Navy manufactured armaments. An explosion at the factory during the war killed dozens of people.

It was on South Tryon Street that Davis first learned of the assassination of Lincoln. He called it "sad news." He said "We have lost our best friend in the court of the enemy." Davis stayed in Charlotte until April 25, 1865. He had just two thousand soldiers with him at the time.

After crossing over I-277 on Tryon Street, turn left onto East Morehead Street. Go two blocks to the YMCA and park in the parking lot. This is the site of the North Carolina Military Academy. Before the war, the academy was commanded by D.H. Hill. A detailed marker is on Morehead Street in front of the building. On June 10, 1861, Hill and a number of the cadets from this school fought and won the Battle of Big Bethel near Yorktown, Virginia. It was the first battle of the war after the attack on Fort Sumter, and many Southerners thought it would be the only one.

After reading the marker at the YMCA, turn left, back onto Morehead, toward I-77. Drive approximately 1 mile to the entrance ramp for I-77 North. Get on I-77 North and head to Davidson.

Drive 19.7 miles on I-77 North and turn off at Exit 30. Follow Griffith Street to Davidson College. Griffith Street dead-ends into Davidson College 1.2 miles from the interstate. Park in a visitor's space on the campus and walk 0.2 mile north on the road running in front of the college (Old Statesville Road, or N.C. 115) to a small cemetery on the left. In the rear of the cemetery will be the grave for Lieutenant General Daniel Harvey (D.H.) Hill.

There are few Confederate generals more puzzling than D.H. Hill. He was an 1842 graduate of West Point and a brilliant general when he was fighting. However, he was someone who could never play politics with his superiors when he wasn't fighting.

During the Mexican War, Hill was cited three times for bravery and promoted three times. He resigned from the Army in 1849 to become a mathematics professor, first at Washington College in Lexington, Virginia, then at Davidson College. He was at Davidson from 1854 to 1859. In 1859, he took the job as superintendent of the North Carolina Military Academy in Charlotte. He left that job to become colonel of the 1st North Carolina Regiment in May 1861.

After his service at Big Bethel, he was rewarded with a promotion to brigadier general. In March 1862, he was promoted to major general. It was then that he started becoming a pain in the side of his superiors. He complained about anything and everything. He was such a complainer that fellow officers used his personality as an excuse for the Confederate Army's defeats and near defeats.

Lee chose not to give Hill a corps command in the Army of Northern Virginia because of Hill's poor attitude. Hill reacted to the slight by trying to resign from the army in January 1863. Only the persuasion of his brother-in-law, Stonewall Jackson, kept Hill in the field. Hill accepted a corps command in the Army of Tennessee under General Braxton Bragg, a decision Hill soon regretted. Even though he had finally received his coveted lieutenant general's rank, Hill began to criticize Bragg. That resulted in Bragg demanding Hill's resignation after the Confederate victory at Chickamauga, even though Hill had been instrumental in the victory there. Hill's promotion to lieutenant general was canceled, and he spent the rest of the war in minor roles. He was present at the Battle of Bentonville.

Hill turned to journalism after the war, authoring North Carolina's volume for *Confederate Military History*. He also served as president of two colleges, including what would become the University of Arkansas. He never apologized for his combative attitude with his fellow officers. He died in 1889. His tombstone reads: "He feared not the face of man, but feared and trusted God with all his heart."

Retrace your route to I-77 and head north to Statesville. Take Exit 50 and turn west onto East Broad Street heading towards town. After 1.5 miles, the street becomes West Broad Street. Two blocks after becoming

West Broad Street, the street runs past Mitchell Community College, founded in 1856. Stoneman's raiders camped around the college buildings on the night of April 13, 1865. Stoneman himself arrived in a carriage, too sick to ride a horse.

While resting in Statesville, Stoneman wrote a report to his commanding officer that described the success of the raid: "I can say that we are much better mounted than when we left Knoxville. The rapidity of our movements has in almost every instance caused our advance guard to herald our approach and make the surprise complete."

Stoneman's raiders stayed in Statesville three days, skirmishing several times with Confederate cavalrymen who rode into town unaware that Federals were around. From here Stoneman's raiders went on to Lincolnton, Taylorsville, and Morganton.

From Broad Street at Mitchell Community College, turn south onto Mulberry Street. Drive 3 blocks to West Sharpe Street and turn right. Drive to 301 West Sharpe Street. This is the house where North Carolina Governor Zebulon Vance was arrested after the war. Federal cavalry returned to Statesville in May. They arrested North Carolina Governor Zebulon Vance on May 13, 1865, as he ate breakfast at his rented house. It was his thirty-fifth birthday. Vance was imprisoned in Washington, D.C., until his release on July 6, 1865. The house where Vance was arrested was relocated from Grace Park to this location. It is opened by request.

This concludes The Piedmont Invasion Tour.

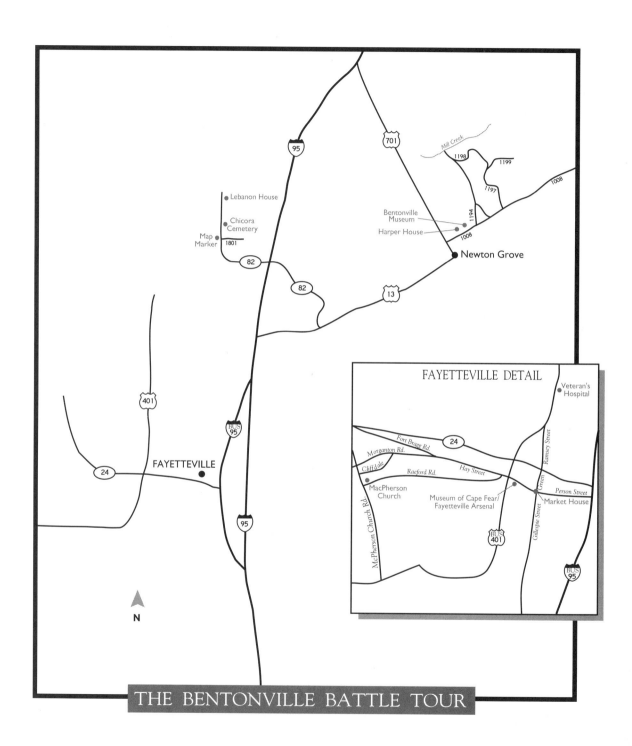

Lebanon House

Chicora
Cemetery

Map
Marker 1801

95

701

Mill Creek

1198

1199

1197

1008

1194

Bentonville
Museum

Harper House

1008

82

82

13

Newton Grove

401

BUS
95

24

FAYETTEVILLE

95

FAYETTEVILLE DETAIL

Veteran's
Hospital

Fort Bragg Rd.

24

Morganton Rd.

Cliffdale

Ramsey Street

Raeford Rd.

Hay Street

MacPherson Church Rd.

MacPherson
Church

Museum of Cape Fear/
Fayetteville Arsenal

Gillespie Street

Green

Person Street

Market House

BUS
401

BUS
95

N

THE BENTONVILLE BATTLE TOUR

The Bentonville Battle Tour

This tour starts in Fayetteville, North Carolina, and includes a visit to the site of the Fayetteville Arsenal, an important Confederate arms factory. From Fayetteville, the tour moves to the Averasboro Battlefield, a small battle where Confederates delayed Sherman's left wing for a full day, almost long enough to set up an ambush at Bentonville. From Averasboro, the tour continues to the Bentonville Battlefield. The Battle of Bentonville was North Carolina's largest Civil War battle, and one of the last battles fought in the war.

Total mileage: approximately 120 miles, including a side trip.

North Carolinians knew Union General William T. Sherman was on his way in the spring of 1865. In early February, he had crossed over the Savannah River from Georgia into South Carolina, and was quickly making his way through the Palmetto State.

They also knew that in South Carolina, Sherman's sixty-three thousand man army had burned, looted, and pillaged everything in its path. Towns and cities like Barnwell, Orangeburg, Columbia, Winnsboro, and Chesterfield had all tasted the torch. Camden and Cheraw, South Carolina, had escaped serious damage, but that was cold comfort. There was no guarantee that Sherman's "bummers" wouldn't continue looting and pillaging once they crossed the Pee Dee River into North Carolina.

By March 3, 1865, the first of Sherman's foragers and cavalry started to filter across the Pee Dee River. Although Sherman had ordered his men to go easy on the Tar Heel state as a means of creating pro-Union sentiment, Union Major General Hugh Judson Kilpatrick's cavalrymen still robbed everyone they saw in towns like Wadesboro and Lumberton. In Lumberton the local Methodist minister was robbed of his finest mare, Kate. The preacher, who apparently kept records of everything, wrote in his diary that he had owned the horse for 5 years, 11 months, and 17 days, and had ridden her 17,102 miles. Both towns lost their train depots and other public stores.

The North Carolinians feared the "bummers" and Kilpatrick's men more than the "regular" Union soldiers. Bummers were the foragers who roamed in front of the army. Officially, they were looking for livestock, grain, and food to feed Sherman's army. Unofficially, since they were usually out of the sight and control of officers, they could be thieves, rapists, and murderers.

Kilpatrick, twenty-nine, was a roguish and unpredictable cavalryman who kept loose reins on his riders. In 1864, he had been in charge of a cavalry raid on Richmond. According to rumor, the purpose of the raid was to kill President Jefferson Davis. He rode his horses and his men so hard that he carried the nickname "Kil-Cavalry." North Carolinians knew they would see flames if he came to their farms.

Still, the wholesale burning of homes and attacks on civilians slacked off as more Federals crossed the river. Sherman, hearing that a civilian had been murdered in Wadesboro when he couldn't produce a watch that already had been stolen by a Federal cavalryman, specifically ordered Kilpatrick to "deal as fairly and moderately with North Carolinians as possible." Sherman learned that Confederate General Joseph T. Johnston was back in command of what was left of the scattered Confederate forces from Mississippi to North Carolina. He knew Johnston would fight him somewhere in North Carolina, so he did not want to create any more animosity among civilians than necessary.

Sherman's army moved northward in the same right and left columns that had proved effective through South Carolina. Small towns like Laurel Hill and Laurinburg were raided, while the town of Rockingham saw a street-to-street battle between Confederate cavalry and Union cavalry and infantry foragers.

On the night of March 9, 1865, one of General Kilpatrick's officers was captured. The man revealed that Kilpatrick himself was staying at the home of a man named Charles Monroe at Monroe's Crossroads a few miles away. The officer, who did not mind talking, also told the Confederates that Kilpatrick was not in a very military mood. He had other things on his mind. He had been spending his nights in the arms of a beautiful woman, who had been with the column since it left Columbia the previous month, and he was now with the woman at Monroe's Crossroads.

A scouting trip to Monroe's Crossroads confirmed the Federal officer's story. The Confederates waited until it was almost dawn, then swooped down upon the Federals who were still sleeping inside their tents. Kilpatrick was inside the Monroe house, in bed snuggling with his South Carolina sugarplum.

Confederate Cavalry Commander Lieutenant General Wade Hampton saw a golden opportunity before him. He could both gain access to the road to Fayetteville, which Kilpatrick's cavalry had blocked, and capture the mutton-chopped braggart who had done so much damage during Sherman's march. Hampton must have figured he could bargain with Sherman for Kilpatrick's return.

Unfortunately, Kilpatrick escaped from the clutches of the Confederates. At the first sound of firing, Kilpatrick padded to the front door of the house in his stocking feet, where he was grabbed by a Confederate soldier. The soldier demanded to know where he could find "the general," and Kilpatrick pointed to a man riding away. Once the gullible Confederate let him go, Kilpatrick leaped astride his horse and fled the house. Clad only in his underwear, the general left behind his boots, pants, shirt, coat, hat, sword, pistol, and his mistress, Marie Boozer.

The twenty-something Miss Boozer, said to be the most beautiful woman in all of Columbia, stood in the door of the farmhouse, clad only in a flimsy nightgown. She watched as the object of her affections ran like a scalded dog. Kilpatrick had not stopped to pick her up, or even to say, "Thank you, ma'am." A courteous Confederate leaped from his horse, covered her with an overcoat, and led her to the safety of a nearby ditch as the battle sent musketballs whining through the house.

Though made in complete surprise, the Confederate attack on Kilpatrick's love nest and his cavalry's camp failed. The Confederates had tried to surround the Federals before the attack, but a swamp bogged down many Confederate cavalrymen. In addition, a nearby Federal infantry regiment came to the relief of Kilpatrick's cavalry before the Confederates could press any advantage. Still, the Southerners were able to open the road to Fayetteville, and ride into the city without incident.

In a sense, the Confederates did win something. Kilpatrick became the laughingstock of the Federal Army, particularly among the Federal infantrymen. The infantrymen called the incident "Kilpatrick's Shirt Tail Skedaddle." Sherman summed Kilpatrick up with the statement, "I know Kilpatrick is a hell of a damned fool, but I want that sort of man to command my cavalry in this expedition."

Marie Boozer did not finish the war with her lover. Sherman sent her to Wilmington at the first opportunity.

Sleeping in one's underwear and coming close to getting captured was not purely a Federal foible. Two days later, Confederate Major General Matthew Butler was surprised by Federal cavalry while he was sleeping in a home in Fayetteville. He threw on his hat, boots, and overcoat, and rode away in a hail of gunfire. Butler did not make fun of Kilpatrick.

Lieutenant General Wade Hampton, commander of Confederate cavalry, was also surprised by the Federals when they rode into downtown Fayetteville. At least Hampton was wearing his uniform. Hampton and seven others stumbled across a sixty-eight-man Federal scouting party that had found its way into the city undetected. Hampton's tiny force killed eleven Federals and captured twelve in fighting on the crowded city street. Hampton himself was said to have killed two of the Federals.

There was not much more fighting to save Fayetteville. The Confederates burned the bridge over the Cape Fear River and evacuated the city. Fayetteville was surrendered on March 11, 1865. Within a day, Sherman ordered the destruction of the arsenal, all railroad property, factories, warehouses, and all but one of the city's mills. Sherman also destroyed the offices of the town's three newspapers, which had supported the war effort. Most of the town's private homes escaped the flames. By March 15, Sherman was on the move again in two main columns. On the right were the 17th and 15th Corps, called the Army of the Tennessee. It was under the command of Major General Oliver O. Howard. On the left were the 14th and 20th Corps, called the Army of Georgia, under Major General Henry Slocum.

At times during the army's march through the state, there was a day's march between the two columns. Confederate General Johnston found that interesting—and tempting.

Johnston's problem was that he did not know where Sherman was heading. The Federals either planned to attack Raleigh, the state capital, or Goldsboro, an important railhead that the Federals had been trying to capture for more than two years.

Johnston chose to wait at Smithfield, a small town between Raleigh and Goldsboro, until Sherman made the direction he was heading in obvious. Johnston ordered Confederate General Braxton Bragg to send his troops moving from Wilmington to Smithfield. Meanwhile, Confederate Lieutenant General William J. Hardee was slowly retreating toward Smithfield with his troops. Hardee had defended Savannah, Georgia, against Sherman's attack on that city before retreating. As Sherman advanced north from Savannah, Hardee continued to retreat through Charleston, Columbia, and the rest of South Carolina.

Hardee stopped his retreat on March 15, 1865, near Averasboro, a small community north of Fayetteville. Though he had less than six thousand men to face more than thirty thousand Federal soldiers, Hardee intended to slow Sherman's advance and to determine the eventual destination of the Federals.

On the morning of March 16, Hardee's men rushed from their earthworks to attack Kilpatrick's dismounted cavalrymen. The Federals were pushed back for awhile until artillery fire and reinforcements drove the Confederates back to their second line of trenches. The Federals attacked the trenches all day but failed to dislodge the Confederates. Hardee held his ground until that night, when he withdrew toward Smithfield. More than a 100 Federals were killed and 500 were wounded, compared to 450 casualties for the Confederates.

That was a heavy loss of manpower for Hardee, but he had gained valuable information. The troops Hardee fought were from Sherman's left wing under Slocum. While the Battle of Averasboro was raging, Sherman's right wing under Howard continued marching northeast, rather than swinging northwest toward Raleigh. This troop movement showed the Confederates that Goldsboro was Sherman's target.

Because it had not stopped to help the left wing at Averasboro, the Federal right wing was now nearly a day's march ahead. The two halves of Sherman's army were separated; the break Johnston had been hoping for was here. The Confederate general hoped to smash Sherman's left wing in an ambush before the right wing could march back to provide help.

Three days later and about twenty miles north of Averasboro, Johnston tested his idea near Bentonville, a small hamlet just north of the Goldsboro Road. Sherman's right wing had already passed by on the New Goldsboro Road, four miles southeast of the Goldsboro Road.

The plan was risky at best. Johnston had just eighteen thousand, dog-tired, hungry men and boys to face the thirty thousand men of Slocum's left wing. What Johnston did have was surprise. He deployed his men along the road to Goldsboro and ordered the Confederate cavalry to harass and slow the Federals until all of the Confederates in the area could group at the site of the ambush.

The cavalry accomplished its goal, and on the night of March 18, 1865, the Federals camped on the ground where Johnston had hoped they would. If Johnston's plan worked, the Federals would march down the Goldsboro Road past heavy woods the next day. The Federals would find the road blocked by a hook-shaped defensive line in front of them. In the woods would be more Confederates ready to sweep in behind the Federals.

The Federals did not suspect that anything other than some cavalrymen were in front of them. Sherman himself told his staff that Johnston was concentrating his army near Raleigh, and that there would be no battle in North Carolina for several weeks, if then. Sherman was so confident the Confederates were nowhere nearby that he left the left wing and rode ahead to catch up with the right wing.

The Battle of Bentonville opened slowly on Sunday, March 19. Federals of the 14th Corps pushed forward, thinking they were facing a few Confederate skirmishers. They were really facing Confederate Major General Robert F. Hoke's experienced division, who had recently evacuated Wilmington. With Hoke was the North Carolina Junior Reserves, boys aged sixteen and younger who had little military training. Some of the advancing Federals moved to their left, thinking they would outflank the Confederates. Instead, they ran into the last remnants of the Army of Tennessee, who fired into the Federals from a range of less than fifty feet. (In 1862, the Confederate Army of Tennessee numbered more than forty-two thousand men. Three years later it could muster no more than eight thousand. The Confederate Army of Tennessee, named after the state, is not to be confused with Sherman's right wing, called the Army of the Tennessee, after the river.)

Johnston had not been ready for the Federal attack. Most of Hardee's command, slowed by muddy roads and a map that was not drawn to scale, was still coming up from the west when the battle started. A rattled Braxton Bragg, seeing the first of Hardee's men arrive, confronted Johnston and demanded that the soldiers be sent to reinforce Hoke on the far left of the Confederate line.

Johnston, frazzled by Bragg's begging, sent the troops (Confederate Briga-dier General Lafayette McLaws's division) without asking Hoke if he needed help. Hoke didn't. McLaws made it to Hoke's position on the left as the Federals were falling back. McLaws's men, who could have been better used in a counterattack from the Confederate center, were now out of place. Bragg, whose poor field decisions lost many major battles for the Confed-erates, once again caused a major mistake.

At this point in the battle, three Confederate soldiers sprang from their lines and ran to the Federals. They explained that they were really cap-tured Federals who had joined the Confederates in hopes of getting close to Federal lines again. They told Slocum that he was facing all of Johnston's Confederate army, not just a few regiments. Slocum thought they were lying, until an officer recognized one of the Confederates as a friend from Syracuse, New York.

With this new information, Slocum sent for the 20th Corps, which was six miles behind him. He also dashed off a note to Sherman and the right wing, describing the pitched battle. (Earlier, he had sent Sherman a note downplaying the engagement in the belief he was facing far fewer Confed-erates than he actually was.) Finally, at 2:00 P.M., the rest of Hardee's com-mand arrived. Johnston was finally ready to engage the confused Federals, who had not fought a full-scale battle since July 1864.

At 2:45 P.M., the last great Confederate charge of the war began when Hardee's men surged forward with flags flying and men lustily shouting the rebel yell. In one sense it must have been very thrilling. In another, it must have been terribly sad.

One Confederate, held in reserve, described the charge: "Several officers led the charge on horseback across an open field in full view, with colors flying and line of battle in such perfect order as to be able to distinguish the several field officers in perfect place. It was gallantly done, but it was painful to see how close their battle flags were together, regiments scarcely larger than companies and the division not much larger than a regiment should be."

Since the Federal 20th Corps had not yet reached the field, the 14th Corps was outnumbered two-to-one by the Confederates. Used to robbing old men of pocket watches instead of facing shooting soldiers, the Federals' left flank crumbled.

Hardee's Confederates then turned their attention to the forty-seven-hundred-man division of Union General James D. Morgan. Morgan's men were entrenched behind a log breastwork in front of Hoke's line. Hoke's division was ordered by Bragg to join the attack on the Federal breastwork in a frontal assault. Despite the attack from two directions, Morgan's men held out until reinforcements arrived, foiling the Confederates' best opportunity to roll up the Union line.

While the Confederates concentrated on attacking Morgan's little log fort, the 20th Corps arrived to rebuild the Union's left flank. Once they arrived, they dug trenches to repel any Confederate attack. When the Confederates attacked the left flank again, the Federals were ready for them. Every available man was in the trenches, including the headquarters guard, whose usual duty was saluting officers. As darkness fell on March 19, the Confederates withdrew.

At 9:30 P.M. that night, about twenty miles away, Sherman learned that Johnston had come very close to destroying half of his army. Sherman was not pleased. He ordered the right wing to the rescue. Johnston's surprise and numerical advantage were now gone.

Little happened on March 20 except for some heavy skirmishing that went in favor of the Confederates. During the night, Johnston redeployed his men closer to Mill Creek, a swollen creek with just one bridge. Johnston could have escaped with his army on the nights of March 19 or March 20, but he refused to leave his wounded men on the battlefield. He was determined to stay until they were safe.

Sherman, who had finally arrived at Bentonville, sat in his headquarters tent and wondered why Johnston had not escaped when he had the chance. As he had been at Averasboro, Sherman seemed almost passive. Instead of attacking and crushing Johnston's army, which he knew was hurting, Sherman was content to wait and see what would happen.

One of Sherman's men was not content to wait. He was Major General Joseph Mower, a career soldier who joined the army as a private in 1846. In February, Mower had, without orders, sent his men into the swamps of South Carolina to try to capture Broxton Bridge on the Salkahatchie River.

On March 21, Mower waited all morning for something to happen. When it didn't, he made something happen on his own. To the surprise of everyone else in the Union army, Mower's division tried to seize the Mill Creek bridge, a bold move that would have cut off the Confederate retreat.

The Confederates, lulled by a day and a half of inaction, were surprised. Mower pushed deep into the Confederate lines. Then, led by General Hardee himself, eighty members of the 8th Texas Cavalry counterattacked the Federals. Reports say the Texans "held their reins in their teeth and a pistol in each hand." Mower's advance was slowed by the Texans, who had just signed up sixteen-year-old Willie Hardee, the general's son, fresh from a Georgia military school. Within minutes, more Confederate cavalry attacked Mower's right and rear, and a Georgia infantry regiment attacked the Federals from the front. Mower pushed to within two hundred yards of Johnston's headquarters before he pulled back with heavy losses.

Among the Confederate wounded was Willie Hardee. He died three days later at a field hospital in Hillsborough, North Carolina. One of the men who sent his regrets to General Hardee was Union Major General Oliver O. "Old Prayer Book" Howard. Howard had taught Willie in Sunday school at West Point.

The night of March 21, Johnston pulled the rest of his army back across Mill Creek and headed toward Smithfield and Raleigh. Twenty-five hundred Confederates were killed and wounded in the battle, compared to Federal losses of fifteen hundred. The Battle of Bentonville accomplished little more than slowing the Federal advance for three days. While the plan was sound, its goal was little more than a pipe dream of a dying Confederacy. Even if Johnston was able to destroy Sherman's left wing, he still would have had to face a very experienced right wing, which would have still outnumbered him more than three to one.

Sherman did not escape unscathed from Bentonville. He was criticized by Washington politicians for allowing a beaten enemy to escape. Sherman shrugged off the criticism. He said his men were tired and in need of rest and new equipment. Their uniforms were in tatters, their ammunition was wet. He knew Joe Johnston was not going far. He could meet and beat him again if necessary. The tour starts in downtown Fayetteville at the Market House, on the intersection of Person and Gillespie Streets. To reach the Market House from Business I-95, take Exit 40 from the south or Exit 56 from the north, both exits lead to downtown Fayetteville. The Market House is easy to find. It sits in the middle of the intersection, and all traffic has to circle around it.

Built in the center of North Carolina's plank-road system, the Market House was constructed in 1832. It was built on the site of the old State House, which was destroyed by a fire in 1831. Before the war, slaves were occasionally auctioned at the Market House when an estate had to be settled or a large debt paid.

Confederate Lieutenant General Wade Hampton and his small band fought with the advance guard of Federal cavalrymen at this spot. Federal bullets crashed into the northwest pillars of the Market House. Confederate bullets crashed into Federals. At least eleven Union soldiers died in this area under the pistols and sabers of Hampton and his staff.

Drive past the Market House to the northwest on Person Street, which becomes Hay Street. Cross Robeson Street and take the next left onto Bradford Street, about 1.0 mile from the Market House. The Museum of the Cape Fear is one block down Bradford Street on the right.

To reach the Fayettevile Arsenal site, walk behind the museum and cross a footbridge over the Central Business District Loop highway. Construction on the arsenal began in 1837 and continued until 1842. By the 1840s, officials in Washington were beginning to rethink the need for an arsenal in the city and downgraded it from a production facility to one that would only store arms.

In April 1861, the North Carolina militia captured the arsenal without a fight from the Federal authorities. Arms-producing equipment captured from the arsenal at Harper's Ferry, Virginia, was shipped to the arsenal in Fayetteville. For the rest of the war, the Fayetteville arsenal was used to manufacture, repair, and modernize muskets. Sherman burned it to the ground on March 11, 1865. Today, only the building's foundations remain. The structure of one of the building's towers has been recreated to give visitors an idea of the size of the original building.

The Museum of the Cape Fear covers the whole history of the region, and includes three display cases on Fayetteville during the war. Two Fayetteville muskets are displayed, as is a Henry rifle captured from the Federals. The personal history and tintype of a Fayetteville soldier who lost his arm at the Battle of Cedar Creek and later drowned in the Cape Fear River gives poignancy to the war.

Return to Hay Street and turn left. Cross over Business U.S. 401 (the Central Business Loop), then take the first left onto Myrover Street. Drive one block to Arsenal Street. Turn right onto Arsenal Street. Arsenal Street soon becomes Raeford Road. Drive west on Raeford Road about 2.5 miles to McPherson Church Road. There is a historic marker there for Lieutenant General Theophilus H. Holmes. Turn right, or northwest, onto MacPherson Church Road. Drive northwest about 1.5 miles to Cliffdale Road. Turn right onto Cliffdale Road. Drive about 100 yards to MacPherson Church on the right, at 3525 Cliffdale Road. Holmes is buried in the churchyard near the church wall.

Theophilus Holmes was one of North Carolina's least publicized, least skilled, and highest ranking generals during the Civil War. An 1829 graduate of West Point, Holmes was a classmate of Robert E. Lee. It is doubtful that Lee had much respect for him at the time. Lee graduated second in that class, while Holmes graduated forty-fourth, out of forty-six cadets. Still, Holmes must have worked hard. He held the rank of major when he resigned from the United States Army in 1861. Lee was only one rank ahead, lieutenant colonel.

Holmes climbed quickly in rank in the Confederacy, probably due to the fact that President Jefferson Davis was a 1828 West Point graduate and a good friend. Holmes was a lieutenant general, just short of a full general, by October 1862.

High rank, however, does not make one a good general. Holmes proved to be a poor field commander and was shuttled off to command the Trans-Mississippi Department, where he also proved to be a poor strategist. He was transferred to Arkansas, then back to North Carolina, where he was given a nice, out-of-the-way command in charge of all reserves. He became a farmer after the war. He died in 1880, surviving classmate Lee by 10 years.

Retrace your route to Hay Street and follow it back to the Market House. At the Market House, turn north on Green Street, which becomes Ramsey Street in three blocks. Drive north on Ramsey Street, or U.S. 401 North. About 3.3 miles from the Market House, turn into the Veteran's Administration Hospital on the right side of Ramsey Street. On the grounds of the hospital are the remains of Confederate earthworks, running from Ramsey Street toward the hospital building. These earthworks were never used by the Confederates, as the city was attacked from the south side, not the north.

Retrace your route on Ramsey Street toward the Market House. At the intersection of Ramsey and Person Streets turn east onto Person Street to leave Fayetteville. In about 0.75 mile, turn north onto U.S. 301/Business I-95 North. Business I-95 North will merge with I-95 North at Exit 56.

Drive approximately 9 miles north on I-95 to the Godwin/Fountain exit, Exit 65. After exiting, turn left, or northwest, onto N.C. 82. Follow N.C. 82 past the U.S. 301 intersection. N.C. 82 will turn north. About 0.6 mile after turning north, slow down. At the intersection of N.C. 82 and West Road, or S.R. 1801, is a large historic marker with a map describing the opening of the Battle of Averasboro. When heading north, the marker will be on the left on a slight curve. Drive slow so you don't miss it. There is a small dirt parking lot at the marker.

The map on the marker is a good tool to study the battle, which was not very complicated. On March 15, 1865, the Confederates started fighting near this spot, then pulled straight back over a distance of about two miles. One of the Confederates captured at this battle was Colonel Alfred Rhett. Rhett had mistaken the Federal cavalry for Confederate cavalry units. He was about to put the soldiers on report for disrespectful language when he realized they were Yankees. Rhett was the son of Robert Barnwell Rhett, the editor of the Charleston *Mercury* newspaper who had pushed for war for more than a decade. When the Federals discovered that, there was some talk of doing something more with Colonel Alfred Rhett than sending him to the rear as a captive. (See The Sea Islands Tour for more information on the Rhetts.)

Look down West Road at the white, two-story house about 200 yards away. It was used as a Federal hospital. Drive 2 miles north on N.C. 82 to the second map marker for the battle, in a small cemetery called Chicora. As you drive down N.C. 82, you will be passing over the location of two other Confederate earthworks used in the battle. Historic markers showing the exact locations of these earthworks have been stolen. At Chicora Cemetery, where fifty-five Confederates rest, are monuments to both North and South Carolina units.

Drive north on N.C. 82 another 0.6 mile to see Lebanon, the home of Farquhard Smith, which was used as a Confederate hospital. Smith's daughter, eighteen-year-old Janie, later wrote that "the blood lay in puddles in the grove, the groans of the dying and the complaints of those undergoing amputation was horrible."

After the battle, the Federals pillaged the house. Miss Janie wrote: "If I ever see a Yankee woman I intend to whip her and take the clothes off her back. I want desolation carried to the heart of their country; the widows and orphans left starving, just as ours were."

Retrace your route on N.C. 82 back over I-95. Follow N.C. 82 southeast about 4.5 miles from I-95 to its intersection with U.S. 13. Turn left, or northeast, onto U.S. 13 and drive approximately 20 miles to Newton Grove. In Newton Grove, drive around the traffic circle to pick up U.S. 701 heading north. Drive 2.3 miles north on U.S. 701 to S.R. 1008. Turn right onto S.R. 1008. A brown sign will point the way to the Bentonville Battlefield site. The state historic site headquarters and museum is on the left, 2.6 miles away. S.R. 1008 is the Goldsboro Road, the road the Sherman's left column marched down in March 1865.

The museum is located next to the Harper House, which was used as a Federal hospital during the battle. More than five hundred Federal wounded and some Confederates were treated at the house. During the battle, one of Sherman's surgeons matter-of-factly commented that he could always tell when he was removing the leg of a cavalryman instead of an infantryman.

Lebanon

The legs of the horsemen were always thin and weak, while hundreds of miles of marching made the legs of infantrymen muscular. He threw both muscular and skinny legs out the windows of the house when he amputated them. Written reports say the pile reached the height of the window.

Interior of Harper House

While many people visit the museum, the house, and the reconstructed trenches across the road, tourists often leave without touring the actual battlefield. Almost all of the Battle of Bentonville took place east of this location. The vast majority of the battlefield's land is in private hands and is under cultivation. A battlefield preservation group raises money to purchase private land to add to the state historic site. Several years ago, Bentonville was named as one of top ten battlefields in the nation under pressure from private development.

The small museum details the Battle of Bentonville and has some artifacts from the battle. The Harper House has three rooms set up as operating rooms. The house is normally locked, but site managers will open it on request.

For some reason, Bentonville and the Harper House have more than their share of ghost stories. Though the site manager says he has never seen anything unusual, many people who claim to be sensitive to paranormal

Harper House

activity have experienced such events at the Harper House. Some claim to have seen stern-looking Mr. Harper standing at the top of the stairs. Others have seen surgeons sawing away limbs.

During the 1930s, two hunters swore that they saw the battle reenacted before them. Much more recently, a reenactor was standing guard on the road when he was surprised by a Federal regiment marching out of the darkness. The officer leading the men did not even look at the sentry when the column smartly turned off the road and headed into the woods. The reenactor, used to seeing his fellow weekend hobbyists sporting beer bellies, was impressed with the battle-hardened, lean look of the Union men. The next morning, he went into the woods to find out who these rough-looking, Yankee reenactors were. The woods where the regiment had marched were empty.

After getting spooked by the creaky floors of the Harper House, cross S.R. 1188 to view the monuments and inspect the reconstructed earthworks. More than 360 unidentified Confederate soldiers were buried on the battlefield. Most of the wounded were carried by rail to hospitals in Goldsboro, Greensboro, High Point, and Hillsborough, where Willie Hardee died. Some original earthworks, constructed by the First Michigan engineers, survive in the woods behind the reconstructed earthworks. A trail leads to them.

At the museum, ask for a driving-tour map of the battlefield, or buy the inexpensive, but detailed, book about Bentonville. The back of the book has a map of the battlefield and details all of the state markers found along the tour.

Continue east on S.R. 1008. In 1865, the village of Bentonville was about three miles northeast of the park. Even then, it was not much more than a general store and a carriage shop with some surrounding houses. About 0.6 mile after leaving the museum parking lot is a marker for the location of twenty-six Federal cannons. These cannons helped check the Confederate attack on the first day of the battle.

At 0.9 mile after leaving the museum parking lot is the location where Confederates attacked Federal positions five times, finally breaking the Union line. Union reinforcements from the 20th Corps crossed the road and drove the Confederates back.

At 1.6 miles after leaving the museum parking lot is the Cole farmhouse. This was the location of heavy fighting on March 19th. Just south of this point was General Morgan's log breastworks, where his Federal division successfully defended against Hoke's and Hardee's Confederate divisions. Also near this point is the location of the first Federal counterattack, led by Brigadier General W. P. Carlin.

Just past this point, at 1.8 miles from the museum parking lot, was the location of Hoke's original line. The line extended from the south, across the road, then turned northwest in a rough, hook shape.

Continue on S.R. 1008 to the intersection with S.R. 1194. Turn left, or northeast, onto S.R. 1194. At the northwest corner of this intersection is a marker for the first Union attack. To the north of that marker is one for the Junior Reserves.

Turn back to the right onto S.R. 1009, the next paved road. This road may not be marked. The Federals advanced as far as this road on the afternoon of March 21. Continue on this road until it intersects with S.R. 1008 again. Turn left, or east, onto S.R. 1008. This is the location where Sherman's left and right wings reunited on March 20, meaning that Johnston no longer had any chance of winning the battle.

Drive 0.7 mile on S.R. 1008 to S.R. 1197, the next road to the left. Turn left onto S.R. 1197, or Bentonville Road. Sherman's headquarters when he arrived on the night of March 20 was four hundred yards to the southeast of this intersection.

Drive 0.3 mile north on S.R. 1197. This was where the Union 17th Corps, commanded by Major General Francis P. Blair Jr., was stationed during the battle. Blair's father, Francis P. Blair Sr., had once offered command of the United States Army to Robert E. Lee. The offer was made in Blair House, today's official guest house of the President of the United States, located across the street from the White House.

At 1.1 miles after turning onto S.R. 1197, turn right onto S.R. 1199. This is a dirt road. At the corner of this intersection is a misplaced marker describing how General William J. Hardee himself led the 8th Texas Cavalry against Mower's Federals. The marker should be another 0.2 mile up S.R. 1197. After 0.3 mile on S.R. 1199, turn left, or north, onto another dirt road called Westbrook Road, or S.R. 1198. This is the same dirt road that Mower used to attack the Confederates. Mower's men pushed hard, even those without shoes. Those under-equipped men had been ordered to stay back, but they refused.

When this dirt road runs into the paved road, follow it until it intersects with S.R. 1009. Turn right, or north, onto S.R. 1009 and drive to the bridge over Mill Creek. The original bridge was to the right of the present-day bridge. Johnston's whole army crossed over this rain-swollen creek on the night of March 21, 1865. After the battle, residents found several mutilated Federal cavalrymen hanging upside down from trees in this area. This was a common retaliation of Wheeler's Confederate cavalrymen. Ghost hunters have reported seeing bodies in the same swamps through the years.

Turn around at Mill Creek Bridge and head south on S.R. 1009. When it intersects with S.R. 1008, turn right and retrace your route to the Harper House. The entire Bentonville battlefield encompasses more than six thousand acres, not much smaller than Gettysburg. However, less than two percent of the battlefield is protected as a state historic site.

If you care to make a side trip, drive from S.R. 1008 back to U.S. 701. Turn south onto U.S. 701 and drive back to Newton Grove. At the intersection of U.S. 701 and N.C. 55, turn west onto N.C. 55 and follow it to the intersection with I-40. Get on I-40 East. Drive about 32 miles on I-40 East and take Exit 373 to N.C. 903. Drive 3.2 miles east on N.C. 903 until it intersects with N.C. 11. Turn left, or north, onto N.C. 11 and drive 1.7 miles to Kenansville. Kenansville was the site of a factory where the Confederates manufactured knives and swords. Nothing is left of the factory today. Just before entering downtown Kenansville on N.C. 11, watch for Liberty Hall and the Cowan Museum on the right.

Liberty Hall was the 1850s plantation of the Kenan family. Thomas Kenan was a United States congressman before the war. His son, Owen Rand, served as a Confederate major and a Confederate congressman. The grounds have been restored to give visitors a feel for the antebellum time period. The Cowan Museum next door has a wide collection of tools used by people before and after the Civil War.

This concludes The Bentonville Battle Tour.

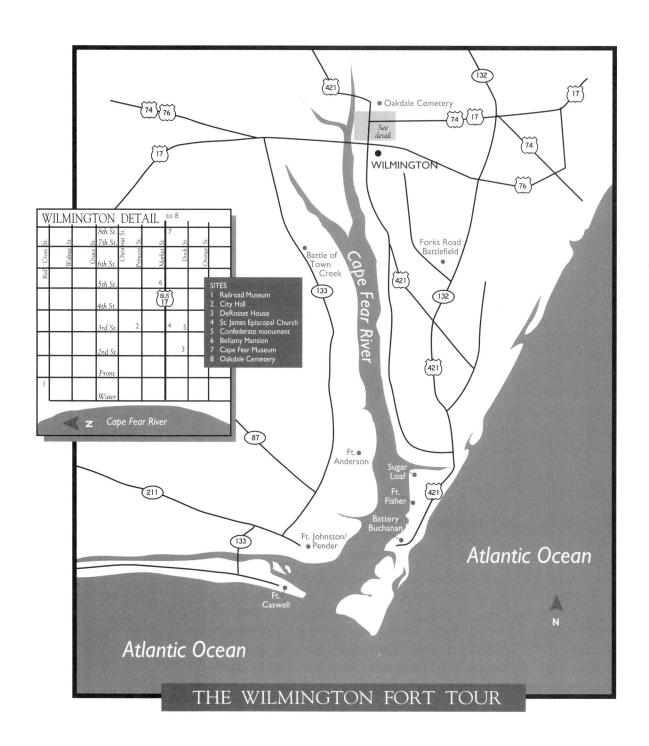

WILMINGTON DETAIL   to 8

	Red Cross St.	Walnut St.	Grace St.	Chestnut St.	Princess St.	Market St.	Dock St.	Orange St.	
8th St.							7		
7th St.									
6th St.									
5th St.						6			
4th St.						BUS 17			
3rd St.			2			4	5		
2nd St.							3		
Front									
Water									
1									

SITES
1 Railroad Museum
2 City Hall
3 DeRosset House
4 St. James Episcopal Church
5 Confederate monument
6 Bellamy Mansion
7 Cape Fear Museum
8 Oakdale Cemetery

N   Cape Fear River

421

132

17

74 76

74 17

17

See detail

● Oakdale Cemetery

WILMINGTON

74

76

● Battle of Town Creek

● Forks Road Battlefield

Cape Fear River

133

421

132

87

421

Ft. ● Anderson

Sugar Loaf ●

Ft. ● Fisher

421

Battery ● Buchanan

211

133

Ft. Johnston/ ● Pender

Ft. ● Caswell

Atlantic Ocean

Atlantic Ocean

N

THE WILMINGTON FORT TOUR

The Wilmington
Forts Tour

This tour starts at the waterfront in downtown Wilmington, where blockade runners docked during the war. From there, it moves to several historic sites in the downtown area, including the Bellamy Mansion, which was occupied by a Federal officer and his tobacco-spitting wife. Also included are stops at the graves of a famous female Confederate spy and a general who sacrificed his own life to be with his men. The tour then moves to Fort Fisher, perhaps the strongest fort ever built on the American continent. The fall of this fort, followed by the fall of the city of Wilmington itself, doomed the Confederacy. The tour then moves across the Cape Fear River to visit Southport, Fort Caswell, and Fort Anderson, a fort that was captured by the Union Navy from the Union Army.

Total mileage: approximately 90 miles, including a ferry ride across the Cape Fear River. Allow at least two days to properly see everything in Wilmington, Fort Fisher, and the other forts in the area.

Virginia-centric Civil War historians spend virtually all their time reviewing the Union Army's four-year campaign to take Richmond. They study the endless procession of Federal commanders who moved toward Richmond from Manassas, from the Peninsula, from Bermuda Hundred, from Fredericksburg, from Chancellorsville, and from Petersburg. They analyze the strategies and tactics of Robert E. Lee, who skillfully maneuvered his outmanned and outgunned Army of Northern Virginia around the Union Army for more than three years. For most of the war, Lee's object was to keep between the Federals and their goal, the Confederate capital. To most casual Civil War historians, and many serious ones as well, the war was fought, won, and lost within a hundred miles of Richmond. However, Robert E. Lee himself would be the first person to admit that his Army of Northern Virginia couldn't have survived more than a few months without the port city of Wilmington, North Carolina.

Wilmington is located on the Cape Fear River, twenty-five miles north of where the Cape Fear empties into the Atlantic Ocean. In 1860, Wilmington was North Carolina's largest city, with almost 10,000 residents (5,200 whites, 3,800 slaves, and 600 free Blacks). The Cape Fear River connected Wilmington with other eastern North Carolina cities. For example, a daily steamship service connected Wilmington and Fayetteville. Steamships also made regular runs from Wilmington to close ports like Charleston, and far away places like New York City. The main prewar exports from Wilmington were "naval stores" such as turpentine, tar, and resin, as well as the South's two leading crops, cotton and rice. Goods imported into the city covered a broader scale, including agricultural implements, fine china, and the latest in European fashions for both men and women.

Once imported goods were unloaded at Wilmington's waterfront, they could be moved easily throughout the whole South by three different railroad lines that terminated in the city. The Wilmington, Charlotte & Rutherford Railroad, still under construction in 1860, cut directly west through the state's interior to the mountains. The Wilmington & Manchester Railroad connected Wilmington to Charleston and Columbia, South Carolina. However, the most important railroad in the city, the state, and the whole Confederacy was the Wilmington & Weldon Railroad. The 161-mile line, one of the nation's longest at the time, began in Wilmington and terminated in Weldon, a small town on the Roanoke River not far from the Virginia state line. (Today, Weldon is located near Roanoke Rapids, North Carolina.) By the end of the war, the Wilmington & Weldon Railroad line was one of the most crucial supply links in the South.

While the Cape Fear River was deep enough for any ship, reaching Wilmington required the skill of an experienced pilot. There were only two channels leading from the Atlantic Ocean to the city and many dangerous passages along the way. The main channel was the Old Inlet to the southwest, which was bordered by Oak Island on the west and Smith Island on the east. The main hazard on the Old Inlet was a treacherous reef called Frying Pan Shoals, located just off of Smith Island on Cape Fear. The New Inlet, formed in 1761 when a hurricane cut through the Federal Point Peninsula, was more shallow than the main channel, but fine for all but the largest ships. The river pilots lived in Smithville (today's more picturesque-sounding Southport). When ships pulled close to the river, the pilots would sail out and safely guide them over the shifting sand bars. Period photos show the pilots to be a rangy, rowdy bunch. Nevertheless, they were crucial to the operation of the port.

When the war started, and President Lincoln announced the blockade of Southern ports, Wilmington was not an immediate target of the small Federal fleet. The larger cities of Savannah, Georgia, and Charleston attracted most of the attention. The first Federal blockading ship did not arrive off Wilmington until July 21, 1861, two months after the other cities.

As the war progressed, however, it became clear to both sides that Wilmington was more important than they first believed. The city was 150 miles closer to the Virginia front than Charleston, 225 miles closer than Savannah. The Wilmington & Weldon Railroad was a direct supply line to the Confederate Army, allowing arms, ammunition, medicines, shoes, blankets, uniform cloth, and other war material to be in Confederate hands within a few days of their arrival at the port.

To keep this supply line open, Wilmington's port and railroad had to be protected from invading Federal forces and blockading ships. Two old forts, Fort Caswell on Oak Island, and Fort Johnston on the Cape Fear River shore in Smithville, were already in place to protect Old Inlet. They had been captured from Federal forces just before North Carolina seceded.

Nothing protected the New Inlet, so construction began in summer 1861 on Fort Fisher, a massive dirt fort on Federal Point. Fisher was not an enclosed fort. It was L-shaped, with the longest side facing the Atlantic Ocean and running south toward New Inlet. The shorter side cut across Federal Point from the Atlantic to the river. By the time Fort Fisher was finished, it was the largest, strongest fort on the American continent. The fort was made of dirt and sand (better for absorbing artillery rounds), and at points, its walls reached heights of forty feet.

Battery Buchanan, a smaller dirt fortification, was placed about a mile south of Fort Fisher at the edge of the New Inlet.

In 1863, the Confederates began construction of Fort Holmes on the other side of the Cape Fear River on Smith's Island (modern-day Bald Head Island). On Oak Island, another earth fort called Battery Campbell was constructed about a mile away from Fort Caswell. Several miles north of Smithville, on the west bank of the Cape Fear, was another large earth fort called Fort Anderson. It was designed to be the final defense of Wilmington should any Federal ships slip past the forts at the river's mouth.

All of the forts except Fort Anderson were constructed so they could shell Federal ships that chased blockade runners into the mouth of the Cape Fear River. The blockade runners were also protected by nature. Since Federal ships did not know the locations of the shoals around the inlets, they rarely chased blockade runners into the river. If blockade runners got close enough to come under the protection of the forts' guns, they had clear sailing into Wilmington.

By 1862, Wilmington and Charleston were the two most important ports for blockade runners. The Confederate Ordnance Bureau, entrusted with bringing in munitions, designated Wilmington as its official port of entry.

Researchers say more than a hundred blockade runners called Wilmington their "home port," although exact figures will never be known. The life of a blockade runner depended directly on the skills of the ship's pilot, captain, and crew. Some blockade runners were captured, run aground, or sunk on their first voyage. Others made dozens of trips, collecting huge profits by buying cotton at five cents a pound, then selling it at fifty cents a pound in foreign ports. Even higher profits were made by bringing in military goods and hard-to-get luxury items on the return trip. However, the risk was high. Eventually, as more and more Federal ships joined the blockade, nearly all of the blockade runners were caught. Federal Navy records show that over the four-year blockade, fifty blockade runners were captured, and another fifty-three were destroyed around the Cape Fear River.

Occasionally, blockade running was even dangerous for the townspeople of Wilmington. In the late summer of 1862, the steamer *Kate* docked in Wilmington, off-loading passengers sick with yellow fever. In three months, more than fifteen hundred cases of yellow fever were recorded. Nearly seven hundred people, 15 percent of the town's population, died. They were all buried in a section of Oakdale Cemetery that is still avoided by many locals today.

Although blockading Union ships was a constant presence for almost two years, Wilmington itself was not seriously threatened until Christmas Day 1864. On that day, after a heavy, day-long naval bombardment of Fort Fisher, Federal forces landed just north of the fort. The soldiers, under the command of Union Major General Benjamin Butler, reported that the fort seemed to have absorbed the Navy's shelling without any damage. Some captured Confederates told Butler's officers there was a large force of Confederate soldiers at the fort, waiting to pounce on the Federals. The news discouraged Butler enough to call off the attack. His army retired without even trying to attack Fort Fisher.

Two weeks later, the Federals returned, this time under the command of Brigadier General Alfred Terry. After failing to go through with the attack on Fort Fisher, Butler had been relieved of command. Yet another huge naval bombardment was unleashed against the fort's dirt walls. This time it had a greater effect. The fort's defenders were stunned by the day-long shelling. The Federals landed unopposed and attacked the fort. The fierce hand-to-hand fighting lasted for hours, as the outnumbered Confederates gave ground grudgingly. Finally, Fort Fisher was surrendered. With the fort's capture, the way to Wilmington, less than twenty miles away, was open for the Federals.

The Confederates in the city evacuated as quickly as they could, rather than try to mount a major defense. On February 22, 1865, one week after the fall of Fort Fisher, the final Confederate forces left Wilmington, and the first Federals arrived and accepted the surrender of the city. On March 14, 1865, the mayor of Wilmington ordered the city to celebrate the return of Federal rule. On April 1, 1865, Robert E. Lee, who could no longer depend on supplies from Wilmington to feed, clothe, and arm his troops, broke out of Petersburg, Virginia, in search of supplies. On April 9, 1865, Lee surrendered his exhausted, starving, and undersupplied Army of Northern Virginia.

The Wilmington Forts Tour starts at the heart of any blockade-running city, the waterfront. Begin the tour at the intersection of Market and Water Streets. There is a tourist information center here where visitors can get a street map of the city.

Drive north for five blocks on Water Street, away from Market Street along the water's edge, to imagine the hustle and bustle that occurred here during the war. The point on the docks where a tourist sternwheeler ties up today would have been where long, narrow steamships with twin sidewheels unloaded their cargo of muskets, artillery shells, uniform cloth, blankets, and luxury goods, like fine English china, during the war. These steamships had a very rakish appearance, with lines that seemed to lean

Wilmington waterfront where blockade runners would dock

backward in order to present a very low profile on the ocean. The smokestacks would telescope, allowing the captain to pull his profile down even lower on days when a calm sea provided no sheltering swells. The most resourceful captains had fuel loads of anthracite coal, which burned hotter and with less smoke than softer bituminous coal. Smoke on the ocean was always a giveaway to Federal lookouts searching the horizon.

While the life of a blockade runner sounds exciting, the lives of the townspeople were not made better by the sudden burst of commerce. The corporations that owned the blockade runners used Wilmington strictly as a port, moving most of the goods quickly inland rather than storing them in town. Sailors, speculators, war profiteers, and prostitutes all flocked to the city, much to the horror of the established townspeople. One writer called Wilmington "the meanest city in the Confederacy."

The Wilmington Railroad Museum is at the intersection of Red Cross and Water Streets, five blocks north of Market Street. While the museum offers only a cursory history of the Wilmington & Weldon Railroad, which terminated a few blocks from the museum, it does offer a wall map showing the railroads in the state in the mid-nineteenth century. Construction of the Wilmington & Weldon Railroad began in 1834 and was completed in 1840. After going through several name changes, the line officially adopted the name Atlantic Coastline Railroad in 1900. Most of the displays relate to the growth of railroading during the early twentieth century.

Assuming you have driven to the Railroad Museum, leave the parking lot on Red Cross Street and drive east three blocks to Third Street. Turn right and drive four blocks to City Hall, 102 North Third Street, at the corner of Third Street and Princess Street. On the morning of February 22, 1865, Mayor John Dawson surrendered the city to Union Major General Alfred H. Terry on the steps of this building. The building is also the location of Thalian Hall, a playhouse that was called Wilmington Hall during the Civil War. The theater opened in 1858. In 1867, the theater was operated by John T. Ford, who had been unable to run Ford's Theater in Washington since the night President Lincoln was assassinated. Thalian Hall is haunted, but the ghosts are Victorian actors who like to watch present-day rehearsals, not Civil War soldiers.

Terry was probably in a good mood on the day he accepted the surrender of the city. A self-taught lawyer who dropped out of Yale once he passed the bar, Terry had no formal military training. He started the war as a colonel of militia from Connecticut. He was present at the first Federal defeat, at First Manassas in July 1861, and at the second Federal victory, the capture of Hilton Head in November 1861. Terry slowly worked his way up in the command structure. His career could have been over in December 1864, when he was part of General Butler's unsuccessful attempt to take Fort Fisher. However, two weeks later, he was put in charge of the second, successful attempt to take the fort. He was promoted to brigadier general in the regular United States Army just four days after the fall of Fort Fisher.

Terry was the first Civil War volunteer officer to attain the rank of major general of the United States Army, an accomplishment that was helped along in large measure by his capture of Fort Fisher and Wilmington. Making general in the "regular army" (as opposed to the large temporary army fielded during the Civil War) was quite an accomplishment for someone who had never been to West Point. In the Federal army, most civilian officers, no matter how good they were, were passed over for promotion in favor of professional officers, no matter how bad they were.

Terry would go on to a long career with the United States Army, although he would have to answer critics who charged he did not properly keep track of the actions of a brash colonel serving in his command in the Department of Dakota in 1876. That colonel was George Armstrong Custer.

In the same block as the City Hall, in a house now lost to time, John Ancrum Winslow was born in 1811. Winslow moved to Massachusetts in 1825. Two years later, at the age of sixteen, he joined the United States Navy as a midshipman. In 1846, he and a friend, Lieutenant Raphael Semmes, both lost their ships while blockading Mexico. The friends later served together on the USS *Cumberland*.

By 1862, Winslow was in command of the warship USS *Kearsarge*, with the duty of sailing the Atlantic to find and destroy Confederate raiders. In June 1864, he was in the Netherlands when he learned a Confederate raider, the CSS *Alabama*, was being refitted in Cherbourg, France. Winslow waited for the *Alabama* off the French coast, until the *Alabama*'s confident commander brought her out to do battle, much to the pleasure of French citizens who lined the bluffs to watch the sea battle.

It was not much of a fight. The *Alabama* was used to fighting merchant ships and whalers. More importantly, its gun powder was old and damp, making its guns no match for the cannons of Winslow's *Kersearge*. Within an hour, Winslow's gunners had shot the *Alabama*'s stern away, and the Confederate ship sank beneath the waves. The *Alabama*'s captain was picked up by an English sailing ship, and he lived to fight another day. The *Alabama*'s captain was Winslow's old messmate, Raphael Semmes. (University of Alabama football fans might not know that their cheer, "Roll, Alabama, Roll," is a line from a Civil War sea chanty describing the career of the Confederacy's greatest sea raider.)

After leaving City Hall, drive one block toward the river on Princess Street, then turn left, or south, onto Second Street. Pass through the Market Street intersection and drive one block to the DeRosset House, located at 23 South Second Street, on the northeast corner of Second and Dock Streets. The house was built in 1841 by Dr. Armand J. DeRosset III, a physician who also headed DeRosset & Company, a shipping company. According to some researchers, the company did its share of blockade running during the war. The house was the headquarters for Confederate General Braxton Bragg at the end of the war. Today, the house is the headquarters of the Historic Wilmington Foundation.

Retrace your route one block on Second Street to Market Street, turning right, or east, away from the river. Drive one block on Market Street to St. James Episcopal Church, built in 1839, which is on the southeast corner of Market and Third Streets. The rector of this church, Alfred A. Watson, was a diehard Confederate. When Union officers ordered him to pray for the President of the United States, Watson refused. His church was confiscated and used as a hospital.

Continue east on Market Street for three blocks to the Bellamy Mansion at 503 Market Street. Many consider this house both a symbol of the city of Wilmington and of the grandeur of the antebellum South.

The Bellamy Mansion was the home of Dr. John D. Bellamy and his wife Eliza. Construction began on the house in 1859. From the beginning, the Bellamy Mansion was intended to be the city's finest house. Constructed

Bellamy Mansion

using free Black and slave labor, the four-story, twenty-two-room house was finally finished and ready for occupancy in February 1861, two months after South Carolina seceded from the Union.

South Carolina's secession was just fine with the wealthy Bellamy, who in addition to his medical practice, owned a large turpentining operation run on slave labor. Bellamy was such a supporter of secession that he bankrolled a bonfire and torchlight parade through Wilmington on December 20, 1860, the night South Carolina seceded. When the new Confederate President Jefferson Davis passed through Wilmington on his way to Richmond, Dr. Bellamy was the head greeter.

At the age of forty-four, Bellamy considered himself too old to back up his Confederate support by actually marching into battle. His sons Marsden, eighteen, and Willie, seventeen, served in the cavalry and infantry.

The Bellamy family was only able to enjoy their mansion for a year before the yellow fever epidemic of 1862 sent them fleeing to Robeson County. The care of the empty house was entrusted to the slave cook, Sarah, while most of the furnishings were crated and shipped inland. The Bellamys

---

returned infrequently during the war, but Sarah must have done a masterful job, as the house was spared from any damage.

After Wilmington's fall to Federal forces, Brigadier General Joseph Hawley, a division commander under Major General Terry, used the house as his headquarters. He liked the house so much that he invited his wife Harriet down from Connecticut to join him. Mrs. Hawley helped the general organize relief efforts around Wilmington.

Over the past 130 years, General Hawley and his wife have sustained a reputation for being "party animals." According to stories passed down through the years, the Bellamy mansion was used for numerous encounters between Union officers and prostitutes. Neighbors reported watching an officer and a prostitute chase each other around the second floor with the shutters open for all the world to see. At another party, a prostitute gave birth on the Bellamy's master bedstead.

When he was not carousing, Hawley did spend at least some time on official business. Though a native of North Carolina, Hawley had grown up in the North and was a staunch advocate of abolition. He spent much of his time trying to figure out ways to transfer the land of former slave holders to the freed Blacks. In the spring of 1865, he invited Supreme Court Chief Justice Salmon P. Chase to the Bellamy mansion to speak before four thousand freed slaves on their enfranchisement rights.

After the war, Bellamy and his wife tried talking the Hawleys into giving back the house. Mrs. Bellamy was shocked speechless when Mrs. Hawley "hawked and spit into the fire" during the course of their conversation. When sweet-talking the Hawleys did not work, Bellamy traveled to Washington to beg for a pardon and the return of his properties. After money changed hands between Bellamy and Union officials, he regained his house and his plantations.

When Bellamy and his wife produced the pardon at the house, the occupying Federal forces left within an hour. At least all but one did. When Mrs. Bellamy threw open an upstairs door, she found a naked woman who had been forgotten in the shuffle. When last seen, the nude woman was running down Market Street, trying to escape the wrath of Mrs. Bellamy.

The only lasting damages the Bellamys discovered from the six-month occupation of their house were tobacco-juice stains on the white marble fireplace mantles. By September 1865, the Bellamys and their ten children, including their Confederate soldier sons, were back in their grand house.

Today, three stories of the grand house are open for touring Thursdays through Sundays. One of the most unusual aspects of the house is the bright red-gold-and-blue carpet that was installed by the Bellamys. Also on the grounds, and undergoing restoration, is a two-story brick building in back of the mansion where the family's house slaves lived.

After leaving Wilmington and the Bellamy Mansion, Hawley enjoyed a meteoric postwar career. He was elected governor of Connecticut in 1866. He was then elected to the United States House of Representatives and spent fourteen years in the United States Senate, before dying in office in 1905. It just goes to show that some politicians can have a sordid past and come out all the better for it.

After leaving the Bellamy Mansion, proceed three blocks east on Market Street to the Cape Fear Museum at 814 Market Street. The museum originally opened in 1898. It was started by the United Daughters of the Confederacy as a way of honoring Confederate soldiers. In 1970, the museum moved to the National Guard Armory. In 1990, a new wing was added, and in 1992, the entire museum was reopened and rededicated to focus on the counties within a fifty-mile radius of Wilmington.

Inside the museum are two historical dioramas that vividly display the Civil War history of Wilmington. The diorama on the ground floor shows a typical day on the Wilmington docks as two blockade runners are unloaded. On the second floor, an eight-minute sound-and-light show dramatizes the Fort Fisher diorama. This show provides a great description of both the December 1864 and the January 1865 battles, and it should not be missed. Both dioramas are more than thirty years old, having once belonged to the now-defunct Blockade Runners Museum at Carolina Beach.

Civil War relics in the museum's collection include a sword belonging to Confederate Brigadier General W.H.C. Whiting. Originally manufactured with "USA" on the hilt, Whiting modified the letters to read "CSA." A musket picked up by a Federal soldier as a souvenir has this inscription carved into the stock: "Taken from the 2nd Battle of Ft. Fisher. Its owner, a Confederate soldier, was killed by a bullet to the head."

A newspaper display at the museum reads: "General Bragg's presence, wherever he has controlled, has been felt as a disaster, an omen of impending evil like a dark, cold, dreary cloud." That sentiment pretty much summed up the feelings of the citizens of Wilmington toward the Confederate commander they inherited in late 1864.

An outside display shows the gearing necessary to run paddlewheel steamboats.

After leaving the Cape Fear Museum, continue east on Market Street for 0.4 mile to the corner of Market Street and Fifteenth Street. Turn left, or north, on Fifteenth Street and proceed six blocks, or 0.2 mile, to Oakdale Cemetery.

If visiting during a weekday, it is best to stop at the office just outside the cemetery gate to obtain a map. Ask the staff for the section and grave numbers of the person being sought. And, before leaving, compare the small map against the large wall map in the office. Directions can be confusing in this huge cemetery because none of the crisscrossing paved and grass roads have been named. The office is open Monday through Friday, 9:00 A.M. to 12:00 noon and 1:00 P.M. to 4:00 P.M.

Drive into the cemetery and bear to the left, then turn right on the first paved road. Drive past two paved roads and stop in front of a grave marker for the Walker family on the right. Walk to the right of the Walker gravestone and past two grass roads until you reach the grave of Captain John Newland Maffitt, Confederate sea raider and blockade runner extraordinaire.

Fittingly born at sea in 1819, Maffitt joined the United States Navy as a midshipman at age thirteen. He was in the United States Navy for twenty-nine years, serving much of his duty on a coastal survey. This was knowledge that would come in handy when he joined the Confederate Navy in 1861, at age forty-two. Maffitt commanded the cruiser CSS *Florida*, which captured twenty-two Union merchantmen in 1863. He later became a blockade runner and commanded five ships, including the *Owl*, a ship he took into Wilmington, Charleston, and even Galveston, Texas. After the war, he became a novelist and a journalist. He died, on land, at age sixty-seven.

About a hundred yards to the north of Maffitt's grave is the mass burial of the victims of the 1862 yellow fever epidemic. On the cemetery map, every plot is marked except for this large blank section.

Get back in the car and continue on the paved road. Slow down as the paved road makes a slow sweeping turn to the left. A third paved road (counting from the cemetery entrance) intersects from the right. Just past that third paved road is a grass road. A gravestone for the Fonvielle family should be in sight. Stop here and walk to the right. Beside the grass road is the grave of Brigadier General John Decatur Barry.

Barry was a twenty-two-year-old graduate of the University of North Carolina when he was elected captain of the 18th North Carolina Regiment. The regiment saw much combat, but Barry stood the test, winning promotion to rank of major after Antietam. At Chancellorsville, his regiment's officer corps was decimated, and he was appointed colonel after the battle. In 1863, he led his men at Gettysburg. After his commanding general was wounded at Cold Harbor, Barry was named a brigadier general. However, he never got to take the field as general. He was wounded himself a few days later and his promotion was rescinded after his commander returned to duty.

Barry never really recovered from his wound. In 1867, he died at age twenty-seven, while making a living as a newspaper editor. There is a sadness to Barry's grave. He is buried all alone with no family around. A small tombstone carries an inscription that is attributed to Napoleon speaking about one of his generals. It reads: "I found him a pygmy and lost him a giant."

While time has forgiven the soldiers of the 18th North Carolina for their mistake, one has to wonder if Barry, who was the regiment's major at the time, ever forgave himself for what happened on the dark evening of May 2, 1863, in the woods around Chancellorsville, Virginia.

Told by brigade commanders they could consider any movement in front of them to be Union soldiers, the nervous men of the 18th North Carolina heard a column of galloping horsemen thundering down on top of them in the darkness. No orders were given, but one shot rang out. That was followed by a volley fired toward the riders. One of the riders shouted that they were "friends." An unidentified voice in the darkness said to ignore that comment and to fire another volley at the riders. A second volley was fired.

The rider most seriously hurt that night was Confederate Lieutenant General Thomas J. "Stonewall" Jackson, whose arm was shattered and later amputated. Eight days later, Jackson would die of pneumonia.

Walk to the left of Barry's grave, while staying on the paved road, and head towards a little "island" of graves bordered by grass roads. This is close to the paved road and the bridge leading to a cemetery annex. In the island is the family plot of Confederate Brigadier General William MacRae. His name does not appear on the tombstones, but cemetery records indicate he is there.

A descendant of Scottish soldiers who claimed ancestry back to the Crusades, MacRae was another officer who joined the Confederate Army as a private and worked his way up to general. His early service was with the 15th North Carolina Regiment.

MacRae was a fighter. He took in three hundred men at Malvern Hill and came out with thirty-five. Even knowing that serving under him was dangerous, MacRae's men were always inspired. One man said "no position was considered too strong to be assaulted if MacRae ordered it."

Although he had two different swords shot to pieces during battle, MacRae was wounded only once. He made a career as a railroad superintendent after the war and died in 1882.

Leaving MacRae's grave, get back into the car and turn left onto the outside paved road that circles the entire cemetery. Drive forward twenty yards, watching on the left for a brick mausoleum on a hill. This hill is about ten feet high, probably the tallest spot in the cemetery. Beside the mausoleum, almost on the edge of the hill, is a small, but prominent, white cross tombstone that reads: "Drowned off Ft. Fisher from the steamer *Condor* while attempting to run the blockade Sept. 30, 1864." Get out of the car and climb the hill to this tombstone.

The front of the tombstone reads: "Mrs. Rose O'N Greenhow, a bearer of dispatches to the Confederate government."

When the war started, Mrs. Greenhow was a wealthy, forty-five-year-old widow living in Washington City (now D.C.). Even as a teenager, the darkly attractive Rose seemed intrigued with power. She counted numerous congressmen, military officers, and even vice presidents like John C. Calhoun among her inner circle. By 1861, she was using the contacts she had built over thirty years into an effective spy network that many historians credit with supplying detailed knowledge of the Union Army's intentions at First Manassas. Mrs. Greenhow was good at collecting information but apparently lousy at concealing her identity as a spy. She was arrested in 1862, and deported to Richmond before she could be tried for treason.

The Confederacy sent Mrs. Greenhow to collect intelligence in England. She was returning to the Confederacy in 1864 when a blockading ship ran the *Condor* down near Fort Fisher. Fearing arrest again as a spy, Mrs. Greenhow tried to make shore in a small boat. The boat capsized, and she was dragged under by the weight of two thousand dollars in gold that she had sewed into her dress. Her body washed up on shore several days later, and she was given a hero's funeral. Someone still thinks of her that way. In 1995, her grave was decorated with a single artificial rose and a new Confederate flag.

Get back in the car and follow the outside road to the first paved intersecting road. Turn left, then turn left again at the next paved road. On the corner will be the grave of Confederate Brigadier General William H.C. "Little Billy" Whiting, the commander of Wilmington's Confederate forces during most of the war.

Graduating first in his 1845 class at West Point, the five-foot-two-inch (thus his nickname) Whiting posted the highest scholastic record ever received by a cadet up to that time. Whiting was a brilliant engineer and was credited with successfully getting General Joseph Johnston's army to First Manassas in time to defeat the Federals in July 1861. He accomplished the feat by skillfully scheduling trains and providing the Confederates with accurate maps of the area.

Whiting likely had the intelligence and nerve for a brilliant military career, but his reputation as a pessimist dogged him from the beginning of the war. Robert E. Lee got rid of Whiting by transferring him to Wilmington in 1862, with orders to improve Fort Fisher. Whiting, with the cooperation of his admiring subordinate, Colonel William Lamb, carried out that order with great success.

Whiting was given one more chance to prove himself as a field commander. In May 1864, he was assigned to fight with General P.G.T.

Mrs. Rose Greenhow's grave

Beauregard against Union Major General Benjamin Butler's forces during the Bermuda Hundred campaign south of Richmond. Accused of being drunk during the battles, Whiting requested his old post back at Wilmington. His request was granted.

Whiting spent the rest of the war strengthening Fort Fisher. Whiting told his men their survival depended on the strength of the fort. They believed him and built the dirt fort into what is likely the strongest fortification ever seen on the American continent.

In one final insult to Whiting's pride and career, he was relieved of Wilmington's command in October 1864. General Braxton Bragg, a close personal friend of President Davis but one of the least respected generals in all of the Confederacy, replaced Whiting. Bragg lost virtually every battle he ever commanded and gave up every city he was ever assigned to defend. Even the battles he won, like Chickamauga in September 1863, turned out badly because he consistently failed to follow up on advantages. When it was announced that Bragg would assume command at Wilmington, a Virginia newspaper printed this headline: "Goodbye Wilmington."

Whiting took his replacement in stride. While he could have asked to go home, he stayed at his post. When the final attack on Fort Fisher was imminent, Whiting rode from Wilmington to Fort Fisher. He brought a simple message to Colonel Lamb: "Lamb, my boy. I have come to share your fate. You and your garrison are to be sacrificed." While his rank entitled him to take over command of the fort, Whiting told Lamb he was there merely to advise, and Lamb remained in command.

During the attack on Fort Fisher on January 15, 1865, Whiting was shot while tearing down a Federal flag. He lingered for almost a month, dying in a prisoner-of-war camp on Governor's Island, New York. He was reburied in Oakdale in 1900.

After viewing Whiting's grave, retrace your route to the outside perimeter road and turn left, toward the front of the cemetery. At the fourth paved road after turning, turn left again. The bronze Confederate monument should be directly ahead. What is interesting about the monument is that the Confederate soldier is resting his wrist across the muzzle of his musket, a clear violation of safety measures. On top of that, the musket is at full cock. The statue soldier is about to blow his hand off. The paved road out of the cemetery is directly behind the Confederate statue. Retrace your route to Market Street and turn right, heading back toward the Cape Fear River. At Third Street, turn left, or southwest. Drive one block to the intersection of Third and Dock Streets.

At this intersection is a Confederate monument designed by Henry Bacon of Wilmington, who also designed the Lincoln Memorial in Washington, D.C. This statue is interesting because it is one of the few Confederate monuments to show a soldier in the actual act of combat. He is reaching into his cap box to cap his musket. Muskets are fired by first pouring a charge of gun powder down the barrel's muzzle. A musket ball is then dropped down and rammed on top of the powder using a ram rod. The soldier then puts a metal cap on a nipple located over the right side of the barrel's breech. When the musket's hammer strikes the cap, a small spark is fired through the breech, setting off the powder and sending the musket ball on its way. While the bronze soldier certainly looks heroic, he is doing it wrong. He is reaching into his cap box with his left hand, a very awkward maneuver since a musket's nipple is always on the right side. Even if a soldier was left-handed, he was taught to pull out a cap with his right hand.

In the same block of Third Street is a historic marker for a house once occupied by a Judah P. Benjamin. Benjamin was a United States senator who also served as Confederate attorney general and secretary of state. Raised in Charleston, Benjamin spent most of his adult life in Louisiana. His connection with Wilmington is very slight.

Proceed southwest on Third Street until it becomes U.S. 421 heading south. About 6.75 miles after leaving downtown, U.S. 421 will intersect N.C. 132, or College Road.

If you care to make a brief side trip, turn left, or north, onto N.C. 132. Drive 3.1 miles to the intersection with Seventeenth Street Extension. Turn left onto Seventeenth Street Extension and drive about 0.75 mile to the next street, Independence Boulevard. On the southeast corner of this intersection, on private land beside a housing development, is the site of Confederate earthworks. Confederate Major General Robert Hoke fought the Battle of Forks Road here before he evacuated Wilmington, and these earthworks were part of the Confederates' main defensive line. Few details of the battle are known, other than Hoke fought a holding action against a Federal force that included at least two thousand Black troops. The Federals advanced on the earthworks from the direction of N.C. 132. All signs of the Federal earthworks have disappeared under the housing development.

Retrace the route back down N.C. 132, past the intersection with U.S. 421, and proceed toward Carolina Beach State Park.

After passing over the Intracoastal Waterway, follow the brown signs for Carolina Beach State Park and turn right, or west, onto Dow Road. The entrance to the park is 0.2 mile south on Dow Road. Turn right onto Masonboro State Park Road. Follow this main road all the way to the parking lot on the Cape Fear River, passing a marina on the right. In the far southwest corner of the parking lot is the start of the mile-long walking trail to Sugar Loaf. Though flat, this walk through sand can be a moderately strenuous. Take water if going in the summer.

Sugar Loaf, a sixty-foot-tall dune of white sand, has been a landmark on the river since the 1760s. During the Civil War, Confederates used it as a camp and signal station. On January 15, 1865, General Robert Hoke and his twenty-two hundred troops were forced to watch and listen to the attack on Fort Fisher from Sugar Loaf. Wilmington's commander, General Braxton Bragg, would not allow Hoke's men to aid their comrades.

A round trip to Sugar Loaf takes at least forty-five minutes, but from the top of the dune, it is easy to imagine what Hoke must have been thinking as he watched the Federals swarming around Fort Fisher. Trenches remain hidden in the woods near the dune.

Sugar Loaf

After leaving Sugar Loaf, return to Dow Road and turn right, or south. At 1.8 miles from the parking lot, there is a warehouse on the right side of the road. A white United Daughters of the Confederacy marker is beside the warehouse, commemorating the men who served at Sugar Loaf.

At 1.0 miles from the United Daughters of the Confederacy marker, turn left, or east, onto Ocean Boulevard. Drive 0.8 mile to U.S. 421, also called Carolina Beach Road at this point. Turn right, or south, onto U.S. 421. The Atlantic Ocean will be just 100 yards to the east.

During the January 1865 attack on Fort Fisher, all of the land in this area would have been under Federal control. The Union landings took place about a mile north of this point, near a fresh-water, spring-fed lake that still exists. Continue driving south, past the Atmospheric Testing Center and a recreational area for the United States Air Force. Much of this area was clear-cut by the Confederates, both to provide lumber to build the bombproofs of Fort Fisher and to provide a clear field of fire against a land attack.

At 3.4 miles from the turn onto U.S. 421 is the entrance to Fort Fisher on the right side of the road. The first building actually encountered, on the north side of the parking lot, houses "Hidden Beneath The Waves," an underwater-archaeology exhibit detailing how divers uncover artifacts from shipwrecks. In front of the building is a cannon recovered from the USS *Peterhoff*, a Union blockading vessel that Federal forces claimed was accidentally sunk by a collision. Confederates claimed they sunk it using shore artillery. Inside the building are displays of artifacts recovered from sunken blockade runners. The closest one can sometimes be seen at extremely low tide off Carolina Beach near the fresh-water lake mentioned above.

The Fort Fisher Visitor's Center at the south end of the parking lot features a slide show explaining the fort's battles, artifacts recovered from the

Shepherd's Battery at Fort Fisher

site, items recovered from sunken ships, and how a Confederate "torpedo," or floating mine, washed up on the beach near Fort Fisher in '64—that is 1964, more than a hundred years after it was constructed and put in the ocean to sink Federal ships.

Both Union and Confederate commanders agreed that Fort Fisher was the best seacoast fortification ever constructed during the war. Although it lacked the grandeur of traditional, five-sided, brick forts like Fort Sumter in Charleston, or Fort Macon in Morehead City, North Carolina, and actually consisted of only two sides, Fort Fisher was remarkable in its strength and value to the Confederacy.

The fort's construction began in earnest in 1862. That year, Colonel William Lamb, a former lawyer and newspaper editor, was assigned to Wilmington to strengthen defenses protecting the Cape Fear River. Lamb was inspired by a book that described a gigantic earth fort built by the Russians during the Crimean War, and decided to recreate the fort on the North Carolina beach. The design was simple: the side of the fort facing the water was a mile-long, twenty-three-foot high wall. Twenty-four cannons would be positioned along the sea side. At the end of the wall was a mound battery soaring more than forty feet into the air, high enough for blockade runners to use as a landmark for finding the New Inlet. The land face, intersecting the sea face near the ocean, ran for a quarter mile from the ocean to the river behind it. The land face had twenty-three cannons, all aimed northward up the beach. This was where any land assault on the fort would occur since the fort was built near the end of Federal Point. The end of Federal Point was protected by the smaller Battery Buchanan. Built with slave, free Black, and soldier labor, Fort Fisher grew stronger with each wheelbarrow of dirt and sand dumped on its walls.

Military engineers had spent the previous fifty years preaching the value of brick forts, never dreaming that the advent of rifled cannons would make these expensive facilities obsolete overnight. A spinning cannon round could burrow deep within the bricks before exploding, possibly blowing a wall down with one shot. A fort built of dirt and sand, however, would absorb that round and cushion the explosion. A wall of sand was only affected by wind and rain, and a few wheelbarrows of sand replaced what nature swept away.

Although Fort Fisher was a formidable defense, Confederate Brigadier General William Whiting, commander of Wilmington, constantly requested reinforcements for his meager force of twenty-four hundred troops. Whiting knew he did not have enough men to defend one of the most strategic cities in the entire South. Knowing that his superiors did not like him, or even believe his warnings that Wilmington would be the object of Federal invasion, Whiting threw his energies into strengthening the city's defenses. It was lucky for the Confederacy that he did. By summer 1864, the Federals, fresh from taking Mobile Bay and heavily involved in besieging Charleston, were ready to turn their attention towards Wilmington.

Wilmington was in trouble, just as Whiting had warned over the past two years. The Confederate powerbrokers, including Robert E. Lee, suddenly realized that Whiting had not been crying wolf. They finally saw that Lee's army would be without its most vital supply line if Wilmington fell. Lee ordered Whiting to hold Wilmington and sent a division under Major General Robert F. Hoke for support.

However, Whiting's victory in finally getting the attention of Richmond was snatched from him. Whether true or not, Whiting carried the reputation of being a drinker and a poor battlefield commander. In October 1864, Whiting was replaced in overall command of Wilmington by Braxton Bragg.

The first attack against Fort Fisher began on December 23, 1864, and involved one of the silliest ideas the Union forces ever tried. Union Major General Benjamin Franklin Butler, a powerful Massachusetts politician who had wrangled command of the Department of Virginia and North Carolina, wanted to blow up Fort Fisher by sending a ship loaded with gunpowder close to the fort. Butler's "engineers" (the term is used loosely) suggested that blowing up three hundred tons of gunpowder could destroy everything within a quarter mile of the explosion, including the thick sand walls of the fort.

An old ship, the USS *Louisiana*, was loaded with 215 tons of black powder and towed to within 300 yards of Fort Fisher. Fuses were set, and the Federal fleet pulled back 12 miles from the fort so they would not be destroyed by the shock waves that were expected from the tremendous explosion. When the *Louisiana* blew up at 2:00 A.M. on December 24, 1864, it woke up the sleeping Confederates in Fort Fisher. That was all.

The real battle opened less than twelve hours later, when thirty Federal ships, mounting more than six hundred guns, opened fire on Fort Fisher's forty-seven guns. Records indicate the Federals fired more than ten thousand rounds at the fort, many of them absorbed in the forgiving sand. Fort Fisher fired less than seven hundred rounds in answer, mainly because the fort had less than four thousand rounds in stock. Lamb wanted to conserve his ammunition to keep any ships from running past him into the New Inlet.

Lamb noticed that the Federals seemed to be aiming at battle flags flying above the fort, so he lowered flags on the sea face and raised them on the far end of the land face. Just as he hoped, the Federal gunners shifted their aim to the flags they could see. Many of the Federal shells sailed harmlessly over the fort and landed in the Cape Fear River.

On Christmas Day 1864, Union Army troops landed about three miles north of the fort, while the Federal Navy continued bombarding Fort Fisher with another ten thousand shells. The troops, under the command of Union Major General Godfrey Weitzel, advanced to within a few hundred yards of the land face. One of Weitzel's subordinates, Brigadier General Martin Curtis, wanted to storm the fort, but Weitzel, a trained engineer, looked at the undamaged ramparts and the intact palisade (a wooden fence with sharpened ends in front of the fort's wall) and thought better of an attack. He sent word out to Butler that an attack could be disastrous.

Butler decided to consult some other "experts" he had with him about the success of a Union attack. The men he asked were Confederate prisoners. Butler asked the men how many soldiers were inside Fort Fisher. Never missing an opportunity to fool a Yankee, the Confederates told Butler the fort was filled with men. Besides that, the prisoners said, Hoke's division was waiting in the woods to pounce on Federal reinforcements.

The truth was that Lamb had less than six hundred men to man forty-seven guns and defend a mile-and-a-half of earthworks against the more than two thousand Federals that had already landed, out of an intended sixty-five-hundred-man invasion force. Hoke's men were not in the woods, but were still at Sugar Loaf, four miles away. Butler could have overwhelmed Fort Fisher if he acted quickly.

Spooked by the Confederates' claims, Butler ordered his men back on board their transports before the soldiers even fired their muskets. Due to heavy seas, at least six hundred Federal soldiers were stranded on the beach for two days before they could be rescued. Butler did not even bother waiting for them to come back aboard ship. He returned to headquarters to prepare an explanation as to why an entire invasion force decided not to attack when they were just three hundred yards from a fort they had been planning to attack for four years. Union General Ulysses S. Grant, commander of all Federal forces, was not happy when he heard about the debacle. Butler was relieved of command.

Lamb was praised by all involved, even the dour Bragg. The fort suffered only two dead and sixty-one wounded after a two-day, twenty-thousand-round barrage by Union gunboats. However, Lamb and Whiting did not rest long. They brought out the wheelbarrows and shovels and put their men to work repairing the minor damage done to Fort Fisher's earth sides.

In two weeks, the Federals returned with more men, more ammunition, and a new, determined commander, Brigadier General Alfred H. Terry. While Butler's force had numbered around sixty-five-hundred men, Terry's numbered nearly nine thousand. On January 12, 1865, fifty-eight Federal gunboats and fourteen transports loaded with troops, light artillery, and siege mortars were sighted off Fort Fisher.

Facing them at the fort was one regiment, the 36th North Carolina Infantry, and a ragtag group of artillerymen from various other units—forces that added up to less than two thousand men. Even Hoke's men were not immediately available. Bragg had withdrawn them from Sugar Loaf after the Christmas Day engagement to participate in a dress parade in downtown Wilmington. Bragg ignored messages to send Hoke's troops back to Fort Fisher. It was on this day that Whiting rode into the fort and told Lamb that he had come to share the fate of the men at Fort Fisher.

The Federal fleet anchored less than a half-mile from the fort and started pouring shells into the land side of the fort, hoping to open holes for the soldiers. Unlike the first attack, this Federal bombardment was very effective. The shelling lasted for two days, killing or wounding at least two hundred men and blowing apart the palisade protecting the fort from ground assault.

While the shelling was going on, Terry was landing six thousand Federal soldiers north of the fort. Also landing were two thousand United States Marines and naval crewman, all volunteers. Actually, their naval commander, Admiral David Porter, volunteered them in an effort to get some glory out of what he expected to be a quick victory.

Bragg rushed Hoke's men back to Sugar Loaf. However, he ordered Hoke not to attack the landing Federals, but to hold his ground and keep the Union forces from advancing on Wilmington.

On Sunday, January 15, 1865, Bragg finally made an effort to reenforce the fort with troops from Wilmington. Bragg, being Bragg, waited until broad daylight to try to land his troops, in full view of the Federal gunboats. Only 350 South Carolinians got ashore, and they had to make their way more than two miles over open beach to reach the safety of the fort. Federal cannon fire chased them all the way. When they arrived, they were too exhausted and shell-shocked to be of any help.

The first part of the Federal assault was undertaken by the strange force of Marines and sailors, armed with pistols and cutlasses. Few of the sailors even carried muskets, as Porter had told them to expect hand-to-hand fighting when they "boarded" the fort at the point where the sea face and the land face intersected. Porter apparently thought he was attacking a sandy pirate ship instead of a twenty-three-foot-tall fort bristling with canister-loaded cannons.

The naval attack must have been an incredible sight for Lamb and his Confederates. They watched as a disorganized mob of sailors charged the strongest part of Fort Fisher like a swarm of locusts. Lamb must have sympathized with them. Serving under Bragg, he knew how stupid commanders could be. That did not stop Lamb from ordering his artillerymen to cut the sailors down as they charged across the open beach. Not a single sailor made it inside the sand walls.

However, things were not going as well for the Confederates on the land face, which was under heavy attack by the organized, battle-hardened Union soldiers who were sweeping out of the distant woods.

Union General Curtis, who had personally led his men to within three hundred yards of the fort just two weeks earlier, was one of the first Union soldiers into Fort Fisher. As he climbed over the wall of Shepherd's Battery near the river, Curtis encountered a Confederate about to fire a ten-inch cannon loaded with canister. Curtis hit the man with a saber and forced him to drop the lanyard.

Within minutes, the battery was overrun, and the fight for the fort shifted to hand-to-hand combat. Soldiers fought with bayonets, rocks, and clubs. Starting from Shepherd's Battery, Federal forces moved toward the sea. Everyone on both sides, officer and soldier alike, was fighting for his life. Whiting was shot twice at the fourth bastion in from Shepherd's Battery. Curtis was shot three times, but he survived to receive the Congressional Medal of Honor. Lamb was shot down with a bullet in the hip. The fighting went on for hours at close range. By 10:00 P.M. the last of the Confederate defenders had given up.

The killing did not end when the shooting stopped. Neither did the dumb mistakes. The day after the battle, two drunken United States Marines wandered into a dark room in the fort to look for souvenirs. They raised their torches high, and likely had just enough time to realize the barrels they were looking at contained black powder. The explosion of thirteen thousand pounds of powder blew them, and an unknown number of other soldiers, to kingdom come.

The Battle of Fort Fisher was costly to both sides. The Federals fired nearly forty thousand naval artillery rounds into the fort. Nearly fifteen hundred Federals were killed, wounded, or missing. Five hundred Confederates were killed or wounded, and fourteen hundred were captured.

Today, the ravages of time and the endless waves of the Atlantic Ocean have taken almost all of Fort Fisher. All of the sea face is gone. It was probably located at least 150 yards into the ocean. The only structure remaining that could be considered part of the ocean side defenses is Battery Buchanan, at the end of Federal Point. But this was a separate battery and not actually connected to the fort. It remains near the Southport ferry.

About two-thirds of the land face has also been surrendered to the ocean. What remains of the land face is the point of the fiercest fighting. Shepherd's Battery has been faithfully recreated from period photos. The wooden walkway over the marsh, taking visitors inside the fort, is in the same place where the fort's gate was protected by a twelve-pound field piece. The recreated wooden palisade protecting the mounds looks just as formidable today as it must have looked to Federal soldiers in 1865.

The future survival of Fort Fisher appears to be assured. In 1993, the government finally decided to build a revetment to try to keep any more of the fort from washing away. As of summer 1995, that construction was going on in front and to the north of the fort.

Not all of Fort Fisher's defenders seem to have left. In the late nineteenth century, when some old Confederates were holding a reunion at the fort, they noticed a man standing on top of one of the ramparts looking out to sea. They waved to him and started walking toward the rampart to see who this comrade was. As they got closer, they paled. All of them recognized the diminutive figure of General Whiting. As they watched, the general slowly disappeared. In more modern times, other people, including some Carolina Beach police officers, claim to have seen Little Billy walking the ramparts of the fort.

Leaving Fort Fisher, get back on U.S. 421, or Carolina Beach Road, heading south, and drive 1.8 miles to the tip of Federal Point to see Battery Buchanan. This was the battery that protected New Inlet. Turn around on U.S. 421, drive 0.1 mile to the ferry station, and catch the half-hour ferry ride across the Cape Fear River to see the forts on the western side.

Leave the ferry dock on the west side of the river on S.R. 1534. Drive 0.7 mile to the intersection with S.R. 1528. Turn left onto S.R. 1528 and follow the signs to Southport, 2.3 miles away. The road becomes Moore Street in Southport.

During the Civil War, Southport was known as Smithville. On the left, coming into town, is the two-story brick building that is the officers quarters for Fort Johnston, or Fort Pender, as it was known by the Confederates. In 1863, the Confederates renamed Fort Johnston in honor of fallen Confederate Major General Dorsey Pender. Just in front of the officers quarters will be St. Phillips Episcopal Church, built in 1860 and used as a hospital by Union forces after taking the town in 1865.

Turn left at the officers quarters onto Davis Street, then left again onto Bay Street and park. In the river, in front of the officers quarters, are what appears to be coquina walls, all that is left of old Fort Johnston, originally built in 1745.

Fort Johnston was taken on January 9, 1861, three months before Fort Sumter was surrendered. Its captors were a force of private citizens from Smithville, who feared that the vital fort at the mouth of the Cape Fear River would soon be reinforced by Federal soldiers. Taking the fort was not exactly a great act of bravery by the citizens. Its entire garrison consisted of one ordnance sergeant, who demanded and received a receipt for the fort and its contents. Six days later, the governor of North Carolina ordered the fort returned to the sergeant, citing the fact that North Carolina was still in the Union and had no right to seize Federal property. Just before North Carolina seceded in May 1861, the citizens returned and took the fort for good.

Fort Johnston, or Fort Pender, was the setting of an interesting raid by Union Lieutenant William Cushing, an amazing Federal Navy officer who may have inspired the creation of today's elite Navy SEALS. In February 1864, Cushing and a small team of volunteers rowed ashore in Smithville with the express purpose of capturing the commanding general of the Cape Fear region artillery. Luckily for the Confederates, the general was in Wilmington that night, so Cushing captured the fort's adjutant instead. When one of Cushing's men returned the next morning under a flag of truce to get some clothes for his prisoner, a Confederate officer proclaimed that the capture was "a splendid affair." The amused Confederate was handed a letter from Cushing to the lucky general expressing Cushing's regret that the general was not at home when the Federals had come calling. (See the River Cities Tour for further details of Cushing's exploits.)

Return to the car, turn around on Bay Street, and drive four blocks west to the corner of Bay and Caswell Streets. Here is the home of Captain T. Mann Thompson, a blockade runner who prospered during and after the war. He built the house with his profits from the war.

Turn onto Caswell Street, heading away from the river. Drive one block, then turn right, or east, back onto Moore Street. Turn left, or north, onto Howe Street and park near the intersection of Howe and Moore Streets to visit the Southport Maritime Museum at 116 North Howe Street. This museum offers a small exhibit on the Civil War, including relics recovered from blockade runners, a two-hundred-pound pile torpedo (driven into the river bottom in hopes that a ship would pass overhead), and an unusual wartime souvenir, a meat cleaver lifted from the mess of the USS *Monitor* by the man who installed the ship's engines. A photo of the river pilots used by blockade runners shows them to be a tough bunch.

Leave the museum and continue north on Howe Street, which becomes N.C. 211. After approximately 2 miles, turn left, or south, at the intersection with N.C. 133. Cross the Intracoastal Waterway, stay straight at the traffic light, and follow N.C. 133 east on the peninsula for 4.9 miles to Fort Caswell, the fort that defended the Old Inlet from the tip of Oak Island. The fort is located on the gated grounds of the North Carolina Baptist Convention. During the day, visitors can get out of their car to see the fort up close if they register at the office. After 5:00 P.M., the administration asks that people remain in their cars. The single-story brick fort is still mostly intact, though the Confederates blew up the powder magazine when they abandoned it in January 1865. The crumbling fort is not maintained as a tourist attraction by the Baptist Convention, so exploring it is not suggested. Stay safe by staying outside the fort.

Construction of Fort Caswell began in 1827, and it must have been a contractor's dream. Construction of a brick fort on a desolate island was inherently difficult, so cost estimates meant nothing. The fort's final price tag was $473,402, more than four times the government's estimate. Designed to mount sixty-four guns and garrison four hundred men, the fort took eleven years to finish.

Fort Caswell was "captured" on the same night that Fort Johnston was in January 1861. Like his comrade at Johnston, Caswell's ordnance sergeant demanded and received a receipt for his fort. When North Carolina Governor Ellis ordered the citizens to return Caswell, the caretaker agreed to accept the fort's return, stating "none of it was broken and none of the ammunition was expended. It was returned in good order."

When the Confederates returned just before North Carolina seceded, the reinforced Federal garrison (it now consisted of three men) was ordered out, and the Confederates took possession. They did not get much. The first Confederate commander of Fort Caswell reported to the governor that the fort was in a sad state of repair.

Fort Caswell protected the Cape Fear River for the entire war, and the Federals seem to have feared it as much as they feared Fort Fisher. It never came under direct attack. Its men fought boredom more than anything. One report describes how the men and officers rushed from the fort when a blockade runner ran aground nearby. The writer describes how everyone got "beastly drunk" from the liquor found on board.

After Fort Fisher fell, Fort Caswell was abandoned without a fight. Its magazine of a hundred thousand pounds of black powder was blown up by the Confederates, making a noise that people in Fayetteville claim to have heard. The men were transferred to the mainland earth fort of Fort Anderson. After the war, two of Fort Caswell's cannons were shipped to Raleigh, where they now flank the Confederate monument at the capitol.

Return to the mainland on N.C. 133 and turn right back onto N.C. 211. Follow N.C. 211 for 0.8 mile, then turn left onto an access road leading to N.C. 133. Turn left, or north, onto N.C. 133.

At approximately 9.6 miles, turn right, or east, onto an access road marked with a brown state historic sign for Old Brunswick Town. Fort Anderson will not be mentioned on the sign. Follow the signs for approximately 2 miles to reach the visitor's center.

Originally designed by Colonel William Lamb, the same self-taught engineer who created Fort Fisher, Fort Anderson was first called Fort St. Phillip, for the church within its walls, then Fort Henderson. By 1864, it was called Fort Anderson, named after Confederate Brigadier General George Anderson, who died from a wound received at the Battle of Sharpsburg in 1862.

Like Fort Fisher, Fort Anderson was designed to fight ships, so its sand mounds and guns faced toward the Cape Fear River. It was never enclosed from the land side, which may have convinced General Bragg not to defend the fort once it was clear it would come under attack from both gunboats and land forces after Fort Fisher fell.

On February 17, 1865, Union Admiral Porter's gunboats started shelling Fort Anderson, while Union Major General Jacob Cox's men prepared a ground assault. As the first Union troops rushed the fort, they discovered it had been abandoned during the night, However, the fort was still being heavily shelled by Union gunboats. A white flag was run up the pole, creating the unlikely situation of the Union Army surrendering to the Union Navy.

Fort Anderson is one of the few remaining Civil War forts that has remained intact over the past 130 years. Its dirt walls appear to be as tall as they ever were. A gravel walkway atop the dirt mounds gives visitors an idea of how formidable this fort would have been had it been fully enclosed. From the mound closest to the river, the white sand of Sugar Loaf is clearly visible across the river. It is likely that the two garrisons signaled each other with flags and bonfires.

The visitor's center has a slide show that concentrates on the colonial history of Brunswick Town, with some details on the Civil War history. A huge cannonball, recovered from the river in front of the fort, gives visitors a sense of the destruction gunboats were capable of delivering. The site is closed on Mondays.

Return to N.C. 133 and head north. At 8.1 miles after leaving Fort Anderson is Town Creek, the approximate site of a Confederate rearguard action during the Wilmington campaign. Near this site, on the afternoon of February 19, 1865, Union Major General Cox and his sixty-five-hundred troops caught up with Confederate Brigadier General Johnson Hagood's twenty-two-hundred soldiers—the men who had abandoned Fort Anderson. Hagood picked a good defensive position on the north side of the creek, after burning the bridge. Hagood could have held Cox for some time, but his scouts missed sinking an old flatboat tied up on the south side of the creek. The Federals found it. While part of Cox's force kept the Confederates looking forward, most of the Union soldiers were taken across the deep creek. The Confederate flank and rear were attacked, and more than four hundred Confederates were captured, before the bulk of Hagood's force could escape.

The next day, the Battle of Forks Road took place east of Wilmington, with Hoke faring little better than Hagood against the overwhelming Federal forces.

General Bragg burned any valuable Confederate stores left in Wilmington, and marched out of the city with what was left of his forces at 1:00 A.M. on February 22, 1865. By midmorning, Federal forces had marched into the city and accepted the surrender of the mayor on the city hall steps.

Continue 7.4 miles on N.C. 133 to the intersection with U.S. 17. Follow U.S. 17 back to Wilmington, just across the river. This concludes The Wilmington Forts Tour.

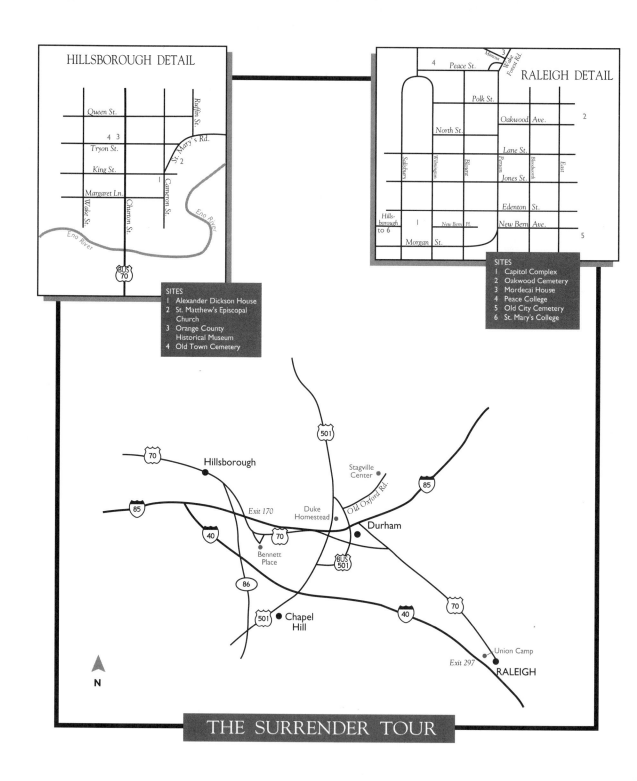

HILLSBOROUGH DETAIL

Queen St.

Rufin St.

4 3

Tryon St.

St. Mary's Rd.

2

King St.

1

Cameron St.

Margaret Ln.

Wake St.

Churton St.

Eno River

Eno River

BUS 70

SITES
1 Alexander Dickson House
2 St. Matthew's Episcopal Church
3 Orange County Historical Museum
4 Old Town Cemetery

RALEIGH DETAIL

4 Peace St.

Mimosa

Wake Forest Rd.

3

Polk St.

Oakwood Ave.   2

North St.

Lane St.

Salisbury

Wilmington

Blount

Person

Bloodworth

East

Jones St.

Hills-
borough
to 6   1

New Bern Pl.

Edenton St.

New Bern Ave.

Morgan St.   5

SITES
1 Capitol Complex
2 Oakwood Cemetery
3 Mordecai House
4 Peace College
5 Old City Cemetery
6 St. Mary's College

501

70

Hillsborough

Stagville Center

85

85

Exit 170

Duke Homestead

Old Oxford Rd.

Durham

40

70

Bennett Place

BUS 501

86

501

Chapel Hill

40

70

Union Camp

Exit 297

RALEIGH

N

THE SURRENDER TOUR

The Surrender Tour

This tour begins in Raleigh at the Farmers Market, which was once a Federal camp. It moves to the state capitol, the state museum, and then to Oakwood Cemetery, the final resting place of four Confederate generals and many other Confederate soldiers. The tour continues past the grave of another Confederate general and several historic buildings in Raleigh before moving to Hillsborough to see the headquarters of Confederate General Joseph Johnston. From Hillsborough, the tour moves to Bennett Place near Durham, where Johnston surrendered to Union General Sherman. It then moves to the Duke Homestead, the birthplace of the tobacco industry that helped pull the South out of poverty after the war. It ends at Stagville Center, a plantation northeast of Durham, where a barn hand-built by slaves still stands as a monument to their skills.

Total mileage: approximately 71 miles.

After Mississippi, Florida, Georgia, and Alabama joined South Carolina in seceding from the Union, North Carolina decided to hold a general election on the issue of whether or not to have a secession convention. The election occurred on February 28, 1861, and a large majority of the people answered "no." When four young men raised a secession flag in downtown Raleigh, an old man shot it full of holes with a rifle.

Still, the issue was not settled, and even peaceful Tar Heels knew something was boiling. The pot overflowed on April 12, when Fort Sumter was bombarded. North Carolina Unionists hoped against hope that the Federal government would pursue peaceful alternatives, but that was not the case. On April 15, 1861, President Lincoln issued a national call for seventy-five thousand volunteers to put down the rebellion. He ordered North Carolina to supply two regiments of militia to be used to invade the rest of the South.

That tore it. Governor John W. Ellis replied: "I can be no party to this wicked violation of the laws of the country and to this war upon the liberties of a free people. You will get no troops from North Carolina."

Governor Ellis ordered the capture of Fort Johnston and Fort Caswell at the mouth of the Cape Fear River. Just weeks earlier, he had forced over-eager militia members to return those forts to their caretakers. At the time, he felt North Carolina had no right to take Federal property since the state was still a member of the Union. This time he would keep those forts, and they would stay in North Carolina's hands for the rest of the war. Ellis also ordered the capture of the United States Arsenal at Fayetteville, a swift move that brought the state thirty-seven thousand stands of muskets.

Raleigh became the center of North Carolina's war effort. When Governor Ellis appealed for volunteers to fight the Union, the response was overwhelming. Eventually, almost 13 percent of the state's population, more than 127,000 men, joined the Confederate army. That was more than the voting-age population. Less than 19,000 North Carolina men were drafted into service. The rest volunteered.

One of the first Confederate units from the state was the 1st North Carolina Volunteers, commanded by Colonel Daniel Harvey "D.H." Hill. The 1st North Carolina Volunteers included many cadets who left the North Carolina Military Academy in Charlotte to see what real war was all about. The 1st Volunteers left the state with a grand parade down Fayetteville Street in Raleigh. The following month, they became the first Confederates to face the Federals in battle at Big Bethel, Virginia. At least one member of the 1st North Carolina Volunteers never made it to Big Bethel. This young Charlotte soldier died of pneumonia in a Raleigh camp on May 11, 1861, nine days before the state seceded. He was the first North Carolina Confederate to die.

Ironically, the first South Carolina Confederate to die was accidentally killed in Charleston, when a bayonet was poked in his eye while he was horsing around in the barracks. Of the fifty-eight thousand soldiers from North and South Carolina that died in the Civil War, the first two never saw a battlefield.

By January 1862, less than nine months after the war started, North Carolina had forty-one regiments in service. By the end of the war, the state had organized seventy-two regiments. However, the last few of these regiments were made up of teenagers and called the Junior Reserves.

While men from all over the state were joining the Confederate Army,

Governor Ellis was turning the capital city into a major manufacturing center. He ordered all of the cotton and wool produced in the state's mills shipped to Raleigh to be made into uniforms. The project was so efficient that, by the end of the war, the state's warehouses contained more than enough uniforms to clothe every man in Robert E. Lee's army—if they were from North Carolina. North Carolina Governor Zebulon Vance refused to release the uniforms to any regiment except those from his own state.

However, while Raleigh was the center of North Carolina's war effort, it was also where the state's peace movement was strongest. By 1863, W.W. Holden, editor of the Raleigh *Standard* newspaper, was suggesting in his paper that North Carolina seek its own peace with the Union. In 1862, Holden had successfully convinced citizens to elect Zeb Vance as governor, with Vance never leaving the Virginia battlefields to campaign for the job. As the war progressed, Holden became dedicated to seeking peace. In 1864, he ran for governor against Vance on a platform of ending North Carolina's involvement in the war. Though North Carolinians were sick of war, they had no stomach for a man who would give in to the Union. Vance garnered nearly fifty-eight thousand votes to Holden's fourteen thousand.

Holden and other Unionist leaders did have some support in the area. The counties near Wake County were hotbeds of Unionist sentiment. Attacks on loyal Confederates became so bad that Confederate soldiers were ordered into Randolph, Chatham, Moore, Montgomery, Davidson, and Alamance Counties to root out deserters and Unionists. The Piedmont Unionists developed elaborate schemes and hiding places to protect themselves. The term "laying out" became common. It meant staying out of the war by hiding in the woods.

As the war continued, conditions deteriorated for civilians in Raleigh. In 1862, a pound of bacon cost 33 cents. By 1865, it cost $7.50 a pound. Flour had cost $18 a barrel in 1862. By 1865, it cost $500.

When Sherman's men appeared on the outskirts of town in the spring of 1865, the citizens of Raleigh were ready to give up.

This tour begins at the Farmers Market in Raleigh, which was the campground for some of General Sherman's army. From I-40 on the west side of Raleigh, take Exit 297 to Lake Wheeler Road. This exit will be marked as the exit for the Farmers Market. Turn north on Lake Wheeler Road, toward downtown. (You will be able to see tall office buildings in this direction.) Drive 0.2 mile to the entrance of the Farmers Market. Turn into the market on Centennial Road. On your left will be the Farmers Market Restaurant. Park and walk to the restaurant.

The Farmers Market was built in 1988 on the 1865 campground of the Union 14th Corps, which was under the command of Union Major General Jefferson C. Davis (no relation to the Confederate president).

Davis, thirty-seven, had been in the army more than half his life, having served in the Mexican War as a private. He was a rarity in the Union Army. He had worked his way up through the ranks to a full corps command without a formal military education from West Point. He was also more than a little rough-edged.

In September 1862, Davis's commanding officer, Major General William Nelson, insulted and slapped Davis (who was then a brigadier general) in a hotel lobby in Louisville, Kentucky. Davis did not bother to file formal assault charges. Instead, he borrowed a pistol and shot Nelson dead. No murder charges were ever filed. The incident did not even keep Davis off the promotion list. He was later named a major general, although the promotion was a "brevet," meaning temporary for the duration of the war.

Davis came under heavy criticism in Georgia during Sherman's "March to the Sea." After his men crossed a creek outside of Savannah, he pulled up the pontoon bridges, leaving hundreds of runaway slaves who were following the army on the other side of the creek. Some slaves drowned while trying to swim the creek. Most of the slaves were captured and returned to their plantations by the pursuing Confederate cavalry.

By the time it reached Raleigh, the 14th Corps was battle-hardened and war weary. It had fought in Mississippi, Tennessee, Georgia, South Carolina, and most recently, at Bentonville, just fifty miles southeast of Raleigh. Davis's men proudly called themselves "bummers," soldiers who lived off the land, scrounging and taking what they could from Southerners. They did not mind raping a woman now and then when they thought they could get away with it, and an occasional civilian murder did not bring rebuke from their officers. What the bummers could not take, they burned. Many were hatless and shoeless. Their uniforms were in tatters. They were tired and ready to go home. In short, they were mean.

On April 17, 1865, General Sherman told his army camped outside of Raleigh the news he had learned earlier that day. President Lincoln had been assassinated. The seventeen thousand soldiers in the 14th Corps camp boiled with anger. Small, but swelling, knots of men swore revenge. One Union soldier wrote in his memoirs that men were willing to "reenlist for 40 years to exterminate the Southern race." The general sentiment among the men was to burn Raleigh to the ground, just as they had done to Columbia, South Carolina.

Nervous officers, under orders from Sherman, refused to let the men leave camp. Governor Vance sent Sherman a letter asking him to spare the city. According to legend, Sherman also had friends in the town. Perhaps he had already proven his point with the burning of Columbia. At any rate, something about Raleigh appealed to Sherman. His officers protected the city, though it took the threat of being fired upon to keep the 14th Corps in line.

The wall on the right side of the entrance to the Farmers Market Restaurant has a display of Civil War artifacts from the site. Included among the relics are numerous unfired bullets, buttons, a musket, and musketband swivels. The wall also has newspaper articles about saving the site, as well as an interesting collection of Civil War photographs.

Another wall is decorated with photographs of old soldiers gathered for Confederate reunions, and of men who lived at Raleigh's Old Soldiers Home. The home was once located about a mile east of Raleigh, near where the State Department of Motor Vehicles is today.

Leaving the Farmers Market, turn left toward town on Lake Wheeler Road. Next to the Farmers Market is Dorthea Dix Hospital, the state's mental hospital founded in 1849. During the 14th Corps' occupation, the soldiers frequently gathered on the lawn of the hospital to listen to a patient play the violin.

Lake Wheeler Road deadends into Saunders Street 0.8 mile from the Farmers Market. Turn left, or north, onto Saunders Street. Proceed to the next light then turn right, or east, onto South Street. Stay in the left lane. You will pass the Memorial Auditorium on the right. A historic marker designates the area as the site of the Governor's Palace. This was the governor's house that was occupied by Sherman on April 13, 1865. One of

Sherman's men described the palace as "a musty old brick building skinned of furniture."

After passing Memorial Auditorium, turn north, toward town, onto Wilmington Street, a one-way street. Proceed seven blocks to Edenton Street, passing the capitol building at Morgan Street. At the next street, turn west onto Edenton Street, also a one-way street. Park at the meters on Edenton Street, or follow the signs for visitors parking. The capitol building is on your left and the North Carolina Museum of History is on your right, midway through the block. The capitol is located on Union Square, bound by Edenton, Salisbury, Morgan, and Wilmington Streets, all one-way streets.

Construction began on the North Carolina State Capitol in 1833, and the building took seven years to complete. Designed in the Greek Revival style, it is one of the least-changed state capitols in the nation. It still houses the offices of governor and lieutenant governor, although the legislature moved to a new building in 1961.

Standing on the west side of the capitol on Salisbury Street, look up at the dome. The capitol was occupied by Union forces on April 13, 1865. One of the first Union soldiers in the building was Lieutenant George Round of the United States Army Signal Corps. Round was ordered to set up a signal station on top of the dome. Climbing up the outside of the building, Round carefully made his way to the domed cupola.

By the time Round made it to the top of the dome, night had fallen. He pulled himself to the top of the dome, then jumped over a small railing. That was a big mistake. What Round couldn't see in the fading light was that he was jumping onto the dome's glass ceiling. As the glass shattered beneath his boots, he grabbed a railing. The lanterns lit inside showed him that it was ninety-seven feet to the floor. He was able to pull himself back to the railing, where he set off his signal rockets.

There was something about the capitol and Lieutenant Round that just did not mesh. Nearly two weeks later, he was again ordered to the top of the building to fire off a series of rockets signaling the surrender of the army of Confederate General Joe Johnston to Union General William T. Sherman. One rocket misfired, and Lieutenant Round leaned over to re-light it. Just as he got close, the rocket's fuse went off, and the rocket

zoomed by Round's face, burning off his eyelashes. The luckless Round continued his duties, finally spelling out with numerous signal rockets: "Peace on earth, goodwill to men." He survived the end of the war and returned home.

A number of statues of Civil War personalities ring the capitol grounds. Follow them in counterclockwise order, starting with the one closest to the west side doors. This is the statue of Henry Lawson Wyatt, a private in the First North Carolina Volunteers Regiment. Wyatt fell at Big Bethel, Virginia (near Williamsburg), on June 10, 1861, just three weeks after North Carolina seceded from the Union. Wyatt was the first Confederate soldier killed in battle, giving credence to the first part of North Carolina's post-war motto: "First at Bethel." Sharp observers will recognize why Wyatt may have been the first Confederate killed. The sculptor put a musket in his hands, but failed to provide him with cartridge or cap boxes to load his weapon. Wyatt was given a hero's burial in Richmond's Hollywood Cemetery.

Near Wyatt's statue is a relief of Samuel Acort Ashe, who never ranked higher than a captain. Ashe was not a famous Confederate, but he must have had influence. At least he had enough friends to get his likeness put up on the capitol grounds on the hundredth anniversary of his birth.

On the west side of the capitol, at the point where Hillsborough Street dead-ends into Salisbury Street, is the Confederate monument erected May 20, 1895, the anniversary of the day the state seceded. The shaft is seventy-five feet tall. At the top is a Confederate infantryman. Two lower figures represent the cavalry and artillery. The monument cost twenty thousand dollars and was unveiled by the granddaughter of Stonewall Jackson. It is flanked by two cannons first captured by Confederates at the Norfolk Naval Yard in 1861, then remounted at Fort Caswell near Wilmington.

The next monument, frequently overlooked since it is closer to the Morgan Street sidewalk than the other statues, is the Confederate Women's Monument. Erected in 1914 by a Confederate veteran, the statue shows a mother at home with her young son. The woman is clutching her missing husband's saber. On either side are reliefs. One shows brave men marching off to war. The other shows the deadly results of warfare, the broken bodies of those same men being carried home from war.

Moving on from this monument, walk east toward the southeast corner of the capitol to the statue of war-time governor Zebulon Vance, who was from Weaverville, near Asheville. Vance was thirty-two when elected to the first of three terms in the governor's office. This statue's older likeness apparently depicts him in the United States Senate, where he served from 1879 until his death in 1894. The statue bears the inscription: "If there be a people on earth given to sober second thought, amenable to reason and regardful of their plighted honor, I believe it is the people of North Carolina."

Near Vance's statue is one of George Washington, the first statue on the capitol grounds, unveiled on July 4, 1857. It and the iron fence surrounding it were respected by Union forces. The two French cannons flanking the statue are of American Revolution vintage, but were in a fort near Edenton during the war.

Across the street from the capitol, at the corner of Edenton and Wilmington Streets, is Christ Church. One local wag, noting that both Confederate and Union forces were equally adept at stealing food, said that the last chicken left in Raleigh in April 1865 was Christ Church's rooster weather vane.

Zeb Vance statue

Near the corner of Fayetteville Street (now a pedestrian mall) and Morgan Street, a foolhardy Texas Confederate cavalryman named Walsh made a series of fatal mistakes on the day the Federals rode into town. First, he stayed too long foraging in the city. Then, when he saw Union General Judson Kilpatrick's cavalry riding up Fayetteville Street toward the capitol, Walsh snapped off five pistol shots before spurring his horse away. The horse fell rounding the corner, and Walsh was captured. Kilpatrick gave him five minutes to write his wife a farewell letter before executing him on the spot. Walsh is buried in the Confederate section of Oakwood Cemetery. Whether that incident sobered the citizens of Raleigh is not known, but there were no further incidents of resistance.

Kilpatrick was not in a good mood anyway. A month earlier, Confederate cavalry had surprised him in bed with a young woman. Kilpatrick abandoned his admirer and escaped by leaping astride his horse clad only in his underwear. Behind his back, Union soldiers called the incident "Kilpatrick's Shirttail Skedaddle." (See the Bentonville Battle Tour for more details on "Kilpatrick's Shirttail Skedaddle.")

Enter the capitol building through the east side doors. The building is open for tours seven days a week. It is closed New Year's Day, Thanksgiving, and Christmas.

Lining the rotunda are busts of two Civil War figures. One is of Matt Ransom, a general who was wounded three times. He later served as a United States senator. The other is of Governor William Alexander Graham, who later served in the Confederate Senate.

The statue of George Washington inside the rotunda is a 1970 copy of one that was first placed in the Capitol in 1815. The original was destroyed by fire in 1831.

While details are sketchy, North Carolina's original copy of the Bill of Rights may have been stolen from the capitol by a Union soldier. The document was first missed when the city was occupied by Union soldiers. As late as the 1920s, a New York lawyer claiming to represent the "owner" of North Carolina's copy of the Bill of Rights was trying to negotiate its sale back to the state. North Carolina's secretary of state curtly replied that the state did not buy stolen property. The document has never been returned. Research on what regiments were nearby at the time indicate that the Union soldier who took it may have been from Ohio.

Across Edenton Street from the capitol is the North Carolina Museum of History. Although it has a wealth of Confederate artifacts and flags in its collection, the museum displays only a few items. The small "Button, Sword, and Pistol" section in the main gallery displays a button from Henry Wyatt's coat; a sword belonging to General James Johnston Pettigrew, the commander of the North Carolinians during the Confederate assault on the third day at Gettysburg; and a pistol belonging to General Bryan Grimes, who ordered the last Confederate attack at Appomattox. Portraits of these men are nearby, as is the original painting of the "Three Colonels" of the 26th North Carolina Regiment. One of the three was Zebulon Vance, war-time governor. The display also shows a smokestack from the ironclad CSS *Albemarle*, armor plating from the ironclad CSS *Neuse*, some artillery shells and muskets manufactured at Fayetteville, and some bayonets manufactured at Kenansville, North Carolina.

On the second floor, a women-in-history exhibit describes the lifestyles of both Black and white women during the Civil War. A photograph of Malinda Blalock, who successfully hid her sex from recruiters to join the Confederate army, is displayed. She served for several months, posing as "Sam," the brother of her husband Keith. (See The Mountain War Part II Tour for more details on the Blalocks' Civil War careers.)

If you have parked near the Capitol, head east for two blocks until intersecting Person Street, a one-way street heading north. Drive north on Person Street to Oakwood Avenue, two blocks north of the Governor's Mansion, which is located at the corner of Person and Jones Streets.

Turn right onto Oakwood Avenue. Drive three blocks east to the 600 block. Turn north, or left, into Oakwood Cemetery on Oak Avenue. This cemetery contains the graves of four Confederate generals and more than twenty-eight hundred Confederate soldiers. Look for a blunt, bulky monument marking the grave of Confederate Major General Robert Frederick Hoke on the hill on the left, located just before the right turn leading to the cemetery office.

Hoke, a native of Lincolnton, North Carolina, was just twenty-three when the war broke out. He immediately enlisted as a second lieutenant and was at Big Bethel. Hoke quickly rose through the ranks and was a twenty-four-year-old colonel when he was wounded during the Chancellorsville campaign. He returned to service as a brigadier general.

Hoke's greatest victory came on April 20, 1864, when his command recaptured the town of Plymouth, North Carolina, and took more than three thousand Union troops captive. Rewarded with a promotion to major general, Hoke fought in Virginia for several months before being transferred back to North Carolina. Hoke was at Wilmington during the Union's invasion of that city. His last action was at Bentonville.

In Hoke's last address to his men, he told them to teach their children that "the proudest day in all your proud careers was that on which you enlisted as Southern soldiers." He died in 1912. (See the River Cities Tour for details on Hoke's retaking of Plymouth, North Carolina.)

Park on Oak Avenue, then walk from Hoke's monument past the cemetery office. If the office is open, get a map of prominent graves. Directly south of the office, on the north end of the Confederate cemetery under an oak tree, is the obelisk marking the grave of Confederate Brigadier General George Burgwyn Anderson.

A native of Hillsborough, North Carolina, Anderson was a 1852 graduate of West Point. He resigned his cavalry lieutenancy in the United States Army in 1861 and was commissioned colonel of the 4th North Carolina Regiment. He was promoted to brigadier general after his service at Williamsburg.

Anderson was engaged in heavy fighting during the Seven Days battles around Richmond and was wounded at Malvern Hill. He returned to command his men at South Mountain and was with them in the Sunken Road, also known as "Bloody Lane," at Antietam in September 1862. During that battle, he was wounded in the foot. The wound was considered slight and Anderson may have ignored it for awhile. The foot was finally amputated in Raleigh after it failed to heal. Infection from the wound claimed Anderson's life on October 16, 1862. Anderson is one of those capable generals historians believe would have made valuable contributions in future battles had he lived.

A short distance to the east of Anderson's grave, under a magnolia tree, is the small, unassuming marker for Confederate Brigadier General Thomas Fentress Toon.

Toon was a twenty-one-year-old senior at Wake Forest college (when the college was located in Wake Forest, North Carolina) when he joined the 20th North Carolina Regiment. He fought at Seven Pines, South Mountain, and Fredericksburg. He was promoted to colonel in time to lead his men during Stonewall Jackson's flank march at Chancellorsville. Toon continued to serve in all of the major actions of the war, including leading the 20th North Carolina Regiment at Gettysburg. His regiment marched to within thirty miles of Washington at the Battle of Monocracy.

On March 25, 1865, Toon was wounded for the seventh time during the night attack on Fort Stedman at Petersburg. He survived the war and lived another thirty-seven years. Toon was state superintendent of education when he died in 1902.

South of Toon's and Anderson's graves are twenty-eight hundred Confederate soldiers, many of whom lie in graves marked with their birth and death years along with their regiments and companies. In the far southwest corner are the graves of several hundred Confederates who were retrieved from battlefield graves at Gettysburg. Reading the years on these gravestones shows that several of the soldiers were just sixteen when they fell.

Towering above these graves is the obelisk marking the remains of North Carolina's most famous regimental colonel. Colonel Henry King Burgwyn, Jr., was a twenty-one-year old who led the 26th North Carolina Regiment after its original commander, Zebulon Vance, was elected governor of North Carolina.

When Burgwyn first took command of the regiment, his men thought the Boston-born, University of North Carolina educated young man to be a "martinet," too strict a disciplinarian. One Confederate general so disliked Burgwyn, dubbed the "boy colonel," that he transferred the 26th Regiment to another brigade. However, Burgwyn's men changed their opinion of him when he led them into battle. Burgwyn was the last member of his regiment to leave the battlefield at New Bern, staying on the enemy side of a stream until all of his men had crossed. (See the Union's Base Tour for more details on this battle.)

It was at Gettysburg that the 26th North Carolina Regiment would go down in Civil War history. The 26th went into battle on July 1, 1863, with more than 800 men. In two days of fighting, it suffered 708 casualties, the most of any regiment on either side at Gettysburg. One of those killed was Burgwyn. On the first day of the battle, he grabbed the regiment's battle flag when it fell to the ground during a fight with the 24th Michigan Regiment at Willoughby Run. When Burgwyn turned to hand the flag to a waiting private, the colonel was shot through both lungs. Burgwyn died without a sound, but with a slight smile on his lips. He was one of fourteen color bearers in the 26th North Carolina Regiment to be shot down in less than a half-hour. The remaining soldiers in the regiment went into action again on the third day of Gettysburg. At the Gettysburg battlefield, the Confederate monument closest to the Federal stone wall on Cemetery Ridge honors the 26th North Carolina Regiment.

Just in front of Burgwyn's Oakwood monument is the grave of an unknown Confederate whose bones were recovered in 1990 from a Virginia battlefield trench. Uniform buttons inscribed with the letters "NC" surrounded by an engraved, starburst design showed him to be a Tar Heel. He was buried with full military honors after a twenty-four-hour memorial service in the capitol building. To the east of Burgwyn are the graves of more Confederates, including several Junior Reserves who were killed at Bentonville. The forced use of these barely trained teenagers proved to even the staunchest Confederates that the war was almost over.

On the far western edge of the Confederate cemetery is a small stone building called the House of Memory. Inside the open building are brass plaques commemorating the North Carolina military dead of all wars, including the Civil War. One plaque is inscribed:

North Carolina Gettysburg dead at Oakwood Cemetery

Not for fame, not for wealth, not for renown.
Nor goaded by necessity, nor lured by ambition, but lured in single
    obedience to duty,
These men suffered all, sacrificed all, dared all and did.
Furl that banner, softly, slowly. Treat it gently. It is holy.
For it drops above the dead.
Touch it not, unfold it never.
Let it droop here, furled forever.
For its people's hopes are dead.

Leave the Confederate cemetery and get back into the car. Drive past the office and up the hill further into the Oakwood Cemetery. Bear left onto Elm Avenue. At the next intersection, make a turn to the left, then an immediate turn to the right onto Willow Avenue. Drive to the intersection with Maple Avenue and turn right. (The cemetery map obtained at the office makes this easy to follow.) Where Maple Avenue and Chapel Circle meet is the grave of Brigadier General William Ruffin Cox, no doubt one of the luckiest, if not hardiest, men in the entire war.

That luck is evident from the fact Cox was wounded eleven times over four years. At least the man who carved Cox's inscription on his obelisk claims Cox was wounded eleven times. Records show Cox was wounded at least five times at the Battle of Chancellorsville.

During the Confederate Army's retreat to Appomattox, General Robert E. Lee noticed the orderly march of Cox's brigade. Lee took off his hat and said, "God bless gallant old North Carolina." On April 9, 1865, Lee decided to make one last attempt to break out of Appomattox, and he asked Cox's North Carolina troops to try it. Cox's men charged the Federals and briefly cleared the road to Lynchburg, before more Federal reinforcements appeared. It was the last Confederate victory of the war.

Cox served in the United States Congress before dying in 1919, one of the last surviving Confederate generals. His obelisk notes that "his soldiers acting under his orders fired the last volley at Appomattox." He is described on the stone as "Warrior Jurist Statesman."

Turn around and leave the cemetery by retracing your route back to Oakwood Avenue. Turn right onto Oakwood Avenue and drive back to Person Street. Turn right on Person Street, which is one-way heading north, and drive 0.6 mile to the Mordecai Historic Village. At this point, Person Street has turned into Wake Forest Road. Turn left onto Mimosa Street and park in the lot in front of the Mordecai House.

The Mordecai House has been a Raleigh landmark since it was originally built in 1785. The house was once the focal point of a plantation that covered thousands of acres (including the land of Oakwood Cemetery). Union troops took food from the grounds during the occupation of the city. Over the years, several historic structures, including the birthplace of postwar president and Raleigh native Andrew Johnson, have been moved to the site to form a small historic village. A one-hour tour of the village is offered.

One block north of the Mordecai House on Wake Forest Road is a historic marker describing earthworks that surrounded the city. Governor Vance ordered the earthworks built to protect Raleigh. Although the marker says the earthworks can be seen one-third of a mile to the west, that area is now a residential neighborhood, and they were not found during a 1995 visit.

Retrace your route south toward the city on Wake Forest Road. Wake Forest Road becomes Blount Street, a one-way street heading south. At the intersection of Blount and Peace Streets, turn right onto Peace Street. Peace College is on the right. The main building of the school, then called Peace Institute, was used as a Confederate hospital.

Return to Blount Street and turn right. Drive seven blocks, passing New Bern Place, and turn left onto Morgan Street, just past the capitol. The road will wind to the left. At the next traffic light, bear right onto New Bern Avenue. On the right side of the 500 block of New Bern Avenue, behind a brick wall, is the Old City Cemetery.

Ignore the drive-in opening on New Bern Avenue as the passage is extremely narrow. Proceed to the next street, Swain Street, and turn to the right. Park along Swain Street near New Bern Avenue. There are roads leading into the cemetery, but they are all extremely narrow. The roads were designed for horse-drawn carriages, not automobiles. Walk into the cemetery from New Bern Avenue.

Walk to the twin obelisks near the front of the cemetery. The obelisks, just west of another obelisk surrounded by an iron fence, mark the graves of Brigadier General Lawrence O'Bryan Branch and his wife. Branch was a Princeton graduate and lawyer before his election to the United States House of Representatives in 1855. He resigned when North Carolina left the Union. He was among the first generals to face Union forces on North Carolina soil when his command at New Bern was defeated by Union General Ambrose Burnside on March 13, 1862.

At Antietam in September 1862, Branch's brigade was part of General A.P. Hill's "Light Division." During the battle, the Light Division made an all-day, 22-mile march from Harper's Ferry to support the Confederates, saving Lee's army from destruction. After Branch's men helped turn back the Federal assault, Branch joined in a meeting with Hill and two other brigadier generals. A Federal sharpshooter noticed the meeting of high-ranking officers and fired at the group. His single shot found Branch's head.

Hill mourned the loss of Branch. He wrote that he would have trusted the forty-two-year-old with command of the whole division. Most military historians think Hill was too generous in his praise of Branch. Branch did not show any great brilliance during the Battle of New Bern, and it is unlikely that he improved much in six months. Branch's son later was elected to the United States House of Representatives, serving the same district his father once represented.

Turn around on Swain Street and cross over New Bern Avenue. Drive one block past New Bern Avenue to Edenton Street. Turn left, or west, onto Edenton Street. After passing the capitol, turn south, or left, onto Salisbury Street. After a half-block, turn right, or west, onto Hillsborough Street. Drive west on Hillsborough Street, which eventually passes North Carolina State University, founded by former Confederate soldiers.

Drive six blocks from the capitol to the intersection of Hillsborough and St. Mary's Streets. St. Mary's College, a female academy during the war, is at this intersection. Union reports said that the young women of St. Mary's waved to the Federals as the soldiers rode past the school on their way to the capitol. The friendly gesture worked. The Federal soldiers told the girls they would be back after the war because they were looking for pretty wives. The girls blushed. No harm came to the young women, or the buildings of St. Mary's College.

Continue west on Hillsborough Street. About 3.5 miles from the capitol is the entrance to I-440 West. Get on I-440 West, then take the first exit, which will point the way to I-40 West.

Travel I-40 West to Exit 266 for N.C. 86. Drive about 7 miles north on N.C. 86 to the town of Hillsborough. Hillsborough is a historic town dating back to pre–Revolutionary War times. It was also the hometown of General George Anderson, who is buried in Raleigh's Oakwood Cemetery, as well as William Graham, who was a prewar governor of North Carolina and a staunch Unionist.

N.C. 86 intersects and merges with Business U.S. 70 near downtown Hillsborough. At this intersection, turn right, or north, onto Business

U.S. 70/N.C. 86, or Churton Street. After passing over the Eno River bridge, turn right, or east, onto King Street. The Orange County courthouse is on the corner. The Alexander Dickson House, now the Hillsborough Chamber of Commerce and Visitor's Center, is two blocks down King Street on the right, beside the United States Post Office.

The Dickson House is a two-story farmhouse that was built in 1790. It has been moved to its present location from its original site two miles southeast. Confederate General Joseph Johnston made his headquarters at the Dickson House when it was in its original location. The original exterior of the house has been preserved. The interior is used for offices and for tourist information. A short video describing Hillsborough's historic significance is offered at the visitor's center.

To view the grave of sixteen-year-old Willie Hardee, son of Confederate Lieutenant General William J. Hardee, stay parked in front of the visitor's center on King Street and walk straight ahead into the parking lot of the Orange County Board of Education Office. Walk to the end of the parking lot, then turn left, crossing over a small wooden bridge into the cemetery of St. Matthews Episcopal Church. Willie's grave is marked by a small, white, flat stone about twenty yards behind the northeast corner of the church. The general's son died of wounds received at the Battle of Bentonville. (See Bentonville Battle Tour for a detailed account of Willie Hardee's wounding.)

Return to your car and retrace your route on King Street back to Business U.S. 70/N.C. 86. Turn right, or north, and go one block to the Orange County Museum at the intersection of Business U.S. 70/N.C. 86 and West Tryon Street.

In the graveyard behind the museum is the grave of William Graham, governor of North Carolina from 1845–1849, and one of the state's leading Unionists. By the time the war started, Graham had spent more than twenty-five years in politics, including holding the vice president's spot on the 1852 presidential ticket of Winfield Scott.

In 1860, Graham was one of the creators of the Constitutional Union party, which ran former Tennessee senator John Bell for president. Graham, knowing that Lincoln's election would lead to a secession crisis, was hoping that Bell would garner enough votes to throw the election into the

United States House of Representatives. He hoped he could convince house members to save the Union by putting the moderate Bell into office.

After Lincoln's election, few other Southern politicians listened to Graham's impassioned pleas to stay in the Union. Graham preached moderation and reconciliation right up to the point when Lincoln issued his demand for all states to supply soldiers to put down the rebellion in the eight seceded Southern states.

"However widely we have differed from, and freely criticized the course taken by these (seceding) states, they are closely united with us, by the ties of kindred, affection and a peculiar interest," Graham said. He reluctantly participated in North Carolina's secession convention and allowed all five of his sons to join the Confederate Army. They all survived the war.

Graham served in the Confederate Congress, where he had the reputation of being anti–Jefferson Davis. After the war, Graham was selected to represent North Carolina in the United States Senate, but the Federal government refused to let him take his seat. He died at age seventy-five in 1875.

Return to Business U.S.70/N.C. 86 and drive north, away from the interstate. Follow N.C. 86 through a residential section of the town until you reach the intersection with Bypass U.S. 70 (Business U.S. 70 will turn to the left before this intersection). Turn right, or east, onto Bypass U.S. 70. Outside of Hillsborough, Bypass U.S. 70 runs into U.S. 70. Drive 8.5 miles from the turn onto Bypass U.S. 70 to the outskirts of Durham. Look for the brown historic-site signs for Bennett Place. Turn right onto Bennett Place Road. Bennett Place is 0.5 mile from the U.S. 70 intersection with Bennett Place Road.

Bennett Place is the site where Confederate General Joseph Johnston surrendered his army to Union General William T. Sherman. Like the McLean House at Appomattox Court House in Virginia, the Bennett House was a chance meeting place for the two opposing generals. On April 16, 1865, Johnston had sent word to Sherman that he wanted to talk surrender terms on the following day. The generals met on the road between Hillsborough and Durham. Looking for a place to talk, they rode up to a farmhouse and asked Nancy Bennitt (over the years the family name has been changed to the more familiar spelling of Bennett) if they could meet

Johnston's headquarters

there. She and her two children went to the outlying kitchen while the two generals conferred alone in the three-room cabin.

At the first meeting, Johnston tried to arrange the terms of a permanent peace, including a pardon for Confederate President Jefferson Davis. At a second meeting on April 18 at the Bennett Place, Sherman agreed to liberal terms. Sherman said Johnston could disband his army, and the Union would recognize state governments, reestablish federal courts, restore political and civil rights, and grant general amnesty to the Confederates. In effect, Sherman agreed to let the ninety thousand soldiers under Johnston's command in the Carolinas, Georgia, and Florida return to the status they had before the war started. (There were less than eighteen thousand in Johnston's army that had fought at Bentonville, but he was in overall command of the forces in those distant states.)

Though the Confederates seemed to be getting a fair shake, it did not mean both sides would immediately be friends again. In the course of negotiations, Sherman absently poured himself a stiff drink of bourbon, but did not offer any to thirsty Confederates. That prompted whiskey-loving John C. Breckinridge, the Confederate secretary of war since February 1865, and a former vice president under President Franklin Buchanan, to remark, "You, sir, are a hog, a damned hog!"

President Davis, who had escaped Richmond and was now in Greensboro, was not satisfied with the surrender terms negotiated by General Johnston, an old political enemy. Davis ordered Johnston to make his escape with his mounted troops and to continue fighting. Johnston disobeyed those orders and returned to the Bennett farm on April 26 to sign the surrender.

By that time, the Washington politicians running the country after President Lincoln's assassination had seen Sherman's suggested surrender terms and refused to recognize them. The politicians were so alarmed at Sherman's liberal terms that some suspected him of treason. Some Northerners actually worried that Sherman might march on Washington and try to take military control of the government.

General Ulysses S. Grant himself rode the train to Raleigh to meet Sherman. Grant told Sherman that Johnston had to accept the military surrender terms agreed to by General Lee at Appomattox. If not, Grant warned, the attacks against the dwindling Confederate army, described by one general as "disappearing like snow in the sunlight," would start anew. Johnston had no choice but to sign the simple military surrender. Though scattered fighting in the country would continue for another month, the two largest Confederate armies had surrendered. The war was over.

The small, two-room museum at the Bennett Place features many artifacts from the Bennitt family, including books the children used to learn to read and the farm's ledger books. Other displays describe the life of the "yeoman farmer," the average North Carolinian during the war. A short slide show describes the war's progress through period art and letters read by actors.

The buildings are all reproductions because the original structures burned in 1923. The reproductions are faithful to the originals, and the recreated Bennitt cabin is built around the original fireplace. A section of the original Hillsborough-to-Durham road rests beside the cabin.

Retrace your route on U.S. 70 West to the intersection with I-85, about 1.75 miles from Bennett Place. Take the entrance to I-85 North. Take Exit 175 off I-85 North, just a few miles north of Bennett Place. After exiting I-85, turn north on N.C. 157. Drive 0.4 mile and turn right, or east, onto Duke Homestead Road. The Duke Homestead and Tobacco Museum is 0.5 mile down this road on the right.

The Duke Homestead and Tobacco Museum is not really a Civil War site, but it demonstrates how some enterprising former Confederates were able to regain economic status in a country that was otherwise devastated by war. Washington Duke was the brother of Robert Duke. Robert Duke was married to the daughter of James Bennitt, the owner of the house where Johnston surrendered to Sherman. Washington Duke resisted service in the Confederate Army until 1864, when he reluctantly left his farm and joined the Confederate Navy. Captured outside of Richmond in the closing days of the war, he made his way back to New Bern and walked home to Orange County (The city of Durham did not yet exist).

When Duke arrived home, he found "the Yankees had stolen everything but a wagonload of tobacco and two blind mules" from his farm.

It is a wonder that the Yankees did not steal the tobacco. Duke noticed the attraction the soldiers had to tobacco, so he started pounding his dried leaves into tiny bits, then weighing the leaves out in one-pound sacks. The Federal soldiers quickly bought all the tobacco Washington Duke and his sons could grow and dry. Even after the Federal occupying troops left the area and returned north, they wrote Duke asking him to ship his tobacco north. The letters often contained money. Their affection for Duke's tobacco was so strong, these Yankees trusted the former Confederate with their money.

Duke may have been an uneducated farmer, but he knew a market when he saw one. Within a decade, he had become a prosperous businessman. He moved to Durham and built a tobacco processing factory that produced enough profits to make the Duke family extremely wealthy. They spent their profits diversifying into all sorts of things, including investing in a newfangled energy source called electricity when the Duke Power Company was launched by the family. The Dukes also had enough money to buy a small college in Trinity, North Carolina. They moved the college and its faculty to Durham, then named the new college after themselves.

Retrace your route to I-85 North and drive to Exit 177-C, the Business U.S. 501 North exit. Drive 2.4 miles north on Business U.S. 501. Bear right at the seventh traffic light after exiting the interstate onto Old Oxford Road. A historic marker on Old Oxford Road will mention the Stagville Preservation Center. Drive north 6.8 miles on Old Oxford Road to a small white sign announcing Stagville Preservation Center. The center is located at 5825 Old Oxford Road.

The Stagville Plantation house was built by Richard Bennehan in 1787, then expanded in 1799. By 1860, the original 4,000-acre plantation had been combined with holdings of the neighboring Cameron family to encompass nearly 30,000 acres. Much of the Bennehan and Cameron properties merged when Rebecca Bennehan married Judge Duncan Cameron in the mid-1800s. The plantation grew tobacco, grain, and livestock, and was the largest plantation in North Carolina. Nearly 900 slaves worked on Stagville Plantation, giving the plantation the dubious distinction of having the largest concentration of slaves in North Carolina. (In 1860, more than 300,000 slaves lived in North Carolina.) While the house appears modest, it was likely the best for miles around.

When the Civil War began, Stagville Plantation was under the control

Slave cabin at Horton Grove

of Paul Cameron, son of Judge Cameron and Rebecca Bennehan Cameron. Paul Cameron was a skilled farmer, and during the war, much of the agricultural output of Stagville was sold to the Confederacy and shipped away to feed hungry soldiers. There are no indications that the plantation was ever attacked. It is likely that General Johnston surrendered his Confederate army before Sherman's Union army ever discovered the vast store of food that was probably stored on the plantation.

All of the slave cabins, storehouses, and other outbuildings that were in back of the Stagville Plantation house have disappeared with time. But the house is preserved, and there is a good slide show that describes how the plantation worked.

Leaving the Stagville Preservation Center parking lot, turn right, or north, onto Old Oxford Road. At 0.7 mile from the parking lot, continue straight onto the gravel Jock Road rather than following the main paved road which turns sharply to the right. Drive 0.2 mile on Jock Road to the Great Barn of Stagville, a 135-foot-long, wooden barn built by slaves in 1860. Once the largest agricultural building in North Carolina, the white barn with a red roof housed mules needed to work the fields.

Turn around and drive 0.1 mile back up Jock Road to a gravel driveway on the right, leading to four wooden cabins and a house. Turn up the driveway and park in front of the house. These are the remains of the slave community of Horton Grove. The two-story, four-room cabins were built by slaves in 1851. Research indicates that one slave family probably shared each of the rooms. Each room measures just seventeen feet by seventeen feet. The fifth building on the site is the Horton House, built in the 1770s. This cabin is typical of the houses built by the small farmers who made up most of North Carolina's population before the Civil War. The Horton House was used later as slave quarters. Nearly eighty people lived in this small community, which existed to serve Stagville Plantation.

Cameron kept good records and left details about the abilities of his skilled slaves. Slaves named George and Cryus were teamsters, able to control six-mule teams that transported crops to market. Matthew was a miller who ground corn into flour. The flour went into barrels made by Solomon, a cooper or barrel maker. Daniel sawed boards and Dandridge, a carpenter, used them to build and repair the plantation buildings. Dandridge may have been the architect and contractor for the barn, which stands just as solidly today as the day it was built.

Retrace your route to Old Oxford Road and then to U.S. 501 and I-85. This concludes The Surrender Tour.

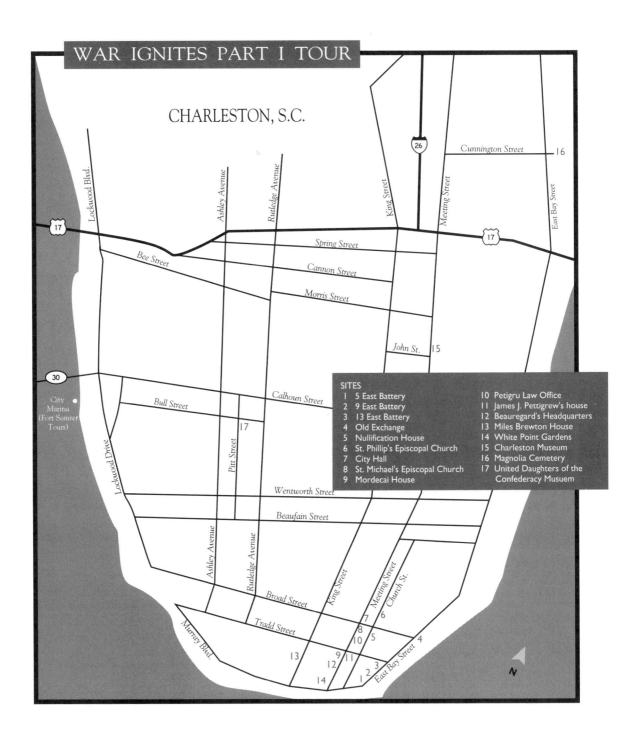

WAR IGNITES PART I TOUR

CHARLESTON, S.C.

Lockwood Blvd.
Ashley Avenue
Rutledge Avenue
King Street
Meeting Street
Cunnington Street   16
East Bay Street
26
17   17
Spring Street
Bee Street
Cannon Street
Morris Street
John St. 15
30
City Marina (Fort Sumter Tours)
Bull Street   Calhoun Street
Lockwood Drive
Pitt Street
17
Wentworth Street
Beaufain Street
Ashley Avenue
Rutledge Avenue
King Street
Meeting Street
Church St.
7
Broad Street   6
8
Murray Blvd.   Tradd Street   10   5
13   9 11   4
12   2 3
14   1   East Bay Street

SITES

1	5 East Battery	10	Petigru Law Office
2	9 East Battery	11	James J. Pettigrew's house
3	13 East Battery	12	Beauregard's Headquarters
4	Old Exchange	13	Miles Brewton House
5	Nullification House	14	White Point Gardens
6	St. Phillip's Episcopal Church	15	Charleston Museum
7	City Hall	16	Magnolia Cemetery
8	St. Michael's Episcopal Church	17	United Daughters of the
9	Mordecai House		Confederacy Musuem

N

War Ignites
Part I Tour

This tour covers Fort Sumter and the historic district of downtown Charleston. The tour starts at the City Marina, where visitors can take a ferry ride to Fort Sumter. After returning from the fort, it moves to White Point Gardens, the Battery, and throughout Charleston's historic district for an extended walking tour of houses and buildings that are significant to Civil War history, including the site of the building where South Carolinians signed the Ordnance of Secession. After returning to the car, the tour continues to the Charleston Museum, Magnolia Cemetery, and the United Daughters of the Confederacy Museum.

Total mileage: approximately 9 miles.

In the South, secession fever had been building for thirty years, ever since South Carolina–native John C. Calhoun first proposed that states could "nullify" federal laws they did not like or else secede. Still, it was not until April 1860 that the idea of states actually leaving the Union became a real possibility.

In that month, at the national convention of the Democratic Party, things came to a head. Some Democratic strategists had decided that Charleston, a hotbed of angry, secessionist rhetoric, should host the convention. That decision was initially promoted as a way to appease Southern firebrands. Today, many historians speculate that the selection of Charleston was really engineered by northern Democrats to settle the question of whether the United States would continue to allow slavery within its borders.

Whatever else it was, the 1860 Democratic National Convention was a zoo. Delegates to the convention overwhelmed the services that Charleston could provide. Innkeepers set room rates as high as they wanted since most of the delegates were visiting Yankees unlikely ever to return. Some delegates stayed at the Hibernian Hall in dormitory-style arrangements. The New York and Massachusetts delegations came down in their own ships with their own prostitutes. Apparently, they were concerned that a Southern city could not provide them with the quality of prostitutes to which they had become accustomed to up north.

The convention was held in Institute Hall, just up the block from the Mills House, the main hotel in town. It was at Institute Hall where the more than six hundred delegates debated on whether to allow slavery in the new territories, and who would best represent the party's interests in that fall's presidential election. More than twenty-four hundred spectators watched.

Pro- and anti-slavery politicians made speech after speech. The Southern politicians promised they would leave the Union if they did not get their way. The Northern politicians were adamant that they would never support slavery. Stephen A. Douglas, the man who had hoped to be a bridge between the two sides, could say nothing to bring the sides together. After seven days, the delegates of eight Southern states walked out, and the convention ended without a candidate. Only after the convention was reconvened in Baltimore weeks later did Douglas get the Democratic nomination.

It did not really matter. Thanks to a split vote between four different parties, Republican Abraham Lincoln was elected president. In his campaign, Lincoln said that, while he would not try to abolish slavery where it existed, he would work against it in the new territories. That was all it took to convince many Southerners that the North was ready to attack slavery and all their other institutions.

Within days of Lincoln's election, actually within hours, South Carolinians were calling for the state to leave the Union. On November 10, 1860, the general assembly approved a bill calling for a secession convention in December. The convention started on December 18, 1860, and was held at Institute Hall in Charleston. Most of the 169 delegates were slave-holding planters. These men represented a minority of South Carolina's citizens, but they stood to lose the most if slavery were abolished or otherwise controlled by the federal government.

The "debate" was actually two days of repeated calls for secession. When the vote actually came, it was unanimous. The signing of the Ordnance of Secession, a remarkably short document, took place at Institute Hall so the crush of spectators could be accommodated. Within minutes, the *Charleston Mercury* newspaper was selling a special edition proclaiming "The Union Is Dissolved."

Of South Carolina's wealthy planter class, only James Louis Petigru, Charleston's most prominent lawyer, who was also a slave holder, seemed to remain a Unionist, even in the face of the countless loud and boisterous parades. Mary Boykin Chesnut wrote in her diary that Petigru was the only man in South Carolina who had not seceded.

Things began to move swiftly after South Carolina seceded from the Union. Major Robert Anderson of the United States Army, commander of Fort Moultrie on Sullivan's Island and Fort Sumter, the unfinished fort in Charleston harbor, was ordered to hold his forts until the situation appeared useless.

Anderson, a Kentucky native who had owned slaves, figured he would never be able to hold Moultrie, a low-walled fort which could be easily attacked on its three land sides. On December 26, 1860, Anderson moved Fort Moultrie's force of eighty-nine men to Fort Sumter. Before leaving Fort Moultrie, he spiked the cannons (drove long metal rods into the holes where sparks would normally fire the gun powder charge). He also set fire to the wooden gun carriages. His final act of defiance was to chop down the fort's flagpole. If a secession government was going to occupy his fort, they would not be using his flagpole.

The next night, a company of South Carolina militia captured Castle Pinckney, a smaller Federal fort just a few hundred yards off Charleston's shore. This was the first seizure of United States government property by the state of South Carolina, more than three months before the war would officially start.

South Carolina spent the next three months preparing for war. The state started rearming Fort Moultrie and building up the gun batteries at Fort Johnson on James Island. "A ring of fire" of more than sixty forts and batteries was constructed on the land masses facing Sumter and on the outskirts of Charleston. One of the most interesting installations was a four-cannon battery designed to float in the harbor. The battery was designed by Clement Stevens, a landlubber banker who would later become a general. Armored by railroad iron, the floating battery was built on the city's waterfront and towed to Sullivan's Island. This forerunner of the ironclad was the first of many military innovations that would be developed during the Civil War.

Not everything went smoothly for the new Confederates. One careless recruit, who ignored his mother's warning about running with sharp objects, was stabbed in the eye with a bayonet while horsing around in the barracks. He died before the war even started. A practicing gun crew on Morris Island accidentally fired on Fort Sumter, sending a cannonball bouncing off the fort's wharf. Their excuse was that they didn't know the cannon was loaded. Embarrassed Confederates hastily and sincerely apologized to the Federals they would soon be trying to kill.

The whole time the South Carolinians were preparing for attack, Anderson and his men at Fort Sumter were mounting guns and eating through their rations. Anderson figured he had enough food to last through the second week of April. After that, he would have to surrender or starve.

The first intentional shot fired by either side came on January 9, 1861, when a Federal supply ship, *The Star of the West*, was fired on by batteries at Morris Island. Two cannonballs hit the ship. The balls did little damage, but they did convince the ship's captain that the Citadel cadets manning the guns had done their homework in artillery class.

By early April, Fort Sumter's rations were almost gone, and Confederate Brigadier General Pierre Gustave Toutant Beauregard, commander of all Confederate forces in the city, knew it. He also knew that he would soon be the center of national and world attention. That pleased the native of Louisiana, who once ran for mayor of New Orleans while still on active duty with the United States Army.

No one ever accused Beauregard of being shy when it came to promoting himself. In January of 1861, he even secured the job as superintendent of West Point, before smarter thinkers in Washington realized that it was not a good idea to put a secessionist Southerner in charge of the United States Military Academy. Beauregard's orders to report to West Point were revoked after one day.

On April 11, 1861, Beauregard sent messages to Anderson formally requesting that he and his men evacuate Fort Sumter. Beauregard was very respectful—Anderson had once been his instructor at West Point. Mindful that Anderson would want an honorable surrender, Beauregard even promised to tell the major when the Confederates were going to begin firing, so Anderson would have proof for his superiors that he was in an untenable position.

Anderson asked if he could surrender on April 15. That was no good for Beauregard. A relief mission of several ships, personally ordered by President Lincoln, would arrive before then, and a resupplied Fort Sumter would have no reason to surrender. At 3:30 A.M. on April 12, 1861, Beauregard sent word to Fort Sumter that the bombardment would begin in one hour. Anderson told his men to hunker down inside their casemates.

The first Confederate round was fired from Fort Johnson. Soon, more than forty cannons were firing on Fort Sumter. From most Confederate positions, it was just a mile away, easy distance for even untrained cannoneers.

Fort Sumter did not actively return fire until daybreak, a move designed to conserve limited ammunition. Captain Abner Doubleday, who did not invent baseball, claimed the honor of firing the first Union cannon in reply. Doubleday was one of five staff officers at Sumter who later went on to become a Union general.

The Confederate shelling continued through the 12th and 13th. It finally ended, after thirty-four hours, around 1:30 P.M. on April 13, 1861. Incredibly, though the fort took many direct hits, no Union soldiers were killed. No Confederates were killed either. More than three thousand artillery shells, some weighing more than forty-two pounds, had been fired during the attack, and no one was killed.

The surrender terms were simple. Anderson and his men were allowed to evacuate the fort, taking all their personal property with them. They were allowed to sail to the northern port of their choice. Anderson was even granted permission to fire a salute to the United States flag as it was lowered from its staff. As the guns were firing, a burning piece of cotton landed in a pile of unfired cartridges. The cartridges exploded, killing one man outright and mortally wounding another. The first two men to lose their lives after the start of the Civil War were accidentally killed by salute cannons.

For the rest of the war, Fort Sumter was occupied by Confederate troops.

Although Union ironclads pounded it in April 1863, and it endured eleven major bombardments from Federal land batteries on James and Morris Islands during the period of August 1, 1863, to September 18, 1864, the fort remained a defiant symbol of secession throughout the war.

Fort Sumter never actually surrendered. On the evening of February 17, 1865, the Confederates evacuated the fort. Sherman's capture of Savannah two months earlier put a large Federal force in Charleston's rear, and Confederate Lieutenant General Hardee was taking no chances that he would be trapped between Sherman and the blockading squadron on the Atlantic.

The rest of Charleston surrendered to a handful of Union soldiers. There was not a lot of the city left to capture. Much of the central core of the city had been destroyed in an accidental fire on December 11, 1861. Houses, businesses, and churches that didn't burn then had been shelled regularly over the previous two years by Federal land batteries on James and Morris Islands.

On the night before Federal troops entered the city, two more fires began on opposite sides of town and burned toward the center. Looting by gangs of deserters and draft dodgers was rampant. When the Federal troops came at daylight, Charleston's mayor practically begged them to take over his city to put an end to the violence.

There was one final irony to the surrender of Charleston. The first Union troops in Charleston were Black. The slaves that South Carolinians wanted to control at the April 1860 Democratic Convention and the December 1860 Secession Convention now ruled over the city.

Start the War Ignites Part I Tour with a visit to Fort Sumter because the tour-boat company to the national monument makes only three trips a day. The boat leaves from the City Marina at 9:30 A.M., Noon, and 2:30 P.M. (In January and February, the boat only makes the 2:30 P.M. trip).

The City Marina is on the west side of the city on the Ashley River. From the intersection of Calhoun and Meeting Streets (two blocks south of the city's visitor's center on John Street), take Calhoun Street west for 11 blocks to Lockwood Drive. Lockwood Drive is located just before going over the S.C. 30 bridge to James Island. Turn left onto Lockwood Drive and follow the signs to the marina.

The boat ride takes about thirty minutes to reach the fort, located in the harbor near the Atlantic Ocean. Along the way, an audio tape describes the early history of Charleston.

The boat passes by some of Charleston's most famous houses on the land point called the Battery. Before the Confederates captured Fort Sumter, cannons facing the fort were placed in White Point Gardens on the point of the Battery. The cannons did not fire at Sumter, nor were they fired upon by the Federals. After passing the Battery, a tiny brick fort appears on the left, several hundred yards offshore from Charleston and in front of the Cooper River Bridge. This is Castle Pinckney, the first Federal installation captured by the South Carolina militia.

On the night of December 27, 1860, Colonel James Johnston Pettigrew and a small force of Charleston militia rowed out to Castle Pinckney. They demanded the fort's surrender from United States Army Lieutenant Richard K. Meade, who held the fort with four brick masons. Meade turned his back on Pettigrew and refused to recognize the authority of South Carolina to take the fort. He even refused Pettigrew's offer to supply a receipt for the fort and its contents. Instead, Meade simply climbed into a rowboat and pulled for Fort Sumter. No blood was shed, although Pettigrew was peeved at how rudely he was treated by Lieutenant Meade.

After capturing Castle Pinckney, Pettigrew, a cousin of Charleston's most prominent lawyer, James Petigru (who preferred the Scottish spelling of the name), returned to his native North Carolina, where he joined the regular Confederate Army. He eventually worked his way up to brigadier general. Pettigrew commanded one third of the Confederate attack staged on the third day of Gettysburg. In North Carolina, the misnamed Pickett's Charge has always been known as the Pettigrew-Pickett-Trimble Assault. (See the Railroad Defense Tour for a more detailed biography on Pettigrew.)

Meade met Pettigrew under more friendly circumstances in 1862. Meade was constructing earthworks at Rainbow Bend on the Roanoke River in northern North Carolina, and Pettigrew was in charge of Confederate forces in the region. Yes, Meade, the regular United States Army lieutenant who had dutifully resisted the South Carolina militia, joined the Confederate Army once the war began. He was the only member of Anderson's officer staff to resign.

Cannon in Fort Sumter

Castle Pinckney played a minor role in the rest of the war. Insignificant as a fort, it was used as a prisoner-of-war camp. Period photographs show Federal prisoners at Castle Pinckney had a relatively good life compared to the overcrowded conditions many Federal prisoners suffered. Today, privately owned Castle Pinckney is not on any tour. Historians say that four cannons remain buried on its grounds.

After viewing Castle Pinckney, move to the right side of the boat to see the site of Fort Johnson, located on James Island at the point of land that comes closest to Fort Sumter. Little remains of the original fort, which fired the first shot of the Civil War, but many are surprised at how close the tip of the island is to Fort Sumter. Sumter was an easy target from Fort Johnson, as well as from Fort Moultrie on Sullivan's Island

While docking at Fort Sumter, move back to the right side of the boat and look towards Sullivan's Island to view Fort Moultrie.

First-time visitors to Fort Sumter are sometimes surprised, maybe even disappointed, at the low, one-story fort. It hardly looks like a structure that could start a war. What many of these visitors do not realize is that today's Fort Sumter is just one-third its original height of fifty feet.

Construction on Fort Sumter started in 1828. The fort's construction was part of a federal government plan to create a string of forts defending the country's harbors. Since there was no solid ground to build on in Charleston's harbor, the construction of Fort Sumter was an engineering marvel. More than seventy thousand tons of rock were dumped on a sandbar to provide the base of the fort. Some of the rock came from as far away as Maine. The construction of the fort took so long that it was not even finished when Anderson occupied it. He spent the first three months of 1861 mounting the fort's guns. Although the fort was designed for 135 guns, Anderson could only mount 65. Even mounting that half-complement took a long time. The fort's full garrison was supposed to be 650 men, but Anderson's force was barely a tenth of that.

The Confederate bombardment in 1861 damaged Sumter's three original stories. Federal bombardments in 1863 and 1864 brought the top two stories down into mounds of rubble. Confederate workers piled the rubble behind the remaining walls, making the fort even more formidable.

The boat stays at Fort Sumter for only one hour, about half the time you need to explore the whole fort, spend time in the excellent museum, and walk around the top to view the range of Confederate positions. To save precious time, visitors might want to skip the park ranger's fifteen-minute history lesson that follows the initial orientation session. The history is covered in the park brochure and in the museum.

Start the tour on the ground level by examining the guns poking through the casemates facing Charleston, more than four miles away. The city's citizens had nothing to fear from these cannons. These guns were aimed to fire on ships that might slip past artillery on the opposite side of the fort.

Walk into the parade ground to examine two, 15-inch Rodmans, an 8-inch Columbiad, and a 10-inch mortar. All are typical of the type and size of coastal artillery that would have been used by Confederates and Federals. The mortar is the type of gun that would have fired the first shot on Fort Sumter. Mortars were siege weapons designed to throw shells high into the air then explode on or just above the ground. Cannons were used to punch through walls and the sides of ships.

Examine the wall in front of the cannon display. The holes in the wall were made by both Confederate and Federal shells. At several points on the wall, solid metal balls and shells have been left where they punched through the brick.

Walk behind Battery Huger, a black concrete structure added after the turn of this century, to view the guns that would have fired on Fort Moultrie to the northeast. A Federal cannon that has been mounted to fire up into the air in an attempt to make it work like a mortar is located at this point. The Confederates tried modifying cannons the same way at Fort Macon in Morehead City, North Carolina. It did not work for them either.

Climb back to the top of Fort Sumter to see how close Fort Moultrie, Fort Johnson, and the Morris Island batteries were. There are several exhibit markers on top of the wall that describe events that are important to the history of Fort Sumter and Charleston.

Somewhere east of Fort Sumter in the Atlantic Ocean lies the CSS *Hunley*, the world's first successful submarine. On February 17, 1864, the *Hunley*, a black, forty-foot-long vessel that was powered by eight men turning a crank hooked to a propeller, sank a Union blockading vessel called the USS *Housatonic*. The submerged *Hunley* rammed the Union ship and left behind a "torpedo," a keg of gunpowder that exploded when the Confederates pulled on a lanyard. The *Housatonic* went down in thirty feet of water, but the *Hunley* never returned.

For nearly a century, historians assumed the Confederate ship was stuck in the Union ship. In the summer of 1995, the *Hunley* was discovered some distance away from the wreckage of the *Housatonic*, leading to speculation that it was returning to Charleston when it sprang a leak. Plans are being developed to try to raise this historic vessel. The *Hunley*'s exact location off Fort Sumter is kept secret to foil relic hunters. (Full-size models of the *Hunley* are located in front of the Charleston Museum and at the South Carolina Museum of History in Columbia.)

Another marker on the south side of the fort describes an ill-advised night amphibious assault by Federal sailors against Fort Sumter on September 9, 1863. The Federal naval commander at Charleston, Admiral John A. Dahlgren, had told the officer in charge of the assault that the Confederates had all but abandoned Sumter. Dahlgren made up this assessment of the fort's defenses out of thin air. He had no idea how many soldiers were behind Sumter's walls.

The Union sailors, assuming they would overwhelm the handful of men they had been told might resist them, attacked at 1:00 A.M. They were surprised to find a full force of Confederates firing from the parapets and tossing an early version of hand grenades. Twenty-one Federals were killed or wounded, and more than a hundred were captured. Not a single Confederate received a scratch. Fort Sumter's commander was Major Stephen Elliott, Jr., who likely felt some satisfaction in the victory. His home in Beaufort, South Carolina, was being occupied by Federal officers at the time.

A sign on the southwest side of Fort Sumter points to Morris Island, a three-mile-long strip of sand. In the summer of 1863, Morris Island was key to the Union's hopes of attacking Fort Sumter and Charleston. At its north end was Battery Wagner, a formidable sand fort that commanded the land strip to the south, as well as the bay to the north and the ocean to the east. On July 10, 1863, the Federals landed more than 10,000 troops on Morris Island. The Union soldiers started a slow, costly push up the island. The first attack made it to within six hundred yards of the battery. The next attack, on the following day, made another two hundred yards. The advance on the remaining four hundred yards cost 339 Federal soldiers their lives. Only 12 Confederates were killed in the attack.

Over the following week, the Federals tried to bombard Battery Wagner into submission. On the night of July 18, 1863, the Federals decided the Confederate position had been weakened enough for a direct frontal assault by 6,000 soldiers. The regiment chosen to spearhead the assault was the 54th Massachusetts, a unit made up totally of Black men, though commanded by white officers. The 54th mostly consisted of northern-born Blacks, including two sons of Frederick Douglass. Douglass was a former slave whose brilliance in organization and rhetoric had convinced Northern politicians to create all-Black regiments.

The night attack was disastrous. The Federals had to run down a narrow strip of land before hitting a water-and-obstacle-filled ditch. The Confederates, who had ridden out the week-long bombardment inside sand-covered bombproofs, fired down into the 54th at point-blank range. More than half of the 600-man regiment were killed or wounded, including its colonel, a rich Bostonian named Robert Gould Shaw.

Shaw's body was stripped, tossed into a ditch with his Black soldiers, and buried. No effort was made by the Confederates to return his body through the lines, as was the custom with high-ranking officers. Shaw's father was not upset by this radical mistreatment of his son's body. Mr. Shaw said he was proud that his twenty-five-year-old son rested with the men he had trained. Total Federal casualties during the attack on Battery Wagner attack were more than 1,500, compared to just 200 Confederate casualties.

Like Fort Sumter, Battery Wagner would never be taken by the Federals in combat. It was abandoned in September 1863, as the Federals landed more reinforcements on Morris and Folly Islands. Battery Wagner washed into the Atlantic Ocean in the last century.

Once Battery Wagner was abandoned, the Federals used Morris Island as the main base for their shelling of Charleston and Fort Sumter. One of the guns mounted in the marsh of Morris Island was an 8-inch Parrott rifle that could lob a 150-pound shell nearly four-and-a-half miles. Nicknamed the "Swamp Angel," the gun rested on a platform designed to float on top of the mud. Although the barrel of the gun burst on its thirty-sixth round, the Swamp Angel was a successful experiment that showed Federal engineers they could put heavy guns into any type of terrain. The citizens of Charleston felt the effects of this experiment over the next eighteen months, as all of the city below Calhoun Street came within easy range of the Federal guns.

From the upper deck, walk down into Fort Sumter's museum to see the artifacts and read the extensive historical displays. The most valuable artifact on display is the United States flag that was flying over Fort Sumter when Anderson surrendered. Four years to the day after he had hauled it down, Anderson hoisted the same flag back above the fort.

As you return from Fort Sumter on the boat, the audio tape will describe some of the early history of Fort Moultrie and go into some detail on Castle Pinckney.

After docking, get in the car and head for the Battery. From the City Marina, turn right, or southeast, onto Lockwood Drive heading toward the city. Drive about 1.0 mile. After passing the Coast Guard Station, turn right onto Chisolm Street. Drive one block, then turn right onto Tradd Street. Drive one block to Murray Boulevard, the road running next to the sea wall along the Ashley River. Turn left, or east, onto Murray Boulevard. This sea wall has protected Charleston since the 1850s.

Follow Murray Boulevard for about 0.7 mile to a convenient parking spot somewhere near White Point Gardens, the city park near the end of the Battery. White Point Gardens starts at King Street.

As you walk along Murray Boulevard, you will notice the mortars pointing toward James Island. During the war, these mortars were located on James Island and used to bombard Charleston. Continue on Murray Boulevard to the intersection with East Battery Street. At this intersection, turn left and head northeast on East Battery Street. The several cannons along the street pointing toward Fort Sumter mark the location of a former battery. A Confederate monument is at the corner of Murray and East Battery Streets.

The northernmost cannon in this battery is the most historic cannon in the city. This eleven-inch Dahlgren, at the intersection of East and South Battery Streets, was recovered by the Confederates from the wreck of the USS *Keokuk*, a Federal ironclad. The *Keokuk* was sunk off Morris Island by Confederates in Fort Sumter.

The recovery of the *Keokuk*'s guns might be the most incredible salvage operation in all of military history. Working at night within two miles of blockading Federal ships, the Confederates spent three weeks cutting open the tops of the ship's two turrets and unbolting two, 14-foot-long cannons. The salvage was all done by volunteers gulping breaths of air then diving into the submerged ship.

Once recovered, the guns were remounted and used by the Confederates. One of the guns was sold as scrap after the war. The cannon in the park was placed there in 1899 as a monument to the Confederate salvagers' hard work and ingenuity. The cannon's squared-off muzzle was created by the Federals when they installed the guns in the *Keokuk*. The turret opening on the ship was too narrow for the cannon's barrel. Instead of enlarging the turret opening, they shaved down the cannon.

The yellow house beside the cannon, at 5 East Battery Street, belonged to Dr. St. Julien Ravenel, a physician who dabbled with inventions in his spare time. Ravenel developed fertilizers and suggested the theory of plowing under cover crops to return nutrients to the soil. He also designed the *David*, a cross between the submarine *Hunley* and a pre-World War II version of a patrol torpedo, or PT, boat. The *David* did not fully submerge, but it did sink low enough in the water to become almost invisible on a dark night.

On October 5, 1863, the *David* severely damaged the armored frigate USS *New Ironsides* by ramming her and setting off a torpedo seven feet below the Federal ship's water line. Several other *David*-type ships were manufactured during the war, but none successfully sank a Federal ship. However, for the next two years, Union ships around Charleston kept close watch for another *David* to come steaming out of the night.

Ravenel's house was built in 1849 and has walls that are thirty-two-inches thick. In 1865, the house needed those thick walls. Retreating Confederates realized that they could not move a huge, thirty-ton, English-made Blakely cannon that was located directly in front of Dr. Ravenel's house. Ignoring Ravenel's protests, the cannon was blown up to keep it out of Federal hands. Ravenel's house escaped serious damage, perhaps due to the thick walls, but in the explosion, a five-hundred-pound piece of the barrel spiraled high in the air, then crashed through the roof of Number 9 East Battery, two houses up the street. The five-hundred-pound piece of can-

Number 9 East Battery

non rests there today, balanced on roof breams above the master bedroom. Built in 1838, the house at 9 East Battery, notable for its thick, white pillars, was one of the first houses built on the lower Battery, acting as proof that the land on the point could support such large structures.

Continue walking on East Battery Street. The house at 13 East Battery Street was built in 1845. As one of the tallest houses on the waterfront, its roof was where many Charlestonians watched the bombardment of Fort Sumter in 1861.

The Edmondston-Alston House at 21 East Battery Street was briefly occupied by General Robert E. Lee after the December 1861 fire. It is now operated as a museum by the Historic Charleston Foundation.

Continue north on East Battery Street until it becomes East Bay Street. During the war, blockade runners and packet boats docked at the wharves on the Cooper River in this region. One of those supply ships was a 147-foot-long, twin-engined boat called the *Planter*. The *Planter* was a shallow-draft boat that was used by Confederates to deliver cargo and messages to the various forts around the harbor.

The *Planter*'s pilot was a slave named Robert Smalls. A native of Beaufort, South Carolina, Smalls was trusted implicitly by the ship's captain, C.J. Relyea. Relyea paid Small's master for the slave's services. Relyea was a predictable man who always wore the same white straw hat and had a habit of standing on his boat's bow with his arms folded across his chest. Smalls noticed those habits and used them to launch the most daring slave escape of the war.

Early on May 12, 1862, Smalls and six other slave crewmen boarded the *Planter*, several hours sooner than they normally would. They built up the fire in the ship's boiler and started upriver, waving to the trusting sentry as if they were on normal business. Instead of continuing on their normal route, they pulled up alongside another steamer and picked up the wives and children of Smalls and the other slaves. They then turned downriver. Smalls put on the captain's white hat and stood in the bow with his arms folded. He was careful to turn his back to anyone he saw on shore or on another boat to hide his black skin.

Smalls slowed the *Planter* as the ship neared Fort Sumter. He wanted the sentries there to see the familiar ship at a familiar time, just before dawn.

He knew the sentries would be less likely to challenge him at the slow speed, rather than if the boat came charging out of the darkness. As the *Planter* neared Fort Sumter, Smalls blew the correct recognition signal on the ship's whistle. When Smalls cruised past the point where the ship normally would have turned south toward Morris Island, he pushed both throttles full ahead and headed to the open sea.

The Federal blockading ships outside the harbor were preparing to sink the charging ship until Smalls hoisted a white flag. Smalls delivered the *Planter*, four cannons that had been removed from Confederate forts, and himself to Federal forces. He was the most valuable prize. Smalls served the Union Navy as the *Planter's* pilot for the rest of the war. His service was invaluable since he knew the depth of dozens of South Carolina's inlets and rivers. He was cited for gallantry in one battle when the white captain of the *Planter* cowered under fire, and Smalls took over control of the ship.

Smalls survived the war, became a politician, and served South Carolina in both state houses and in the United States House of Representatives. He moved back to Beaufort where he bought his master's former home. He died in 1915. (See The Sea Islands Tour for more details on Smalls's life.)

At 122 East Bay Street, at the intersection with Broad Street, is the Old Exchange, which served as Charleston's post office during the war. Confederate postal displays are located inside the building.

Turn left, or west, onto Broad Street and walk two blocks to Church Street. Turn left and walk one block to 94 Church Street. In the 1830s, John C. Calhoun gathered with other South Carolina leaders at this location to discuss and refine their beliefs in nullification.

Turn around on Church Street and walk north, crossing over Broad Street. Continue to 146 Church Street, which is St. Phillip's Episcopal Church, built in 1835. During the war, St. Phillip's bells were melted for their steel, and the steeple was used as a Confederate lookout. The steeple was also used as an aiming point for Federal artillery on Morris and James Islands.

In the church's cemetery across the street, located in the shade of a spreading oak tree, is the tomb of John C. Calhoun. (See The Dead Generals Tour for details on the life of Calhoun.)

Leave the cemetery and continue walking north on Church Street to Cumberland Street. Turn left, or west, onto Cumberland Street and walk one block to Meeting Street. Turn left, or south, and walk down Meeting Street. Walk to 134 Meeting Street. On the left side of the street in the first block, is a modern building with a plaque on the wall identifying it as the location of Institute Hall, the place where the Ordnance of Secession was signed. Institute Hall burned in the December 1861 fire.

Continue walking south to 115 Meeting Street, located at the intersection with Queen Street. This is the Mills House Hotel. The present building, although taller than the original Mills House, looks similar to the hotel that was the main lodging for delegates at the 1860 Democratic Convention.

During the December 1861 fire, the Confederate general in charge of Charleston's defenses watched the city burn from the roof of the Mills House. He became concerned that the hotel might burn next, so he walked to the lobby to evacuate. To his alarm, he saw a number of women and babies still in the lobby. Grabbing one child and directing his staff to grab others, the group fled out a back door through a hail of sparks.

It may have been this brush with death that caused Robert E. Lee's newly grown beard to turn white. Lee's newly purchased horse, Greenbriar, also survived the fire in a nearby stable. Lee renamed the horse Traveler.

Next door to the Mills House on Meeting Street, to the south, is Hibernian Hall, a fellowship hall for Irish-born Americans. The hall was rented by Democratic delegates and used as a dormitory at the 1860 convention.

Continue south on Meeting Street to the intersection with Broad Street. The county courthouse on the northwest corner of this intersection still shows some signs of Federal shell damage on the lower right portion of the wall facing Broad Street. On the northeast corner is City Hall, which was hit four times during the Federal bombardment.

On the second floor of City Hall is the city council meeting room, which is open to the public. The walls are graced with several large portraits and busts of Civil War characters. The most prominent is an original portrait of Confederate Brigadier General P.G.T. Beauregard, thought to have been painted before the war started. However, even before the war, he likely knew his service at Charleston would make history—in the background of

St. Michael's Episcopal Church

the painting is Fort Sumter. A cannon in the foreground of the portrait is aimed at the fort.

Another painting shows a vibrant John C. Calhoun, who was actually quite ill when the painting was done. A bust that is popular with visiting teenagers is of Charleston lawyer and Unionist James Petigru. Petigru's shoulder-length hair makes him resemble a rock-and-roll icon. Outside the City Council chambers is another, less dramatic portrait of Beauregard.

Leave City Hall and cross Broad Street to St. Michael's Episcopal Church, on the southeast corner of the intersection of Meeting and Broad Streets. The church was used as a sighting point for Federal artillery and was hit at least once. A shell crashed through the roof then through the pulpit, knocking off the front of the pulpit. The front piece was sent north for a while, where it came into the possession of Julia Ward Howe, writer of the *Battle Hymn of the Republic*. She gave it to a northern church, which later returned it to St. Michael's.

Leave the church and continue walking south on Meeting Street for a short distance until reaching St. Michael's Alley. Turn left onto St. Michael's Alley. At 8 St. Michael's Alley is the former law office of James Louis Petigru, and his cousin, James Johnston Pettigrew. Petigru likely lived in this 1849 house after his home on Broad Street was destroyed in the 1861 fire.

Though he was a slave owner, Petigru was a staunch Unionist. He stood alone among South Carolina's prominent politicians during the secession debates. He died in 1863. He lies buried in St. Michael's Cemetery behind his house and law office. His lengthy tombstone inscription includes the line "He withstood his people for his country, but his people did homage to the man who held his conscience higher than their praise."

Return to Meeting Street and cross to the west side, then walk south to 69 Meeting Street. This is the Poyas-Mordecai House, bought in 1837 by Moses Cohen Mordecai, a Jewish blockade runner. By the end of the war, his wholehearted support of the Confederacy had bankrupted him, but he quickly regained his fortune after moving to Baltimore. He did not forget the sacrifice of South Carolina. In 1870, he financed the removal of the bodies of eighty-four South Carolinians from Gettysburg. They were reburied in Charleston's Magnolia Cemetery under tombstones he purchased.

Continue south on Meeting Street to the intersection with Tradd Street and turn left. At 59 Tradd Street is the home of James Johnston Pettigrew, the commander of North Carolina's soldiers during the Confederate charge on the third day at Gettysburg.

Return to Meeting Street and head south again. At 37 Meeting Street is the house playfully called "The Bosoms," or "The Double-Breasted House," for obvious reasons. Built sometime around 1760, the house was owned by Otis Mills, who operated the Mills House. In 1861, Mills offered the house to Beauregard as a headquarters. Beauregard stayed here through 1863, until the Federals started shelling the city. He then moved north out of range. The general tethered his own cow, brought all the way from Louisiana, in the back of this house. Why he did not trust the milk from South Carolina bovines has never been determined.

The Bosoms, Beauregard's headquarters

Continue south to One Meeting Street. This is the Middleton House, built in 1846 and owned at one time by William Middleton. William Middleton also owned Middleton Place Plantation north of Charleston. During the war, the house was occupied by a company of Confederate marines. When the Middleton family asked them to leave, the marines politely, but firmly, declined.

Continue to the intersection of Meeting and South Battery Streets. At this intersection, on the edge of White Point Gardens, is a monument to the Confederate Navy that is also a working water fountain.

Turn west onto South Battery Street, walk one block, then turn right, or north, onto King Street. Walk one block to 27 King Street. This is the Miles Brewton House. Built in 1769, the Georgian-style house has the distinction of having served as unwilling host to the commanders of two conquering armies in two different centuries. The British occupied it during the American Revolution, and the Union occupied it after the fall of Charleston. The iron spikes on the fence were designed to keep out rebelling slaves.

Anti-slave devices found on Charleston homes

Turn around, walk down King Street, and retrieve your car. Then return to Meeting Street.

Drive fourteen blocks north on Meeting Street. Just past the intersection with Calhoun Street, on the left, is the Old Citadel, which is being restored into a hotel. This was once the location of the military academy that trained many of South Carolina's Civil War officers.

Drive one block on Meeting Street to the intersection with John Street. On this intersection, at 360 Meeting Street, is the Charleston Museum. A full-scale model of the *Hunley* is in front of the museum. It is not difficult to imagine the courage it took for nine men to crawl into this cramped, narrow boiler, then crank themselves out into the open ocean to attack a Federal warship.

Inside the museum are excellent exhibits on the slave trade, and cotton and rice cultivation, as well as displays of artillery, muskets, and swords. One of the more unusual exhibits shows mule shoes designed to help the beasts walk through the mud.

Leave the museum and continue driving north on Meeting Street. Start clocking mileage while passing the Cooper River Bridge at U.S. 17. At 1.4 miles north of the bridge, turn right onto Cunnington Street, just after passing over a railroad track. Continue two blocks and enter Magnolia Cemetery.

Inside the cemetery, take the road to the right side of the lake. On the right is the Confederate section, guarded by a statue and two cannons cast by the Tredegar Iron Works in Richmond, Virginia. The statue was erected by Mrs. Mary Ann Snowden, a Charlestonian who wanted to honor "her" boys. A close examination of the plaque on the statue shows pictures of tombstones with readable names, including the name of Mrs. Snowden. Behind the statue are the graves of several unknown Confederate sailors who were discovered several years ago buried under the parking lot of the Citadel's football stadium. The bodies were moved to Magnolia Cemetery and reburied with full military honors.

Follow the road past the Confederate section to the cemetery's office, where a detailed map showing Confederate graves can be obtained. The office was once the Magnolia Umbra farm house.

About 30 yards in front of the office under an obelisk is the grave of Confederate Brigadier General Micah Jenkins. Jenkins, the number one graduate in his 1854 Citadel class, started his own military academy in York, South Carolina. He left that school in 1861, when he was named colonel of the 5th South Carolina Regiment. After First Manassas, he formed the Palmetto Sharpshooters, a regiment made up of the best riflemen from several other regiments. At the age of twenty-six, he was named brigadier general and given command of a division in Lieutenant General James Longstreet's First Corps.

Jenkins fought well with Longstreet and was at his side during a reconnaissance ride in the dark during the Battle of the Wilderness in May 1864. Nervous Virginians fired on the horsemen, wounding Longstreet in the throat and Jenkins in the head. Jenkins was ordering his men forward in an imaginary battle when he expired a few hours later. He was twenty-eight years old. His obelisk makes no mention of his accidental death.

Directly east of Jenkins's grave, across three dirt streets and underneath a large oak tree, is the Hunley Circle. The bodies of Horace Hunley, inventor of the submarine, and the two crews who drowned before the machine could be perfected lie here. Hunley's family purchased the plot and paid for the burial of all of the men, whose names are listed on a small monument.

Follow the grass road beside the circle counterclockwise to the Rhett family cemetery and the resting place of Robert Barnwell Rhett. During the 1850s, Robert Barnwell Rhett was likely the South's number one secessionist. (See the Sea Islands Tour for more details on Rhett.)

Continue following the grass road counterclockwise to the grave of Confederate Brigadier General Arthur Manigault, two plots down from the Rhett plot. Manigault helped supervise the construction of the batteries around Charleston. He served as an aide to Beauregard before taking command of the 10th South Carolina Regiment. Manigault spent most of the war in the Army of Tennessee, winning promotion to brigadier general in 1863. In November of 1864, he was severely wounded in the head at the Battle of Franklin in Tennessee. He never returned to active duty. He was a planter after the war and died in 1886.

Retrace the road back past the cemetery office, almost to the entrance to the cemetery. This time, follow the road to the left side of the lake. Stop under a spreading oak tree, near a sign pointing the way to Green Hill, and look for the grave of Confederate Brigadier General Roswell Sabine Ripley. Ripley was a native of Ohio and a 1843 graduate of West Point who married a Charleston girl in 1852. Figuring that marriage is thicker than home-state ties, Ripley threw his lot with the Confederacy. He was in command of all the forts in South Carolina for almost a year. Ripley was severely wounded at Sharpsburg and did not do much for the rest of his military career. He died in 1887.

Follow the same road until it almost intersects with another road. Several graves before this intersection, under a white marble crypt that is distinguished by tips at each corner, is the grave of Confederate Brigadier General James Conner. Oddly, his own grave makes no mention of his rank, but his daughters' graves state that their father was a general.

A native of Charleston, Conner was the powerful United States attorney for South Carolina when the war started. He resigned and entered service as a captain in the Hampton Legion. He was later made colonel of the 22nd North Carolina Regiment, creating the rare occasion when someone from South Carolina was given command of a North Carolina regiment. Conner's leg was broken at Seven Pines, but he returned to command two months later. The same leg was hit again at Cedar Creek in October 1864 and was amputated. After the war, Conner was elected attorney general of South Carolina. He died in 1883.

While the cemetery map shows a grave for Confederate Brigadier General Clement Stevens, he was moved to Pendleton, South Carolina, after

Magnolia Cemetery

the war and reburied beside his brother-in-law, Confederate Brigadier General Barnard Bee.

After viewing Conner's grave, leave Magnolia Cemetery and retrace your route back to Meeting Street. Turn left onto Meeting Street and drive back towards downtown. Ten blocks after passing the Cooper River Bridges, and just after passing Marion Square on the right, turn right onto Calhoun Street and drive four blocks to Pitt Street. Turn left, or south, onto Pitt Street. Drive one block and cross over Bull Street. After crossing Bull Street, the first building on the left, at 34 Pitt Street, is the Marian Hankel Kindergarten, the temporary location of the United Daughters of the Confederacy Museum. Before Hurricane Hugo hit in 1989, the museum was located in the Market Hall at the intersection of Market and Meeting Streets. Market Hall's renovation is scheduled to start in 1996.

On Saturday and Sunday afternoons, visitors can find one of the best collections of Confederate relics outside of the Museum of the Confederacy in Richmond at this museum. More than fifteen original Confederate uniforms, most donated by the soldiers who wore them, are on display. Many of the tags describing the uniforms are written in the soldiers' own hands.

A rare piece in the museum's collection is the state's first secession flag, a blood red banner with a crescent moon in the corner pointing toward a star in the center. This flag flew from the Custom House the morning after the Ordnance of Secession was signed. The first and last Confederate flags that flew over Fort Sumter, the key to the door of Sumter, and a signal flag from the fort are also in the collection. The collection includes Civil War guns and swords, as well as personal items such as one soldier's cloth and wash soap.

This concludes the War Ignites Part I Tour. Part II of the tour begins on the grounds of the Citadel.

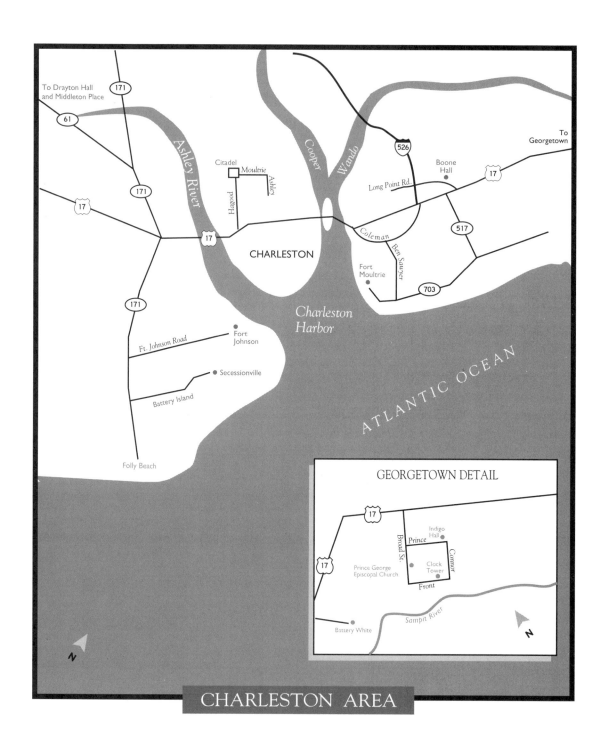

CHARLESTON AREA

War Ignites
Part II Tour

This tour covers the forts and historic sites on the outskirts of Charleston. It begins at the Citadel museum and library, where artifacts and paintings from this historic military school are on display. It then moves to the plantation houses of Drayton Hall, which was not burned by Federals, and Middleton Place, which was. From Middleton Place, the tour travels to Folly Beach, where a Federal invasion force landed, then to James Island, the site of the Battle of Secessionville and Fort Johnson. It continues across the Cooper River to Fort Moultrie on Sullivan's Island and Boone Hall Plantation. The tour ends with a side trip to Georgetown.

Total mileage: approximately 160 miles, including the side trip to Georgetown.

This tour picks up where the War Ignites Part I Tour ends, focusing on the sites outside of downtown Charleston. It should be taken after Part I. If taking this tour before taking the War Ignites Part I Tour, read the historical overview of that tour to understand the war in Charleston.

This tour starts on the grounds of The Citadel. From the intersection of Meeting and Calhoun Streets in downtown Charleston, drive 7 blocks west on Calhoun Street to Ashley Street and turn right, or north. Drive 14 blocks on Ashley Street to Moultrie Street and turn left. Moultrie Street leads directly to The Citadel.

The military school has been in this location since 1922. It first opened in 1842 at Marion Square, just north of the intersection of Meeting and Calhoun Streets.

At the beginning of the war there were 224 Citadel alumni. Of those men, 209 joined the Confederate Army. Four were promoted to general, and 19 headed regiments. Almost all of the rest served as officers. The school's most accomplished alumni during the war were Brigadier General Johnson Hagood (class of 1847), Brigadier General Micah Jenkins (class of 1854) and Brigadier General Ellison Capers (class of 1857).

After passing through The Citadel's gates, the first building on the right, at 171 Moultrie Street, is the school's museum. The museum shares the building with the school's library, which has several paintings of cadets in battle in Virginia and South Carolina.

The museum covers various periods in the school's history. There are some relics and photographs related to the Civil War, although all of the school's early records were lost in 1865. Someone at the school figured Charleston would be attacked by Sherman. All of the records were boxed up and sent away for safekeeping—to Columbia. The records were lost as Columbia went up in flames.

One of the more amusing relics from the early days of the school is a cadet's pen-and-ink drawing of a girls' school that was once located across from the old Citadel on Meeting Street. In one window, a gaggle of girls is giggling and waving. The headmaster of the girls' school is slamming down another window in disgust at the attention the cadets are paying his young students. At a third window, a mysterious young woman is standing silently, staring at the artist. Tradition says that this young woman was the artist's future wife.

Leave The Citadel by turning around on Moultrie Street. Turn right, or south, onto Hagood Avenue, the first street encountered after passing through the gate. Drive south on Hagood Avenue, past Johnson Hagood Stadium, one of the few football stadiums named after a Confederate general rather than a monied alumnus looking for a tax write-off. Follow Hagood Avenue to U.S. 17 and turn right, or southwest, to cross the Ashley River.

Immediately after crossing the river, bear right, or north, onto S.C. 61. Continue on S.C. 61 to the plantation of Drayton Hall, about 12 miles after leaving The Citadel.

Thomas Drayton commissioned Drayton Hall in 1738, when he was just twenty-three years old. At one time, the rice, indigo, and cotton plantation covered several hundred acres. It also served as the center of operations for thirty other Drayton-family properties, including some plantations that covered more than a thousand acres each. Drayton Hall was the family's primary residence before the war. They inexplicably moved their primary residence into Charleston at about the same time many Charlestonians were moving to the country to escape Federal shelling.

The family used a ruse to keep their house from being burned by the Federals. According to family legend, the Draytons hoisted yellow fever flags outside the property, keeping the Federal soldiers at bay. The house is unique in that it has never been officially "restored," meaning that historians can study the original architecture and interior confident that only age has changed it.

Continue north on S.C. 61 for 4 miles to Middleton Place. During the American Revolution, Henry Middleton was one of the leading politicians of South Carolina. He represented the state in the Continental Congress, and his son signed the Declaration of Independence. All the while, they were building Middleton Place. The plantation and its gardens must have been grand, but modern-day visitors can only get a taste of the original. All of the estate except one, still-magnificent wing of the house was burned by Federal troops in 1865.

After leaving Middleton Place, retrace your route south on S.C. 61. About 3 miles after passing under I-526, S.C. 171 intersects S.C. 61 from the left. Continue south on the combined road, then bear right onto S.C. 171, following the signs for James Island and Folly Beach. Drive to Folly Beach,

Drayton Hall

a distance of about 9 miles. Many of the Federal soldiers who attacked Morris Island first landed on Folly Beach. Without renting a boat and approaching Morris Island from the ocean, this is as close as visitors can get to the site of Battery Wagner.

Retrace your route on S.C. 171. About 2.9 miles after leaving Folly Beach, there is a yellow flashing light warning of the presence of a fire station. Just before reaching the station, there is a road to the right called Battery Island Road. Turn right onto Battery Island Road. After 0.5 mile, the road bears left and becomes Old Military Road. Drive 0.2 mile and take the second right onto Fort Lamar Road into a housing development. Drive 1.0 mile on Fort Lamar Road. A raised area of land that could be part of Fort Lamar is behind a locked gate on the right, near the end of the road. A development sign advertising lots is in front of the land. While there are no state historic markers describing it, this is the site of the Battle of Secessionville, a little-known but critical battle that kept Charleston from being captured by the Federals in 1862.

Fort Lamar was constructed by Confederates on the Secessionville Peninsula by piling up the marsh mud and installing six cannons. When the fort was built, the citizens of the little community of Secessionville (named after a movement of younger planters leaving older planters, not for the state's secession from the Union) laughed at the Confederates. The residents never imagined that any Federals would try to attack across the watery bogs.

They were wrong. Three brigades consisting of thirty-one hundred Federals rushed the fort in the predawn hours of June 16, 1862. When the Federals attacked, most of the five-hundred-man Confederate garrison was a half-mile away trying to bring in more cannons. The remaining Confederate artillerymen fired their cannons point blank into the Federals, as the Confederate infantrymen ran along a narrow causeway to get back to their posts. Luckily, the marsh mud did its job. It was so thick that the Federals could not deploy properly to attack the fort on all sides. By the time the Federals could get into position, more Confederates had arrived. By 9:30 A.M., the Federals had retreated, leaving more than a hundred dead in front of Fort Lamar. The Federals may have underreported their dead in order to cover up the debacle. The Confederates claimed at least three times that many Federals were killed, while the Confederates lost only twenty men. The swamp swallowed many Federals, who are likely still there.

Had Fort Lamar fallen, the way to Fort Johnson would have been clear. Beyond Fort Johnson was Charleston. The tenacity of a few hundred Confederates and an expanse of several square miles of mud saved the city from capture.

Return to S.C. 171 and head north, toward Charleston. Watch for Fort Johnson Road, about 1.8 miles on the right. Turn right and drive to the end of the road, approximately 4.8 miles. At the end of the road is the site of Fort Johnson. Park in a visitors spot at the South Carolina Wildlife and Marine Resources Department and walk directly east through a break in the trees to the beach, passing a stone marker noting Fort Johnson's role in the war. From the beach, Fort Sumter can be seen about 1.25 miles to the east. Even Sumter's flagpoles are visible at this distance, demonstrating what an easy target it was for Confederate gunners at Fort Johnson.

Retrace your route back to S.C. 171 and again head north. After almost 2 miles, bear right onto S.C. 30 and head north into the city. This road leads over a relatively new bridge across the Ashley River that directly links James Island with Charleston. Once in the city, S.C. 30 becomes Calhoun Street. At the intersection with Meeting Street, turn north. Drive 11 blocks north on Meeting Street to U.S. 17. Take U.S. 17 North across the heart-quickening (if not heart-stopping) Cooper River Bridge, a soaring 2.5-mile-long steel structure that takes travelers to Mount Pleasant and Sullivan's Island, site of Fort Moultrie. (For those looking for a wider, modern alternative across the Cooper River, I-526 can be reached by driving north on I-26. I-526 East leads across the river.)

If you are still breathing after crossing over the Cooper River Bridge, make the first right onto S.C. 703, or West Coleman Boulevard. Follow the signs to Sullivan's Island. On Sullivan's Island, S.C. 703 splits to the right and left. Turn right and follow the signs to Fort Moultrie at the end of S.C. 703. The fort is about 6.5 miles after crossing the Cooper River Bridge.

Fort Moultrie was first built of palmetto logs and sand in 1776 to protect Charleston from British attack. In June of that year, the fort's thirty smooth-bore cannons drove off a frustrated British fleet mounting two hundred guns. British shells that hit the fort were absorbed into the spongy palmetto trees without doing much damage, while American shells splintered the British ships. South Carolina was so enthralled with the combat performance of its native tree that it became part of the state flag. A second Fort Moultrie, built on the same site, was swept away by a hurricane.

In 1809, a third Fort Moultrie was started on the site. The third fort was the one Major Anderson abandoned in December 1860. Disregarding the few additions made to the fort from the Spanish-American War through World War II, the fort still looks much like it did during the Civil War.

Before walking into the fort, visitors should first see the twenty-minute movie on the history of Fort Moultrie at the visitor's center. The movie does a very good job of describing all three forts that were located at the site, right up to Moultrie's decommissioning in 1947. The tour of Fort Moultrie is self-guided.

One helpful aspect of the fort's tour is that all of the Civil War guns mounted or displayed at the fort list the range and the weight of the projectile they would have thrown. Several cannons rest on the ground outside the fort on Cannon Walk. Included on the grounds are eight- and ten-inch Parrott rifles. These guns had a range of eight thousand yards and were the type used by the Federals on Morris Island to shell Charleston and reduce Fort Sumter to rubble. By contrast, the Confederates' ten-inch Columbiad cannons had a range of only fifty-six hundred yards. A comparison of the two cannons shows how much coastal artillery advanced during the war. Allow at least an hour at the fort, as the artillery buffs will spend a lot of time studying the cannons.

Leave Fort Moultrie and retrace your route on S.C. 703. Drive 4.7 miles from the fort on S.C. 703 to a bridge called the IOP (Isle of Palms) Connector. Turn left onto S.C. 517 at the bridge. At 8.5 miles from Fort Moultrie, turn right, or north, onto U.S. 17. After just 1.0 mile, turn left, or northwest, onto Long Point Road, which leads to the entrance for Boone Hall Plantation.

Boone Hall charges admission and is not really a Civil War site. However, the house was used to portray Confederate Orey Main's plantation home in the television movie *North & South*. Boone Hall also has several original, brick slave cabins that demonstrate how close the slaves lived to their work and their masters.

At Boone Hall, and all along U.S. 17 in this region, visitors will find Black women making and selling sweet-grass baskets. This art, handed down through the generations, was brought over by the slaves from Africa.

Boone Hall slave cabin

This concludes the War Ignites Part II Tour. If you care to end the tour with a side trip to Georgetown, 56 miles away, leave Boone Hall and turn left, or north, onto U.S. 17. About 24 miles from Boone Hall is the Francis Marion National Forest, Hurricane Hugo's bulls-eye in 1989. Trees knocked down by the hurricane still rest on the ground in this area. Several people lost their lives in McClellanville, a tiny fishing village just off U.S. 17.

At 56.3 miles from Boone Hall, turn right, or east, at the sign for Battery White. This turn is about 6 miles after passing over the North Santee River. Stop at the gate to Belle Isle Plantation and pick up a visitor's pass to visit Battery White. This was a small, earth battery built by the Confederates to protect Winyah Bay, the body of water formed at the mouth of the Great Pee Dee River and the Waccamaw River. The battery is in front of a clubhouse, about 0.4 mile after passing through the gate.

Nothing happened at Battery White, which probably accounts for its excellent preserved condition. One gun, a smoothbore ten-inch Columbiad, is still mounted there, pointing out to Winyah Bay. While the cannons here were never fired in anger, a Union warship still went down within their range.

On February 28, 1865, Admiral John A. Dahlgren (inventor of the cannon that bears his name), was having breakfast on board his flagship, the USS *Harvest Moon*, when a mine exploded under the ship's keel. The ship settled quickly in the bay. During some extremely low tides, the smokestack of the *Harvest Moon* can still be seen.

Dahlgren was embarrassed. He had told his men to ignore the threat of Confederate mines in the bay. Up to this point, none of them had exploded.

Retrace your route back to U.S. 17 and continue north. Follow U.S. 17 across the Sampit River and into Georgetown. Continue on U.S. 17 to the intersection with Broad Street and turn right. Drive 2 blocks on Broad Street to Prince George Episcopal Church. Park and walk into the cemetery behind the church. In the first row of the cemetery is the grave of Confederate Brigadier General James Trapier.

Trapier, a native of Georgetown, graduated third out of forty-five cadets in his 1838 West Point class. He served in the United States Army for about ten years before leaving to become a planter. He stayed active in the militia and bought much of the heavy coastal artillery used to bombard Fort Sumter.

Despite his high class ranking at West Point, Trapier was not a good military commander. He briefly served in command of Florida until the legislature there returned a vote of "no confidence" in him. He was transferred to a field command in Mississippi, where he failed to impress his superiors. In November 1862, he was sent back to South Carolina, where he remained the rest of the war. He died in December 1865.

Leave the church and continue on Broad Street for 2 more blocks to the intersection with Front Street. Turn right and drive 2 blocks to 1003 Front Street. This is the Kaminski House Museum. Though the present-day museum has nothing to do with the Civil War, this was once the home of Captain Thomas Daggett, the Confederate officer who developed the torpedo that sank Dahlgren's *Harvest Moon*.

Clock tower in Georgetown

Turn around on Front Street and drive 3 blocks to a clock tower. In 1862, a Federal gunboat cruised up the Sampit River to look over the town. As the gunboat made a slow turn upriver, a valiant, perhaps foolhardy, woman climbed the clock tower to unfurl a Confederate flag. Such defiance had been known to get some towns shelled, but the gunboat commander did nothing in retaliation. In the building below the clock tower is the Rice Museum. The museum describes how difficult it was to cultivate and process rice. A map shows how virtually all of the land in the region was underwater and in rice cultivation. After the war, with the disappearance of free slave labor, the industry collapsed.

Beside the Rice Museum, at 633 Front Street, is an antique store that was the building where Daggett put together his torpedoes. Daggett, a Massachusetts native, survived Dahlgren's wrath and became a successful businessman after the war.

Continue on Front Street past the Rice Museum for 2 blocks to the intersection with Cannon Street. Turn left onto Cannon Street. Drive one block to the intersection of Cannon and Prince Streets. At this intersection is the Indigo Society Hall. The society was founded before the American Revolution to educate children. This building was built in 1857 and was occupied by Federal troops in 1865, who destroyed the hall's library. Instruction of children did not start again until the 1870s. The second house east of the Indigo Society Hall, at 417 Prince Street, was used as a Union hospital immediately after the war.

This concludes the side trip to Georgetown.

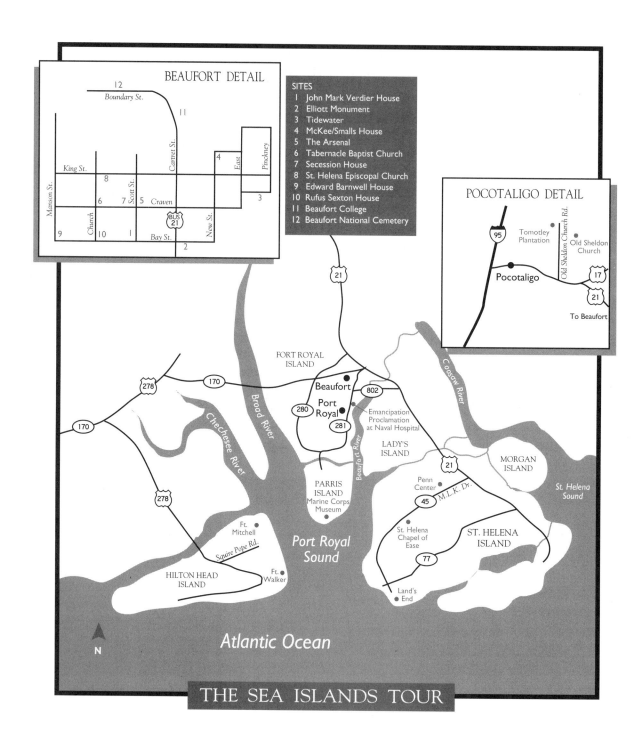

BEAUFORT DETAIL

Boundary St.

King St.

Manson St.

Church

Scott St.

Carret St.

Craven

New St.

Bay St.

East

Pinckney

BUS 21

12

11

4

3

8

6 7 5

9 10 1

2

SITES
1 John Mark Verdier House
2 Elliott Monument
3 Tidewater
4 McKee/Smalls House
5 The Arsenal
6 Tabernacle Baptist Church
7 Secession House
8 St. Helena Episcopal Church
9 Edward Barnwell House
10 Rufus Sexton House
11 Beaufort College
12 Beaufort National Cemetery

POCOTALIGO DETAIL

95

Tomotley Plantation

Old Sheldon Church Rd.

Old Sheldon Church

Pocotaligo

17

21

To Beaufort

21

FORT ROYAL ISLAND

170

278

170

170

278

Broad River

Chechesee River

Beaufort

Port Royal

280

281

802

Emancipation Proclamation at Naval Hospital

Beaufort River

Coosaw River

LADY'S ISLAND

MORGAN ISLAND

St. Helena Sound

21

Penn Center

45

M.L.K. Dr.

St. Helena Chapel of Ease

ST. HELENA ISLAND

77

Land's End

PARRIS ISLAND

Marine Corps Museum

Port Royal Sound

Ft. Mitchell

Squire Pope Rd.

Ft. Walker

HILTON HEAD ISLAND

N

Atlantic Ocean

THE SEA ISLANDS TOUR

The Sea Islands Tour

This tour starts on Hilton Head Island, which the Federals captured early in the war. It then moves to the excellent museum at the United States Marine Corps base on Parris Island. From there, it travels to a historic spot near the town of Port Royal where many freed slaves started their new lives. It then continues to Beaufort, an important commercial center before the war that was captured by Federal forces. Since the Federals did not burn Beaufort, many of the Civil War sites there have been preserved. From Beaufort, the tour moves north and ends at the forgotten battlefields of Pocotaligo.

Total mileage: approximately 105 miles. It would be best to take this tour in two days, allowing time to see Beaufort's beautiful homes.

In 1861, there seemed to be two types of people living on and around the sea islands off the lower South Carolina coast: Black slaves and white masters. Census records from 1860 show that more than eighty percent of the residents of the region were slaves. Some ten thousand slaves lived on the plantations found on the dozens of islands around Beaufort, which included Hilton Head, Parris Island, Lady's Island, and St. Helena Island.

While rice was a popular cash crop in the swampy islands, cotton made the region famous all over the world. The slaves cultivated a particularly fine strain that was named for the region, sea island cotton. Compared to the shorter fibers of upland cotton, sea island cotton was renowned for its long, delicate, silk-like fibers. When picked, sea island cotton was usually left in bags rather than baled so as not to damage the fibers. Sea island cotton seeds were sometimes removed by hand, rather than running the bolls through the teeth of the cotton gin, as was commonly done with most upland cotton.

Planting, cultivating, and harvesting such a delicate crop was extremely labor-intensive, but the labor supply was not a problem. Most planters did not even plow their holdings with horses. Slaves with huge-headed hoes did that work.

Although the sea island planters were wealthy in land and slave holdings, building cash wealth from growing cotton was never assured. One planter calculated that over forty years, he had made little more than four-percent profit from his agricultural holdings. Still, planters put every acre they could under cultivation. By 1860, cotton covered so much of the lower South that the region imported thirty-million-dollars worth of food supplies each year from Western states. Planters did not mind buying food instead of growing their own because the large Northern textile industry depended on a steady supply of cotton fiber.

The worldwide popularity of cotton drove Southern politicians to new heights of rhetoric. In 1858, South Carolina Senator James H. Hammond declared to Northern senators: "You do not dare make war on cotton! No power on earth dares make war upon it. Cotton is King!"

Three years later, the North not only dared to make war on cotton, it attacked the heart of the cotton growing region, the sea islands of South Carolina.

By 1861, Hilton Head Island was carved up into twenty-four cotton plantations bearing names like Calibogia, Grass Lawn, Cotton Hope, Myrtle Bank, Coggins Point, and Seabrook. Two planters with no sense of the picturesque named their plantations Possum Point and Fish Haul.

When the war started in April 1861, the sea island planters knew they were vulnerable to Union attack from the sea. By June, the Confederates were building Fort Walker at Coggins Point Plantation on Hilton Head and Fort Beauregard two miles across the water at Bay Point on Phillips Island. The sand forts were supposed to defend the entrance to Port Royal Sound. The theory was that no Union vessels would try to pass through the narrow waterway if they knew the forts were guarding it.

Military theories do not often stand up in practice. On November 6, 1861, Union Flag Officer Samuel F. Du Pont arrived at Port Royal Sound with a fleet of seventeen warships and transports. With him was an invasion force of twelve thousand infantry and six hundred marines.

The next morning, Du Pont began his attack from the warships, concentrating his artillery fire on Fort Walker's twenty-three guns. The most accurate Union fire came from the USS *Pocahontas*, commanded by Commodore Percival Drayton. Drayton was brother to Confederate Brigadier General Thomas F. Drayton, commander of Fort Walker and owner of Fish Haul Plantation, located just a few hundred yards behind the fort.

In less than three hours, Fort Walker's guns were disabled. Seeing no hope, the fort's defenders abandoned their defenses and retreated to the mainland. Eleven Confederates were killed in the attack and forty-eight were wounded. The Union losses were just eight killed and twenty-three wounded.

The defenders of Fort Beauregard, under the command of Beaufort resident Stephen Elliott, Jr., heard the cheers of the Union soldiers and the singing of "Yankee Doodle." They didn't need orders to tell them to abandon their outpost. They spiked their guns and headed for Beaufort. The Union soldiers, who had done no fighting, simply walked ashore and took possession of Hilton Head.

For the remainder of the war, Hilton Head was an important coaling station and dry dock for Union ships enforcing the blockade along the Atlantic coast. At one time, more than ten thousand Union soldiers garrisoned the island. Some regiments occasionally left the island on raids as far away as Jacksonville, Florida.

The Sea Islands Tour starts at the Hilton Head Visitor's Center at 100 William Hilton Parkway. The visitor's center is found on the right side of U.S. 278, just 0.3 mile after crossing the bridge from the mainland. The museum offers two different guided bus tours of forts that played roles during the war. One tour is of the remains of Confederate Fort Walker and Union Fort Sherman. The other tour visits the remains of Fort Howell, a 1864 Union fort adjacent to Mitchelville, the first town built for freed slaves. The forts are on a private residential compound with guard gates.

There is one fort on Hilton Head that is easily accessible to the driving tourist, although it is also on private property. Fort Mitchell was a small earth fort built in 1862 by the Union Army on a bluff overlooking Skull Creek. The fort was designed to protect the nearby dry dock from Confederate raids.

To reach Fort Mitchell, turn right from the Hilton Head Visitor's Center onto U.S. 278 and drive about 200 yards. Turn left, or north, onto Squire

Pope Road, the first road to the left. Proceed until reaching the Hilton Head Plantation gatehouse. Tell the guard that you want to visit Fort Mitchell or Old Fort Pub. The guard will issue a pink pass restricting the car to travel only to those locations. Once the visit is over, you must leave the plantation. Driving through the neighborhoods without a valid pass is a trespassing violation .

Take the second left after the gatehouse. The fort is about 0.5 mile away.

Fort Mitchell is a small earth fort on Skull Creek. It has an excellent self-guided tour, with numerous signs explaining Civil War–fort construction. One sign even lists all the Union regiments stationed on the island during the war. Two 24-pounder cannons have been placed in the fort with signs explaining the guns' complete history from their manufacture to their placement in the fort.

During the war, the Federals drove wooden pilings from the fort all the way across Skull Creek to Pinckney Island to prevent Confederates from sending gunboat raiders up the creek. They need not have bothered. Fort Mitchell never fired a shot during the war.

Touring the fort takes no more than fifteen minutes. The Old Fort Pub next door to Fort Mitchell has a fair collection of Civil War photographs on the wall.

After leaving Fort Mitchell, there is little else of the Civil War for the driving tourist to see on Hilton Head. Retrace your route to the gatehouse, wave at the guard, and return to U.S. 278 on Squire Pope Road. Turn right on U.S. 278 and cross over the bridge to the mainland.

Drive north on U.S. 278 until it intersects with S.C. 170. Get on S.C. 170 heading north to Beaufort. S.C. 170 passes over the Broad River on a mile-long, narrow, two-lane bridge. During the war, Union forces patrolled the Broad River. On at least two different occasions, the Federals ran up the river to attack Pocotaligo, a railhead 30 miles inland from Beaufort.

After driving 13 miles on S.C. 170, turn right onto S.C. 802. Drive 6 miles on S.C. 802 to Parris Island. In daylight, tourists will see the island, once occupied by a half-dozen cotton plantations. The twenty thousand Marine recruits who do eleven weeks of boot camp on the island every year first see it in the dead of night.

Follow the signs to the guard gate and stop to request a driving tour map. If the Civil War is your only interest, the Parris Island Marine Corps Museum is your destination.

To reach the museum, take the first right after passing under the large pipes (hidden by a Marine Corps sign) running over the road. The museum is one block away, directly across the street from the campus Burger King.

On the left after entering the museum is a map showing Civil War engagements on the sea islands. Beside the map is an exhibit showing the uniform styles United States Marines wore during the war. Down a hallway is an entire room set aside for the Civil War history of the nearby sea islands. In this room, visitors can see the expected, such as photographs of the warring Drayton brothers, and the unexpected, such as a print of General Robert E. Lee. Lee was in South Carolina from November 1861 to March 1862 to help plan a defense from Union attack. While he was in the Beaufort area, Lee bought a horse to help him inspect the numerous earth forts and trench lines scattered around the low country. He renamed the horse Traveler.

On two back walls are photographs of Beaufort taken during the Union occupation. The pictures show that most of the surviving structures in the city seem to have changed very little from that time.

Touring all of the Parris Island Marine Corps Museum takes at least two hours. The rest of the museum tells the history of the United States Marine Corps from the American Revolution right through Desert Storm, with extensive exhibits on both World Wars, Korea, and Vietnam.

Retrace your route to S.C. 802 and drive north toward the town of Port Royal. Follow the signs to the entrance of the United States Naval Hospital. Stop at the gate for permission to visit Fort Fredricka. The road to the fort starts at the guard gate and winds through the base housing, then ends at the fort in about 0.5 mile. There is little left of this sixteenth-century fort other than the tabby foundation. It is what happened around the fort on January 1, 1863, that makes this point of land one of the most significant in history.

It was here, on the grounds of what was then part of the Smith Plantation, that the Emancipation Proclamation was first read in a public forum. The proclamation freed all slaves in states that were then in rebellion.

Apparently, the freed slaves instantly understood what freedom meant. According to one account, after the Federal commander in Beaufort finished reading the document, a single voice in the crowd of newly freed men and women started singing "My Country 'Tis of Thee." Within a few bars, all who knew the song joined the singing. For the first time in their lives, the freed slaves could share the joy of living in the "sweet land of liberty."

This point of land is doubly historic, as it was the training camp for the 1st and 2nd South Carolina Volunteers, the first two Black regiments raised during the Civil War. The 1st South Carolina was organized in May 1862, nearly nine months before the 54th Massachusetts Regiment was raised among free Blacks living in the North.

The 1st South Carolina Volunteers was raised by the district's commander, Union General David Hunter. Hunter took it upon himself, without authorization from President Lincoln and several months before the Emancipation Proclamation was issued, to declare that all the slaves in South Carolina, Georgia, and Florida were free. At the same time, he started his own personal draft, ordering Black men into a military training camp. Lincoln, nervous that freeing the slaves would send the wrong message to border slave states still in the Union, rescinded the order within the week and ordered the Black regiment disbanded. Against orders, Hunter kept one company in uniform. When Lincoln finally was ready to start raising troops among the freed Blacks, that company formed the basis for the 1st South Carolina.

Later commanded by Colonel Thomas Wentworth Higginson, a Massachusetts abolitionist, the 1st South Carolina demonstrated to a skeptical Federal military bureaucracy that Black soldiers could—and would—fight Confederates. From his sea island base, Higginson led his men on raids as far away as Jacksonville, Florida. His regiment occupied that city in 1863 and successfully disproved charges that they had set the city on fire. The fire was actually started by white Union soldiers.

In his 1869 book, *Army Life In A Black Regiment*, Higginson never missed a chance to take digs at white officers and soldiers who did not like serving with a regiment made up of freed slaves. Once, a skittish white colonel reported that he had stumbled onto a large Confederate camp filled with white tents. The nervous officer sent for reinforcements. Higginson's 1st South Carolina Volunteers rushed to the location and swooped down on the camp—which turned out to be a woman hanging her white sheets after washing. Higginson, proving even an abolitionist could have a sense of humor, described the incident as "The Battle Of The Clothes Lines."

Unfortunately, these first Black troops developed an early image problem that was not of their making. That image was created by Colonel Robert Montgomery, commander of the 2nd South Carolina Volunteers, another regiment of freed slaves who made their camp near the 1st South Carolina on Smith Plantation.

Montgomery was a fiery veteran of the Kansas Jayhawk wars who counted abolitionist John Brown among his friends. While other officers were training the freed slaves to be Union soldiers, Montgomery was leading his lesser-trained men on raids to free other slaves. Freeing slaves was reluctantly condoned by the military leaders back in Washington, but Montgomery also burned the plantations he raided, and destroying private property was not yet accepted as a war practice.

On one raid up the Combahee River to Edisto Island, a few miles north of Beaufort, Montgomery took along a tiny, turbaned Black woman who was known as "the little general." The woman guided him to the area's rice plantations, and the raid freed nearly eight hundred slaves. The woman's real name was Harriet Tubman, a fearless escaped slave who spent her life leading other Blacks to stops on the Underground Railroad.

On another raid, Montgomery's men burned Darien, Georgia, a tiny coastal town just north of St. Simons Island. Colonel Robert Gould Shaw, the horrified commander of the Black 54th Massachusetts Regiment, refused to let his men take part in the destruction (a scene accurately depicted in the movie *Glory*).

Over the last two years of the war, 180,000 or more Black soldiers were mustered into the Union Army. Black soldiers eventually numbered twenty percent of all Federal forces.

Turn around from Fort Fredricka and drive back through the base housing, past the guard house, and return to S.C. 802 heading northeast toward Beaufort. Drive 0.3 mile and turn east, or right, onto S.C. 802/U.S. 21, crossing over the bridge leading to Lady's Island. Follow this road to the traffic light. At the light, turn right, or east, onto U.S. 21. After crossing Chowan Creek, you are on St. Helena Island.

St. Helena, Fripp, and Phillips Islands were all abandoned quickly by the white plantation owners once Fort Walker on Hilton Head Island fell to the Federals. Former slaves laughed for years at stories of how their owners, who had watched the battle from Fort Beauregard on Phillips Island, turned over buggies in their rush to get back to the mainland.

One former slave from a St. Helena Island plantation remembered asking his mother why it was thundering in a cloudless sky. Knowing it was cannon fire (slaves referred to the battle as "The Big Gun Shoot at Bay Point"), his mother replied to the six-year-old boy, "That ain't no thunder. That is Yankee come to give you freedom."

At 5 miles after turning onto U.S. 21, turn right, or south, onto Martin Luther King Drive, or Land's End Road. Drive approximately 0.7 mile on this road to Penn Center (named for Pennsylvania Quaker William Penn). Park at the museum on the right side of the road.

Only one building at Penn Center, the Brick Church across the street from the museum, is original to the Civil War. The other original buildings all deteriorated with age and were torn down.

In early 1862, a shipload of fifty-three people calling themselves Gideonites arrived from Boston and New York. These people came to Beaufort with a noble mission. These young idealists, almost all under the age of twenty-five, intended to teach freed slaves how to read, write, and live on their own. Their goal was a simple one: to teach the sea island freedmen how to be free.

The first school opened at The Oaks plantation, about a mile away from the Penn Center and now a private residence. Over the course of several months, the Gideonites scattered throughout the plantations, teaching youngsters in the day and the adults at night after they had come in from the fields. They also did what they could to instill the work-for-wages ethic in the former slaves.

Within months of the Gideonites' arrival, other teachers came to the sea islands to help the slaves. These teachers included Laura Towne and Ellen Murray of Philadelphia, and a free Black woman from Massachusetts named Charlotte Forteen. These women would devote almost forty years to teaching the Blacks of the sea islands. Forteen surprised the former slaves with her cultured manners. They thought she acted too much like a master's wife. At first, some hired servants refused to wait on her, believing that she was putting on airs. However, Forteen's concern for them soon changed their minds.

In 1864, a prefabricated school building was shipped from the North and set up at the Penn Center, allowing more students to be taught under one roof. Before the school was built, some classes were held in the Brick Church, built in 1855 by local planters.

Today, Penn Center houses a small museum and a research library dedicated to the sea island Black culture. The museum traces the origin of many of the slaves on the islands to Sierra Leone, a country in western Africa. Some of the evidence of these origins included similar methods of weaving baskets and many common or similar words shared in the African and sea island Gullah languages.

To many listeners, Gullah, still spoken by native Black sea islanders, sounds similar to the lyrical or musical accents of the Caribbean. Gullah's own rules of grammar and distinctive words for everyday objects makes the language an interesting, living artifact of pre-Civil War life on the sea islands.

From the parking lot at the Penn Center museum, turn right, or south, onto Martin Luther King Road and drive 0.3 mile. The tabby ruins of St. Helena Episcopal Chapel of Ease are on the left. Built in the mid-eighteenth century as a branch church of St. Helena Episcopal Church in Beaufort, the Chapel of Ease was abandoned by the white planters after the Federal invasion. When one of the Gideonites died from fever the first summer, he was entombed in the Fripp mausoleum found on the grounds. The chapel was destroyed in a brush-burning accident a few years after the war.

Continue south on Martin Luther King Road to Land's End, literally the end of the island. Now covered with summer homes, this part of St. Helena was once a docking area for Union warships. It was also the area where many of the Black regiments camped and trained. Today, there are no visible remains from the Civil War.

Land's End was on the Jenkins Plantation, adjacent to the Tombee

Plantation. Tombee was a sea island plantation that is described in the book, *Tombee—Portrait Of A Cotton Planter*. The book, published in 1986, included the daily journal of plantation owner Thomas B. Chaplain. The Tombee Plantation house is a private residence and is not visible from the road.

Retrace your route back to U.S. 21. Turn left, or west, onto U.S. 21 and drive toward Beaufort, approximately 9 miles away. Fripp Island, to the east, was home to more sea island cotton plantations. However, the entire island is now under private management, and day tourists are turned around at the gate.

The kindly Fripp family, who acquired title to the island in the 1700s, would likely frown on how the average tourist is barred from their island today. William Fripp, known to his neighbors as "Good Billy" Fripp, must have been a kind and gentle man to own the reputation that has outlived him all these years. Another Fripp, Captain John, gathered all his slaves after "The Big Gun Shoot at Bay Point," and frankly told them what had happened. He told them he was leaving, but that they were free to stay on their plantation. He suggested they ignore the cotton crops and plant food.

Follow U.S. 21 into Beaufort. At the S.C. 802 intersection, U.S. 21 turns into Business U.S. 21.

First laid out in 1712, Beaufort quickly became a major agricultural city due to the local indigo crop. Indigo is a plant that produces a bright, blue dye when processed. By the late 1790s, the Elliott family of Beaufort had perfected the development of sea island cotton. Within a few decades, scores of cotton plantations were operating on the sixty islands fanning out from the city.

Though growing and selling cotton was always a risky pursuit, Beaufort slowly became a home for the rich. Plantation owners, wary of staying on the marshy islands during the "fever season," would move to their Beaufort homes for the summer. By 1860, the city boasted dozens of large, two- and three-story homes that rivaled the best houses in Charleston. That same year, the eventual fate of the owners of those homes was being sealed with the help of one of their own, Robert Barnwell Rhett, Sr.

Rhett was a classic Southern "fire-eater." Champion of nullification (voiding federal laws when they conflicted with state laws), he first discussed

South Carolina seceding from the Union in the 1830s and 1840s in response to higher tariffs and abolitionist sentiment in Washington. In 1851, he took over the United State Senate term of the deceased John C. Calhoun. His views on secession were so radical for the time that he lost support and resigned the seat in 1852.

By 1857, Rhett was owner of the *Charleston Mercury* newspaper, a pulpit he used to preach secession. When it became clear that Lincoln would be elected in 1860, the South's deepest fears about abolitionists in control of the Federal government were fanned by Rhett and his newspaper. He hosted meetings of like-minded politicians in his Beaufort home, where the men wrote drafts of the secession ordnance that would eventually withdraw South Carolina from the Union. He also wrote an article titled "Address To The Slave-Holding States." In the article, Rhett gave the reasons why he felt South Carolina was justified in leaving the union, and called on other southern states to follow. That article described Rhett's vision of a second union made up of Southern states—the Confederacy.

In 1861, Rhett led South Carolina's delegation to the Confederate convention in Montgomery, Alabama. At the convention, Rhett proposed that only slave-holding states should be allowed in the Confederacy and that all trade should be free of tariffs. Rejected as a radical by the other Confederate leaders, Rhett was refused a cabinet post. When the Union invaded the sea islands, he lost both his plantation and his home in Beaufort.

Rhett spent much of the war criticizing Jefferson Davis from the editorial pages of the *Mercury*. He rejected any idea of compromise with the North, which he always thought Davis favored. After the war, Rhett left his native South Carolina and moved to a Louisiana plantation, where he died a bitter, proud man in 1876. He is buried in Charleston.

Rhett was certainly not the only Beaufort resident to lose his home in the Federal occupation. The Federal officers set about turning Beaufort into a headquarters for the region. Union generals such as David Hunter, Rufus Saxton, and Isaac Stevens appropriated houses for their official residences. They also used at least sixteen plantation homes and two churches as hospitals yielding a thousand beds.

Beaufort's homes were spared the destruction that befell hundreds of other Southern homes because the city was captured before "total war" became part of the Federal government's strategy. Many of Beaufort's homes were sold during and immediately after the war to pay "war taxes." During the war, the United States Tax Commission figured out the cost of the conflict, then assigned each state a portion of the cost based on its population. That included South Carolina, even though the state had seceded from the Union that was imposing the tax.

Since Beaufort and Hilton Head were two areas under Union control, the Tax Commission sold the property of the plantation owners to help make up South Carolina's contribution. Union officers, Northern cotton agents, and even former slaves bought the fine houses once owned by the wealthy planters. Usually the houses went for rock-bottom prices and "those in the know" got the best deals.

After crossing over the bridge from Lady's Island on Business U.S. 21, turn right onto Bay Street and park. Walk west on Bay Street. One block west of the bridge, at 801 West Bay Street, is the John Mark Verdier House, also called the Lafayette House. Since the house was so near the dock and the ferry leading to Lady's Island, Union forces used it as a military headquarters. Sherman likely visited the house during his short stay in the city. Tour books of all of Beaufort's historic houses can be purchased here.

Turn around and walk east on Bay Street. On the east side of the bridge in a grassy park beside Bay Street is a marker and cannons recognizing the accomplishments of Beaufort native son Confederate Brigadier General Stephen Elliott, Jr. The cannons are not of Civil War vintage.

Get back in the car and drive east one block on Bay Street to New Street. Turn left, or north, onto New Street. Drive two blocks, then turn right onto Craven Street. Drive one block and turn left onto East Street. Drive another block and turn right onto Federal Street, then continue approximately a block-and-a-half to 302 Federal Street. This is Tidewater, the 1830 residence of William "Good Billy" Fripp.

Continue driving on Federal Street until it intersects with Pinckney Street. Turn north on Pinckney Street and drive three blocks to Hancock Street. Turn left, drive two blocks, then turn south, or left, onto East Street. Just after turning onto East Street, make a quick right onto Prince Street. Drive one block to 511 Prince Street, formally called the Henry McKee House. It is also the postwar home of a more famous Beaufort resident,

Congressman Robert Smalls. When he first lived in the house, Smalls was a slave, not a congressman.

In May 1862, Smalls, a twenty-two-year-old slave living in Charleston, made Civil War history when he stole the *Planter*, a 150-foot-long boat armed with two heavy cannons. Smalls not only delivered the *Planter* to a delighted Union blockading squadron, he also brought four cannons and two hundred pounds of ammunition that were on the *Planter*'s deck, awaiting transfer to a fort. What makes Small's feat even more interesting is that he pulled off the caper by successfully posing as a white man. (See the War Ignites Part I Tour for more information on Small's daring escape.)

Smalls returned to Beaufort after the war. Using the $1,500 he was paid in prize money for delivering the *Planter* to the Union, he bought his master's old house at 511 Prince Street. From there, he launched a career in politics, including three terms in the United States House of Representatives. While serving in Washington, Smalls persuaded Congress to expand the naval station on Parris Island. The United States Marines are glad he did. That naval station eventually became the training center for all United States Marines east of the Mississippi River.

Smalls did not hold a deep grudge against his former masters. When the elderly, confused Mrs. McKee came to Smalls's door thinking she still owned the house, Smalls allowed her to move into her old room. She lived with the Smalls family the rest of her life.

Leaving the McKee-Smalls House, continue on Prince Street to the intersection with New Street and turn left, or south, toward downtown. Drive three blocks, then turn right onto Craven Street. Cross busy Carteret Street, or Business U.S. 21, and stop at 713 Craven Street on the next block.

Behind the bright yellow walls at 713 Craven Street is the Beaufort Arsenal, first constructed in 1795. Inside the arsenal is what is described by residents as "Beaufort's attic," a varied collection of artifacts and art work. There is little in the museum directly related to the Civil War, except for the full-length oil portrait of Brigadier General Stephen Elliott, Jr., and some postwar reminiscences of a well-known area slave.

Drive two blocks west on Craven Street to Tabernacle Baptist Church at 907 Craven Street. The church itself is a postwar structure. A bust of Robert Smalls faces the sidewalk outside of the church. The bust is inscribed:

Secession House

"My race needs no special defense for the past history of them and this country. It proves them to be equal of any people anywhere. All they need is an equal chance in the battle of life." Smalls is buried behind the bust. His grave marker is surprisingly simple. It has no mention of his life as a slave, the hijacking of the *Planter*, or his postwar political career.

Drive another two blocks west on Craven Street to the Secession House at 1113 Craven Street. This house was the prewar home of Edmund Rhett, a former United States senator and the brother of Robert Barnwell Rhett, Sr., the "Father of Secession." Numerous secessionist meetings took place in this house, including the last meeting of Beaufort's delegates before they left for the Secession Convention.

Drive to Church Street, just past the Secession House, and turn right, or north. Drive two blocks to St. Helena Episcopal Church at 501 Church Street. During the war, Union troops removed the pews of the church and built a loft at the mezzanine level, creating a two-story hospital. The fact that St. Helena was a church did not protect it—the church organ was destroyed by Union troops. Such desecration by invading forces was nothing new, however. During the American Revolution, British forces used St. Helena as a horse stable.

St. Helena Episcopal Church is the final resting place for two Confederate generals. One is a native son and the descendent of one of Beaufort's most prominent families. The other has one of the saddest stories of the war.

Brigadier General Stephen Elliott Jr., the native son, is buried beneath an obelisk that lies on the King Street side of the church. As you face the church's steeple on King Street, the obelisk is to the right.

At the start of the war, Elliott was a thirty-one-year-old planter living on Parris Island and enjoying the results of his family's experiments with developing sea island cotton. He had attended Harvard for a time and eventually graduated from South Carolina College in Columbia. His only military training came from his prewar experience as captain of the Beaufort Volunteer Artillery. Meetings and drills were held at the Beaufort Arsenal. Elliott spent the first three years of his Confederate service in South Carolina. He was transferred to Petersburg, Virginia, in May 1864. On July 30, 1864, Elliott's brigade had the misfortune of being stationed right over tons of gunpowder, which had been placed there by Federals who dug a five-hundred-foot tunnel under Confederate lines. Hundreds of Elliott's men were blown to bits. He was badly wounded, but he stayed with his men during the following Battle of the Crater. Elliott recuperated and returned to service just in time to join General Joseph Johnston's army at Bentonville, where he was again wounded. He never really recovered from his wounds. He died in February 1866 at the age of thirty-six.

The other general buried at St. Helena Episcopal Church is Confederate Lieutenant General Richard Heron "Fighting Dick" Anderson. Anderson's grave lies at the rear of the church. It is a rectangular monument, surrounded by a wrought-iron fence.

Anderson, a native of Sumter County, South Carolina, was a soldier virtually all his life. An 1842 graduate of West Point, he served in the Mexican War and was a captain in the United States Dragoons when he resigned in 1861 and joined the Confederate Army. Anderson first served in Florida until he was transferred to the Army of Northern Virginia in early 1862. He became one of Robert E. Lee's most dependable generals.

According to his biography, General Anderson failed to follow orders from General Robert E. Lee on only one occasion. At Chancellorsville, Lee ordered Anderson's division forward three times. Each time, Anderson did not move. When Lee went to Anderson himself to demand that he move forward, he saw that Anderson's thinly spaced men were holding a vital place in the line. If Anderson had followed Lee's orders, the Confederates would have opened a hole for a counterattack. Lee apologized for his orders, saying, "My noble old soldier, I thank you from the bottom of my heart (for not following orders)."

At Gettysburg, Anderson's division took a portion of Cemetery Ridge on the second day, but he was forced to fall back when reinforcements did not arrive. On the third day of the battle, Cemetery Ridge would again be attacked in the Pettigrew-Pickett-Trimble Assault. Had Anderson been supported on the second day, this assault, also known as Pickett's Charge, might not have been needed, and Lee might have won Gettysburg.

In the heat of battle at Cold Harbor in 1864, Lee sent a courier to ask Anderson how he was doing. Anderson only had time to give a verbal reply, "Give my compliments to General Lee and tell him I have just repulsed the enemy's thirteenth charge."

When Lee offered Anderson command of the Confederate cavalry after the death of General J.E.B. Stuart, Anderson politely turned the general down. Anderson told Lee that he had grown to love the men of his infantry division, and he wanted to stay with them for the rest of the war.

When Anderson's command was smashed at the Battle of Sayler's Creek in early April 1865, he escaped and reported to Lee for further orders. Lee, upset at the collapse of his army, waved Anderson away without even speaking to him. Anderson was ordered home the day before the surrender at Appomattox to await orders that never came. In one sense, Anderson was spared the agony of surrendering. Yet, he never experienced the closure of the war that he had fought bravely for four years.

A soldier all his life, Anderson did not know how to do anything else. He tried and failed at farming. He was so poor that he did not have the money to take the train to Charleston to visit his wife's grave. His only son became a wanderer, finally committing suicide somewhere in the West.

Anderson finally found a job as a day laborer on the railroad. Recognized by the president of the railroad as a lieutenant general who had once commanded one-third of the Army of Northern Virginia, Anderson was soon shifted to other jobs. When he was offered a job as a phosphate agent in Beaufort, the fifty-eight-year-old Anderson finally found postwar stability. He died of an apparent heart attack on a very hot day, just three weeks after moving to town in 1879.

Anderson was buried at St. Helena Episcopal Church, but the townspeople did not immediately recognize the sacrifices he had made for his state. His grave was unmarked until 1887, when a sympathetic former comrade paid for the monument that now rests over his grave. The fence was added later, a gift from an admiring Union officer who fought against Anderson at Gettysburg. Anderson is one of the least-known of Lee's generals because he wanted it that way. A shy, unassuming man, Anderson was often urged by his subordinate generals to write more battle reports claiming credit for victories. Anderson preferred to fight rather than write. When he was not in battle, he practiced a calming hobby. Lieutenant General Richard Heron Anderson sewed and patched his own uniforms.

After leaving the cemetery, turn west from the church onto King Street. Continue three blocks to Monson Street. Turn left, or south, and drive two blocks to Bay Street. Turn left, or east, onto Bay Street, heading back towards downtown. At 1405 Bay Street is the Edward Barnwell House, built in 1785. During the war, a signal station was set up on the roof and a telegraph office operated in one of the front rooms.

Drive two blocks to 1203 Bay Street. This is the John A. Cuthbert House, one of the two Beaufort houses Union General Rufus Saxton bought at tax sales during the war. A professional soldier, 1849 West Point graduate, and ardent abolitionist, the Massachusetts-born Saxton never received much battlefield experience. He was a better quartermaster and recruiter of former slaves.

General William T. Sherman spent the night of January 23, 1865, in Saxton's house when his army swung by and rested for a few days around Beaufort before pushing on to Columbia. It is doubtful that Sherman would have stayed longer with Saxton since he did not think much of Black soldiers, and he definitely disliked abolitionists. Sherman once commented, "Massachusetts and South Carolina had brought on the war and I would like to see them cut off from the rest of the continent and hauled out to sea together."

In Beaufort, Sherman's army, which had been living in the field without resupply for more than two months, had several confrontations with the Black garrison troops, who rarely left the islands except for occasional plantation raids. Sherman's men believed they were fighting for the preservation of the Union, not for the abolition of slavery, and certainly not for the rights of Black men to put on the same uniform. One Beaufort resident, possibly a cotton agent, wrote of Sherman's army: "They are strange, rough looking, unshaven and badly dressed like a gang of coal heavers, when compared to the trim and snug fellows here, who have nothing to do but guard duty with white gloves. These western marauders were flopping through the streets, roaring out songs and jokes, making snide comments to all the tidy civilians and overflowing with merriment and good nature. Their clothes are patched like Scripture Joseph's. Hats without brims, hats without crowns. It was a treat, I assure you, to see some real soldiers who had won battles."

Beaufort College Building

Continue east on Bay Street for five blocks until reaching Carteret Street, or U.S. 21. Turn left, or north, leaving the historic district. At 808 Carteret Street, on the right, is the Beaufort College Building. The building was constructed in 1852 and is now the administration building for the University of South Carolina at Beaufort. During the war, the Beaufort College library was shipped north, as were the libraries in many of the houses occupied by Federal forces. In fact, the Gideonites complained that Union officers and cotton agents had stolen all of the books in the region, leaving the slaves nothing to learn to read. Once stripped of its books and furniture, Beaufort College was used as a hospital. Following the war, the Freedman's Bureau was based in the building.

As you continue east on Carteret Street, the road makes a sharp turn to the left, or west, and becomes Boundary Street (it is still U.S. 21). Drive about 0.5 mile on Boundary Street to the Beaufort National Cemetery. The cemetery is located at 1601 Boundary Street and is surrounded by a brick wall. This cemetery was one of the first twelve national cemeteries authorized by Abraham Lincoln in 1863. Buried here are 117 Confederate prisoners of war and more than 7,000 Union soldiers. Some 4,000 of these soldiers are unknown. The cemetery office has maps showing the location of known gravesites.

More than half of the soldiers in this cemetery died from two deadly diseases. Malaria was a common disease along the coast, killing planters

Sheldon Church

and slaves alike long before the war started. Dysentery was a soldier's camp disease, characterized by diarrhea that caused dehydration.

Leaving Beaufort, continue driving north on U.S. 21 for 16 miles to the intersection with U.S. 17. Bear left, or south, onto U.S. 17. Approximately 0.5 mile on the right is Old Sheldon Church Road. Turn right and drive 2 miles to the ruins of Old Sheldon Church. There is no parking lot, just a paved shoulder large enough to accommodate four cars.

First built in 1757, Sheldon Church was burned in 1779 by the British Army. The church's members continued to worship in the burned-out structure until 1826, when the church was rebuilt. On January 14, 1865, the Union 15th Corps under General John Logan burned the church again. The reason for the destruction of the remote church is a mystery.

Today, the church has one service a year on the second Sunday after Easter.

Continue on Old Sheldon Church Road for 0.9 mile to the gate for Tomotley Plantation. This is private property, so do not drive past the gate. However, you can still view the broad avenue of oaks that has welcomed plantation visitors for nearly 170 years. This land was first deeded to Edmund Bellinger in 1698. Bellinger donated the land for Old Sheldon Church. By 1860, there were 138 slaves living on the plantation. Today, no buildings from the Civil War survive on the plantation. The plantation was also burned by the 15th Corps.

Retrace your route to U.S. 17. Turn right, or west, onto U.S. 17. Drive about 7 miles to the point where U.S. 17 meets I-95 at Pocotaligo. During the war, this was the site of an important Confederate rail station. Robert E. Lee helped design the defenses for the station in 1862 before he left for Richmond. The Federals attacked the area in 1862 and 1864. In the 1864 attack, they may have used Old Sheldon Church Road to try to sneak up on the Confederates.

The earthworks from these little-studied battles are on private property. A mention of Robert E. Lee's four-month assignment in the area to strengthen defenses is found on a historic marker nestled between the gas stations and restaurants on the left side of U.S. 17, just before reaching I-95. As noted earlier, it was for his assignment in this area that Lee bought his horse Traveler.

This concludes The Sea Islands Tour.

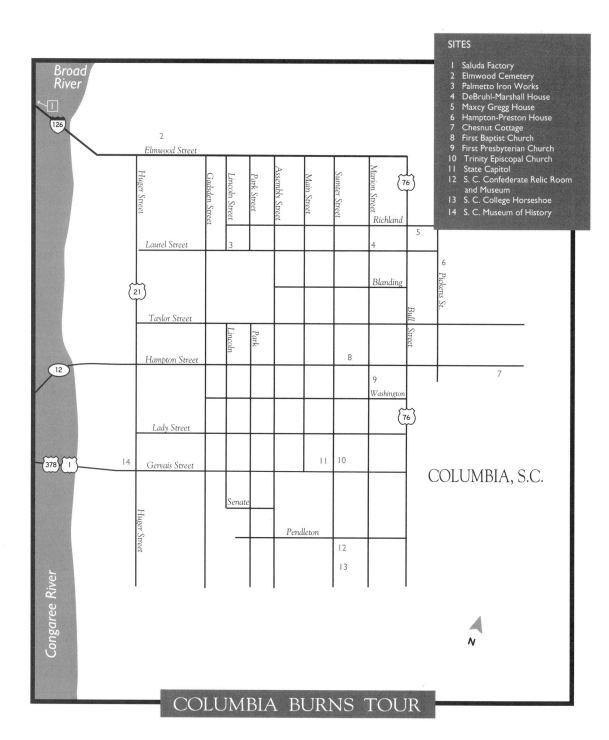

SITES

1 Saluda Factory
2 Elmwood Cemetery
3 Palmetto Iron Works
4 DeBruhl-Marshall House
5 Maxcy Gregg House
6 Hampton-Preston House
7 Chesnut Cottage
8 First Baptist Church
9 First Presbyterian Church
10 Trinity Episcopal Church
11 State Capitol
12 S. C. Confederate Relic Room and Museum
13 S. C. College Horseshoe
14 S. C. Museum of History

Broad River

Congaree River

Elmwood Street

Huger Street

Gadsden Street

Lincoln Street

Park Street

Assembly Street

Main Street

Sumter Street

Marion Street

Richland

Laurel Street

Blanding

Pickens St.

Taylor Street

Lincoln

Park

Bull Street

Hampton Street

Washington

Lady Street

Gervais Street

Huger Street

Senate

Pendleton

COLUMBIA, S.C.

N

COLUMBIA BURNS TOUR

Columbia Burns Tour

This tour covers Columbia, the capital of South Carolina and the object of William T. Sherman's wrath in February 1865. The tour starts in a zoo, at the site of a cotton mill that was burned by Sherman's army. It continues to the graves of two Confederate generals, then visits several historic houses that were spared from Federal torches. It then travels to a church that was a hotbed of secession and a cemetery containing the graves of a general turned preacher, a general turned governor, and a general named "States Rights." Across the street from the cemetery is the South Carolina Capitol, which was hit by six Federal cannonballs. It then proceeds to the nearby South Carolina Relic Room, with a collection that includes several Civil War artifacts, and the University of South Carolina, the alma mater of many Southern heroes. The tour ends at South Carolina's state museum.

Total mileage: approximately 10 miles. The tour should require the whole day, as there is a lot to see.

On February 15, 1865, the sixty-three thousand men of General William T. Sherman's army were within three miles of what many of them considered their ultimate goal, the capital of South Carolina.

Many of the Federal soldiers, and maybe some of their generals, had decided to make an example of Columbia. The destruction of a handful of small towns and scores of plantations and farms had not attracted enough attention or given enough satisfaction. Perhaps something a little bigger would be necessary. A town with a prewar population of eight thousand, and a refugee-swollen population of twenty thousand, could fit the bill.

The shelling of Columbia started on February 16, 1865, much to the surprise of the city's mayor, who had not been contacted by Federals demanding the city's surrender. The unauthorized shelling even surprised Sherman, who rode up to Lexington Heights on the west bank of the Saluda River to find out what was happening. The captain in command of the artillery said he had seen Confederate cavalry moving in the streets. That was unlikely since the Confederate cavalry had retreated some time earlier. Sherman ordered the captain to tighten his aim and shoot only at the unfinished capitol building about three miles away.

Sherman expected little actual fighting in the city and selected Union Major General John Logan's 15th Corps as an occupation force. On the afternoon of February 17, 1865, a pontoon bridge over the Saluda River was completed. Just before crossing, Sherman received his first civilian message asking for mercy for the city. The message was from Sister Baptista, the mother superior of a Catholic convent in the city. Sister Baptista informed Sherman that she had taught his daughter at a convent school in Ohio. Sherman wrote a note back assuring her that no private property, least of all a Catholic school, would be harmed by his men.

The 15th Corps must not have gotten the word. As they marched across the river, no more than fifty yards behind Sherman, most of them were chanting: "Hail Columbia, happy land. If I don't burn you, I'll be damned!" Sherman must not have heard the voices of fifteen thousand men threatening the city. He never looked behind him.

Many of the citizens were glad to see the Federals, at least they made it appear so. They sang "Yankee Doodle" and waved United States flags. Some citizens did a stupid thing. They gave the troops liquor—lots of it.

Other citizens were not at all pleased with the arrival of the Yankees. Emma LeConte watched as the United States flag was raised over the capitol building near where she was living at South Carolina College (now University of South Carolina). "Oh, what a horrid sight. What a degradation! After four long bitter years of bloodshed and hatred, now to float there at last! That hateful symbol of despotism!" she wrote in her diary. When she got her first look at real live Yankee soldiers she wrote, "We cannot look on them with anything but horror and hatred—loathing and disgust!"

Miss LeConte was not selected to serve on the mayor's welcoming committee.

The troops soon made themselves very unwelcome. As soon as they stacked arms, the men scattered, going house-to-house in search of food and valuables.

While his men were ransacking homes, Sherman went visiting. He remembered that an old female acquaintance lived in Columbia. When he arrived at her home, he was surprised that it was untouched, when all of the houses around it had been ransacked by his troops. He asked the woman how she had managed to keep his men at bay. She showed Sherman a book of watercolors he had given her long ago. He had given it as a gift and signed it, "W.T. Sherman, First Lieutenant, Third Artillery." Impressed that the woman had kept the book and was smart enough to show it to any prowling Federals, Sherman ordered a guard put on the house for the rest of his stay in Columbia. With her, at least, he kept his word.

At the end of the day, Sherman told the exhausted mayor, who had been following the general around like a puppy, "You may lie down to sleep, satisfied that your town shall be as safe in my hands as if wholly in your own."

Again, Sherman did not keep his word. Before he could climb into bed that night, the general noticed the shadows of flames dancing on the bedroom wall. His men had been in the city less than eight hours.

While the Federals claimed the Columbia fire probably was started by smoldering cotton fires started by retreating Confederates, evidence suggests at least twenty fires were started in different parts of the city by Federal soldiers. Other fires sprang up from sparks carried by an unusually strong wind that night.

Even as the city burned, soldiers plundered, sometimes waiting to see what valuables women would bring with them while evacuating their burning houses.

Sister Baptista, the nun who was promised protection by Sherman, finally led thirty little girls out of the convent's school just as the building burst into flames. They first went into St. Peter's Catholic Church. They fled the church when it was set on fire by soldiers. Those flames were extinguished, but Sister Baptista thought staying inside the church was too risky. She took the girls into the cemetery, where they huddled among the tombstones for the night.

Several buildings on the South Carolina College campus caught on fire, including a hospital. The hospital's wounded were forced to hobble out into the cold. Those who could not walk perished.

Stories about the night Columbia burned are filled with tales of heroism, terror, and even some humor. A lady and her maid were yelling at marauding soldiers when one soldier stopped to help. He chased the other soldiers out from each room of the lady's house. He told the lady he would stay with her and keep out all invaders if she would give him just one thing from the house.

"Please take anything you wish. We owe everything to you," the relieved woman said.

The soldier ran upstairs and reappeared a few minutes later wearing a purple velvet cloak, a doublet, and white satin hose, the costume the woman's husband had once worn to a ball. The last the women saw of the soldier was when he left at dawn, waving goodbye with a flourish of his purple cloak. One wonders if any Confederates at the Battle of Bentonville the following month noticed they were shooting at Sir Walter Raleigh.

The day after the fire, Sherman wrote that the sun rose "bright and clear over a ruined city." He estimated that half of the city's buildings had burned. An actual count by city officials tallied 460 burned buildings and houses, about one-third of the city's structures. The fire ran from the Old State House up Main Street (called Richardson Street at the time) to Elmwood Street. The worst destruction was on either side of Main Street, from Senate to Laurel Streets. A Federal major wrote in his diary that "Columbia will have bitter cause to remember the visit of Sherman's army." He predicted it would be a century before the city would recover.

Sherman went to the Catholic church, where he found the little girls huddled around Sister Baptista. The general took the nun's hand and said, "Oh, there are times when one must practice patience and Christian endurance."

According to one of the girls, who later wrote about the incident, the mother superior, her robe burned and scorched from the flames, stared at the general from beneath her hood. "You have prepared for us one of those moments, General," she said evenly, without malice in her voice. "This is how you kept your promise to me, a cloistered nun?"

Sherman, who commanded the second largest army on the American continent and had fought and beaten thousands of Indians and Confederates, was left stammering by a single woman of God.

Sherman offered to let Sister Baptista have any of the remaining unburned houses in the city for her girls. After admonishing Sherman that he had no right to give her any houses since he did not own any in Columbia, she selected the John S. Preston house. Preston, who had run South

Carolina's conscription service, abandoned the city during Sherman's approach. His house was now occupied by Union Major General John Logan, commander of the 15th Corps.

Logan looked up from his breakfast that morning to see a line of little girls dressed in dirty white dresses being led up the walk by a nun. He was enraged that a nun and some little girls could put him out of his headquarters, particularly since he had already prepared the mansion for burning by rolling barrels of pine pitch into the basement. He cursed Sister Baptista and the little girls and ordered them out of his house. From under her habit, the nun pulled out Sherman's order giving her possession of the house. Logan cursed again, but ordered the barrels removed. Once again, a single nun had defeated a powerful Union general.

This time, Sherman kept his word to Sister Baptista. She and the girls were bothered no more. However, they were saddened at how the Federal officers treated John Preston's beautiful house. Fine paintings were slashed, mustaches were drawn on portraits, and statues were smashed.

Sherman always publicly denied responsibility for the fire in Columbia, even though his men had burned every other town they marched through with his approval. He wrote, "Though I never ordered it and never wished it, I have never shed many tears over the event, because I believe it hastened what we all had fought for, the end of the War."

There was one last incident during the city's occupation, an act of stupidity that must have made many Columbians chuckle. Sherman ordered all of the abandoned Confederate ammunition in the arsenal thrown in the river; he was afraid that blowing it up might injure his men. As the powder and shells were loaded onto wagons for the short ride to the water, one clumsy soldier dropped a box of black powder. Whether he was smoking or not will never be known, but somehow, a flame ignited the powder trail the soldier had unwittingly left behind him as he walked between the wagons and the arsenal. The flame burned up the powder trail right to the wagons. The resulting explosion killed more than twenty Union soldiers and wounded a large number, more than had been lost in the almost bloodless assault on Columbia.

Three days after they had arrived, Sherman's army moved out. When they had first entered the city, crowds of people had lined the streets to cheer them. When they left, the same crowds lined the blackened, smoldering streets to jeer them.

The Columbia Burns Tour starts at the Riverbanks Zoological Park off I-126/U.S. 76, across the Broad River from Columbia. From I-126, take the Graystone Boulevard exit and follow the signs to the zoo. While it may seem strange to visit a zoo for a Civil War tour, this is the only way to see the ruins of the Saluda cotton-cloth mill and stand on the hill where Federal artillery shelled the capitol building. There is an admission charge.

Once inside, pass the lions and tigers and bears. Go to the west side of the zoo to find the footbridge over the Saluda River. (Just below the zoo, the Saluda River runs into the Broad River to form the Congaree River.) The old stone pilings of a bridge the Confederates burned can be seen on the left, or south, side of the footbridge while walking to the west bank.

On the other side of the river, follow the asphalt path 0.3 mile north to the ruins of the Saluda factory. The path borders the river and is a moderate up-and-down hike.

Just before reaching the mill site, the main trail makes a short turn to the left. A cave is visible high on the rocks. This is Sherman's Rock. Legend says that Sherman himself slept in the cave the night before he entered the city. While now inaccessible to park visitors, it is large enough to hold several men.

Get back on the trail toward the river and follow the sound of rushing water to the factory site. Large rock foundations show where the mill was located. The Saluda factory was built in 1834 and was one of the first water-powered textile mills in South Carolina. During the war, it was used to make woolen and cotton cloth used in uniforms and blankets for the Confederate Army. A building foundation to the left marks the spot where the wool and cotton was prepared before taking it into the mill. Sherman's men destroyed the mill after using it to fire on Confederate pickets on the other side of the river. It was rebuilt in 1874, but it burned again in 1884. It was never rebuilt after that.

Sherman's men did not think much of the women who worked in the factory. One Union officer, who was looking forward to meeting some young damsels in Columbia, wrote: "It would be difficult to find elsewhere than at this place a collection of 250 women so unkempt, frowzy, ragged, dirty, and altogether ignorant and wretched. Some of them were chewing tobacco; others, more elegant in their tastes, smoked. Another set indulged in the practice of dipping." This unimpressed fellow did not get any dates from the women.

Retrace the trail back past Sherman's Rock for 0.2 mile to the botanical gardens on top of the hill. This is the location of Camp Sorghum, a prisoner camp for captured Federal soldiers, so named because that was what the soldiers most often ate (sorghum is a type of sugar cane). Sherman's men became enraged when they saw the dilapidated condition of the prison where thirteen hundred Federals had been held. Without waiting for orders from Sherman, some of the Federals set up their cannons on the hill and began firing at the city from this spot.

A shuttle bus will take you back down the hill to the walkway across the river.

The zoo is one of the best in the Southeast and is worth the price of admission.

Leave the zoo and head east into town on I-126/U.S. 76. After crossing the Broad River, get into one of the two left lanes for U.S. 76 East, which becomes Elmwood Avenue. Elmwood Cemetery can be seen on the left, less than 1.5 miles from the zoo. After crossing an overpass, there is a left turn lane at Lincoln Street that allows a U-turn.

This is the site of the old state fairgrounds, which was used as a training camp for Confederate soldiers early in the war. When the training camp was moved north of Columbia, the fairground's buildings were used as a hospital and a medicine factory. The factory was run by Joseph LeConte, a professor of chemistry and geology at South Carolina College. He was the father of Emma LeConte, the diarist who was not pleased when the Yankees arrived in town. Some munitions were also manufactured near the site, away from the hospital buildings.

After the war, the fairground's buildings were used by the Democratic Party for rallies. The Democrats were trying to wrest control back from the northern-controlled Reconstructionist. It was at these fairgrounds that Wade Hampton relaunched his political career. The political term "waving the bloody red shirt," which reminded Southerners of their war losses, was first used on these grounds. All of the houses and buildings on the grounds today were built near the turn of the century. They illustrate how the city finally started to recover from the war and the fire.

Make the U-turn and veer to the right onto Elmwood Avenue. Elmwood Avenue now runs parallel to U.S. 76. Take the second entrance into Elmwood Cemetery. Visit the office and get a map and instructions on how to find the graves of Brigadier General Maxcy Gregg and Brigadier General Milledge Luke Bonham.

After getting a map, follow North Road, a main cemetery road, all the way to the Confederate portion of the cemetery. The Confederate section is marked by a wrought-iron arched entrance. These graves are guarded by a monument reading "The death of men is not the death of rights that urged them to the fray." Turn your back to the Confederate cemetery and face the office, which is to the southwest. Bonham's grave is about 100 yards away, slightly to the left and beyond a triangular-shaped piece of land intersected on all sides by paved roads. On the other side of the triangle is a larger section of graves. Bonham is on the left side of this larger section, two graves in from one intersecting road and three graves in from another. (These directions make sense when looking at the map. Bonham's and Gregg's graves are both marked on the map.)

When the war started, Bonham was a forty-seven-year-old Mexican War veteran who had been both a United States Congressman for South Carolina and a general in the militia. In other words, he was a perfect politician for a state that would shortly need a war-time governor. Bonham had filled out the unexpired congressional term of his cousin, Preston Brooks. Brooks resigned his office after beating Massachusetts Senator Charles Sumner over the head with a cane in 1856.

Before General P.G.T. Beauregard arrived, Bonham commanded all of the soldiers in Charleston harbor. Beauregard was a professional soldier with a West Point degree, but Bonham did not like being replaced by professional soldiers.

Bonham performed well at First Manassas, but continued to clash with the West Pointers. He resigned from the army in January 1862 to become a Confederate congressman. In the fall of that year, he was elected governor of South Carolina.

Like his neighboring governor, Zebulon Vance of North Carolina,

Bonham fussed with the Confederacy over control of his state's troops. Bonham appears to have been a good war governor and is credited with keeping his state supplied as best he could. After his two-year term of office was over, Bonham returned to the field and fought in the Carolinas' campaign. He was state railroad commissioner until his death in 1890.

Bonham's grave seems modest for an ex-governor. It is a common military marker, which credits him as a general in the "Army of The Potomac." No, this is not a mistake. While the north's largest army went by this title, it was also the name of a Confederate army at First Manassas.

To reach Maxcy Gregg's grave, drive down the road towards the office, just to the east of Bonham's grave. This unmarked road is roughly parallel to North Road. Stay on the road as it curves right. Stop a few graves past an intersecting road on the left and look for a family tombstone for the Pelham family on the left. (Again, the map makes these directions easier.)

To the rear of the Pelham-family tombstone is the grave of Confederate Brigadier General Maxcy Gregg. Gregg rests under a large white cross. His monument reads: "If I am to die now, I give my life cheerfully for the independence of South Carolina."

Maxcy Gregg's house

Gregg was also a forty-seven-year-old Mexican War veteran at the start of the war. Before the war began, he was a lawyer, and he was a signee of the Ordnance of Secession.

By December 1861, Gregg was commissioned a brigadier general and given command of a brigade of three South Carolina regiments. Two more regiments joined his command in the spring. Gregg's men developed a reputation for fighting hard. At Fredericksburg in December 1862, a mistake in troop placement put Gregg's unprepared men in a hole in the line. As Federals poured through, and Gregg tried to rally his troops, he took a musketball to the spine. He lingered for two days before dying on December 15, 1862.

Like Stonewall Jackson, Gregg is often thought of as a charismatic general who motivated his men. Had he not died, he might have made a difference in future battles. Gregg was one of three signees of the Ordnance of Secession who became a battlefield general during the War. Almost all the others were too old to fight, or considered themselves too old to fight.

Leave Elmwood Cemetery by turning left onto Elmwood Avenue, which runs parallel to the four-lane U.S. 76, an elevated highway at this point. At the first unmarked street heading south, turn right and cross under U.S. 76. After crossing under U.S. 76, turn left onto the access road that now parallels U.S. 76 on the south side. Drive east on the access road until reaching Lincoln Street in three blocks. Turn right, or south, onto Lincoln.

The South Carolina governor's mansion is on Lincoln Street, one block south from the intersection with Elmwood Avenue. The governor's-mansion complex covers almost two blocks on the right, from Calhoun Street to Laurel Street. Built in 1855, the governor's residence first served as the officer's barracks at a state-operated military school called the Arsenal Academy. The building was first occupied by South Carolina's governor in 1879.

Continue driving south on Lincoln Street for another block. At the corner of Lincoln and Laurel Streets is the former site of the Palmetto Ironworks, built in 1850. The Palmetto Ironworks was the first and largest iron foundry in South Carolina. During the war, the foundry produced swords and the Palmetto muskets, which were distributed to South Carolina regiments. A palmetto-shaped proof mark was stamped into the lockplate of the musket, making it one of the few muskets that could be traced to the troops who carried it. This whole region is known as Arsenal Hill.

Turn left, or east, onto Laurel Street. Drive five blocks to the intersection of Laurel and Marion Streets. The house on the corner of Laurel and Marion Streets, at 1401 Laurel Street, is the Debruhl-Marshall House. Built in 1820, it served as the headquarters for Confederate General Joseph Johnston for a brief time in 1865. Local stories claimed Federal soldiers set a fire in the attic, but Mrs. Marshall sweet-talked them into putting the fire out. Historians who checked the attic 130 years later found charred attic trusses.

Turn left, or north, onto Marion Street and drive one block to Richland Street. Turn right, or east, and drive two blocks. The house at 1518 Richland Street, built in 1840, belonged to Brigadier General Maxcy Gregg. The house is now used for offices. Continue on Richland Street to Pickens Street and turn right, or south. Drive two blocks to the corner of Pickens and Blanding Streets. The house to the left, with grounds covering the block bounded by Pickens, Blanding, Henderson and Laurel Streets, is the Hampton-Preston House. The address of this museum is 1615 Blanding Street. Built in 1818, the house was purchased in 1823 by Wade Hampton, Sr., the grandfather of Confederate Lieutenant General Wade Hampton III. The house and its four acres are open for hourly tours Tuesday through Saturday.

In 1863, the house was inherited by Hampton's daughter, Mrs. Caroline Hampton Preston. She was the wife of John S. Preston. This was the fine house that the cursing Union Major General John Logan was forced to turn over to Sister Baptista and her little girls. While Logan's belief in the "Almighty" and "Everlasting Heaven or Hell" is unknown, it just does not seem like a good idea to curse someone who goes by the title "Mother Superior."

Tour guides at the Hampton-Preston house report ghostly happenings from time to time, such as lights being turned on and sounds coming from the floors. The ghost is not Wade Hampton III. While the general may have visited the house frequently, he lived in a house outside of Columbia that was burned to the ground by Federals.

After visiting the Hampton-Preston House, drive two blocks south on Pickens Street to Hampton Street. Turn left, or east, on Hampton Street and drive two blocks to 1718 Hampton Street, a small white house on the right side of the street.

A historic marker describes the house, built in 1850, as a home where Mary Boykin Chesnut stayed for a time during the war. Some of her famous memoir, *Diary From Dixie*, published in 1886, may have been written here. In her diary, Mrs. Chesnut, the wife of a military advisor in Richmond, kept track of famous Confederates and offered her perceptive views on the declining fortunes of the Confederacy. (See the Sherman's Exit Tour for more details on the Chesnuts.) Jefferson Davis addressed a crowd of citizens from the house's front porch in October 1864. The house is now a bed-and-breakfast.

Turn around on Hampton Street and drive west for three blocks to the intersection with Marion Street. Turn left onto Marion Street and park near the intersection. Walk back to Hampton Street and turn left. Continue walking to the First Baptist Church at 1306 Hampton Street.

Built in 1859, this massive brick structure, with its bricked columns, was a frequent meeting place for secessionists in the fall and early winter

First Baptist Church

TOURING THE CAROLINAS' CIVIL WAR SITES

of 1860. Charleston lawyer and Unionist James L. Petigru was once walking near the church when he was stopped by a passerby. The man asked Petigru if he knew the location of South Carolina's insane asylum. Petigru pointed to the church, where secessionists were filing in for a meeting.

Return to Marion Street and walk two blocks south to the First Presbyterian Church at 1324 Marion Street. The church is on the left. In the graveyard beside the 1853-era church is an unusual monument. It looks like a stone column that should be supporting some building—which is exactly what it is. The column was retrieved from the ruins of the Old State House, burned by Sherman's troops. It was transported to the church, where it was used as a monument to Confederate soldiers. A metal plaque mounted on the stone column lists the names of men from the church's congregation who served in the Confederate Army. Twenty-four of the seventy-five men listed died while in service. The list includes one dentist and a Ph.D.

After viewing the Presbyterian Church, retrieve your car. Drive one block past the Presbyterian Church to the intersection with Lady Street. Turn right, or west, and drive one block to Sumter Street. Turn left, or south, onto Sumter Street. Drive one block to Trinity Episcopal Cathedral at 1100 Sumter Street. Park along Sumter Street.

This church was one of the first Episcopal churches formed in South Carolina after the American Revolution. In 1812, a group of Columbians formed the first Episcopal parish in the upcountry, away from Charleston and Beaufort. The small wooden church grew so rapidly that the present building was constructed in 1847. The church continued to grow even during the Civil War. During the war, the tops of the iron spires were melted down and given to the Confederate forces to make cannonballs.

The graveyard contains the graves of three Confederate generals: Lieutenant General Wade Hampton III, Brigadier General Ellison Capers, and Brigadier General States Rights Gist.

Hampton, commander of the Confederate cavalry after the death of J.E.B. Stuart, is found near the northwest corner of the cemetery. He is in the Hampton plot, across from the Hampton-Preston plot. His concrete-covered vault has four columns around it.

Born in Charleston in 1818, Hampton was destined to be a leader in

Trinity Episcopal Church

South Carolina. His grandfather had been a leader in the Revolutionary War and the War of 1812. Hampton served in both houses of the South Carolina Legislature. By 1861, he was the largest landowner and richest man in South Carolina. Unlike many others in his position, he was not content to sit back and let the young men do the fighting. At the age of forty-three, he organized and paid for the creation of the Hampton Legion, a combined force of infantry, artillery, and cavalry.

Hampton commanded his legion at First Manassas. He was wounded in that battle, but returned in May 1862 to command a brigade in the Peninsula Campaign. He was promoted to brigadier general in May 1862 and was soon transferred to the Confederate cavalry, where he remained for the rest of the war. He was wounded at Gettysburg and promoted to major general in August 1863. After J.E.B. Stuart's death, Hampton commanded the cavalry of the Army of Northern Virginia. He was promoted to lieutenant general just two months before the war ended.

Hampton, a graduate of South Carolina College, had no military training, yet he was one of only two South Carolinians who achieved the rank of lieutenant general. The other was West Point–graduate Richard H. Anderson.

Unlike most generals, Hampton was known as a general who liked to fight rather than stay behind the lines. He owned a huge cavalry saber that he used in combat. He claimed that on several occasions he used it to slay Federal soldiers.

Hampton was elected governor in 1876, then served as United States senator from 1879 to 1891.

After viewing Hampton's grave, walk down the dirt path toward the church. The grave of Brigadier General States Rights Gist will be near the intersection of the lane leading from Hampton's grave and one heading east-and-west.

Gist's unusual name was really not all that strange during the 1830s, when John C. Calhoun was preaching states' rights from the pulpit of the United States Senate. According to historians, many young boys of that period had the name. Casual inquiries of historians does not reveal what Gist's friends called him.

States Rights Gist was the cousin of Governor William H. Gist, the

South Carolina governor just before the Ordnance of Secession was signed in December 1860. After graduating from South Carolina College, Gist spent two years at Harvard Law School, finishing in 1854.

Gist started practicing law in South Carolina, but he also began to prepare for the day he knew would come. He became a brigadier of state militia troops, conscious that his given name would one day become the rallying call for war. After secession, his first military assignment was as state adjutant and inspector general, in charge of training the state's troops. He then served General Barnard Bee as an aide at First Manassas, and took over command of Bee's South Carolina brigade when Bee was shot in the battle. He was appointed a brigadier general in March 1862 and transferred to Mississippi. For the rest of his career, Gist served in the Army of Tennessee.

Gist met his end in the disastrous frontal assault made against heavily entrenched Union forces at Franklin, Tennessee, on November 30, 1864. Likened to the charge made by Confederates at Gettysburg, this attack was made over nearly a mile of even flatter ground. Gist's body was first buried in Franklin, but was later moved to Columbia.

Make your way to the rear wall of the cemetery. Alongside the last walk near the north end is the grave of Brigadier General Ellison Capers. Capers is better remembered by Episcopalians as the bishop of South Carolina during the 1890s, and by historians as the author of the South Carolina volume for the *Confederate Military History*.

Twenty-four-years old at the start of the war, Capers was a graduate of the South Carolina Military Academy. In 1861, he was elected major of a regiment that took part in the bombardment of Fort Sumter. He was later elected colonel of the 24th South Carolina Regiment. He served in the Army of Tennessee with Gist.

Upon Gist's death at Franklin, Capers was named brigadier general, but it was a short appointment. The war was over just five months later. Capers developed a deep sense of religion during the war, and he became a minister. That may have caused some problems in his family, since the religion he chose was Episcopal. His father was a Methodist bishop. After the war, Capers still kept in touch with his military friends, serving as chaplain of the United Confederate Veterans.

Star marking spot where Federal shell hit the capitol

A plaque inside the church lists all the church's members who died on Civil War battlefields. The oldest is just thirty-four-years old.

Cross Sumter Street to view the South Carolina Capitol. On the southeast side is a large statue of Lieutenant General Wade Hampton on his horse. The statue's base lists all of his battles. On the west side of the capitol building, there are six brass stars that seem to have been randomly placed on the granite walls. These stars mark the six spots where Federals shells struck the building during the short artillery barrage the day before the Sherman occupied the city. The large Confederate statue on the north side of the building was unveiled in 1879.

Return to Sumter Street and walk south for two blocks to the intersection of Sumter and Pendleton Streets, the corner of the University of South Carolina Campus. The South Carolina Confederate Relic Room is located at 920 Sumter Street on the southeast corner of this intersection.

The bottom floor of this two-story structure is totally devoted to Confederate relics. Included in the collection are Wade Hampton's hat, riding gauntlets, and Whitney pistol; more than a dozen battle flags of South Carolina regiments; and a Palmetto musket and saber, both manufactured in Columbia.

The saber carried by General Micah Jenkins is also in the collection. The point of the sword was shot off in battle. Rather than replace the sword, Jenkins treasured it as his "sword of prophecy." He believed that as long as he carried that sword, he would be protected from death. He was wrong. Jenkins was accidentally shot in the head by Virginians during the Battle of the Wilderness.

Jenkins's coat is also in the collection. Its buttons are from the Kings Mountain Military Academy, a school he helped found in York, South Carolina just before the war.

One very historic battle flag on display is that of the 2nd South Carolina Volunteers, one of the first Black regiments founded in the country. (See The Sea Islands Tour for more details on the 2nd South Carolina Volunteers.)

The oddest relic in the collection has to be the second upper molar of General Beauregard, extracted from his mouth in 1890. Not long ago, a dentist visited the museum, saw the tooth, and correctly diagnosed the general's health problem more than 100 years too late: the general had not been flossing.

The second floor of the Relic Room has a few exhibits pertaining to the Civil War, including a medical chest, and the uniform coat of General Gabriel Rains.

While in the neighborhood, walk to "The Horseshoe" 25 yards south of the Relic Room. This is the U-shaped original campus of South Carolina College, now the University of South Carolina. Most of the buildings are marked with signs describing when they were constructed and how they were first used. Some of these buildings were ransacked by Federal soldiers. The hospital that was burned the first night of Sherman's occupation was on the east side of campus. The South Caroliniana Library, near Sumter Street, was designed by Washington Monument–architect Robert Mills. Today, it contains an extensive collection of books and manuscripts on the Civil War.

Leave campus and return to your car. Assuming you have parked in front of Trinity Episcopal Church, drive south on Sumter Street two blocks to Pendleton Street. Turn left onto Pendleton Street. Drive one block to Marion Street and turn left. Drive two blocks on Marion Street to Gervais Street and turn left, or west. Continue seven blocks to the intersection of Gervais and Huger Streets.

At the northeast corner of Gervais and Huger Streets is an old brick building that was once a Confederate printing plant. Millions of dollars worth of Confederate currency were printed at this site. The building was burned by Sherman's troops, rebuilt, and then abandoned. In 1995, it was scheduled for demolition, until historians rallied to save it from the wrecking ball.

Just past the printing plant at 301 Gervais Street is the South Carolina State Museum, housed in the old Columbia Mill Building. The Columbia Mill was the first totally electric textile mill in the world.

Central to the museum's Civil War collection is a working model of the CSS *Hunley*, the world's first successful submarine. In 1864, the *Hunley* sank a Union blockading vessel in Charleston harbor. (See the War Ignites Part I Tour for details on the CSS *Hunley*.)

The museum's model of the *Hunley* is cut away to show how the eight-man crew sat on a long bench and pulled on a crank that turned the vessel's propeller. The model was built by prison inmates in the 1960s as part of South Carolina's celebration of the Civil War Centennial. The state hauled the model around to various cities for the celebration.

Mechanical engineers might wonder about the *Hunley*'s stability. According to the few surviving drawings of the submarine's plans, all of the men sat on one bench, rather than alternating benches to balance their weight. Speculation is that the real *Hunley* had some sort of ballast chamber on the opposite side to compensate for the men's weight.

The other prize in the museum is one of the few surviving original copies of the Ordnance of Secession. The document was taken by a Federal soldier and had been on display in Keokuk, Iowa. In 1990, Iowa sold the copy back to South Carolina.

The museum has one six-pound cannon on display. It rests on a carriage that purists will recognize as inauthentic. Like the *Hunley* model, the cannon carriage was made during the centennial by prison inmates. One wonders how smart it was to give prison inmates access to a cannon, but here it is.

Another cannon that should go on display in 1996 is a ten-pound Parrott rifle, one of four such cannons discovered buried in Chester, South Carolina, in 1986. When all four of the cannons were brought to the museum for cleaning, a surprised—then nervous—museum staff discovered that each of the guns was jammed with live rounds. The cannons were kept emersed in a water tank until experts could clean the guns out without blowing the building down.

Palmetto muskets, Palmetto rifles, and Palmetto sabers, all manufactured in Columbia, have their own cabinets, located next to a display that highlights Union weapons. A cased set of Morse carbines, a rifle manufactured in Greenville, South Carolina, is also on display. Only eight Morse carbines are known to exist.

A collection of very attractive presentation swords is on display, including one sword given to General Barnard Bee in 1854 for his service in the Mexican War. Nine of these ornate swords were given to South Carolina officers by the state. Seven have been found. Bee's sword features a bust of John C. Calhoun on the hilt.

Other exhibits show goods recovered from sunken blockade runners, a cane presented to South Carolina Congressman Preston Brooks to replace the one he broke over the head of Massachusetts Senator Charles Sumner in 1856, and a photo of Camden soldiers wearing Palmetto stickpins in their hats.

Future plans for the museum include a detailed display on the burning of Columbia, and an exhibit showing how doctors performed operations on the battlefield.

This concludes the Columbia Burns Tour.

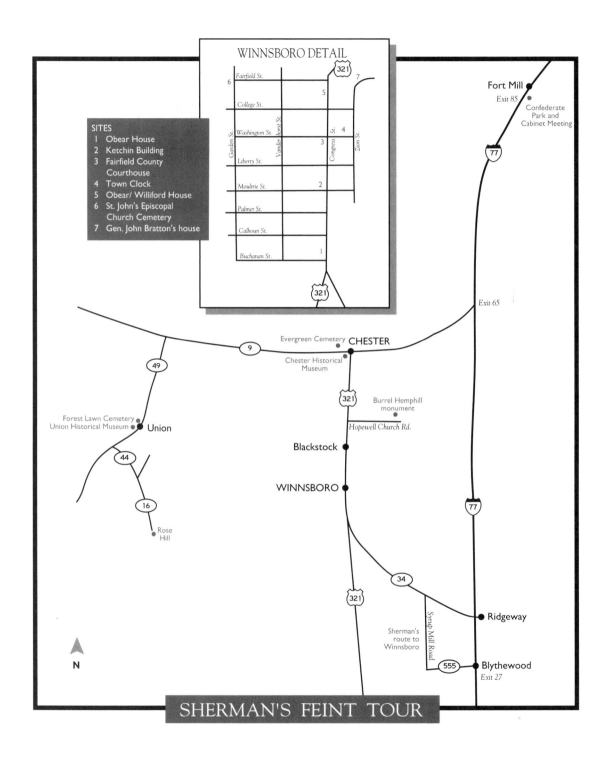

WINNSBORO DETAIL

Fairfield St.
College St.
Washington St.
Liberty St.
Moultrie St.
Palmer St.
Calhoun St.
Buchanan St.

Garden St.
Vanderhorst St.
Congress St.
Zion St.

321
7
6
5
4
3
2
1

321

SITES

1. Obear House
2. Ketchin Building
3. Fairfield County Courthouse
4. Town Clock
5. Obear/ Williford House
6. St. John's Episcopal Church Cemetery
7. Gen. John Bratton's house

Fort Mill
Exit 85
Confederate Park and Cabinet Meeting

77

Exit 65

Evergreen Cemetery **CHESTER**
9
Chester Historical Museum

49

321

Burrel Hemphill monument

Forest Lawn Cemetery
Union Historical Museum **Union**

Hopewell Church Rd.

44

Blackstock

16

WINNSBORO

Rose Hill

77

34

321

Syrup Mill Road

Sherman's route to Winnsboro

Ridgeway

555 Blythewood
Exit 27

N

SHERMAN'S FEINT TOUR

Sherman's Feint Tour

This tour starts in Blythewood, South Carolina, just north of Columbia on I-77. It then follows Sherman's original route to Winnsboro, a town occupied by his whole army. It travels to a monument erected to a slave killed by Federal soldiers before moving on to Chester, the site of a Confederate cemetery. The tour continues to Union, where the table the Ordnance of Secession was signed on and another general's grave are located. From there, the tour proceeds to Rock Hill, the site of one of the last Confederate cabinet meetings and the location of a monument to loyal slaves.

Total mileage: approximately 155 miles.

When William T. Sherman and his sixty-three thousand, lean, mean soldiers entered South Carolina in late January and early February 1865, there was virtually nothing to stop them. Confederates made small, desperate stands behind the Salkehatchie and North Edisto Rivers (See The Dead Generals Tour for details on these battles at Broxton Bridge and Orangeburg, South Carolina), but their depleted regiments were simply no match for whole Union armies. Sherman's army was so overwhelming, Confederate General Joseph Johnston compared it to the one commanded by Julius Caesar.

South Carolina was open, and Sherman's men made the most of it. They took their revenge on the first state to secede from the Union at every tiny farm, large plantation, and small town from Savannah to Columbia. Hardeeville, Estill, Poctotaligo, Barnwell, Bamberg, Blackville, Orangeburg, Midway, Lexington, and countless other crossroads villages suffered from the looting and burning of the Union invaders.

In Barnwell, as Federals looted her home, a woman complained: "We expect civil treatment from gentlemen." A Union soldier replied: "There are no gentlemen in the Union Army. We are all convicts turned out to end the rebellion." The woman then said: "Then officers will treat us like ladies." The soldier ended the conversation with a chilling: "You'll find the officers are worse than the men."

And it was so. Letters and reports from Federal officers made it clear that they believed South Carolina was a "hellhole of secession," and that they cared little what their men did. Even Union chaplains approved of the punishment the army doled out to the civilians of South Carolina. After the war, Sherman said that he did all he could to protect private property, but he couldn't be held responsible when his men ignored his orders. He claimed he personally damaged only one piece of private property during the whole campaign, a chair that he broke up to feed a fire.

Some soldiers did worse than burning and looting. Occasional violence against civilians was always possible during the march, particularly at the hands of Sherman's "bummers," the foragers who operated in front of the main regiments. One story describes how a detachment of Confederate cavalry were riding near Aiken when they came upon a grief-stricken farmer. His daughter had been raped and killed by Federal soldiers. The Confederates captured the seven Federals and cut their throats, leaving them in a ditch with a note pinned to their chests describing their crime. Sherman ordered his officers to respond by executing an equal number of Confederate prisoners for every Union soldier found butchered.

Sherman knew his force was larger than anything the Confederates could muster on their best day. In fact, Sherman's sixty-three-thousand-man army was more than twice as large as Robert E. Lee's army, which was trapped in Petersburg, Virginia, by Union General Ulysses S. Grant.

Still, Sherman wanted to be careful. He was deep in hostile territory, hundreds of miles from supplies and any other Union forces. He had to keep the Confederates guessing what he would do next.

After leaving Columbia, Sherman's next objective was either Raleigh or Goldsboro in northeast North Carolina. However, to keep Confederates in North Carolina from concentrating their forces in the northeast part of the state, he decided to "feint" directly north of Columbia in the direction of Charlotte, North Carolina. A feint is a military movement that fakes the army's true direction.

After three days in Columbia, Sherman's men headed north. In their path lay the little town of Winnsboro, South Carolina. When the Federals left Columbia a smoldering ruin on February 20, 1865, there was no reason for civilians in their path to believe a better fate awaited them.

Sherman's Feint Tour begins at Exit 27 on I-77 in the town of Blythewood, just north of Columbia.

At Exit 27, turn west off I-77 onto S.C. 555. Within a few hundred yards west of the interstate, pass Sandy Level Church on the right, which was there during the war. At 0.9 mile after leaving the interstate, turn right, or north, onto Syrup Mill Road. This is the same route Sherman and his right wing, made up of the thirty thousand men in the 17th and 15th Corps, took on the way to the town of Winnsboro, about 13 miles away. The left wing, the 20th and the 14th Corps, used another road.

As the Union soldiers marched toward Winnsboro, they saw smoke on the horizon. This was the work of the bummers, who were already burning the town. The men started double-quick marching in order to reach Winnsboro before the bummers had destroyed not only the buildings in town, but more importantly, the food.

More than thirty buildings in Winnsboro were burned before the Union soldiers could put out the flames. Still, it could have been worse. Citizens wrote of bummers having "snowball fights" with flour, and of ham hocks that were soaked with fuel and set ablaze before the regular Federal regiments moved into town. However, most of the town escaped destruction, as more than two hundred antebellum homes still stand today.

At 8.7 miles from the interstate, Syrup Mill Road runs into S.C. 34. About 6 miles to the right is Ridgeland, a small town briefly occupied by Confederate troops as they retreated northward. Several fine houses in the city were ransacked by Sherman's men, but most survive today. Turn left, or northwest, from Syrup Mill Road onto S.C. 34 and drive towards Winnsboro. S.C. 34 intersects with Business U.S. 321 just outside of the town limits. Follow Business U.S. 321 North into Winnsboro.

At 3.8 miles after turning onto S.C. 34 is Fairfield Animal Hospital on the left. In the war, this large house was known as Sweet Briar. The bummers quickly surrounded the house and rode repeatedly through its gardens, trampling the flower beds. Although the foodstuffs had been hidden, a young slave girl showed the Federals where everything was stored. The

Courthouse in Winnsboro

Winnsboro Town Clock

top of a carriage was torn off and its seats piled high with hams, silver, and other goods. What could not be carted off was destroyed. Jugs of molasses were poured into the piano and on the rugs in the house.

Follow Business U.S. 321 for 1.7 miles past the animal hospital. On the left side of the road, just after passing Buchanan Street, is the Josiah Obear house. The house was built in 1855, and purchased in 1870 by the Obear family. It was in this house that Katherine Obear wrote *Through the Years in Old Winnsboro*, a book that detailed Winnsboro during the Federal occupation.

At this point, Business U.S. 321 is called Congress Street. Continue to 231 South Congress Street, located 2 miles past the animal hospital on the left. This is a two-story brick building called the Ketchin Building. The building now houses the Fairfield County Historical Museum, which has some Civil War exhibits and a genealogy section. Built in the early 1830s as a private house, the building was operated as a girl's school by Mrs. Catherine Ladd during the war. She often headed Winnsboro's efforts to raise money to buy supplies for the Confederacy. The strong-willed Mrs. Ladd persuaded the Federals to protect her girls from the bummers. During the Federal occupation, she asked for, and received, a guard for the building.

Continue to the intersection of Congress and Washington Streets. At the southwest corner of this intersection is the Fairfield County Courthouse, built in 1823 and designed by Robert Mills, who also designed the Washington Monument in Washington, D.C. Much of the building's grandeur, in the form of its columns and circular stairs, were added after the war. During the war, the sheriff of the county saved the records in the courthouse from destruction by putting them in bags. He then tied the bags under the hoop skirts of his wife and daughters.

Across the street from the courthouse is the Winnsboro Town Clock, first installed in 1837. The town claims it is the oldest continually running clock in America.

Drive one block north on Congress Street. In the middle of the block bordered by College and Fairfield Streets is Winnsboro's handsome, white-columned town hall. During the war, it was the Obear-Williford house. Katherine Obear wrote that she watched from this house as the streets filled with Federals "until it was a sea of blue." A bolder teenager, Lilla Carroll, watched the Federals ransacking the houses from the Obear porch. Lilla broke into loud singing with the proud, defiant, Southern woman's anthem "Palmetto Hat." The song begins with: "Oh yes, I am a Southern girl—I glory in the name."

For some reason, the Federals set fire to Winnsboro's Christ Episcopal Church. As the church burned, the Federals noticed a freshly dug grave. They unearthed it, pried open the coffin lid, and propped up the newly deceased so he could watch his church burn to the ground.

Things got so bad in Winnsboro that Federal soldiers of the 20th Corps arrested Federals soldiers of the 17th Corps for looting. Sherman refused to take control. He excused one wild regiment from Missouri with a simple "I would have pardoned them for anything short of treason." He later wrote: "No general ever was or will be successful who quarrels with his men."

Continue north on Congress Street after passing the town hall. At the intersection with Fairfield Street, turn left, or west and drive two blocks. Here, at the intersection of Fairfield and Garden Streets, is the cemetery of St. John's Episcopal Church, the final resting spot for Confederate

Brigadier General John Bratton. The exact location of his grave cannot be given, as the older part of the cemetery where Bratton is buried is padlocked.

Bratton was Winnsboro's doctor when he enlisted as a private in the 6th South Carolina Regiment. He was later elected colonel of that regiment. Wounded and captured at the Battle of Seven Pines, Bratton was imprisoned for a few months until he was exchanged. He was promoted to brigadier general in June 1864, just a month after his mentor, Confederate Brigadier General Micah Jenkins, was accidentally shot and killed by Confederate troops during the Battle of the Wilderness. Bratton was in command of the largest Army of Northern Virginia brigade surrendered at Appomattox. Bratton left medicine after the war for politics, winning election as a congressman. He was defeated in his bid for governor in 1890. He died in 1898.

Retrace your route to Congress Street. Turn right, or south, onto Congress Street and drive one block to College Street. Turn left, or east, onto College Street and cross over the railroad tracks. At the next block, turn left onto Zion Street, then turn right onto Bratton Street after driving one block. On the corner of Zion and Bratton Streets is Wynn Dee, a house that was built prior to 1777. This house was the pre-war home of John Bratton.

During the Federal occupation of the town, a rusty Revolutionary War saber was discovered in a trunk in the basement of the Bratton house. The women who were staying at the house were threatened with arrest for hiding weapons. Wynn Dee was set on fire, but the flames were extinguished by some loyal servants. Federal soldiers rode their horses through the house, pulling down a hallway staircase.

Retrace your route back to Congress Street, or Business U.S. 321. Turn right, or north, and drive out of Winnsboro on Business U.S. 321, which will merge with U.S. 321 on the north side of town. Drive about 15 miles north on U.S. 321 to Hopewell Church Road, which intersects from the right. Before reaching Hopewell Church Road, you will pass two exits from U.S. 321 for the small town of Blackstock, South Carolina. Turn right, or east, onto Hopewell Church Road, also designated S.C. 12-36. Drive 2 miles and pull into the parking lot for Hopewell Reformed Presbyterian Church.

In front of the church is a small stone monument to Burrel Hemphill. The monument reads: "In memory of Burrel Hemphill, killed by Union soldiers Feb. 1865. Although a slave, he gave his life rather than betray a trust. He was a member of Hopewell." According to his family, Hemphill was a slave of Robert Hemphill, who owned twenty-two hundred acres near the church. When the Federals arrived, the Hemphill family fled, and Burrel was left in charge of the plantation. Burrel buried the family silver in the woods, but was caught by Union soldiers on his return. According to his grandson, who witnessed the incident, Hemphill refused to tell the Union soldiers where to find the loot. The angry Federal soldiers dragged Burrel to a spot near the church, hanged him, then shot his body for target practice.

Monument to slave at Hopewell

Burrel Hemphill's murder was not unusual. It is ironic that Sherman, who freed thousands of slaves during his march, allowed his men to harm hundreds of Blacks. Official records and personal accounts detail the rapes and murders of slaves all along the march. The most notorious and best-documented case of mistreatment occurred when Union General Jefferson C. Davis's corps was marching through Georgia. They came upon rain-swollen Ebenezer Creek, about 35 miles west of Savannah. The Federals told all of the escaped slaves who were following them to stand to one side while the soldiers marched across the pontoon bridge. As the last soldier crossed, the Federals pulled up the bridge behind them. Hundreds of slaves were now on the wrong side of the creek, with Confederate cavalry in hot pursuit. Some of the slaves dove into the creek and were drowned. Most of them were captured by the Confederates and returned to their owners. Sherman did not even reprimand his general for the deaths of the slaves.

Retrace your route to U.S. 321. Turn right, or north, onto U.S. 321 and drive about 10 miles into Chester, South Carolina. Follow Business U.S. 321 when it intersects with U.S. 321. Continue on Business U.S. 321 to the intersection with Business S.C. 9. Three miles to the east on S.C. 9, in an inaccessible private cemetery, is the resting place of Confederate Brigadier General John Dunovant.

Dunovant was one of the few generals during the war who had served in the Mexican War and worked his way up through the ranks. He was a sergeant in the Mexican War who received a commission as a captain in the regular army. He resigned that rank when the Civil War started and accepted the rank of colonel with the 1st South Carolina Regulars. He was at Fort Moultrie during the barrage on Fort Sumter.

While the details are hazy, Dunovant was cashiered for drunkenness in 1862, but then reinstated by Governor Pickens as colonel of the 5th South Carolina Cavalry. In this role, Dunovant won praise. After the battle of Cold Harbor he was promoted to brigadier general. During an engagement on October 1, 1864, Dunovant insisted that he be allowed to lead his men on a frontal assault of some Federal positions south of Richmond. He had been criticized for some mistakes made earlier that week and may have been trying to regain his stature in the eyes of his superior officers. In the assault, Dunovant was shot dead by dismounted Union cavalrymen.

Turn left onto Business S.C. 9 from Business 321. Drive 0.4 mile to the sign for Evergreen Cemetery. Near the sign, turn right, or north, onto Cemetery Street. Follow Cemetery Street for 0.3 mile and turn into the cemetery's first entrance. Bear to the right and go over a hill to see the graves of fifty-four unknown Confederates, one 86-year-old veteran who wanted to be buried with his comrades, and one known Federal soldier.

The Union soldier is nineteen-year-old Charles F. Emerson of the 15th Maine Volunteers, who first joined the Union Army at the age of fifteen. He died of "lung fever" while acting as part of the town's occupation force. Every Memorial Day, Emerson's grave is marked with an American flag. Though he died among enemies, he is remembered by friends.

Retrace your route to Business S.C. 9. Turn right, or west, onto Lancaster Street, or Business S.C. 9, and drive into the town of Chester. Cross the railroad tracks and continue on this road, which is now called Gadsden Street, to the top of the hill. Park the car along Gadsden Street.

At the top of the hill on Gadsden Street is Monument Square. The Confederate monument, erected in 1905 reads: "Time may crumble this monument, but time cannot dim their glory." Behind the monument, marked with a historic marker, is the Davega Building. Civil War–diarist Mary Boykin Chesnut rented an apartment in this building for a few days after the end of the war. It was here that General and Mrs. Chesnut likely entertained Varina Davis, the wife of Confederate President Jefferson Davis, as she fled south in advance of her husband.

Chester is an example of how things happen every day in the South to remind people of the Civil War. Nine years ago, a construction crew was digging near the old railway depot in Chester. Four Parrott cannons, some of the best guns the South ever manufactured, were unearthed by the construction.

The cannons were transferred to the state museum in Columbia, where researchers blanched—each of the guns was crammed with several live shells. Apparently, retreating Confederates felt the guns would end up in Union hands. They jammed them tightly with rounds so the guns would be too dangerous to try to disarm, making them useless to the Federals. The guns were then buried near the train depot, where they rested for 125 years. Money is being raised to display three of the cannons on Monument Square. The fourth cannon will be displayed in the state museum in Columbia.

Retrieve your car and turn left on Main Street, the road running in front of the Davega Building. Drive one block to the intersection with Business S.C. 9 and turn right. Drive one block on Business S.C. 9, then turn right onto McAliley Street. Drive one block to 107 McAliley Street. This is the Chester County Historical Society Museum. The collection includes Confederate Fayetteville and Richmond muskets, captured Federal Henry and Springfield rifles, cartridge boxes, canteens, battle flags, and a soldier's wallet.

Retrace your route to Business S.C. 9. Turn right and drive out of town. Business S.C. 9 becomes S.C. 9 outside of town.

About 18 miles out of town, bear left onto S.C. 49 and follow it through the small mill town of Lockhart, South Carolina. Continue on S.C. 49 to the town of Union, about 9 miles southwest of Lockhart.

While driving into Union, slow down and look to the left in the 400 block of Main Street, or Business S.C. 49. A United Daughters of the Confederacy marker is in front of General and Mrs. Henry Wallace's white, two-story house. The house is unnumbered, but is at about 430 East Main Street. Confederate President Jefferson Davis dined there on his escape south.

In the next block, the 300 block of Main Street, is the Union County Historical Foundation Museum, open in the afternoons on the first weekend of the month, except December and January. The museum is on the second floor of the American Federal Bank. In the museum collection is the table on which South Carolina's Ordnance of Secession was signed. Attorney Benjamin Arthur from Union agreed to write out the Ordnance since he had the best handwriting of all the delegates. Arthur requested that he receive the table as a reward for his good penmanship. The museum also displays two Confederate battle flags from companies raised in Union.

Continue west on Main Street to the intersection with Pinckney Street at a traffic light. Turn right, or north, onto Pinckney Street and drive two blocks to Forest Lawn Cemetery, at the corner of North Pinckney Street and Wedgewood Court. Turn right onto Wedgewood Court and drive one block, then turn left onto the access road into the cemetery.

Park on the access road in the rear of the cemetery. Walk toward three tall obelisks near a small cluster of trees. The obelisks are near the front center of the older part of the cemetery. Here, under a crypt-like monument beside a berry tree, lies Confederate Brigadier General William Henry Wallace.

A lawyer and legislator who supported secession, Wallace enlisted as a private in the 18th South Carolina Regiment in 1861, but was soon named lieutenant colonel. Wallace handled himself well during the war. A military disaster, over which he had no control, made Wallace famous among Southern officers. On the night of July 30, 1864, four companies of his regiment were blown to bits when four tons of gunpowder exploded beneath them in the trenches of Petersburg. The gunpowder had been placed there by a team of Pennsylvania coal miners who tunneled under the Confederates.

Wallace survived the explosion and was promoted to brigadier general. He surrendered with Lee at Appomattox. After the war, Wallace resumed his political and legal career. He served three more terms in the state house and then became a circuit judge. He died in 1901 at the age of seventy-four.

There is a sadness to Wallace's grave. Beside him lay his wife and three infant daughters. If the Wallaces had any children who lived to be adults, they are not buried in the family plot.

Retrace your route to Pinckney Street and turn left, or south. Cross over

Main Street and continue driving south on Pinckney Street for several blocks until reaching the intersection with Sardis Road at a traffic light. Tabernacle Church is on the northeast corner of this intersection. To the right is a highway road sign giving the distance to Rose Hill. Turn right, or west, onto Sardis Road. Drive about 8 miles southwest from this intersection to Rose Hill, the antebellum home of Governor William H. Gist. This is now a South Carolina state historic site.

Gist built the home in 1832, naming it Rose Hill after the rose garden he planted for his wife. The garden still exists in back of the house. Gist also planted the magnolia trees and boxwoods in front of the house. The plants are laid out in a maze pattern popular in English-style gardens in the 1860s.

Gist, a planter and slave holder, was an ardent secessionist. It ran in the family. His cousin was Confederate Brigadier General States Rights Gist, a name that was somewhat common for men born during the 1830s.

William Gist was South Carolina governor the two years before the state seceded, and he lobbied hard for secession during his term of office. He often visited other governors to ask for their support. He finally made his case, but too late for him to have the honor of being governor when South Carolina finally left the Union on December 20, 1860. Gist signed the Ordnance of Secession as just another private citizen.

There is one odd thing about Gist's signing of the Ordnance. In 1776, a proud John Hancock signed the Declaration of Independence in very large letters so King George of England could read it. Former Governor Gist's signature on South Carolina's Ordnance of Secession is one of the smallest ones on the document. The man spent his entire term of office lobbying for secession, but his signature is tiny compared to other names.

The Gist family cemetery is on Sardis Road about 1.0 mile further south of Rose Hill, set back in the woods, but accessible from the road. The Gists had twelve children, but only four survived to adulthood. One of their adult sons was killed while leading the 16th South Carolina Volunteers during the Battle of Knoxville, Tennessee.

Retrace your route on Sardis Road back to Union. Continue to the intersection with Pinckney Street and turn left. Follow Pinckney Street to Main Street, which is also S.C. 49. Turn right and follow S.C. 49 back to

Lockhart. When S.C. 49 intersects with S.C. 9 in Lockhart, turn east on S.C. 9. and drive to Chester. Drive through Chester to the intersection of S.C. 9 and I-77. The total distance from Rose Hill to I-77 is about 45 miles.

Drive north on I-77 for about 20 miles. Take Exit 85 off I-77 to S.C. 160. Drive east on S.C. 160 toward the town of Fort Mill, South Carolina.

At 1.3 miles from the interstate, on the left, is the large, rambling, brick house of Colonel William Elliott White. On April 27, 1865, Confederate President Jefferson Davis accepted the resignation of his treasury secretary, George Trenholm, at this house. The resignation occurred during a cabinet meeting held on Davis's flight south from Richmond. The normally dour Davis showed he had a sense of humor when Trenholm resigned. When Davis told Postmaster General John Reagan that he was also being appointed treasury secretary, Reagan wondered aloud if he could handle both jobs.

"Don't worry, there's not much left for the secretary of the treasury to do. There's but little money left for him to steal," Davis laughed.

Davis himself spent the night in the nearby house of the Springs family. With all the Yankees in the world chasing them, Davis, Reagan, Secretary of State Judah Benjamin, and Secretary of War John C. Breckinridge spent more than an hour on their hands and knees playing a game of marbles with the two young Springs boys. The Springs boys were amazed that these powerful men knew all the rules about marbles.

At 2 miles from the interstate, S.C. 160 intersects Main Street. Turn north onto Main Street. At the corner of Main Street and S.C. 160 is Confederate Park, a small park with four statues and a cannon.

The Confederate statue, erected in 1891, may have the wildest-looking eyes of any statue ever erected. The pupils are large and deep set. The soldier's eyelids appear to be missing. He is also missing his canteen. Perhaps thirst has driven this Confederate to his agitated state.

Next to that statue is a monument to Confederate women. A relief shows a woman with her hands clasped in prayer. At her feet is a furled flag. The sides of the monument feature some extremely bad poetry about "heroines among the gloom of war" and two lines from a song of the period: "Many are the hearts who are weary tonight wishing for the war to cease."

Next to the women's monument is one "dedicated to the faithful slaves" who "guarded defenseless homes, women and children in the struggle for principles for our Confederate States of America." One side of the monument shows a woman holding a child. The other side shows a man sitting on a log with a sickle in his hands. In the background are sheafs of wheat.

The last monument is to the Catawba Indians. The names of Indians from the area who fought for the Confederacy are listed. The Catawbas did not have their own regiment, as the Cherokees in western North Carolina did.

Just a few miles north of Fort Mill is where Sherman's feint towards Charlotte reached its northernmost point. Federal cavalry burned a railroad bridge over the Catawba River, which separates North and South Carolina, then turned east toward Chesterfield and Cheraw to link up with the rest of Sherman's army. The feint had worked. The Confederates in North Carolina had no idea where Sherman was going. They would soon find out.

This concludes the Sherman's Feint Tour.

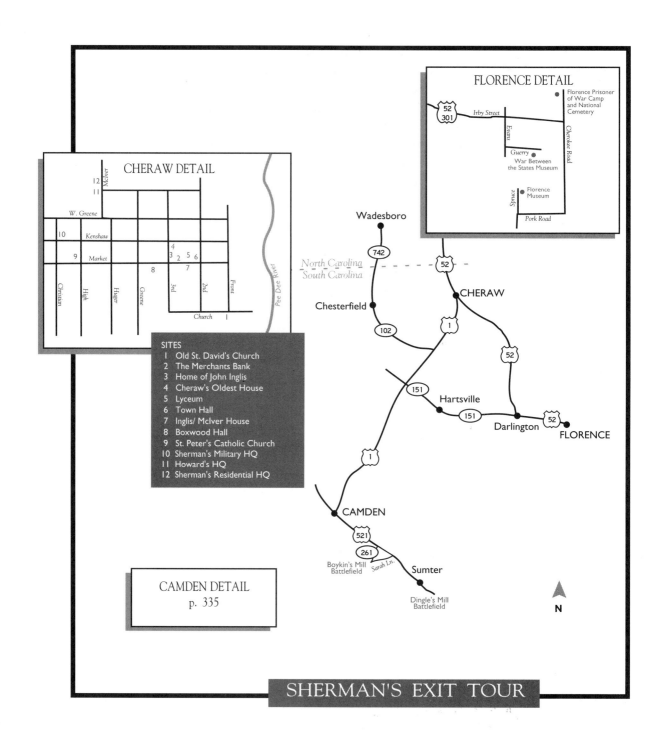

FLORENCE DETAIL

52 301 — Irby Street
Evans
Cherokee Road
Guerry
Florence Prisoner of War Camp and National Cemetery
War Between the States Museum
Spruce
Florence Museum
Pork Road

CHERAW DETAIL

12
11
McIver
W. Greene
10 Kershaw
9 Market
8
4
3 2 5 6
7
Christian
High
Huger
Greene
3rd
2nd
Front
Church 1
Pee Dee River

SITES
1 Old St. David's Church
2 The Merchants Bank
3 Home of John Inglis
4 Cheraw's Oldest House
5 Lyceum
6 Town Hall
7 Inglis/ McIver House
8 Boxwood Hall
9 St. Peter's Catholic Church
10 Sherman's Military HQ
11 Howard's HQ
12 Sherman's Residential HQ

Wadesboro
742
North Carolina
South Carolina
52
CHERAW
Chesterfield
102
1
1
52
151
Hartsville
151
Darlington
52
FLORENCE
1
CAMDEN
521
261
Boykin's Mill Battlefield
Sarah Ln.
Sumter
Dingle's Mill Battlefield
N

CAMDEN DETAIL
p. 335

SHERMAN'S EXIT TOUR

Sherman's Exit Tour

When Sherman's army left Columbia on February 20, 1865, it appeared it was heading directly north towards Charlotte, North Carolina, allowing residents in the towns northeast of Columbia to breathe a little sigh of relief. However, it was only a brief respite. Sherman was only "feinting" north, faking his true direction in an attempt to keep the Confederates from concentrating their forces against him. Once Sherman left Winnsboro, South Carolina, just north of Columbia, most of the sixty-three thousand men in his column turned northeast.

On February 24, 1865, the town of Camden, South Carolina, saw its first bluecoats. The only resistance in the town came from some Confederate cavalrymen, who fired at the Federals from Hob Kirk's Hill, the site of a Revolutionary War battle.

In Camden, the Federals burned the railroad depots, a bridge, two thousand bales of cotton, food warehouses, and a flour mill. As they had at every stop along the way, the soldiers raided the houses of residents. One of the houses they entered belonged to the ninety-three-year-old father-in-law of Mary Boykin Chesnut. The old blind man was protected by a slave who refused to leave his side, though invited along by the Federals. Of the old man, who struck out at the Federals with his cane, Mrs. Chesnut wrote, "This old man is of a species that we will see no more; the last of the lordly planters who ruled this Southern world. His manners are unequaled still, but underneath this smooth exterior lies the grip of a tyrant whose will has never been crossed."

Most of Camden escaped the torch, but the town did suffer financially. Wagons loaded with gold and Confederate bonds were discovered in the woods near the town. Most of the loot was turned over to the Union corps commanders. Still, the soldiers who found the wagons seemed to be a little more flush with cash for the rest of the war.

The army's movement north toward the town of Cheraw was slowed by heavy rains that turned every creek into a river and every low spot into a swamp. The water was so cold in some places that a thin sheet of ice formed which the soldiers smashed with their shoes.

The cold, rain, and constant sniping of Confederate soldiers put Sherman's men in a foul mood as they approached the towns of Cheraw and Chesterfield. At a town meeting on November 15, 1860, Chesterfield had been the first South Carolina town to publicly support secession. Cheraw was the home of two men who had led the secession movement.

Cheraw, founded in 1768 on the banks of the Pee Dee River, was a rich little trading village. During the war, the town became the destination of many of Charleston's wealthiest families who were escaping the Federal bombardment. Many of the Charlestonians' prized possessions were taken to the town, including a considerable quantity of imported European madeira wine.

When Confederate Lieutenant General William J. Hardee retreated from Charleston, he brought his small force of ten thousand soldiers to Cheraw. Hardee's army had tons of black powder and many cannons with them, which Hardee hoped to transfer to a railroad in North Carolina. Also with Hardee's force were many young, frightened teenagers called "kid soldiers." These young men had never even heard a gunshot. It was an indication of how far down the Confederacy had sunk.

The Federals entered Cheraw on March 3, 1865, skirmishing with retreating Confederates in the streets of the town. One diarist thought it was hailing on his roof. He walked outside and discovered it was indeed hailing—musketballs from Federal troops. "The streets filled with bluecoats. They seemed to spring from the ground," wrote one woman.

Hardee's men skirmished with the Federals all the way down to the Pee Dee River. As the Confederates retreated, they burned the covered bridge over the river. The Confederates did not have time to destroy any of their extra ammunition. One Federal report claimed seventeen pieces of artillery, two thousand muskets, and one building containing ammunition were captured from the Confederates. The report did not mention a second Confederate ammunition dump in an open ravine near the river. Some unsuspecting Federals would find that soon enough.

Sherman's men captured eight wagonloads of madeira, which found its way to Sherman's headquarters. Nearly every officer except Sherman spent the first night in Cheraw drinking and singing. It was not until the next morning that Sherman's generals realized that he had not approved of their revelry. One staff general started to apologize, but Sherman waved his hand without even looking up from his breakfast.

"Never mind explaining. Just see that the like of that doesn't happen again," Sherman said.

While visiting with a local family, Sherman was asked by the host what he intended to do next.

"I have sixty thousand men out there. I intend to go pretty much where I please," was the answer.

Not all of Sherman's soldiers would go with him. Down on the Pee Dee River, intoxicated soldiers found some small cakes of gunpowder lying on top of the ground. They proceeded to light the cakes, creating what was commonly called a "gunpowder jollification." Small piles of black powder lit in the open air do not explode, but make a great "puff" of sound and a white cloud of smoke. Watching the action creates a few seconds of fun. That is assuming, of course, that there is not a trail of black powder leading from one of those little cakes down to a ravine piled high with tons of the stuff. Six soldiers and, perhaps, some Cheraw civilians were lost in the explosion, which blew out the windows of every house near the river.

Sherman threatened to execute the mayor and burn the city in retaliation for the deaths of his men, until he realized the incident was merely a repeat of what had occurred just a few days earlier in Columbia. Since leaving Savannah, Sherman had lost more men in self-induced explosions than had been lost to Confederate gunfire.

However, Cheraw was the scene of at least one act of Federal retaliation. Union soldiers found the dead body of one of their men with the message "Death To Foragers" pinned to his coat. Earlier, Sherman had issued a standing order that one Confederate prisoner would be executed for every Federal soldier found executed. The major of the dead Federal initially refused to pick a Confederate for execution. He thought the soldier, unpopular among his own mates, might have been murdered by another Federal. Sherman threatened the major with court-martial unless he followed the order.

An old prisoner, the father of nine girls and a Methodist minister, who claimed he had never even been in combat, drew the black slip of paper that marked him for execution. The major tried to tie his hands, but the man asked for no restraints. The major handed him a handkerchief and told the prisoner to drop it when he finished his prayers.

According to a Wisconsin solider who watched the scene: "As the smoke floated away among the tall pines, our boys looked with sadness upon the bleeding corpse of a brave old man who had met death unflinchingly and heroically for the crime of another man. If the old man had bounded away into the forest, we'd never have run a step to catch him."

After leaving Cheraw, Sherman's army passed into North Carolina at five different points fanning out from the town.

The Sherman's Exit Tour begins in Camden, about 34 miles northeast of downtown Columbia. From I-20 East, take Exit 92 to U.S. 601/U.S. 1. Drive 5 miles north on U.S. 601/U.S. 1 into Camden. Turn left, or north, onto Broad Street, or Business U.S. 601. Continue to the Camden Archives and Museum at 1314 Broad Street, located 0.3 mile north of the intersection of Business U.S. 1 and Broad Street.

The archives has several Civil War–related artifacts, including the flag of a locally raised cavalry regiment, and a few artifacts recovered from the grave of Sergeant Richard Kirkland, "The Angel of Marye's Heights."

Leave the car parked at the Camden Archives and Museum for a short walking tour. Just south of the museum, at 1310 Broad Street, is the Joshua Reynolds House, one of the oldest houses in town. Now a bed-and-break-

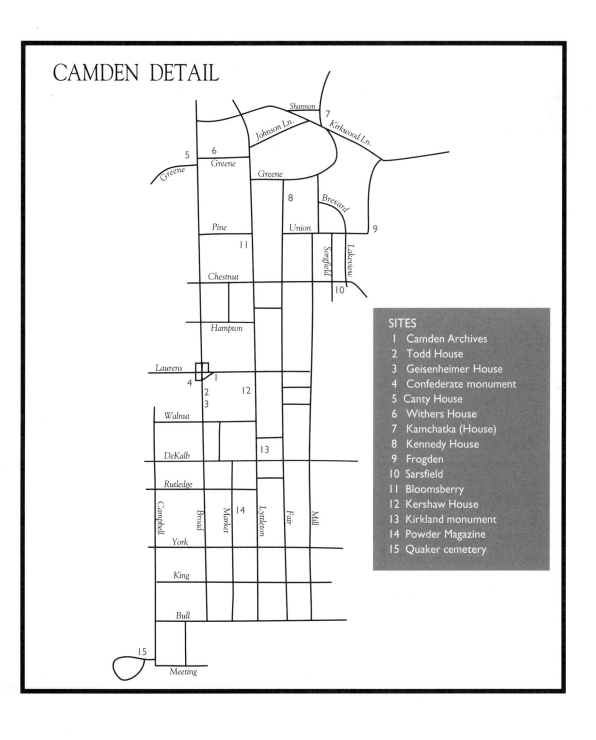

CAMDEN DETAIL

SITES
1 Camden Archives
2 Todd House
3 Geisenheimer House
4 Confederate monument
5 Canty House
6 Withers House
7 Kamchatka (House)
8 Kennedy House
9 Frogden
10 Sarsfield
11 Bloomsberry
12 Kershaw House
13 Kirkland monument
14 Powder Magazine
15 Quaker cemetery

Shannon
Johnson Ln.
Kirkwood Ln.
Greene
Greene
Greene
Brevard
Pine
Union
Songfield
Lakeview
Chestnut
Hampton
Laurens
Walnut
DeKalb
Rutledge
Campbell
Broad
Market
Lyttleton
Fair
Mill
York
King
Bull
Meeting

George Todd's house

fast, the house was also once owned by Dr. George R.C. Todd, a Confederate surgeon and the brother of Mary Todd Lincoln, wife of Abraham Lincoln.

Local historians have few details about Todd's stay in Camden, other than that his hospital was on Broad Street. A newspaper account written in 1923 reported he disliked his brother-in-law the president.

South of Todd's house, at 1204 Broad Street, is the Geisenheimer House. This was one of two identical houses that were once connected with a second-floor passageway that provided cover for a carriageway underneath. In 1923, one of the two houses was razed. This house was used as a hospital during the war. It may have been the hospital run by Dr. Todd.

Cross over to the west side of Broad Street and walk north to Monument Square, at the intersection of Laurens and Broad Streets. Laid out in 1798, the square actually has two monuments, one to Confederate soldiers and one to a soldier who died in the Mexican War. The Confederate monument, erected in 1883, has a dove of peace on top of it. The inscription reads: "They died for home and country. Erected by the Women of Kershaw County to the men who died in the Confederate War defending the rights and honor of the South."

Retrieve the car and drive 0.8 mile north to Greene Street. Turn left, or west, and continue to South Hill at 606 Greene Street. The view will not be good. Much of the house, built in 1830, is obscured by trees and shrubbery. South Hill was the summer home of Confederate Brigadier General James Cantey, a native of Camden who moved to Alabama shortly after the Mexican War. Cantey led the 15th Alabama Regiment during Stonewall Jackson's Shenandoah Valley campaign before being transferred to the Army of Tennessee. He died in Alabama in 1874.

Retrace your route to Broad Street. Turn left on Broad Street, drive for a short distance, then turn right to return to Greene Street on the east side of Broad Street. Continue to 414 Greene Street. This is the house of Judge Thomas Jefferson Withers, a signer of the Ordnance of Secession. The view of this house is also obscured by shrubbery.

Continue east on Greene Street to Lyttleton Street. Turn left on Lyttleton Street, drive for a short distance, then turn right onto Johnson Lane, a dirt road. Follow Johnson Lane to Kirkwood Lane. Turn right onto Kirkwood Lane, then pull over at 108 Kirkwood Lane. This is Kamchatka, a house named for a region in Siberia by its first owner, Confederate Brigadier General James Chesnut. Chesnut was the husband of diarist Mary Boykin Chesnut, who wrote *Diary From Dixie*. The diary was a detailed daily account of the war through the eyes of a woman who knew most of the principal government and military leaders in the Confederacy. In 1981, this diary was republished as *Mary Chesnut's Civil War*. The book won the 1982 Pulitzer Prize in history, ninety-six years after the death of its author.

Confederate Brigadier General James Chesnut, Jr., was a forty-six-year-old, Princeton-educated lawyer and legislator when the war began. Already a veteran of the South Carolina house and senate, he was elected to the United States Senate in 1858, but he resigned two years later in order to participate in the secession convention. He served as an aide to General Beauregard at the bombardment of Fort Sumter. In 1862, he joined the staff of President Jefferson Davis. He was made a brigadier general in 1864, although he never actually commanded troops. He was active in reconstruction politics and was a key supporter of Wade Hampton during Hampton's effort to wrest control of South Carolina politics back from the Republicans. Chesnut and his wife, Mary Boykin Chesnut, are both buried in a family plot near Camden that is inaccessible to the public.

Now surrounded by other houses, Kamchatka was located in the country when it was built in 1854, thus the name.

Continue on Kirkwood Lane for a very short distance, then take an immediate right, or south, turn onto Kirkwood Street. This street curves around to the west and intersects with Greene Street. Turn right, or west, onto Greene Street. Drive one block, then turn left, or south, onto Fair Street. The second house on left, at 1818 Fair Street, is The Sycamores, the home of Confederate Brigadier General John D. Kennedy.

When the war erupted, Kennedy, a twenty-one-year-old Camden native, had just opened his law practice. He enlisted as a captain in the 2nd South Carolina Infantry. When the regiment's first colonel, Joe Kershaw of Camden, was named brigadier general, Kennedy was promoted to colonel. Kennedy served under Kershaw through many battles in Virginia, until the South Carolina regiment was called home to fight Sherman. Kennedy was promoted to brigadier general on December 22, 1864. After the war, he returned to Camden and was elected to Congress, but could not take his seat because he would not take the oath of loyalty to the federal government. He later served as lieutenant governor of South Carolina and general counsel to Shanghai in the administration of President Grover Cleveland. He died in 1896 and is buried in Camden.

After viewing Kennedy's house, drive south on Fair Street for one block to the intersection with Union Street. Turn left and drive to where Union Street dead-ends into Ancrum Road. At this intersection, at 1010 Union Street, is Frogden, another of the Chesnuts' Camden homes, built about 1848. The road leads into the side of the property, so details are hard to see. The house actually faces the stables.

Turn around on Union Street and drive two blocks to the intersection with Sarsfield Street. Turn left, or south, onto Sarsfield Street. The property on the immediate left is Sarsfield, the last of the Chesnuts' houses in Camden. The property covers the entire block. Mary Chesnut finished *Diary From Dixie* in this house, and General Chesnut died here. The house can be completely circled by driving around the block.

Drive one block on Sarsfield Street to the intersection with Chesnut Street and turn right. Drive three blocks to the 300 block of Chesnut. There, in a small park, is a six-columned, pantheon-style fountain dedicated to the six Confederate generals from Camden: James Chesnut, James Canty, Zach Deas, John Kennedy, Joe Kershaw, and John B. Villepigue. Deas and Canty are the only two generals not buried in Camden.

Deas was a cousin of Chesnut who moved to Alabama as a youth. He served in the Mexican War and recruited the 22nd Alabama Infantry at his own expense. He served his military career in the Army of Tennessee. After the war, he joined the New York Stock Exchange. He is buried in New York City.

After viewing the fountain, turn right, or north, at the next block onto Lyttleton Street and drive to 1707 Lyttleton Street. This is Bloomsbury, originally built as an in-town summer house by James Chesnut, Sr., the father of the Civil War general. The best view of any of the Chesnuts' properties in Camden is of Bloomsbury.

Turn around and drive south on Lyttleton Street to 1305 Lyttleton Street, the Joseph Brevard Kershaw House.

Joseph Kershaw, a native of Camden, Mexican War veteran, successful lawyer, veteran state legislator, and delegate to the secession convention, needed just one more accomplishment to make his life complete. That was to become a Civil War general. He was named colonel of the 2nd South Carolina Regiment, then promoted to brigadier general in less than a year. Less than three years after that, he was promoted to major general. Kershaw was captured at Sayler's Creek and spent three months in a Federal prison camp. In the fall of 1865, he was reelected to the state senate. He later served as a judge and was postmaster of Camden when he died at age seventy-two in 1894.

Joseph Kershaw House

Drive south on Lyttleton for two more blocks to the intersection with Hampton Street. Turn left onto Hampton Street and continue to Hampton Park, a city park. Park and walk to the Richard Kirkland Memorial, erected in 1911 by the National Humane Alliance in memory of Sergeant Richard Kirkland for his heroism of December 13, 1862. Its cost was partially paid for by pennies collected from Camden's school children. "Greater love hath no man than this," reads the monument's inscription. While most Confederate and Union monuments are essentially useless statues of soldiers, the Kirkland memorial was designed, and still used, for a useful purpose—a water fountain for horses and dogs. The memorial once stood on a busy street in Camden, where grateful animals slurped their appreciation.

Sergeant Richard Kirkland was a nineteen-year-old Camden native with Kershaw's brigade at the Battle of Fredericksburg. On December 13, 1862, Union General Burnside ordered a frontal assault up a hill, over open ground, against Confederates stationed behind a stone wall. After the disastrous charge, thousands of wounded Federals lay moaning in front of the wall. The moans of the wounded grew in Kirkland's ears until he could stand it no longer. He gathered canteens from his fellow soldiers, then leapt the wall and distributed water to the Federal wounded. Kirkland's friends watched, expecting him to be cut down by Federal fire. Once the Federals realized that the Confederate soldier was giving water to their wounded, all firing on both sides stopped. For his bravery, Kirkland was dubbed "The Angel of Marye's Heights." Kirkland was killed nine months later at the Battle of Chickamauga in September 1863.

Retrace your route to Lyttleton Street, turn left, and drive one block to DeKalb Street, or Business U.S. 1. Turn right, or west, onto DeKalb Street and drive one block to Market Street. Turn left, or south, and drive two blocks. In the 900 block of Market Street is the old powder magazine, built in 1859 on the outskirts of town. Its hollow-wall construction promoted ventilation to keep the black powder dry.

After viewing the powder magazine, drive to the end of the block. Turn right, or west, onto York Street. Drive one block, then turn left, or south, onto Broad Street, or U.S. 521 South. Drive to the 200 block of South Broad, about three blocks, and turn right onto Meeting Street. Continue another two blocks to the Quaker Cemetery.

The Quaker Cemetery has one of the best leases of any piece of property in the world. In 1759, a man named Samuel Wyly leased the cemetery to the Quakers for 999 years at a yearly rental of one peppercorn. The Quakers then leased it to the city of Camden for 99 years at the cost of one dollar a year.

Enter the Quaker Cemetery on Quaker Avenue. On the left side of the first intersection, near the entrance and under a large cross, is the grave of Brigadier General John Bondenave Villepigue.

A native of Camden, Villepigue was a 1854 graduate of West Point whose first duty was fighting Indians in Kansas, Nebraska, and Utah. He joined the Confederacy in 1861 and was wounded while commanding the artillery at Fort McRee in Pensacola, Florida, in November 1861. In March 1862, he was promoted to brigadier general. He commanded Fort Pillow on the Mississippi River and held it against overwhelming odds before being forced to retreat. He died of "fever" on November 9, 1862, one of the few generals to give in to illness during the war.

Continue straight on Quaker Avenue to the intersection with Wylie Avenue. To the right, under a light pole and just before reaching a circular drive, is the grave of General John D. Kennedy. The tombstone looks like a scroll with a sash laid across it.

After viewing Kennedy's grave, walk back a few paces to Memorial Avenue and turn right, or south. A few yards down on the right is a large monument to Richard Kirkland. This is a reburial. What little of his remains that could be found were transferred years ago from his abandoned family gravesite to this well-kept memorial.

Cross over Memorial Drive and walk east about 15 yards to the tombstone of General Joseph Kershaw. Lucrecia Kershaw's name is on the back of the tombstone, which can be seen from the road. For some reason, no mention of Kershaw's military service is on the stone. This seems unusual in light of the fact that he fought throughout the entire war and was praised by his commanders and subordinates.

Get back in the car and drive out of Quaker Cemetery on Quaker Drive. Turn left on Campbell Street and continue to the Jewish Cemetery next to the Quaker Cemetery. In front of the Jewish Cemetery is a large white obelisk in memory of Marcus Baum, the thirty-one-year-old aide to Brigadier General Joseph Kershaw. Baum was killed on May 6, 1864, during the Battle of the Wilderness in northern Virginia. Baum was with Lieutenant General James Longstreet when the group was accidentally fired on by Confederate troops. Confederate Brigadier General Micah Jenkins, buried in Charleston, was also killed. Longstreet, Lee's First Corps commander, was severely wounded.

Baum's body was never recovered. His family erected this monument, which reads, "His bones now mingle with the dust upon that field of honor that his memory is enshrined. The qualities of his nature, well constructed like his brief career in the defense of his adopted country, formed a fitting tribute to his life."

Exit the Jewish Cemetery and turn right on Campbell. Continue to the intersection with Meeting Street and turn left. From Meeting Street, turn right, or south, onto U.S. 521. At 3.6 miles south of Camden, turn right, or southwest, onto S.C. 261. Continue for 4.5 miles to the site of the Battle of Boykin's Mill, one of the last battles of the war fought in South Carolina. The battlefield is 4.5 miles after turning onto S.C. 261.

Sherman suspected that Confederate supplies were being hidden in the swamps south of Camden, and although the war was obviously winding down in early April 1865, he worried that pockets of resistance could continue if the supplies reached Confederate troops. Sherman ordered the Union commander at Hilton Head to find and destroy any remaining railroad cars and locomotives in South Carolina. Union Brigadier General Edward E. Potter was given two brigades of troops, about twenty-six hundred men, and ordered to move inland from Georgetown, South Carolina. One of the brigades was made up of Black soldiers, including the remaining veterans of the 54th Massachusetts and the 32nd United States Colored (formerly the 1st South Carolina Volunteers, the first Black regiment raised from freed slaves. See The Sea Islands Tour for more details about the 1st South Carolina Volunteers.)

There were very few Confederate troops available to stop Potter's Federals. At Dingle's Mill, a few miles below Sumter, a force of 575 militiamen and home-guard troops threw up some earthworks at the creek. They dragged three obsolete cannons to the works and did their best to barricade themselves in for the fight. Potter's men clashed with the Confederate defenders on April 9, 1865, the day Lee surrendered at Appomattox. The two Confederate officers who knew the most about artillery were killed. When they fell, the militia scattered, and all three of the elderly guns were captured.

For a week, Potter followed his orders, searching the swamps for trains. On April 17, Potter and his men moved to Camden, doing some damage to houses and stores. The next day, he moved back south toward Manchester, South Carolina, where he heard a large number of cars and locomotives were hidden. On their way, the Federals ran into a thrown-together force of about 250 home guards and recovering wounded at Boykin's Mill.

This Confederate force had one purpose: to try to slow the Federal advance so the railroad cars could be moved. The Confederate commander, Colonel A.D. Goodwyn, who was home recovering from a wound, chose his defenses well. He put his troops behind a swamp and a mill pond. The only way the Federals could attack was along a narrow road that the Confederates covered with their two cannons. To make the swamp even more difficult for the Federals, Goodwyn released some water into it from the mill pond.

The Federals tried to slide alongside the pond's dam, where the ground was drier, but Confederate sharpshooters in rifle pits beside a church on high ground shot them down as they neared the mill. For six hours, the Confederates held the pond and the road, until the Federals were guided to a crossing around the pond, well out of the range of the Confederate muskets. Once they were flanked, the Confederates withdrew.

At least twenty-two Federals were killed, including the last Federal officer killed in the war, Lieutenant Edward L. Stevens of the 54th Massachusetts Regiment. Stevens might have been smart enough to attend

Harvard, but he was not smart enough to know that you do not stay astride your horse in full view of Confederate sharpshooters. He was picked off by a rifleman stationed at the church.

Potter's force was delayed, but not enough. He found 21 locomotives and 268 cars near Manchester, several miles away. All were destroyed. While some historians wonder why such a large numbers of cars and engines were concentrated so far from the battlefields, it is likely that Federal raiders had already destroyed the tracks further north, and that there was no place for the trains to run. Potter's men also burned five thousand bales of cotton, five thousand bushels of corn, and other private and public property.

Three days later, a flag of truce was exchanged between the forces in the area and all fighting ceased.

Boykin's Mill battlefield has changed very little. The mill pond is still there. The road from Camden still passes through a nearby swamp. The battlefield is marked by one of the few, if only, obelisks commemorating both sides. Erected by the 54th Massachusetts reenactment unit, the marker mentions Burwell Boykin, a fifteen-year-old volunteer of the South Carolina Home Guard, and lists all of the Federal and Confederate regiments that were engaged in the battle.

Today, Boykin's Mill has a little general store, a restaurant, and a broom shop that has become an unofficial museum about this battle and the battle at Dingle's Mill.

Leaving Boykin's Mill, drive east on Sarah Lane, the road running between the general store and the broom shop. The house on the high ground on the east side of the hamlet was the location of the Confederate cannon. The church on the left is in the same location where Confederate rifle pits were located to shoot across the mill pond.

Drive east on Sarah Lane to return to U.S. 521, about 10.5 miles after leaving Boykin's Mill battlefield. Turn right, or south, onto U.S. 521.

Follow U.S. 521 through Sumter, making sure to follow the highway when it turns right, or southeast, in town at Cole's Restaurant. The Dingle's Mill battlefield is 5.6 miles from this point. Follow U.S. 521 south 1.0 mile past the intersection with U.S. 15. At this point, U.S. 521 turns right at a stop sign. Follow U.S. 521 another 0.1 mile to the battlefield. Two cannons and a historic marker are placed on the high ground close to the creek that the Confederates defended. The creek is a short walk east in front of the cannons. There is no sign of the mill that was once on the site.

One story from the battle at Dingle's Mill tells of a nervous teenager who arrived at the trenches. He looked over at a group of veteran soldiers sitting down to a picnic lunch. One waved him over. "Help yourself son. If we must die, let it be on a full stomach," the man laughed.

Lieutenant McQueen, a veteran who was home recuperating from a wound, was nonchalant about the upcoming battle. He was seen leaning on his cannon and chatting with his crew while twirling his glasses around by the earpiece. Several hours later, he was killed instantly when the very first Federal artillery shell tore off his arm and shoulder. The other experienced artilleryman, Lieutenant Pamperya, died soon afterwards when a musketball hit him in the head. The Confederate crews tried to carry on, but their guns were hopelessly outclassed. One gun crew tried to make their old cannon fire by holding a slow-burning pine knot over the torch hole.

Retrace your route north on U.S. 521 all the way back to Camden and the intersection with U.S. 1. From the intersection of U.S. 521 and U.S. 1 in Camden, drive north on U.S. 1 to Cheraw, South Carolina, about 50 miles away.

Upon entering Cheraw, drive east on U.S. 52/U.S. 1, which becomes Market Street. Stop at the Chamber of Commerce at 221 Market Street (actually a half-block to the right of Market Street) to pick up two keys. One will be to Old St. David's Church. The other will be to the Lyceum Museum. A city map showing all of the town's houses is also available there. (If visiting on the weekend, call the chamber during the week to make arrangements about obtaining the keys.)

Get back in the car and drive east on Market Street until it dead-ends into Front Street. Turn right, or south, and follow Front Street two blocks to Old St. David's Church and cemetery.

St. David's was established in 1770 and was the last Anglican church built in South Carolina under the colonial rule of England's King George III. The present building was completed in 1774. During the Civil War, both sides used the church as a hospital and a campground. In the 1970s, preservationists used a drawing of the church that appeared in northern newspapers during the war to faithfully restore the church. Today, the church is used for special occasions such as weddings. Before leaving the church, be sure to relock the door.

At the left rear of the church is the South's oldest Confederate monument, erected in 1867, less than two years after the war was over. It was built at a time when the town was still under Federal occupation. Erected by the Ladies Memorial Association, the monument's original inscription to "Confederates" was rejected by the Federal officer in charge of the city. The women decided to reword the inscription so that "Confederate" would not appear on the monument. The monument addresses the visitor with: "Stranger—Bold champions of the South revere their tombs with love. Brave heroes slumber here." On another side is the phrase: "They have crossed over the river and they rest in the shade of the trees." It probably went right over the occupying Federals' heads that those were the death-bed words of Stonewall Jackson.

Old St. David's Church

Perhaps the subtlest touch of defiance by the clever ladies is on a third side of the white obelisk. That side shows a full-grown tree that has been blown over. Half of its roots are out of the ground—and half are still in the earth. The inscription is: "Fallen—Not Dead." The symbolism is unmistakable to any rural Southerner, but likely missed by an urban Northerner. A tree pushed over by a heavy wind (an overwhelming Federal force) may appear to be dead; but, if half of its roots remain in the ground, the tree will live a long, normal life. The ladies were implying that while the Confederacy may have been defeated, the South was not dead. The Federal officer approved this second design, apparently oblivious to its rebellious symbolism.

Leave St. David's cemetery and turn right from Front Street onto Church Street. Drive a long block to the Pee Dee River at Riverside Park. To the left, or north, in the ravine beside the park was the Confederate ammunition dump that was accidentally blown up by the Sherman's men. The covered bridge burned by retreating Confederates was located straight ahead.

After viewing the river and ravine, retrace your route back up Church Street to Second Street. Turn right onto Second Street, drive two blocks, and park before reaching Market Street.

Walk north to Market Street and turn left, or west. Walk on the south side of Market Street to 232 Market Street. This is the site of the Merchant's Bank (now First Citizens' Bank). The main part of the bank was built around 1835. It still has a carriage step in front. As might be expected in such a rich farming area, the bank was once the largest one in South Carolina outside of Charleston. Near the end of the war, the bank's vault was used to store currency that was evacuated from towns threatened by Sherman. The original vault is still inside, although the bank uses it more for storage than to protect money from raiding Yankees. As befits a town that played an early role in leading South Carolina out of the Union, the bank was the last in the south to honor Confederate currency. It took the virtually worthless money right up to the bitter end.

Cross Market Street and walk one block north on Third Street (just west of the bank) to 226 Third Street, the one-time home of John Inglis, a signer of the Ordnance of Secession. When Inglis heard that Federals had put a ten-thousand-dollar bounty on his head, he fled the town with his daughter. Only his wife and mother remained at the house. When the grand old lady refused to leave, the Federals put her in a wheelbarrow and pushed her down the street. The Federals did not burn Inglis's house, which may be an indication that Sherman had started to soften his stand against the Confederates by the time he reached Cheraw.

Continue walking north on Third Street. At 230 Third Street, on the southeast corner of the intersection with Kershaw Street, is Cheraw's oldest house, probably built prior to 1790. An addition to the house in the 1840s was added by a family that used to entertain the father of President Woodrow Wilson. The family who lived here during the war had six sons who fought for the Confederacy. Remarkably, all of them returned from the war, with one dying a year later. The family's father planted a single magnolia tree in front of the house to honor his dead son, and five magnolias in a row in the back to honor his living sons. The trees survive today. When the present owner put in a bid for the house, one of the stipulations in the seller's contract was that the buyer not cut down any of the magnolias.

Turn around and retrace your route down Third Street to Market Street. Walk east on Market Street past the bank to a small brick building called the Lyceum (a Greek word for a public lecture hall). Built around 1820 as a chancery court, it was used later as a lending library and as the town's first telegraph office. During the war, commanding officers from both sides frequently sent telegraph messages from the building. On April 8, 1865, the building was depicted in a *Leslie's Weekly* illustration showing Union cavalrymen racing into town shooting at Confederate skirmishers. In the drawing, dead horses lie everywhere in the streets, an accurate account according to eyewitnesses.

Use the chamber of commerce key to let yourself into the one-room museum. The collection offers an excellent overview of early life in the region, as well as life during the war.

Two of the early protagonists for secession lived in Cheraw, Henry McIver and John Inglis. Both men signed the Ordnance of Secession, enough of a reason for both of them to get out of town when the Federals arrived. The pen McIver used to sign the Ordnance is in the Lyceum, as well as a gavel used during the meeting. One display at the museum is an excellent map showing the movements of all of Sherman's four corps during their march through South Carolina.

Other relics include a muster roll for a Chesterfield County company of the 8th South Carolina Regiment, an illustration from *Leslie's* showing Federal soldiers camping outside St. David's Church (this was the illustration used as a guide for restoring the church), and receipts signed by the cashier of the Merchant's Bank describing amounts of money turned over to the Confederate States.

A note from a smart-aleck Federal soldier is also displayed. Discovered years later in the back pages of the minutes book of the Merchant's Bank, the note reads: "Remember my southern friends when this foul Southern War is over that you invested your surplus bunk in a very poor war when you got it into your head to secede and you have satisfied yourselves that Southern rights would have been better served by sticking with the Old Union. Remember when you look at the deserted truck in Georgia and South Carolina that William Sherman was your best friend." It was signed by "Almost A Southerner."

Be sure to relock the door on your way out of the Lyceum, and hang onto the key for now. Walk east on Market Street. Next door is Cheraw's Town Hall, built approximately in 1858 (since Sherman burned all of

Chesterfield County's records, the age of the buildings and houses in the county are estimated). Dominated by four, two-story-tall wooden columns and an outside staircase of wrought iron leading to the second floor, the Town Hall is one of the most prominent buildings in town. The Masons, the Cheraw Lyceum (the society that built the museum), and the town itself all contributed funds for the construction of the building, with the understanding that it would be used for private and public meeting space.

The Masons were granted a ninety-nine-year lease on the second floor. The Masonic symbol can be seen in the ironwork there. In those early days, the open second floor was used for everything from lodge meetings to ice cream socials to plays to graduation ceremonies from the public school. The building can be seen in the same *Leslie's* illustration that shows the street fighting. The building is open to the public, though no official tours are offered.

Walk in back of the Town Hall to the corner of Second Street and Wall Street and look for the law offices of Miller Ingram. The office has an official address of 204 Market Street, though it is a half-block north of Market Street. Miller Ingram has his own free Civil War museum located in a spare room of the old Hotel Covington, built in 1910. The museum has an extensive collection of artifacts that Ingram discovered at river-wreck sites. Ask the receptionist at the office for permission to see the relic room.

Walk back to Market Street and cross to the south side. Directly across the street from the Town Hall is Market Hall, built around 1837 as a public market. The tiny white building to the west of Market Hall was once used as a law office by John A. Inglis and Henry McIver. This building once was located on Front Street, and it is one of the few survivors of the explosion of the ammunition dump.

Continue walking west on Market Street for a block-and-a-half to the house at 317 Market Street, known as Boxwood Hall. Built prior to 1820, one of Boxwood Hall's owners put his hams in the attic of the house to save them from the Yankees. The hams started to drip fat that permeated the walls. To this day, the house's owner has trouble making paint stick to the walls because of the 130-year-old pig fat on them.

Boxwood Hall

Turn around and walk east on Market Street, stopping at the Chamber of Commerce at 221 Market Street to return the keys to the Lyceum and St. David's Church.

Pick up your vehicle and drive west on Market Street to 602 Market Street. This is the location of St. Peter's Catholic Church, built around 1840. Faint saber marks can be found in the church's wooden columns. Some soldiers tried to start a fire in the right rear of the church's interior. The charred floor timbers can still be seen.

Continue west on Market Street for one block to Christian Street. Turn right, or north, on Christian Street and drive one block to Kershaw Street. Turn right and continue to 612 Kershaw Street, the Matheson Memorial Library. This library was built in 1810 as a private school funded by the Cheraw Academical Society and the Masons. Sherman used it as a military headquarters during his short stay. He posted signs on all the trees telling common soldiers to stay off the property unless they had official business at the headquarters.

General Oliver O. Howard's headquarters

Drive to the next street, High Street, and turn left, or north. Continue to the intersection with West Greene Street and turn right, or east. Drive to the next intersection and turn left onto McIver Street.

The house at 135 McIver Street, built in 1815, is Enfield, a wedding present from Eramus Powe to his daughter. Union General Oliver O. Howard used this house as his headquarters during his stay. A ghost story associated with this house claims that a slave girl was standing on the porch when a Federal officer rode his horse up and tossed her his reins. When she failed to catch them, he shot her. Through the years, owners have credited unusual noises in the night to the girl. So far, she has not really bothered anyone, other than to wake them up at night or make noise while they are talking on the phone.

Two houses further up the street, at 143 McIver Street, is a home once owned by Mr. Powe. During the war, it was owned by Henry McIver. Sherman used this house as his sleeping quarters, probably because the house was out in the country at the time. Sherman may have wanted to get away from the hustle and bustle of downtown Cheraw.

While staying in the house, Sherman took great pleasure in playing with the McIver children. He was bouncing one child on his knee when he noticed that the small boy was staring intently at the general's head. When Sherman asked the lad why he was staring, the honest little boy said, "I don't see any horns. You are supposed to have horns."

Turn around and head back down McIver Street, which becomes Huger Street. Take Huger Street to Market Street, which is two blocks away.

This concludes the tour in Cheraw, but visitors may want to stay longer to see all of Cheraw's historic sites. The town has forty-five different antebellum houses and historical stops.

To leave Cheraw, turn right, or west, onto Market Street, which is also U.S. 52/U.S. 1. Follow this road until U.S. 52 turns south. Drive south on U.S. 52 towards Darlington, about 32 miles away. About 5 miles outside of Cheraw is a historic marker for the home of Colonel Ellerbe Boggan Crawford Cash. Cash was a colonel of the 8th South Carolina Regiment, but he is better known as the last officially recognized winner of a duel in South Carolina. In 1880, Cash killed Colonel William Shannon after a now-forgotten argument. After this duel, officers of the state and members of the bar were required to take an oath that they had not participated in a duel since January 1, 1881.

On the outskirts of Darlington, take Business U.S. 52 South into town. As you enter Darlington, look to the left for a large wall mural depicting life in old Darlington. One block behind this building/mural is the Darlington County Historical Commission, housed in an old brick jail. The building houses a vast collection of photographs chronicling Darlington's history.

One of the photos is of Henry "Dad" Brown, just two years before his death. The photo shows an old Black man posing with a snare drum. Brown knew how to use that instrument. He was a free Black man who drummed for three different South Carolina Confederate regiments, including one of the very first units to organize, the Darlington Guards. Serving with the Darlington Guards, Brown would have been present at the firing on Fort Sumter.

Once the three-month enlistment with the Darlington Guards expired, Brown joined the 8th South Carolina Regiment. He later transferred to the 21st South Carolina. By law, Brown could not carry a weapon, but he was apparently quite proud to carry a drum. His commander at First Manassas said that when Brown saw the enemy, he played the "long roll" (a constant drumming call to get men into line) so long that he had to be ordered to stop. Brown sent all of his pay home to his wife in Darlington.

After the war, Brown became an undertaker rather than return to his previous job as a brick mason. He eventually became somewhat wealthy. His obituary in 1907 claims that many of his white soldier friends came to him when they were experiencing hard times during Reconstruction, and he always gave them some money if they needed it. Upon his death, Brown's surviving regimental members went to his house and escorted his body to the funeral home. An honor guard stood by his body all night. The service was given by a white and a Black minister, and about a third of the people attending his funeral were white.

The service of slaves and free Blacks in the Confederate Army is probably the least studied aspect of the war. Thousands of slaves served the Confederacy by digging trenches and building forts. These slaves did not perform such service willingly and most were not paid for their labor.

Hundreds of body servants went to war with their officer masters, with duties ranging from tending horses to serving as regimental cooks. Some were trusted to go back and forth from home to exchange mail and bring back supplies.

The slaves, free Blacks, and mulattoes who actively fought against the Union confound many historians. At least two regiments of free Blacks who owned slaves themselves organized in Louisiana and offered their services to the Confederacy. Their help was refused. At Gettysburg, a Black Confederate sniper killed many Federals before he was killed himself. More than thirty Black wagon teamsters surrendered with Lee at Appomattox. In the confusion of the Confederate retreat from Petersburg, these men could have slipped away as easily as thousands of Lee's white soldiers did, yet they remained until the end.

To view Henry Brown's grave, drive south on Business U.S. 52 through downtown Darlington until it runs into U.S. 52. Turn right, or north, onto U.S. 52 and drive to the intersection with S.C. 340 at the Big Apple Inns Motel. Turn right, or east, onto S.C. 340. Take the first left onto Washington Street, then the next right onto Jeffrey Street. Follow Jeffrey Street to a cul-de-sac, 3.7 miles from the museum. Brown's obelisk is on the left of the cul-de-sac, between two brick houses. It does not list his service record.

Retrace your route to U.S. 52. Turn left, or south, onto U.S. 52 and drive towards Florence, South Carolina.

Follow U.S. 52 into Florence. The road becomes Irby Street, or U.S. 52/U.S. 301. Near the center of old downtown, just after passing the city/county government building on the left, turn right onto Evans Street. Drive six blocks and turn left onto Guerry Street. Continue to 107 South Guerry Street, the War Between the States Museum.

The museum includes examples of Confederate money from every state; some chain and cannonballs from the *Pee Dee*, a Confederate gunboat that was built near Cheraw; a replica of the prisoner of war camp that was in Florence and relics from the site; and a small collection of weapons. The most unique relic in the collection is a snuff box. That by itself is not all that interesting, but when it was found, the box contained some money and a letter that is now on display. The letter reads: "Momma—It is cold here on the River. Won't be long until I come home. I am sending you this money to help. I kept it in the can and hid it at night. Take it. We are supposed to move out today and move to Charleston." The note was not signed, and there was no indication why the money was never delivered.

Retrace your route to Irby Street and turn right. Continue to Cherokee Road and turn left, or north. Drive 1.0 mile to the Florence National Cemetery. Like many other Civil War–era national cemeteries, the Florence cemetery started out as a prison camp. More than twenty-eight hundred of the twelve thousand Federal prisoners kept in Florence died of disease. At least one of them was a woman, Florena Budwin. Budwin is believed to be the first woman buried at a Federal military cemetery.

Mrs. Budwin disguised her sex to join her husband in a Pennsylvania regiment, and both were captured. She apparently continued to hide her sex at Andersonville, even after her husband died. She was transferred to Florence, and her true identity was discovered during a routine examination by a Confederate doctor. The doctor put Budwin to work as a nurse. She died of pneumonia on January 25, 1865, just one month before all sick prisoners were released to the north. Her tombstone stands in the middle of the cemetery, along many long rows of unmarked, unknown Union soldiers.

Retrace your route back on Cherokee Road, crossing over Irby Street. At 1.5 miles from the cemetery, turn right, or west, onto Park Road. Follow Park Road for 0.2 mile to Spruce Street and turn. In the 600 block of Spruce Street is the Florence Museum.

Among the museum's small Civil War collection are the two propellers of the *Pee Dee*. This wooden gunboat did very little during the war other than try to cover the retreat of Hardee's army at Cheraw by firing exactly one round toward the Federals.

One display includes a cynical letter from a prison guard who wrote: "Savannah has gone up the spout. The papers are saying that it was of no importance in a military point of view. Now, when Charleston and Wilmington go up, they will be of no importance either."

This concludes the Sherman's Exit Tour.

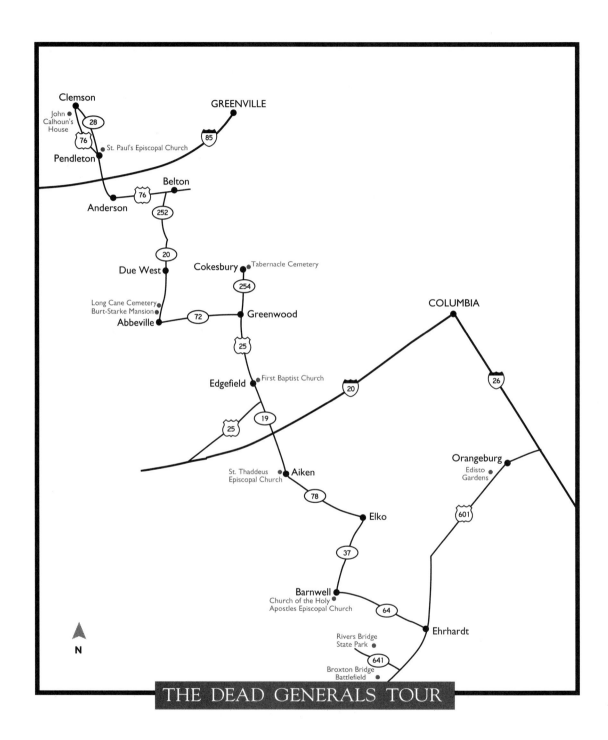

Clemson
John Calhoun's House
28
76
St. Paul's Episcopal Church
Pendleton
GREENVILLE
85
Belton
76
Anderson
252
20
Due West
Cokesbury
Tabernacle Cemetery
254
Long Cane Cemetery
Burt-Starke Mansion
72
Greenwood
Abbeville
25
COLUMBIA
Edgefield
First Baptist Church
20
26
25
19
Orangeburg
Edisto Gardens
St. Thaddeus Episcopal Church
Aiken
78
Elko
601
37
Barnwell
Church of the Holy Apostles Episcopal Church
64
Ehrhardt
Rivers Bridge State Park
641
Broxton Bridge Battlefield

N

THE DEAD GENERALS TOUR

The Dead Generals Tour

This tour starts in Clemson, South Carolina, at the home of John C. Calhoun, the inspiration for future secessionists. From there, it moves down the road to Pendleton, the final resting place of two generals, including one who gave Stonewall Jackson his nickname. The tour travels to Abbeville, the site of the last formal meeting of the Confederate cabinet, and continues to Cokesbury to view the graves of two generals, including one who was the hero of the war's first major land battle. It then travels to Edgefield and the graves of a Confederate general and a South Carolina politician whose caning of a Massachusetts senator angered the North and amused the South. From Edgefield, the tour moves to Aiken, the site of a street battle and another general's grave. It continues to Barnwell to see yet another general's grave before moving to Ehrhardt, the site of preserved Confederate earthworks at Broxton Bridge and Rivers Bridge. The tour ends in Orangeburg.

Total mileage: approximately 235 miles.

This tour begins at the home of a man who had been dead for eleven years by the time the Civil War started. He may have been dead for a generation, but the secessionists who removed South Carolina from the Union in December 1860 were following the blueprint drawn by John C. Calhoun more than thirty years before the war.

Calhoun was never president, but he did serve in almost every other office. He was a congressman (1811–1817), secretary of war (1817–1825), vice president (1825–1832), senator (1832–1843 and 1845–1850), and secretary of state (1844–1845). He also had a great head of hair. Every portrait of Calhoun concentrates on his great, flowing locks, no doubt cultivated to look like a lion's mane.

Ironically, this son of a cotton planter first heard secessionist principles at Yale University and at a Connecticut law school during a period when the North was contemplating leaving the Union. He wrestled between the conflicting ideas of a strong Federal union and states' rights for years, before finally coming down on the side of the states' rights. Once he made up his mind, his support was unwavering. He had a rock-bottom belief in the rights of individual states to decide what is best for their citizens. This

John C. Calhoun's house

belief evolved into the theory that citizens should be able to "nullify" any law based on the United States Constitution that they did not like. The theory continued that if three-fourths of the states ratified any amendment that gave disputed power to the Federal government, then the opposing states could secede from the Union by repealing their ratification of the Constitution.

Calhoun tested his theory of nullification in 1832. Calhoun, and many other South Carolina politicians, felt that a national tariff only protected the interests of Northern manufacturers, and South Carolina should not be forced to pay it. He demanded the tariff be dropped, and threatened that South Carolina would secede over the issue. However, no other Southern states backed up his threat. When President Andrew Jackson threatened to invade South Carolina if the state tried to secede, Calhoun backed off.

Calhoun did not stop trying to unify the South, however. He shifted his attention to the issue of slavery, demanding that no interference must ever be made to stem its spread. He even warned that the South was prepared to go to war "when you reduce the question to submission or resistance."

Calhoun's home, Fort Hill, has been preserved and is located on the campus of Clemson University in Clemson, South Carolina. From I-85 west of Anderson, South Carolina, take the exit for U.S. 76/S.C. 28 and head north toward Clemson. Drive 8.5 miles to a sign for Perimeter Road with other directions for parking for Clemson Stadium. Turn left onto Perimeter Road. Drive 2.6 miles to Williamson Street, just 0.3 mile after passing through a traffic light. Turn right, or north, onto Williamson Street. Continue to Palmetto Boulevard and turn right again, then take the next left onto Fernow Street. The house is on the corner of Fernow Street and Calhoun Drive. It may be difficult to find a parking spot. Turn right onto Calhoun Drive and drive to the intersection with Fort Hill Street. There may be some parking spots along Fort Hill Street.

Calhoun lived at Fort Hill for more than twenty-five years. The house was built in 1803. Calhoun lived there from 1825 until his death in 1850. It was inherited by Thomas Clemson, his son-in-law, who gave South Carolina the land to start Clemson. The house is open every day for tours, but don't even attempt to visit the site on a football Saturday.

After touring the house, retrace your route back to Perimeter Road and turn left. Follow Perimeter road to U.S. 76 and turn right, or south. Within 0.1 mile, turn left, or south, onto Business S.C. 28.

At 5.1 miles after leaving Calhoun's house, turn left, or east, onto Queen Street from Business S.C. 28. Park the car to visit the Pendleton Historic Commission on the corner of this intersection. Inside are brochures for all the area attractions and some small Civil War displays. One display is of a hundred-dollar Confederate bill that features the image of Lucy Holcomb Pickens, a Pendleton native and wife of Civil War South Carolina Governor Francis Pickens. Calhoun's image also graces the hundred-dollar bill.

The same display case shows a revealing letter from a Confederate soldier to his sister in Pendleton. Written just after Gettysburg, the man writes how hungry he is. It is an excellent first person account of life in the field with Lee's army.

Leaving the little museum, continue two blocks on Queen Street to St. Paul's Episcopal Church. On the west side of the church, beside each other, are the graves of two brothers-in-law, Brigadier General Barnard Bee and Brigadier General Clement Stevens.

Although a native of Charleston, Bee really considered himself a Texan. His father had moved the family there to become the secretary of state when Texas was still a republic. Bee graduated from West Point in 1845, far down in class ranking. He fought in Mexico and was fighting Indians when he left the army in March 1861 to join South Carolina's forces. Why he joined a South Carolina unit instead of a Texas one is a bit of a mystery. Bee was made a brigadier general on June 17, 1861, just a month before the war's first big clash at First Manassas.

In that battle, Bee's troops were falling back in disarray under pressure from superior Federal forces. Bee was trying to think of something to stem the tide when his eye caught another regiment in his rear that was not moving. Behind the regiment, astride a little sorrel horse, was a general clad in a blue uniform. Bee sang out to his troops, "There stands Jackson like a stone wall! Rally round the Virginians!"

There have always been two theories about this famous rallying cry. One theory claims that Bee was trying to impress his troops with how coolly the Virginians were holding their ground as the Federals advanced toward them. The other theory is not at all popular with Virginians. Some historians believe Bee was really cursing Jackson for keeping his troops in the rear when Jackson could plainly see that the South Carolinians were being cut to pieces. One wonders if Bee's next most famous call would have been: "Jackson, get your butt down here and help me shoot these Yankees!" History will never know. Within minutes, Bee was cut down. He died the next day, without knowing that he had created the most famous nickname any general bore during the war. Lieutenant General Thomas E. Jackson, jokingly called "Tom Fool" to that point, would be remembered as "Stonewall" Jackson forevermore.

Bee's brother-in-law, Clement H. Stevens, was born in Norwich, Connecticut, in 1821, but the family soon moved to Pendleton, the hometown of his mother. At the start of the war, he was a banker in Charleston and married to Bee's sister, giving him some clout in securing a good position in the army. Stevens was the designer of the "floating battery," the wood-and-iron battery that floated in the water and was used against Fort Sumter.

Wounded at First Manassas while serving as an aide to his brother-in-law, Stevens impressed someone enough to secure a commission as colonel of the 24th South Carolina Infantry. He fought with that unit at the Battle of Secessionville on Morris Island south of Charleston. He was then transferred west, where he fought at Vicksburg and Chickamauga. He was wounded again at Chickamauga. Somewhere along the way, his men started calling him "Rock." Stevens returned to duty as a brigadier general on January 20, 1864. His luck finally ran out on July 20, 1864, when he received his last and fatal wound at the Battle of Peachtree Creek, at today's downtown Atlanta. He died five days later, three years and three days after his brother-in-law.

Retrace your route back to Business S.C. 28. Turn left and follow Business S.C. 28 to the intersection with U.S. 76. Turn south onto U.S. 76 and drive to Anderson. In downtown Anderson, 15.4 miles from St. Paul's Episcopal Church, U.S. 76 turns left, or east toward Belton. Continue east on U.S. 76 for 5.1 miles to the intersection with S.C. 252. Follow the right fork onto S.C. 252. Drive 5.6 miles to the intersection with S.C. 20. Turn right, or south, onto S.C. 20 and drive through Due West, a charming little town that seems to be made up almost entirely of Erskine College.

After leaving Due West, drive another 6.3 miles, towards Abbeville, and look for Long Cane Cemetery on the right. The terrain hides the cemetery from view until you are almost upon it, so watch for graves close to the road.

The entrance to the cemetery is on the south side. From S.C. 20, make a sharp 120-degree turn to the right into the cemetery's main entrance. The cemetery road will point toward a large magnolia tree and a grave topped by a Celtic cross (a cross with a circle around the top portion of it). The most famous Confederate graves are in that area.

Under the magnolia tree, beneath a crypt-like monument, lies Brigadier General Samuel McGowan, who served in the Mexican War and in the state house for fourteen years before joining the Confederate Army at age forty-two. He was one of the ranking militia officers at the bombardment of Fort Sumter and was made a colonel of the 14th South Carolina Regiment. He was promoted to brigadier general after Brigadier General Maxcy Gregg was killed at Fredericksburg in December 1862. McGowan took over Gregg's brigade. (See the Columbia Burns Tour for details on the career of Maxcy Gregg.) McGowan led a charmed life, surviving four wounds. He was with Lee at Appomattox and returned to politics after the war. He was elected to the United States Congress, but was refused his seat by Northerners trying to keep former Confederates out of office. He later served on the South Carolina Supreme Court, a position he held until four years before his death in 1897. The stonecutter that carved McGowan's inscription seems to have succumbed to wound inflation. While most histories say McGowan was wounded four times, his monument says seven times.

Just three graves north from McGowan is Thomas Chiles Perrin, the first man to sign South Carolina's Ordnance of Secession.

Return to S.C. 20 and continue into Abbeville. To the right of the first stoplight in Abbeville, across from a cannon in a little traffic island on the left, is the Burt-Starke Mansion. This house was the site of the last formal meeting of the Confederate Cabinet on May 2, 1865. In the meeting, Confederate President Jefferson Davis met with Secretary of State Judah P. Benjamin, Secretary of the Navy Stephen Mallory, Postmaster General John H. Reagan, Secretary of War John C. Breckinridge, and four other brigade generals.

Burt-Starke Mansion

During the meeting, Davis still professed hope of continuing the fight. Though there were barely two thousand soldiers accompanying Davis as he fled south, the president thought these troops could form the nucleus of a new army. One by one, the generals told Davis their men were not willing to continue to fight for a now-lost Confederacy.

"Then why are you still in the field?" Davis asked.

"We are here to help you escape. Our men will risk battle for that, but they won't fire another shot to continue the war," answered Brigadier General Basil Duke, a cavalryman who had once invaded Indiana and Ohio with Brigadier General John Hunt Morgan. Davis made one more plea for his generals to rally their men for the Confederacy. They stared at their boots and did not answer.

A bitter Davis then said, "All is lost indeed. I see that the friends of the South are prepared to consent to her degradation." He went up to his room. At that point and on that date, May 2, 1865, the Confederate States of America officially ceased to exist.

Davis stayed in the Burt-Starke Mansion in the same room that his wife

Varina had used several days earlier when she passed through the town.

From Abbeville, Davis fled south into Georgia. Benjamin, Mallory, and Breckinridge, the remaining members of his cabinet who had accompanied Davis to Abbeville, would leave him two days later. Most of the escort would disband.

Davis finally caught up with his wife in central Georgia on May 7. On May 10, 1865, the party was captured near Irwinville, Georgia.

Davis's capture was big news in the north, but there was one person in the Davis party whose capture was not mentioned in the newspapers. His name was Jim Limber.

Jim was a Black playmate of the Davis children. He had been living as a member of the family ever since Mrs. Davis rescued him from the streets of Richmond when she saw him being beaten by an older Black man. When the Davis family was captured, Jim was taken away kicking and screaming from what he considered his family. Mrs. Davis tried to find Jim after the war but was never successful. They never saw each other again.

There is something unusual about Abbeville. The first signer of the Ordnance of Secession was Thomas Perrin. His house once stood across the street from the Burt-Starke House. If you count the first signature on the Ordnance as the first act of war, and the dissolution of the Confederate Cabinet as the last act of war, you could make a case that the war started and ended in Abbeville. (The town of Chesterfield, South Carolina, claims to be the site of the first town meeting where secession was demanded.) The Burt-Starke Mansion is only open Friday and Saturday afternoons.

Continue south through Abbeville on S.C. 20, driving around the unique town rectangle. Continue to the intersection with S.C. 72, about three blocks south of the rectangle. Turn left, or east, onto S.C. 72. Continue on S.C. 72 to the town of Greenwood.

In Greenwood, about 15 miles after leaving Abbeville, turn left, or north, onto S.C. 254 toward Cokesbury. Drive 3.8 miles north on S.C. 254, then watch for a historic marker on the right for Tabernacle Cemetery.

At the marker, turn right, or east, onto a dirt road and drive 0.3 mile to Tabernacle Cemetery. This is the resting place of Confederate Brigadier General Nathan G. "Shanks" Evans and his brother-in-law, Brigadier General Martin W. Gary.

Evans is an unusual case. He is credited both with saving the South from its first defeat, and being one of the worst generals to put on the Confederate uniform. Nicknamed "Shanks" at West Point for his puny legs, he graduated next to last in the class of 1848. He then spent several years fighting Indians in the West.

At Fort Sumter, Evans served as adjutant general of all of South Carolina's troops. By First Manassas, he had risen to the rank of colonel. In that battle, Evans and his two regiments, serving under General Bee's command, were the first ones to figure out the Federal plan to turn the Confederate left flank. Without waiting for orders, Evans moved his two regiments into the breach, where they held the Federals until the rest of the Confederates could form for battle. It was during this slow, fighting retreat that Bee exclaimed "there stands Jackson like a stone wall!" Most historians credit Evans's quick thinking for saving the whole Confederate Army.

In October 1861, Evans did well again at the Battle of Balls Bluff, Virginia. His troops drove the Federals so far so fast that some Union troops were pushed back over the bluff and drowned in the Potomac River. He was promoted to brigadier general for that action, and the Confederate Congress gave him an official thanks.

However, Evans's career nosedived in late 1862. In command of troops at Kinston, North Carolina, during a Union raid toward Goldsboro, he forgot the placement of his troops. When attacked by an overwhelming force of Federals, Evans pulled back his troops on his left flank. He then shelled the positions still occupied by his troops in the center and right flank. He was accused of being drunk during the action, and it was a charge that stayed with him for the rest of his career. Evans was court-martialed for cowardice, but acquitted. His reputation shot, Evans did little for the rest of the war. He was called up for battle again, but he fell off his horse and was injured. He died in 1868 at the age of forty-four.

Evans is buried under a white obelisk that lists "Wichita Kansas 1858" without explanation. It may have to do with either a favorable action report or a wound he received while fighting Indians. "Balls Bluff" is also listed, probably because he was in command at this battle.

Evans's brother-in-law, Martin Gary, carried the nickname "Bald Eagle" since he was bald except for his beard. A graduate of Harvard, he was a lawyer and a legislator when the war started. Like his brother-in-law, Gary performed admirably at First Manassas, stepping in to command his regiment when both his colonel and his lieutenant colonel were wounded. Gary was later given command of Hampton's Legion, a combined infantry, artillery, and cavalry force.

Gary was promoted to general in 1864. His troops were the last to leave Richmond on the retreat and acted as an escort to President Jefferson Davis on his flight south. Gary resumed his political career after the war and died in 1881. One wonders what West Point–educated Evans must have thought of the great success of his brother-in-law, who had no military training whatsoever.

Gary's monument lists thirty different battles. He is recognized as "Jurist, Patriot, Hero, Statesman." His brother, who was mortally wounded in 1863 while in command of Battery Wagner near Charleston, is buried beside him.

President Davis and the cabinet spent the night of May 1, 1865, in the Cokesbury home of General Gary, who had accompanied Davis south. It was at Gary's house that General Braxton Bragg caught up with the fleeing party. Davis was overjoyed to see his old friend Bragg, but he was the only one. The rest of the party had grown weary of Bragg's four-year record of excuse-ridden defeats. Breckinridge was particularly pained to see Bragg. He had served under the man and hated his guts.

Leave Tabernacle Cemetery and turn left, or south, on S.C. 254 to return to Greenwood. In Greenwood, turn left, or south, onto U.S. 25, about 3.5 miles after leaving Tabernacle Cemetery. Drive about 38 miles south on U.S. 25 to Edgefield, South Carolina. In Edgefield, turn left, or south, at the first traffic light in town to continue following U.S. 25. Drive one block south, then turn left onto Aiken Street. Drive one block on Aiken Street to a stop sign. The First Baptist Church is straight ahead. To reach the church, turn left at the stop sign, drive no more than 20 yards, then turn right onto Church Street. The church's address is 212 Church Street.

In the left rear of the church cemetery, next to the Confederate dead, is a family plot surrounded by a brick-and-iron-work fence. A tall obelisk marks the grave of South Carolina Congressman Preston S. Brooks.

Brooks made a name for himself on May 22, 1856, by caning United

States Senator Charles Sumner of Massachusetts. On May 20, 1856, Sumner, a well-known abolitionist, made a speech on the Senate floor claiming that South Carolina Senator Andrew P. Butler had taken "the harlot Slavery as his mistress." Sumner went on to say that if the state of South Carolina were to suddenly disappear "civilization might lose little." Two days later, Brooks, who was Butler's cousin, walked into the Senate chambers carrying his gutta-percha (an early type of rubber) cane. He used it to conk Sumner over the head—repeatedly.

The incident became a media event throughout the nation. Brooks received dozens of canes as gifts, including one inscribed with "Hit Him Again!" The Republicans used the event as a publicity machine for nearly four years. Sumner himself claimed the caning so injured him that he could not return to his seat for years.

Once the war started, however, Sumner made a miraculous recovery and jumped into war affairs with both feet. He was a leading advocate for harsh treatment of the South during Reconstruction. He died on the Senate floor in 1874, not of a cerebral hemorrhage caused by the caning eighteen years earlier, but from a heart attack. Sumner had outlived his attacker by seventeen years.

The monument to Brooks lays it on a little thick: "The whole South unites with his family in deploring his untimely end. Earth has never pillowed upon her bosom a truer son, nor heaven opened wide her gates to receive a manlier spirit. Preston S. Brooks will be long, long remembered as one who the virtues loved to dwell."

Closer to the back corner of the church cemetery, and surrounded by iron work, is the grave of Confederate Major General Matthew Butler, a nephew of Senator Andrew Butler, who was the man initially insulted by Sumner. General Butler knew where to butter his bread. Besides being the favorite nephew of a United States Senator, he married the daughter of South Carolina Governor Francis Pickens. In 1861, he resigned his seat in the state legislature to join Hampton's Legion as a captain of cavalry. By August 1862, he was in command of the 2nd South Carolina Cavalry. He fought hard in the world's largest cavalry battle at Brandy Station, Virginia, in June 1863, but lost a foot to an artillery shell.

He returned to action early in 1864 and was promoted to brigadier general. Helped into the saddle once he healed, Butler again commanded his cavalry. He was promoted to major general in September 1864. In March 1865, Butler was almost captured in Fayetteville, North Carolina, when he was caught sleeping at a house by Federal cavalry. He threw an overcoat on over his underwear and rode away to safety.

Butler returned to politics after the war. He was appointed United States Senator in 1876 when his old cavalry commander, Wade Hampton, gave up his Senate seat to become the governor of South Carolina. Butler served three terms as senator, until he was defeated in 1892. In 1898, Butler joined General Joe Wheeler as the second former Confederate general reactivated by the United States Army to fight in Cuba during the Spanish-American War. He died in 1909 at the age of seventy-three.

Whoever wrote the epitaph on Butler's monument must have been inspired by Brooks's stone. Butler's inscription reads: "Knightliest of the knightly since the days of old has kept the light of chivalry alight in hearts of gold."

Retrace your route back to U.S. 25. Turn left, or south, heading towards Aiken. About 6.1 miles after leaving Edgefield, U.S. 25 intersects with S.C. 19 and curves away to the right. This is a confusing intersection. Follow S.C. 19 south toward Aiken. At 14.7 miles from this intersection, S.C. 19 becomes Laurens Street on the outskirts of Aiken.

Though no historic marker mentions it, Aiken was the scene of a street battle on February 11, 1865. Union Major General Judson Kilpatrick's cavalry was surprised on both flanks by Confederate Major General Joe Wheeler's cavalry. Kilpatrick had been warned repeatedly that Wheeler's men were in the area possibly trying to set up a trap, but the man known as "Kil-Cavalry" for his hard driving of men and horses could not have cared less. Dozens of Kilpatrick's men were cut down by Confederate gunfire before they even had a chance to draw their pistols. Those who could still breathe turned tail and galloped off, with the Confederates in hot pursuit.

Kilpatrick led the scramble out of town, with several Confederates riding amongst the Federals in an attempt to pull the general off his horse and take him prisoner. If there was one thing Kilpatrick always did well, it was ride his horse away from Confederates. He escaped. More than ninety Federals were taken prisoner. Kilpatrick's hat was also captured.

Follow Laurens Street into downtown Aiken. Turn right onto Richland Street at the first major intersection downtown. Drive one block on Richland Street to St. Thaddeus Episcopal Church, which is on the left. In the left rear of the cemetery, along a wall, is the grave of Confederate Brigadier General Gabriel Rains, the inventor of the torpedo. (See The Union's Base Tour for a detailed biography of Rains).

Oddly, Rains's grave has only a standard military marker, a humble monument to a man whose inventive genius kept the South ahead of the North in the field of explosives.

Turn around and follow Richland Street east out of Aiken. Richland Street becomes S.C. 78. Continue driving east on S.C. 78 until reaching the small town of Elko, 24.9 miles from Rains's grave.

In Elko, turn right, or south, onto S.C. 37. At 7.8 miles outside of Elko, S.C. 37 runs into U.S. 278/S.C. 64 and turns east. Follow this road into the town of Barnwell. Barnwell was visited by Kilpatrick's Union cavalry in February 1865. In a letter to Sherman, Kilpatrick wrote, "Barnwell's name has been changed to Burnwell."

In Barnwell, follow the road signs for U.S. 278/S.C. 64 through town. At the separation of U.S. 278/S.C. 64, turn left to follow S.C. 64 (U.S. 278 continues straight). Drive one block. On the right corner of this intersection is the Church of the Holy Apostles Episcopal Church, founded in 1848. In the left rear of the church, under an obelisk, is the grave of Confederate Brigadier General Johnson Hagood.

A native of Barnwell, and one of The Citadel's most famous Civil War soldiers, Hagood had been practicing law for eleven years when the war started. He was named colonel of the 1st South Carolina Volunteers and was at Fort Sumter during the bombardment. He served around Charleston until being promoted to brigadier general in July 1862.

Hagood was transferred to Virginia in 1864, where his men fought in the trenches of Petersburg and at Cold Harbor. In December 1864, his troops were sent to support Fort Fisher, North Carolina. They performed poorly in that battle, refusing to come out from their bunkers after the Federal shelling had stopped. Hagood ended his career fighting under Confederate General Joe Johnston at the Battle of Bentonville in North Carolina.

Hagood ran for South Carolina comptroller general in 1876. In 1880, he

General Johnson Hagood's grave

was elected South Carolina governor, following the term of Wade Hampton. Hagood may be the only Civil War general to have a football field named after him, The Citadel's Johnson Hagood Stadium in Charleston, South Carolina. He died in 1898.

Continue driving southeast on S.C. 64 for 22 miles to the town of Ehrhardt, South Carolina. In Ehrhardt, S.C. 64 intersects U.S. 601, a major highway. Turn right, or south, onto U.S. 601.

Before leaving town or a telephone, you will have to call ahead to see the battlefield and excellent, preserved earthworks of the Battle of Broxton Bridge. The land is on private property behind a locked gate, but the owner of the property, Gerald Varn, will conduct a tour of the Broxton Bridge battlefield for a small fee. Call 800-437-4868 to set up an appointment to see the grounds.

Once the appointment is made, continue driving south on U.S. 601. Drive 1.5 miles past the intersection of U.S. 601 and S.C. 641 to the Broxton Bridge Plantation Bed-and-Breakfast. At the bed-and-breakfast, turn right onto a dirt road, where you will be met by Gerald Varn.

Broxton Bridge was one of the points where Confederate Major General Lafayette McLaws chose to defend the Salkehatchie River against Sherman's march. The river was usually not very large, but it was flooded on February 3, 1865, giving a tactical advantage to the Confederates. The Federals had to wade through several hundred yards of flooded swamp before even reaching the deep river.

At Broxton Bridge, the Confederates built a strong earth fort on the northeast side of the river, then extended rifle pits and sharpshooter entrenchments along the road that led down to the bridge. Any Federal trying to wade the river and swamp was in Confederate range for a long time. Union Major General Oliver O. Howard, commander of the right wing of Sherman's army, saw the Broxton Bridge earthworks and said they were the strongest he had ever encountered.

Without orders, Union Major General Joseph Mower pushed his men into the swamp in front of Broxton Bridge, where they were subjected to artillery fire. Since he could not directly attack Broxton Bridge, Mower moved his troops further up the river. He tried to cross first at Rivers Bridge, where he was repulsed again. Mower and his men finally moved back south along the river and waded across two miles upstream from Broxton Bridge (on the grounds of Broxton Bridge Bed-and-Breakfast). Mower then flanked the Confederates at Broxton Bridge. The hopelessly outnumbered Confederates were forced to retreat, heading north toward Columbia

Today, the earthworks and enclosed fort at Broxton Bridge may be the best examples of original Civil War fortifications remaining in South Carolina. The fort itself extends for at least 150 yards, and the places where twelve cannons were mounted are still visible. Standing on the bank of the river and looking back at the fort, the trench line is sobering. Federals, struggling in knee-deep swamp water, would have seen the same thing—a formidable structure. The earthworks for the sharpshooters are still at least ten-feet tall.

If the owner of Broxton Bridge is unavailable, it is still possible to see local earthworks at Rivers Bridge State Park. To reach Rivers Bridge State Park, turn left, or north, onto U.S. 601 from the Broxton Bridge Bed-and-Breakfast. Drive about 1.5 miles to the intersection with S.C. 641. Turn left, or west, onto S.C. 641 and follow the signs to the park, about 5.1 miles away. The park is closed on Tuesdays and Wednesdays.

Rivers Bridge, several miles north of Broxton Bridge on the Salkehatchie River, had an earthwork mounting seven cannons. This is where Mower's men and other Union troops first tried to cross the river in a failed frontal assault. When they received heavy fire from the earthworks, the Federals split their forces and looked for two crossings that were not defended. They found them, waded the river, and flanked the Confederates at both Broxton Bridge and Rivers Bridge.

After seeing the trenches at Rivers Bridge, retrace your route back to U.S. 601. Turn left, or north, onto U.S. 601 and drive towards Orangeburg, 31 miles away. This would have been the same general route that Sherman's sixty-three thousand soldiers took towards Columbia. At 14 miles after leaving Ehrhardt, just below Bamberg, U.S. 601 merges with U.S. 301. Continue north on U.S. 301/U.S. 601.

After crossing over the North Edisto River into the outskirts of Orangeburg on U.S. 301/U.S. 601, take an immediate left fork onto Russel Street. Once on Russel Street, take an immediate left turn into Edisto Gardens. Park in the parking lot along the right side of the street.

Today, this is a peaceful city park, with rose gardens where rifle pits once were. In February 1865, it was a battleground where six hundred Confederates resisted the advance of Sherman's army for two days. The Confederates had an advantage in the battle because the North Edisto River, which is usually only about thirty-yards wide, was flooded beyond its banks, and the Confederates had burned all the bridges.

Eventually, as it always did, Sherman's army found shallower fords, out of the range of the Confederate riflemen. The Federals crossed the North Edisto River, driving the Confederates northwest towards Columbia. Orangeburg was occupied by Union forces on February 12, 1865. All of the town was looted, and about half of it was burned.

One building that Sherman specifically ordered protected was an orphanage, filled with children from Charleston whose fathers and mothers had died during the war. One witness reported that Sherman was moved to tears when he saw the three hundred frightened children eating their breakfast of cornmeal mush and molasses. Apparently, to keep the children from concentrating on the burning and destruction going on outside their windows, the orphanage master ordered them to sing their regular morning songs. Even Sherman's hardened men broke down and agreed not to burn the building when they heard the singing.

This concludes The Dead Generals Tour.

Appendix

NORTH CAROLINA

Chambers of Commerce and Visitors Bureaus

Asheville Travel and Tourism Office
P. O. Box 1010
Asheville, N.C. 28802-1010
704-258-6109
800-257-1300

Boone Convention and Visitors
Bureau
208 Howard Street
Boone, N.C. 28607
704-262-3516
800-852-9506

Burke County Visitors Information
Center
P. O. Box 751
Morganton, N.C. 28680-0751
704-437-3021

Cape Fear Coast Convention and
Visitors Bureau
24 North Third Street
Wilmington, N.C. 28401
910-341-4030
800-222-4757

Capital Area Visitors Center
301 North Blount Street
Raleigh, N.C. 27601-2807
919-733-3456

Carteret County Tourism Development Bureau
P. O. Box 1406
Morehead City, N.C. 28557
919-726-8148

Charlotte Convention and Visitors
Bureau
122 East Stonewall Street
Charlotte, N.C. 28202
704-334-2282
800-231-4636

Cherokee Visitors Center
P. O. Box 460
Cherokee, N.C. 28719
800-438-1601

Craven County Convention and
Visitors Bureau
219 Pollock Street
P.O. Box 1413
New Bern, N.C. 28563
919-637-9400
800-437-5767

Durham Convention and Visitors
Center
101 East Morgan Street
Durham, N.C. 27701
919-687-0288

Elizabeth City Area Chamber of
Commerce
502 East Ehringhaus Street
Box 426
Elizabeth City, N.C. 27909
919-335-4365

Fayetteville Area Convention and
  Visitors Bureau
245 Person Street
Fayetteville, N.C. 28301-5733
800-255-8217

Greensboro Convention and Visitors Bureau
317 South Greene Street
Greensboro, N.C. 27401
910-274-2282

Halifax County Tourism Development Authority
P. O. Box 144
Roanoke Rapids, N.C. 27870
800-522-4282

Greater Haywood County Chamber
  of Commerce
P. O. Box 125
Waynesville, N.C. 28786
704-456-3021

Greater Hendersonville Chamber of
  Commerce
330 North King Street
Hendersonville, N.C. 28739
704-692-1413

High Point Convention and Visitors Bureau
P. O. Box 2273
High Point, N.C. 27261
910-884-5255

Johnston County Convention and
  Visitors Bureau
P. O. Box 1990
Smithfield, N.C. 27577
919-989-8687

North Carolina Travel and Tourism
  Division
430 North Salisbury Street
Raleigh, N.C. 27611
919-733-4171
800-VISIT NC

Orange County Visitors Center
150 East King Street
Hillsborough, N.C. 27278
919-732-8156

Outer Banks Chamber of Commerce
P. O. Box 1757
Kill Devil Hills, N.C. 27948
919-441-8144

Rowan County Convention and
  Visitors Bureau
215 Depot Street
Box 4044
Salisbury, N.C. 28145-4044
800-332-2343

Southport-Oak Island Chamber of
  Commerce
4841 Long Beach Road SE
Southport, N.C. 28461
910-457-6964

Washington-Beaufort   County
  Chamber of Commerce
102 West Stewart Parkway
Box 665
Washington, N.C. 27889
919-946-9168

Washington County Chamber of
  Commerce
701 Washington Street
Plymouth, N.C. 27962
919-793-4804

Wayne County Chamber of Commerce
P.O. Box 1107
Goldsboro, N.C. 27533-1107
919-734-2241

Winston-Salem Convention and
  Visitors Center
601 West Fourth Street
P.O. Box 1408
Winston-Salem, N.C. 27102
910-725-2361
800-331-7018

*Museums, Parks, and
Historic Sites*

Beaufort Historic Site
100 Turner Street
Box 1709
Beaufort, N.C. 28516
919-728-5225

Bellamy Mansion Museum of History and Design Arts
503 Market Street
Box 1176
Wilmington, N.C. 28402
910-251-3700

Bennett Place
4409 Bennett Memorial Road
Durham, N.C. 27705
919-383-4345

Bentonville Battleground
P.O. Box 27
Newton Grove, N.C. 28366
910-594-0789

Brunswick Town State Historic Site
  (Fort Anderson)
8884 St. Phillips Road, SE

Winnabow, N.C. 28479
910-371-6613

Cape Fear Museum
814 Market Street
Wilmington, N.C. 28401
910-341-4350

Carolina Beach State Park
P.O. Box 475
Carolina Beach, N.C. 28428
910-458-8206

Carteret County Museum of History
and Art
100 Wallace Drive
Morehead City, N.C. 28557
919-247-7533

Duke Homestead and Tobacco Museum
2828 Duke Homestead Road
Durham, N.C. 27705
919-477-5498

Duplin County Cowan Museum
P.O. Box 158
Kenansville, N.C. 28349
919-296-2149

Fayetteville Independent Light Infantry Armory & Museum
c/o 433 Hay Street
Fayetteville, N.C. 28301
910-433-1914

C.E. Fonvielle Company (Civil War tour of Wilmington)
307 North Front Street
Wilmington, N.C. 28401
910-772-9372

Fort Branch
S.R. 1416
Hamilton, N.C. 27840

919-792-3001
* open Saturdays and Sundays from
1:00 P.M. to 5:30 P.M.

Fort Caswell
North Carolina Baptist Assembly
100 Caswell Beach Road
Oak Island, N.C. 28465
910-278-9501

Fort Fisher State Historic Site
1610 Fort Fisher Boulevard
Box 169
Kure Beach, N. C. 28449
910-458-5538

Fort Macon State Park
P.O. Box 127
Atlantic Beach, N.C. 28512
919-726-3775

Greensboro Historical Museum
130 Summit Avenue
Greensboro, N.C. 27401
910-373-2043

Guilford College
5800 West Friendly Avenue
Greensboro, N.C. 27410
910-316-2000

Josephus Hall House
226 South Jackson Street
Salisbury, N.C. 28144
704-636-0103
* open Saturdays and Sundays from
2:00 P.M. to 5:00 P.M.

High Point Historical Museum
1805 East Lexington Avenue
High Point, N.C. 27262
910-885-6859

Historic Halifax
P.O. Box 406
Halifax, N.C. 27839
919-583-7191

Hubie Bliven Wildlife Art
Rt. 1, Box 1624
543 Ananias Dare Street
Manteo, N.C. 27954
919-473-2632

Liberty Hall
P.O. Box 634
Kenansville, N.C. 28349
800-755-1755

Lincoln County Museum of History
403 East Main Street
Lincolnton, N.C. 28092
704-732-9055

Mendenhall Plantation
603 West Main Street
Jamestown, N.C. 27282
910-454-3819

Mordecai Historic Park
One Mimosa Street
Raleigh, N.C. 27604
919-834-4844

Museum of the Albemarle
1116 U.S. 17 South
Elizabeth City, N.C. 27909
919-335-1453

Museum of the Cape Fear
801 Arsenel Avenue
Fayetteville, N.C. 28305
910-486-1330

Museum of the Cherokee Indian
U.S. 441 North
Cherokee, N.C. 28719
704-497-3481

New Bern Academy Museum
P.O. Box 1007
New Bern, N.C. 28653
919-638-1560

New Bern Civil War Museum
301 Metcalf Street
New Bern, N.C. 28650
919-633-2818

CSS *Neuse* and Governor Caswell
   Memorial
P.O. Box 3043
Kinston, N.C. 28502
919-522-2091

North Carolina Maritime Museum
315 Front Street
Beaufort, N.C. 28516
919-728-7317

North Carolina Museum of History
5 East Edenton Street
Raleigh, N.C. 27601
919-715-0200

North Carolina State Capitol
Union Square
Raleigh, N.C. 27603
919-733-4171

Orange County Museum
P.O. Box 871
Hillsborough, N.C. 27278
919-732-2201

Pettigrew State Park
Route 1 Box 336
Creswell, N.C. 27928
919-797-4475

Port O Plymouth Museum
302 East Water Street
Plymouth, N.C. 27962
919-793-1377

Greater Raleigh Convention and
   Visitors Bureau
P.O. Box 1879
225 Hillsborough Street, Suite 400
Raleigh, N.C. 27602
919-834-5900
800-849-8499

Rowan Museum
116 South Jackson Street
Salisbury, N.C.
704-633-5946

Somerset Place
P.O. Box 215
Creswell, N.C. 27928
919-797-4560

Southport Maritime Museum
P.O. Box 11101
Southport, N.C. 28461
910-457-0003

Stagville Center
P.O. Box 71217
Durham, N.C. 27722-1217
919-620-0120
* closed weekends

Wayne County Museum
P.O. Box 665
Goldsboro, N.C. 27530
919-734-5023
* closed Mondays, Wednesdays, and
   Fridays.

Woodfield Inn
Box 98
Flat Rock, N.C. 28731
704-693-6016

Woodside Inn
P.O. Box 197
Milton, N.C. 27305
910-234-8646

Wilmington Railroad Museum
501 Nutt Street
Wilmington, N.C. 28401
910-763-2634

Zebulon Vance Birthplace
911 Reems Creek Road
Weaverville, N.C. 28787
704-645-6706

SOUTH CAROLINA
*Chambers of Commerce
and Visitors Centers*

Abbeville County Visitors Council
P.O. Box 533
Abbeville, S.C. 29620
803-459-2181

Greater Aiken Chamber of Commerce
P.O. Box 892
Aiken, S.C. 29812
803-641-1111

Bamberg County Chamber of Commerce
P.O. Box 907
Bamberg, S.C. 29003
803-245-4427

Barnwell County Chamber of Commerce
P.O. Box 898
Barnwell, S.C. 29812
803-259-7446

Historic Beaufort Foundation
P.O. Box 11
Beaufort, S.C. 29901
803-524-6334

Greater Beaufort Chamber of Commerce
P.O. Box 910
Beaufort, S.C. 29901
803-524-3163

Cheraw Visitors Bureau
221 Market Street
Cheraw, S.C. 29520
803-537-8425

Chester County Chamber of Commerce
P.O. Box 489
Chester, S.C. 29706
803-581-4142

Greater Chesterfield Chamber of Commerce
P.O. Box 230
Chesterfield, S.C. 29709
803-623-2343

Historic Columbia Foundation
1601 Richland Street
Columbia, S.C. 29201
803-252-7742

Darlington Chamber of Commerce
P.O. Box 274
Darlington, S.C. 29532
803-393-2641

Fairfield County Chamber of Commerce
P.O. Box 297
Winnsboro, S.C. 29180
803-635-4242

Georgetown Chamber of Commerce
Drawer 1776
Georgetown, S.C. 29442
803-546-8436

Hartsville/Society Hill Tourism
P.O. Box 578
Hartsville, S.C. 29551
803-332-6401

Hilton Head Chamber of Commerc
P.O. Box 5647
Hilton Head Island, S.C. 29938
803-785-3673

Kershaw County Chamber of Commerce
P.O. Box 605
Camden, S.C. 29020
803-432-2525
800-968-4037

Orangeburg County Chamber of Commerce
P.O. Box 328
Orangeburg, S.C. 29116-0328
803-534-6821

The Pee Dee Tourism Commission
P.O. Box 3093
Florence, S.C. 29502
803-669-0950

Pendleton District Commission
P.O. Box 565
Pendleton, S.C. 29670
803-646-3782

Ridgeland Chamber of Commerce
P.O. Box 1267
Ridgeland, S.C. 29936-1267
803-726-8126

South Carolina Historical Society
100 Meeting Street
Charleston, S.C. 29401-2299
803-723-3225

Museums, Parks, and Historic Sites

Anderson County Museum
Old Courthouse on Main Street
Anderson, S.C. 29624
803-260-4737
* closed weekends

Beaufort Arsenal Museum
713 Craven Street
Beaufort, S.C. 29902
803-525-7077

Boone Hall Plantation
P.O. Box 1554
Mt. Pleasant, S.C. 29465
803-884-4371

Broxton Bridge Battlefield
P.O. Box 97
Ehrhardt, S.C. 29081
800-437-4868
* can be toured by appointment only

Burt-Stark Mansion
306 North Main Street
Abbeville, S.C. 29620
803-459-4297
* open Friday and Saturday afternoons

John C. Calhoun House Museum
c/o Clemson University Visitors Center
103 Tillman Hall
Clemson, S.C. 29634
803-656-4789

Camden Archives and Museum
1314 Broad Street
Camden, S.C. 29020
803-425-6050

The Charleston Museum
360 Meeting Street
Charleston, S.C. 29403-6297
803-722-2996

The Citadel Museum
171 Moultrie Street
Charleston, S.C. 29409
803-953-6846

Civil War Walking Tour of Charleston
17 Archdale Street
Charleston, S.C. 29401
803-722-7033

Columbia Downtown Business Association
1426 Main Street
Columbia, S.C. 29201
803-733-8345

Drayton Hall
3380 Ashley River Road
Charleston, S.C. 29414
803-766-0188

Fort Sumter/Fort Moultrie Boat Tours
205 King Street
Charleston, S.C. 29401
803-722-1691

Fort Sumter and Fort Moultrie National Parks
Drawer S
Sullivans Island, S.C. 29482
803-883-3123

Hampton-Preston House
c/o Historic Columbia Foundation
1601 Richmond Street
Columbia, S.C. 29201
803-252-7742

Miller, S. Ingram, Jr.
204 Market Street
Cheraw, S.C. 29520
803-537-6565
* operates private relic collection in Cheraw, South Carolina. Open by appointment on week days.

The Lyceum
* contact the Cheraw Visitors Bureau

Middleton Place
Ashley River Road
Charleston, S.C. 29414-7206
803-556-6020

Parris Island Museum
Marine Corps Recruit Depot
Parris Island, S.C. 29905
803-525-2951

Penn Center
P.O. Box 126
St. Helena Island, S.C. 29920
803-838-2432

The Rice Museum
P.O. Box 902
Georgetown, S.C. 29442-0902
803-546-7423

Riverbanks Zoo
P.O. Box 1060
Columbia, S.C. 29202
803-779-8717

Rivers Bridge State Park
Rt. 1
Ehrhardt, S.C. 29081
803-267-3675

Rose Hill Plantation State Park
Rt. 2 Sardis Road
Union, S.C. 29379
803-427-5966

South Carolina State Museum
301 Gervais Street
Columbia, S.C. 29201
803-737-4935

South Carolina State Parks
1205 Pendleton Street
Columbia, S.C. 29201
803-758-3622

United Daughters of the Confederacy Museum
Marian Hankel Kindergarten
34 Pitt Street
Charleston, S.C. 29402
803-723-1541
* temporary location

War Between the States Museum
107 South Guerry Street
Florence, S.C. 29501
803-669-1266
* open Wednesdays and Saturdays

Bibliography

Arnett, Ethel Stephens. *Confederate Guns Were Stacked (at) Greensboro, North Carolina*. Greensboro, N.C.: Piedmont Press, 1965.

Barrett, John Gilcrest. *Civil War in North Carolina*. Chapel Hill: The University of North Carolina Press, 1963.

————. *North Carolina as a Civil War Battleground*. Raleigh, N.C.: Department of North Carolina Cultural Resources, 1980.

————. *Sherman's March Through the Carolinas*. Chapel Hill: The University of North Carolina Press, 1956.

Bradley, Mark L. "Last Stand in the Carolinas," *Blue & Gray Magazine*. Columbus, Ohio: Blue & Gray Enterprises, December 1995 (pages 9–72).

Branch, Paul, Jr. *The Siege of Fort Macon*. Morehead City, N.C.: Herald Printing Company, 1994.

Brimlow, Judith, ed. *South Carolina Highway Historical Marker Guide*. Columbia, S.C.: South Carolina Department of Archives and History, 1992.

Cromie, Alice Hamilton. *A Tour Guide of the Civil War*. Chicago: Quadrangle Books, 1964.

Crow, Vernon H. *Storm in the Mountains*. Cherokee, N.C.: Press of the Museum of the Cherokee, 1982.

Current, Richard, ed. *Encyclopedia of the Confederacy*. 4 vols. New York: Simon & Schuster, 1993.

Davis, Burke. *Sherman's March*. New York: Random House, 1980.

———. *The Long Surrender*. New York: Random House, 1985.

Elliott, Robert G. *Ironclad of the Roanoke*. Shippinsburg, Pa.: White Mane Publishing, 1994.

Faust, Patricia L. *Historical Times Illustrated Encyclopedia of the Civil War*. New York: Harper & Row, 1986.

Flood, Charles. *Lee: The Last Years*. Boston: Houghton Mifflin & Company, 1981.

Fonvielle, Chris. "The Last Days of Departing Hope," *Blue & Gray Magazine*. Columbus, Ohio: Blue & Gray Enterprises, December 1994 (pages 10–59).

Gibson, John M. *Those 163 Days*. New York: Coward-McCann, Inc., 1961.

Glatthaar, Joseph T. *The March to the Sea and Beyond*. New York: New York University Press, 1985

Gragg, Rod. *Confederate Goliath: The Battle for Fort Fisher*. New York: HarperCollins Publishers, 1991.

Hill, Daniel Harvey. *Confederate Military History: North Carolina*.

Hill, Mitchel, ed. *Guide to North Carolina's Historical Markers*. Raleigh, N.C.: North Carolina Division of Archives and History, 1990.

Hinshaw, Seth B. *The Carolina Quaker Experience*. Ramseur, N.C.: North Carolina Friends Historical Society, 1984.

Hollowell, J.M. *War Time Reminiscences and Other Selections*. Goldsboro, N.C.: The Goldsboro Record, 1939.

Howe, W.W. *Kinston, Whitehall, and Goldsboro Expedition*. New York: n.p., 1890.

Jones, Katharine M. *When Sherman Came*. Indianapolis, Ind.: The Bobbs-Merrill Company, Inc., 1964.

Jones, Terry L. *Lee's Tigers*. Baton Rouge: The Louisiana State University Press, 1987.

Jordan, Weymouth T. *The Battle of Bentonville*. Wilmington, N.C: Broadfoot Publishing Company, 1990.

Keys, Thomas B. *The Uncivil War*. Biloxi, Miss.: The Beauvoir Press, 1991.

Kozak, Ginnie. *Eve of Emancipation*. Beaufort, S.C.: Eagle Press, 1994.

LeConte, Emma. *When the World Ended*. Oxford: Oxford University Press, 1957.

Leland, Jack. *60 Famous Houses of Charleston, South Carolina*. Charleston, S.C.: The News & Courier and The Evening Post, 1970.

Lesser, Charles H. *Relic Of The Lost Cause*. Columbia, S.C.: South Carolina Department of Archives and History, 1990.

Noffke, Jonathan. "The Civil War Years at the Bellamy Mansion," brochure. Bellamy Mansion, 1995.

———. "The Rebirth of a Landmark," *Wilmington Coast* magazine. Raleigh, N.C.: VSD Communications, Winter/Spring 1996.

Rose, Willie L. *Rehearsal for Reconstruction: The Port Royal Experiment*. Indianapolis, Ind.: The Bobbs-Merrill Company, Inc., 1964.

Rosen, Robert N. *Confederate Charleston*. Columbia: The University of South Carolina Press, 1995.

Shiman, Phillip. *Ft. Branch and the Defense of the Roanoke Valley 1862–1865*. Hamilton, N.C.: Ft. Branch Battlefield Commission, 1990.

Sterling, Dorothy. *Captain Of The Planter*. Garden City, N.Y.: Doubleday & Company, 1958.

Thompson, N.S. *Historic Resources of the Lowcountry, A Regional Survey of Beaufort County, S.C., Colleton County, S.C., Hampton County, S.C., Jasper County, S.C.* Lowcountry Council of Governments, Yemassee, S.C., 1979.

Trotter, William. *The Civil War in North Carolina*. 3 vols. Greensboro, N.C.: Signal Research, 1988.

Tucker, Glenn. *Front Rank*. Raleigh, N.C.: North Carolina Confederate Centennial Commission, 1962.

Underwood, George C. *History of the Twenty-Sixth Regiment of North Carolina Troops in the Great War 1861-1865*. Goldsboro, N.C.: Nash Brothers. Reprint, 1978.

Van Noppen, Ina W. *Stoneman's Last Raid*. Boone, N.C.: North Carolina State College, 1961.

Walker, C. Irving. *The Life of General Richard Heron Anderson of The Confederate States Army*. N.p.: Art Publishing, 1917.

Warner, Ezra. *Generals in Blue*. Baton Rouge: The Louisiana State University Press, 1959.

————. *Generals in Gray*. Baton Rouge: The Louisiana State University Press, 1959.

Wheeler, Richard. *Sherman's March*. New York: Thomas Crowell Publishers, 1978.

Wilcox, Arthur, and Warren Ripley. *The Civil War in Charleston*. Charleston, S.C.: The News & Courier and The Evening Post, 1966.

Wilson, Clyde N. *Carolina Cavalier*. Athens: The University of Georgia Press, 1990.

Witt, J.V. *Wild in North Carolina*. Springfield, Va.: J.V. Witt, 1993.

Wooding, Frank. *Maryland Cracker Barrel*. Boonsboro, Md.: 1994.

Young, Rudolph. "Black Confederates in Lincoln County, North Carolina." *Journal of Confederate History* (1995).

Index